PENGUIN BOOKS

A PLACE CALLED CANTERBURY

Dudley Clendinen was a national reporter and editorial writer for *The New York Times*, assistant managing editor of the *Atlanta Journal-Constitution*, and a columnist for the *St. Petersburg Times*. He is the editor of a book of essays, *The Prevailing South*, and the author of the text for a book of photographs, *Homeless in America*. He is coauthor of *Out for Good: The Struggle to Build a Gay Rights Movement in America*. His own essays are collected in various anthologies. He lives in Baltimore.

He can be contacted by e-mail at finddudley@aol.com.

Praise for *A Place Called Canterbury*

"Affectionate, touchingly empathetic . . . He conveys fascination with the way Canterbury Tower was full of formidable, interesting people 'meeting one another for the first time, at almost the end of their lives.' . . . He populates the book with brightly drawn characters who give the place its reigning mood, 'a slow, good-humored dottiness and dignity.'"
—Janet Maslin, *The New York Times*

"Cleninden's brilliant writing is . . . engaging and informative."
—*The Seattle Times*

"Cleninden's book chronicles the circumstances in America that have led seniors to come together in 'assisted-living' facilities. The stories in *A Place Called Canterbury* range from painful to humorous to incredible."
—*The Herald Tribune*

"Humor, sometimes in the most unlikely places . . . suffuses Clendinen's Canterbury tales, which in the end are about people finding grace, courage, and community in the new world of old age. An insightful guide for those trying to help their aging parents with life's final challenges."
—The Associated Press

"A book that stands apart from so much of what is being written about aging in this country."
—*The Baltimore Sun*

"*A Place Called Canterbury* should be required reading for anyone with aging parents or anyone who wonders what old age will be like. And there are no better role models than the residents of Canterbury. These are people who understand the importance of living in the present moment. Canterbury is a microcosm of a generation." —*The Atlanta Journal-Constitution*

"*A Place Called Canterbury* will touch you at several levels. It takes us face to face with a brave new world we are dealing with. Sweet, often painful in its detail, Dudley's *Canterbury* is a tale for us all." —*The Tampa Tribune*

"Cleninden tackles the great confused mess of elderly care . . . putting faces and emotions to a complex issue." —*Booklist*

"*A Place Called Canterbury* is a glorious piece of wisdom literature. Masterful . . . Beautifully written . . . A probing examination of the meaning and texture of extended old age." —*Naples Sun Times*

"Brilliant. A must read." —*Tampa Bay Metro*

"*A Place Called Canterbury* tells many a funny, touching, and surprising tale and sheds light on the issues of aging that touch nearly all of us." —*St. Petersburg Times*

"Cleninden [writes] poetic prose and [has a] knack for crafting illuminating word portraits." —*Tennessean*

"After reading [*Canterbury*], you will look at your parents or grandparents with fresh eyes and renewed compassion." —*The Charlotte Observer*

"Clendinen has written a modern masterpiece. It isn't about old age. It's about all of us, a brilliant celebration of what it means to be a human being. I laughed and wept and was changed by reading *A Place Called Canterbury*. I'm buying copies for my family, my friends, their parents, and all our children. It is a gift to be shared, this wonderful, wonderful book." —Linda Ellerbee, journalist and author

"If you've ever had a mother, you will love this book." —Roy Blount Jr., author of *Long Time Leaving: Dispatches from Up South*

"Canterbury's walls rock with geriatrics who live every moment to its fullest, with tales of food from cloudlike biscuits before church to snacks after sex and martinis with social debate. Through it all, the elegance and humor of a generation who laughed and loved through a depression and a great war, surviving to live and die with grace, will have you laughing and crying. You will love every morsel of the Canterbury tales." —Nathalie Dupree, television cooking host and cookbook author

A PLACE CALLED

Canterbury

TALES OF THE NEW OLD AGE IN AMERICA

Dudley Clendinen

PENGUIN BOOKS

PENGUIN BOOKS

Published by the Penguin Group

Penguin Group (USA) Inc., 375 Hudson Street, New York, New York 10014, U.S.A.

Penguin Group (Canada), 90 Eglinton Avenue East, Suite 700, Toronto,
Ontario, Canada M4P 2Y3 (a division of Pearson Penguin Canada Inc.)

Penguin Books Ltd, 80 Strand, London WC2R 0RL, England

Penguin Ireland, 25 St Stephen's Green, Dublin 2, Ireland (a division of Penguin Books Ltd)

Penguin Group (Australia), 250 Camberwell Road, Camberwell,
Victoria 3124, Australia (a division of Pearson Australia Group Pty Ltd)

Penguin Books India Pvt Ltd, 11 Community Centre,
Panchsheel Park, New Delhi – 110 017, India

Penguin Group (NZ), 67 Apollo Drive, Rosedale, North Shore 0632,
New Zealand (a division of Pearson New Zealand Ltd)

Penguin Books (South Africa) (Pty) Ltd, 24 Sturdee Avenue,
Rosebank, Johannesburg 2196, South Africa

Penguin Books Ltd, Registered Offices:
80 Strand, London WC2R 0RL, England

First published in the United States of America by Viking Penguin,
a member of Penguin Group (USA) Inc. 2008
Published in Penguin Books 2009

1   3   5   7   9   10   8   6   4   2

Grateful acknowledgment is made for permission to reprint excerpts from *My Darling Margy: The World War II Diaries and Letters of Surgeon Charles Francis Chunn, MD*, edited by Celeste Chunn Colcord. © 2005 The Scuppernong Press. By permission of Celeste Chunn Colcord.

THE LIBRARY OF CONGRESS HAS CATALOGED THE HARDCOVER EDITION AS FOLLOWS:
Clendinen, Dudley.
A place called Canterbury: tales of the new old age in America / Dudley Clendinen.
p.   cm.
ISBN 978-0-670-01884-0 (hc.)
ISBN 978-0-14-311530-4 (pbk.)
1. Older people—United States—Social conditions.   2. Old age—United States.
I. Title.
HQ1064.U5C5143 2008
305.260973—dc22   2007044546

Printed in the United States of America
Set in Bembo with Goudy Sans
Designed by Daniel Lagin

For my beloved Whitney, and for Christopher, with love,
from Grandmother, and from me

And for David Halberstam and David Rosenbaum,
who should have lived much longer

CONTENTS

INTRODUCTION:
Canterbury and the New Old Age | ix

1. Good-bye, Mother, Hello | 1
2. The Importance of the Moment | 24
3. A Place Unto Itself | 40
4. A Reason to Be Alive | 61
5. The Cocktail Hour | 78
6. Last Communion | 89
7. The Dining Room Waltz | 100
8. In Case of Fire | 114
9. Going Home | 124
10. The Plumbing Problem | 137
11. Meanwhile, Back in the Tower | 152
12. Looking for a Man | 168
13. Sex and Satisfaction | 184

14. "Laugh, Even If Your Heart Is Breaking" | 194

15. Sleeping with the Sweetso | 219

16. When They Were Children | 229

17. When They Were in Love | 244

18. Body Parts | 258

19. War and Survival | 279

20. I Can't Find My Wife | 293

21. The Best-Laid Plans | 303

22. Miss Osama | 326

23. He Wants Our Ashes | 336

EPILOGUE:
Hello, Mother, Good-bye | 345

ACKNOWLEDGMENTS | 367

Canterbury and the New Old Age

In 1994, Mother finally relented and agreed to sell the brick and white clapboard house with a deep cedar-shingle roof, dormer windows, climbing ivy, and sheltering oaks that it had taken her twenty-two years to find, and in which she had lived for twenty-six years with my father, her beloved Jobie. Yes, she would move to Canterbury. She was not an impulsive woman. Boy, was she not. But he was dead. They had been married for forty-eight years. He was silver haired and pink and dignified, twinkly when he had a drink in his hand, and my mother had adored him. She was a romantic. She saw him as a Viking. She wanted to go up on his funeral pyre. Southern Methodists turned Episcopalian, however, don't get to heaven that way, and so Mother did the next best thing: arranged for a funeral service at St. John's, with priests, acolytes, an organist, six pallbearers, twelve honorary pallbearers, Holy Communion, and a series of prayers and hymns calculated to put people on their knees, lift them up, and—if all went well—reduce them to tears. At the end, as my father's casket was carried down the aisle, amid much blinking and snuffling in the silence that followed "My Country, 'Tis of Thee," Mother moved out the side door on her cane with a kind of sad, granite elegance, and made for the limousine, to follow the hearse to the cemetery at Myrtle Hill, where her parents were waiting. It was her family plot.

At the house afterward, surrounded by family and close friends, with everyone drinking and luncheon for thirty coming out of the kitchen, she looked radiant and content. "She's on a widow's high," someone said, watching her. We were celebrating Jobie, and it made her glad. It is later—when the funeral lunch is done, the glasses and plates washed and put up, the friends departed, the notes and letters of condolence all read—when the phone stops ringing with calls of love and concern and the children and grandchildren go back home, that depression sets in. Then, even if she is living in the city where she was born, as my mother was in Tampa, Florida, even if she has a daughter and son-in-law, two grandchildren, a maid twice a week, a yardman three or four times a month, and hundreds of friends and acquaintances there, as Mother still did, the widow is, for the first time in decades or generations, alone in her space. A lot of women, whatever their circumstances, fall apart then. A lot of men do, too.

I never once saw Mother weep. I'm sure she did, but not in front of us. She never whined, never complained of feeling lonely. Never prattled on to us, to her friends, or to strangers about how darling and wonderful my father had been, and what a difference he had made. She filed all that away somewhere inside. She was strong. He was well known. And she knew better than to be a bore.

There were a few weeks of occasional damp-eyed silences. She didn't go out in public for a while, and when she did, her face sometimes crumpled for just an instant when she returned for the first time to someplace they had usually gone together. Otherwise, she seemed determined to carry on as before, with this difference: She was learning to drive, shop, cook, dole out pills, pay bills, and arrange life for one instead of two. To sit at the breakfast table in the bay window of the kitchen by herself in the morning, with just Larkspur, the parakeet, for company, looking out at the garage, which was sagging, and the terrace, which needed sweeping; to take her lunch into the little library with its couch and reading lamps and quiet bookshelves at midday, if she wasn't having lunch out somewhere; to carry her glass of iced vermouth into the softly breezy, green-and-white sunporch with its old wicker rocking chairs in the evening, where she could sit as they had at that hour—and notice the cobwebs on the eaves outside. He wasn't there to tease and divert her, and absorb her attentions. It must have been hard, because Mother was very verbal, accustomed always to checking on Dad, feeding and watering and cheering him up.

"Jobie, dear?" I can hear her calling, room from room. "*JO*-bie?"

At night, often after cocktails and dinner out with old friends, she came home to the house, which was silent except for the hum of the window air conditioners in summer, and the soft chirping and chuckling of Larkspur. She would cover him. Lock the doors. Turn out most of the lights. Slowly climb the graceful stairs she loved so much. Pull herself into the golden four-poster bed she had gotten an old cabinetmaker to make for them forty years before. Open a book. Doze off. Sleep fitfully as the shadows of the branches outside the windows moved across her bedspread in the moonlight. Wake up alone.

No complaints. She didn't believe in it. She had always been equal to the occasion, whatever it might be. She was a southern woman of her generation, strong, resilient, skilled in finding a way to meet the need, without seeming to be looking. "You can catch more flies with honey than with vinegar, darling," she told me once. But she knew how to be direct, too. When she became president of the Tampa YWCA in the mid-1960s, it was segregated. My father had supported integration on the editorial page since the Supreme Court's *Brown v. Board of Education* decision a decade before—not an easy thing for a southern editor of a Virginia-owned paper—and Mother was determined to integrate the Y, which would mean close contact in the locker room and swimming pool. A fervent white Christian on her board, with a rich redneck husband and a country club pool to go to, said if those little colored children came into the Y, she would have to take her children out.

"Sarah," Mother said, "it's not your children who need the Y." The integration proceeded. She led other community groups, too. She was never idle. She had never slept well. But she never seemed to tire. The strength of the family, a flowering magnolia since she came of age in the Great Depression, she was a woman of seductive charm, an amused and charitable heart, steely determination, and canny intent. I think of her as a sort of cross between Scarlett O'Hara and Florence Nightingale. She was diminutive and shapely, with good legs; perfect teeth; a mass of luxuriantly curly dark hair that turned silver black and then silver gray as she aged; lovely, soft, slightly olive skin; large, lively hazel-blue-green eyes that became gradually more gray blue with the years; and the ability to light up almost any room she entered. Mother had always managed their social and cultural and domestic calendar, particularly after my father retired. She was used to being in control. She didn't know how not to be. And Tampa was her town. There was no reason, from her point of view, why she couldn't just keep on.

Except that she was seventy-five when my father died and, for at least ten years, had been falling apart, a piece here, a piece there. She'd lost about four inches in height. Her vertebrae were collapsing. She fainted, tumbling down the front hall stairs. Then she did it again. Coming out of the symphony one night, a long-legged old man took an arm to steady her, and then stepped off so fast—for Mother—that she wobbled out of control and crashed into the azaleas. She had advanced osteoporosis, which was tilting her both forward and sideways. She had gotten bent and frail and crooked, anemic and impossibly arthritic, subject to spells and little strokes, off balance, a little hard of hearing, running into things with her old silver gray car, slower all the time.

And there was another problem. When she opened the checkbook to pay bills, there didn't seem to be enough money in it. Life for one—when you still live in the same place, in the same way, with the same expenses—doesn't cost that much less than life for two. When one of the two dies, however, the income can shrink a lot. My father, like many men of his generation, had worked for the same company, the *Tampa Tribune,* for most of his career. Fifty-five years. For more than half that time, he had been editor, and then chairman of the editorial board. He was eligible, I suppose, for the best pension they gave the editorial staff. But because my mother's family tended to die early of heart disease, and his to live long, they had chosen the survivor plan that would pay the most if he survived her. They calculated that he would—a matter of genes. They forgot to consider that Mother was the only one among her parents and siblings who had never smoked, and that most of the ancestors with longevity on my father's side were spinster sisters who lived together in a decaying plantation house in Alabama, raised their own chickens, put up their own vegetables, and didn't drink. Bad analysis. Big drop in the monthly checks when Dad died.

Mother's response to all this, of course, was extra portions of the usual: a merry look, a jam-full social calendar, a talent for turning life's trials into funny stories, and a good dressmaker. With the right clothes, a sense of humor, and a dazzling smile, she knew, you could hide almost anything. Including the willpower it took to look that way.

"Your mother looks just wonderful," friends who saw her around town told me on the phone.

That way of managing had served women like her—and their husbands—through the Depression, World War II, the trying decades of the second half of the twentieth century, and often the deaths of those husbands. But as the century drew to an end, these women and their remaining men found themselves adrift in a zone of space and time they didn't know awaited them: the New Old Age. It was a territory they weren't prepared to inhabit. They all thought that—like their parents—they'd be dead by now. But life had gotten longer.

Some of us children, on the other hand—unencumbered by the rewards our mothers and fathers were enjoying for having grown so old (creaking bones, creeping dementia, fuzzy vision, dulled hearing, narrowing arteries, and failing friends)—had come to think of our parents as omnipresent and eternal, sort of like clouds and mountains, religion, football, chocolate cake, and Tampa Bay. My father, the newspaperman, a nonromantic, almost spoiled that notion by dying in January 1991, six years after retiring. He was eighty. Dad had probably worked too long, and as he got older, his blood pressure went up. He developed arthritis in his hands and feet, mild diabetes, and the family tendency toward sludgy blood. His eyes grew vague, his veins and arteries encrusted, his motions slower, and one morning, like an old Buick with high mileage, no available new parts, and a lot of rust, he blew a hose while still in bed with Mother. I was in New York. She phoned me as she lay there beside him, perhaps even before she called the ambulance.

"Dudley," she said, her voice dead calm, "you need to come now. *Now.*"

I caught a plane, and over the next twelve days, as we sat in his hospital room, my father expired in increments, with a few words, some murmurs, a lot of alarming long rattles, and a sigh. We pulled his intravenous tubes and let him go, because the rupture had been in his brain—a big bleed. The medical director of the hospital, an old friend who had hunted and fished with Faulkner as a boy in Mississippi—and who knew my father well—encouraged us to do it, because Dad would not have come back. But his body might have lived, and for a very long time.

It would have been more of a shock if it had been Mother. Dad was sort of distant. Mother had always been the anchor. Day and night, for the nearly two weeks that my father lay in that room, she left only once, to get her hair done. It was—as I came to realize—the single most important appointment in the calendar of a woman of her age and manners. Except for those two hours, she stayed with him day and night, sitting silently, sleeping wakefully in the chair—watching him, getting up to stroke his head, to pat his hand, to talk to him about things. She kept sentinel as he slipped away, hour by hour—and managed to look elegant and enduring and tragic the entire time.

After his death, as Mother stayed on in the house she loved and grew more frail, I got more and more worried. There were many conversations—phone calls, visits, letters, even memos—and finally, in 1994, perhaps to placate my sister, Melissa, and me, and because even Mother had to realize that her vision of the lovely widow in her lovely old house had gotten too hard to maintain, she agreed to change her life. She would sell the house and move to the place where many of her friends had gone.

Canterbury Tower. It is a kind of time zone, a never-never land, a small, cream-colored, obsessively well-run geriatric apartment tower and nursing wing, a last communal home, standing in a green patch of grass and trees, across a broad boulevard from an arm of Tampa Bay.

Canterbury had opened in 1977, three years before my wife, Nancy, and I moved to New York, but I hadn't noticed. I had no reason to be interested then. The place I knew from childhood where old people sometimes went to live was the "Old People's Home." A quiet, old-fashioned exercise in noblesse oblige, originally founded in the 1890s, and now simply called the Home, it was by the 1950s, when I began to visit there, a rambling old stucco building of two or three stories, with high ceilings, individual or shared rooms, a dining room with ceiling fans, big overhanging trees, and deep shaded porches lined with rocking chairs, in which gently sat poor old white ladies in cotton dresses, and a few bent old white men in cotton pants. You had to be able to pay something to get in, and something a month, but like the local Children's Home, it was a nonprofit, subsidized institution, supported and run by a group of business- and religious people—Episcopalians, Baptists, Catholics, Methodists, and Jews—for a certain class of the elderly in need. It was one way that communities in small towns and cities— in this case a southern city—provided housing for older people of little means in the last part of the nineteenth century and first part of the twentieth. It came about almost fifty years before Social Security and corporate and public-sector pensions began to give people some guaranteed income to live on. And long before the federal housing programs were created, at the height of the civil rights movement in the mid-1960s, as part of President Lyndon B. Johnson's Great Society. Those programs encouraged construction of low-rent apartments for the elderly low income and poor *of all colors.* That made them different from the Old People's Home, where one of my grandmother's friends lived and made a little money babysitting children like my sister and me.

The low-rent housing for the elderly that began to be constructed in Baltimore, where I now live, and then in cities across the country in the late 1960s and the 1970s, often took the form of plain, or brick-faced, concrete buildings of ten to fifteen floors, with two hundred or more modest studio and one-bedroom apartments in each. Sponsored by churches or synagogues, community organizations, unions that wanted to provide housing for retired workers, or other groups willing to create nonprofit corporations to take advantage of the low-interest, long-term federal loans being offered under the Section 202 program, that housing now exists in almost every city and town in America. Most cities have a number of buildings. The rents are kept below market rates, and the basic requirements for admission are that the applicants be sixty-two—which doesn't sound old anymore—and be able to pay the rent. The apartments were intended for the low- or modest-income elderly: widows, retired blue-collar or public service workers, people living on fixed incomes or in reduced circumstances. It was essentially the same economic class that had been served by the Home, and places like it—of which there were not enough—before the federal government got involved.

There was another Great Society program created in the 1960s called Section 8, designed to subsidize housing for the poor, ages eighteen and up. Those who qualify and are at least sixty-two often live in designated apartments in the Section 202 buildings, with most of their rent paid by the government.

Regardless of whether the government considers them poor or not, the main, and often only, source of income for many of the older people living in those buildings seems to be Social Security. I serve on the board of a senior building of 280 apartments in Baltimore, one of the first in the nation built under the federal 202 program, and when we conducted a simple survey in 2005, to try to find out more about our residents, we discovered that the monthly incomes of those who answered our questions were in the range of just $600 to $900 or $1,200 a month. Most were toward the lower end. Many people in the building have incomes of $10,000 a year or less.

The federal government sets certain standards for the construction and maintenance and management of buildings like ours, and there are regular inspections. But the staffing and services in our building and others like it that I have visited are minimal. There may be a beauty parlor operator who rents space in it, or a doctor or medical group, or a small convenience store operator, but there may not be. There may or may not be an inexpensive restaurant or café that rents space, or some food service. There may be a community food group that brings in a cheap lunch or early dinner for those who sign up. But there may not be. There may be an intercom, but there are no resident medical or nursing or emergency support services, or any housekeeping or other personal services provided within the apartments. They are basic apartment buildings with small residential spaces, some nice group spaces, but little support structure, and an aging population of residents who, if they live long enough, will have to move to nursing homes for the help they will need each day—in bathing, dressing, cleaning, cooking, eating, and taking the right medicines at the right times.

The nursing homes to which they will go are the ones that take Medicaid—the federal/state program that pays for nursing care for the elderly poor. To qualify for Medicaid, someone has to demonstrate essentially no assets and low income. Then he or she pays all but a few dollars of that income each month toward the nursing home bill, and Medicaid pays whatever its formula allows as the balance.

I discovered how the equation works when my father's two older sisters, my aunts Carolyn and Bessie, who were sweet, dotty, and going blind, deaf, and senile, almost burned down their house in Tampa one night in late December 1992. Mother and I went to the hospital and found them, dazed and smoky. It was the year after my father died. It was only a month after I had persuaded them to sign living wills and legal papers giving me power of attorney to act for them if I needed to. I had no idea the need would come so quickly.

But Mother had told me that Bessie had been staying in bed all day for months. And Carolyn had been seen wandering down the middle of their street.

For about eighty-five years—except for a few months when each had been married, at different times, decades before—they had always lived together. They were old-fashioned, southern country Christian ladies, eccentric, stubborn, and naive. Carolyn, who had worked as a legal secretary, had always cared for Bessie, who was nervous and silly, and mostly unemployable. They did not want to go to a nursing home. They wanted to go back home. They couldn't, I said. It was partly burned, and full of water and soot. Well, they could live in the maid's apartment in the garage, Carolyn said, as if that made perfect sense. It was full of termites and falling down, I said. They wanted to be together. So I put them in the only nursing home I could find on short notice that would take them both and keep them in the same room, even though Bessie, who had no money, would be a Medicaid patient, and Carolyn, who had some, would not be. Very shortly, though, Carolyn's savings were gone. All each of them had was her monthly check, and Medicaid. Bessie got $232 from Social Security. Carolyn got a federal pension of $405 a month, and a check from Social Security for $360. She had worked all her life. They each had to pay all but $35 a month—which they were allowed to keep in an account as spending money—to the nursing home. Medicaid dealt with the balance.

The cost of nursing home care is a giant part of the federal Medicaid budget, which itself takes a huge bite out of the whole federal budget. But the Medicaid formula, which differs state by state in how much it will pay, almost always pays less per month than high-quality nursing care actually costs, regardless of where the nursing home is. For that reason, commercial, for-profit nursing homes that accept Medicaid patients are less well staffed and equipped—in order to make a profit—than nursing homes that can charge more because they do not accept Medicaid. In other words, the quality of care in facilities that accept Medicaid is less than in those that charge more, to a more affluent clientele.

That shouldn't surprise. The retail cost of top-flight individual nursing care can be astronomical. In early 1993, a few months after Bessie and Carolyn entered Bay to Bay Nursing Home in Tampa— where care was priced at about $1,300 a month, recreation often meant ten wheelchairs hub to hub in front of an old television, and Bessie shattered an eyeball when another patient pushed her and her head hit the hard tile floor—my ninety-year-old cousin Florence was hospitalized in Clearwater with a lung infection. She and her husband, Louie, had moved there to a house on the bay after he retired from the United Nations in the early 1970s. After some years, Louie died, but Florence, a University of Chicago graduate and charter subscriber to the *New Yorker,* had remained fiercely intellectual and independent until the infection felled her. In the hospital, she was diagnosed with end-stage respiratory disease. She wanted to take some pills and die. She belonged to the Hemlock Society. That had always been her plan. Instead, released to hospice care, with registered nurses around the clock in her own home, she became the prisoner of a system that hid her pills and kept her alive for $15,000 a month—of her own money.

And that was in 1993. Florence's care was costing almost $14,000 more a month than Carolyn and Bessie's, and none of them was happy. When they all died, three and four years later, Florence's house had been sold. Her savings were gone. They were all in nursing homes. But Bessie and Carolyn had gotten so demented that only Florence, whose mind stayed sharp while her body fell apart, knew exactly where she was.

"I'll tell you," she said, "this is really hell."

Canterbury and other nonprofit life-care facilities were created to offer comfortable living and good nursing care by yet another formula. It was one designed to serve not the poor (like Bessie) or the shabby genteel (like Carolyn), but the middle class (like Florence and Louie), at a price that they could afford when they entered and that would not impoverish them in the end. The equation on which life-care facilities are based is an actuarial bet—a gamble. It doesn't matter at what age over sixty-two a person wants to enter, but new residents have to be able to walk through the front doors on their own power. No wheelchairs. They have to have enough money to afford the sizable down payment due when they come in, and enough income for the fee they contract to pay each month. The down payment buys them no equity, so if they die soon, they lose. Their estates get back some, but less and less for the first two years, and then none. But if they live long, they win, especially if they end up in the nursing wing, because the nursing care costs no more—except for the extra meals, pills, and nursing supplies—than the monthly apartment fee.

If not an entirely new vision, it was at least a highly evolved version of the basic idea of the Old People's Home. Founded and run as a nonprofit institution by the same kind of local religious and businesspeople as the ones who oversaw the Home, Canterbury looked and felt very different. It was housed in a vertical modern building, at a good address on the bay, with spacious apartments, a swimming pool, security guards, cocktail parties, good food, covered parking for the residents' well-cared-for cars, and an attached nursing wing. It was probably as representative of the best of community-based, nonprofit care across the country in the latter part of the century as the Old People's Home was of the first, but Canterbury wasn't just senior housing, and it wasn't just a nursing home. It was both in combination, with a lot of amenities to make it attractive.

Life-care (also called continuing-care) facilities began to open just as my father and his peers reached retirement age. My father was born in 1910. He had gone to work full time in 1929, the year the Great Depression began, having had to drop out of college after his freshman year, despite being on a full scholarship, to help support his mother and sisters. He was twenty-five when Social Security was created, in 1935. He and his friends—most of them men, in an era when most married women didn't work, and most of them managers, or successful salesmen, or business owners or white-collar professionals who prospered in the economic boom after World War II—were the first generation to spend almost all their working lives paying into Social Security. The system had begun paying monthly benefits in 1940, but they were the generation that reached retirement age just as Social Security checks began to swell with the newly mandated annual cost-of-living increases. That's the point at which Social Security income began to grow by 25 percent or more a decade. They were also the first generation to build meaningful pensions from long careers with corporations that had developed pension plans while they worked there. A lot of them also had houses to sell. Many, like my parents, had built or bought little houses in the years after the men came home from the war, with financing help from the Veterans Administration and the Federal Housing Administration. They had traded up to bigger houses as the decades passed, the economy expanded, their home equity increased, and they earned more money. The cash they got from selling their last houses, and the Social Security and pension checks that started coming the first or fifteenth of every month, gave my parents and their friends some freedom of choice in old age, even if they didn't have stocks or investments to sweeten the odds.

Many of them had been born at home, in their parents' beds, but they became the first generation to be freed of the idea that you were born in your parents' house and died in your children's—as my father's mother had, at Carolyn and Bessie's house. World War II, with the huge social dislocations it caused, and the ones that followed, mainly in the 1960s, had shaken families up, spreading their members and successive generations around the country. We children don't all live close to our parents anymore, and their new financial freedom meant that they didn't have to come live with us when they got old—as so many of their parents and their grandparents had done. They didn't have to live in an old people's home, either. They could live, within limits, where they pleased.

That was a relief, and the people who began to come to Canterbury Tower, from the time it opened in late 1977 through the eighties and nineties, did so for one of several good reasons. They didn't feel close to their children. Or they did, and didn't want to spoil the relationship. Or they had no children. Or they had children they wanted to be closer to. Mostly, however, they came to places like Canterbury because life had begun to feel fragile to them, and they wanted to be more secure, in a place they thought they could afford.

My mother was frail. Given her deteriorating bone structure and fainting spells, I knew she needed support, and would need more. But my father would never consider Canterbury. It depressed him. "I don't want to be around all those *old* people," he said. After he died, I worked on Mother to make the move. It took three years. I never knew what finally persuaded her. She was very stubborn. But when she saw what happened to Bessie and Carolyn, and to Florence, and watched me deal with them, she decided in early 1994 to make out a living will and to grant me her power of attorney. And that November, she moved to Canterbury.

I didn't realize, even after all my prodding, and research into comparative costs and services, and interviews with friends whose parents had granted them power of attorney, and long memos about all of this to Mother, what a change it would make. But the move began not just a very different phase of her life and her expectations of it, but also of our relationship and, more important, who was supposed to be in charge. Mothers like mine—southern mothers of a generation that was raised to flatter men, to reflect their identity, but, in fact, to manipulate and control them, and the families they produced—did not teach their children to take over when the time came. They didn't want to be taken over. They might want to be waited on, they might want to be provided for, but that wasn't the same thing.

And so we began a very complicated dance, a polite and formal sort of minuet, round and round, in which she, as usual, tried to exercise the lead without seeming to, and I, without seeming to, tried to take the lead without stepping on her feet.

My mother was an artful and enormously stubborn person. She had been very resistant to Canterbury, and she had the option that women in her situation often do—of stalling on decisions. Husbands frequently have no choice. God—or nature—snatches them away, years before they might have moved. But widows usually can choose or not to give up the houses that have been their homes, their nests, and chief creations, and it can be a hard choice to make. When Mother finally did agree, she had a troop of friends already at Canterbury. But our particular luck was that Helen Hogan Hill, a widow and family friend who had moved from Marietta, Georgia, into the north front apartment on the fifth floor sixteen years before, when she decided that she was tired and ready to be pampered, had decided to move again—this time to a smaller apartment. Helen had always been glad of her decision to sell her house and go to Canterbury, where there was a whole staff of people to take care of her.

"When I realized I wasn't in charge anymore," she said, "I felt better."

She decided she would feel better yet if she spent less money each month, so she gave up her two-bedroom, two-bath apartment and moved three floors down to a one-bedroom unit overlooking the building's entrance. Now she could keep tabs on everyone coming in or going out the front doors.

For her signature on a contract, $88,000 in cash, and $1,505 a month, Mother took apartment 502, Helen's old space. It landed her, by luck of the draw, in the middle of what I came to think of—as I visited and listened on the phone to her tales of life at Canterbury—as a special kind of soap opera.

As the years passed, the courage and grace and willingness to change that are required to negotiate passage through this New Old Age began to seem an exquisitely poignant and gritty and dear kind of odyssey to me. Our parents were increasingly what my friends and contemporaries and I talked about. Their drama had become the central drama of our lives. It was a drama—and a comedy—that I felt a part of, and that I wanted to be more of. The feeling grew, and after a time, I decided that there was a book of tales in Canterbury, about a new time in life, and that I should try to be there, with Mother and her friends, as much as possible to experience it and to tell it.

It has taken a while. I have now lived part-time in Florida, in that stubby little building, since the beginning of this century, with a crowd of people I have come to know as brave and pithy and funny, but, *uhm,* not young, and who have to flip the levers on their mailboxes in the lobby each morning to let the front desk know that they're still alive.

I was fifty-five when I started this experience. The average age in Canterbury is eighty-six. That's a difference. But I wanted to know what it was like to live out the New Old Age—roughly, the new last decade that advances in modern medicine and public health have given to the generation of the Great Depression and World War II, and perhaps also to us, their children, and our children, and all who follow. I wanted to experience growing older in America as it more often happens today, in ways that are so different from when our parents' own parents grew old. I have been at it now since January 1, 2000. In that time, particularly in the first five years, I spent almost four hundred days and nights living the life of Canterbury. I still go, and as time passed, the residents of the building, and the people who cared for them—people like Murphy, the maintenance man and bus driver, who was from rural southern Illinois; Chanh, the senior dining room waitress, a refugee from Vietnam; Carlos, the security chief, a retired U.S. Army first sergeant from Puerto Rico; and Ernestine, who sang songs of love and spiritual comfort to the oldest and sickest residents, songs she both made up and learned in church and on the farms across the bay to which her parents brought her from Mississippi when she was young—came to regard me with a kind of tolerant curiosity. We grew familiar to one another, and also fond. We have drinks. We have meals. We do our laundry. We spend time in the hospital, the nursing wing, the church, the bar, the living room, and the temple. We laugh and we get sad. We talk about children, work, health, fear, love, and money. We share the stories of our lives.

There are people there I have known all my life, to whom I feel very close. There are people I've met and have grown to like, or to love. Some are really funny. Some are deeply dramatic and wise. Some are simply interesting. Some aren't easily loved. But I set out to be their diarist and chronicler. As my mother's son and custodian,

I discovered how unprepared I was for this experience, and for my responsibilities in it. As a writer, I discovered that none of us is prepared.

No generation before has lived so long, accumulated so much, grown so independent in old age, or become so demented, as have our parents. No generation of children has ever been as large as ours, the baby boomers, or as dazzled and daunted and consumed by the apparently endless old age of parents as we have been by ours. Year by year, the New Old Age draws more of us into it. It is a growing national set of tales. This, as well as I can fashion it, is the very personal story of that time, at just one place, called Canterbury.

A PLACE CALLED CANTERBURY

CHAPTER ONE

Good-bye, Mother, Hello

SPRING 1998

Mother was in her bedroom, dressing to go out for dinner with friends on the Wednesday evening before Easter when things changed. She had been in her front corner apartment at Canterbury, five floors up, for three and a half years. It had become her nest, and usually, when we talked, she sounded happy as a canary in a tree. It looked out over the bay, at Davis Islands, and to the left, across the water, at downtown Tampa. She had come to like having the security, the supportive staff, the convenience of the dining room, in a building with so many old friends and new people to know. But everyone has a favorite place, and the Tampa Yacht & Country Club, where they were going that night—where she had been going since she was young—was hers. Two miles south of Canterbury on the bay, nested among ancient oaks, looking out at the ship channel down to the Gulf of Mexico, it was where people and things had altered the least. When you're getting slow and fragile and feeling out of touch—and it takes a while to put yourself together—it's a comfort to go to a familiar place, where the food is good and people know you and are glad to see you're still alive.

The members, the club, the staff had all grown old together. Mother was 83. The club—the favorite watering hole for old families on the south side of town (and cheaper than the golf club because it didn't have a golf course to maintain)—was 94. The staff was loyal, and like the members, aged with the place. Herbert, the club host, was 99. He had worked there more than half a century, had his own house, drove his own car, and took his much-younger lady friend out dancing. He looked 72. A *young* 72. He would live to be 107.

The informal dining room, with its brick floor, beamed ceiling, and captain's chairs, was the favored room of the actual young— children, teenagers, twenty- and thirty- and forty-somethings in tennis and cycling gear, boat clothes, shorts and casual pants, and knit shirts. But at lunch and at night, it was the softly blue-carpeted formal dining room, with its padded chairs and big white-framed windows looking out at the landscaped terrace and pool, the marina, and the bay beyond, that was filled with Mother's crowd—men and women in their eighties and nineties who had come together in Tampa after World War II to make babies, money, and a life. Dressed for dinner, sitting over cocktails with dyed and puffed and purchased hair, tucked faces, lasered eyes, titanium hips and knees, and propped-open arteries whooshing with miracle drugs, they flashed porcelain and acrylic smiles across the room as they spotted one another through trifocal glasses and implanted lenses. They waved gaily or politely, if a little stiffly (arthritis), and leaned close to make spirited, carefully enunciated conversation—most of which most of them could hear if their hearing aids were working right. Like Mother, some of them looked just wonderful.

The old friends coming to take her to the club that night were younger. Vic was just 73, Lee 69. They were lithe and pencil-lean, he in a jacket and bow tie, she in a snowy white silk blouse and pearls. Vic swam every day. He and Lee were in the club gym together three times a week. They were going to live forever. They needed to. They had to check on their mothers. Hers was 94 and prickly, still living in her hometown in the Florida Panhandle, about three hundred miles northwest. His was 102, still living alone in Ocala, almost one hundred miles northeast from Tampa, doing her own shopping and writing her own checks. Vic had been retired for more than a decade. His father had been dead for forty-five years. He hadn't inherited a dime. And every year, for Mother's Day, he and Lee spent two days driving around the state, visiting their mothers. They weren't alone. Several of my mother's friends had parents in their second century.

This was Florida, discovered by the Spanish explorer Ponce de Leon in 1513, in vain search of the Fountain of Youth. I don't know why he thought there was one. But eventually, something else happened. People started getting older. When I still lived in Tampa, just off the Bayshore, Frannie, our neighbor across the street, played tennis until she was 83. She worked out at the gym until she was 88. She pushed weights. She didn't feel old. Her mother, a pastor's wife and widow, had lived to be 105. She stayed in her own house until she was 104. She shopped, cleaned, went to church and out to lunch with the children of friends. The friends were dead. And every week she visited people she knew in nursing homes, to give them a little comfort and company. When she was 102, though, she quit. It wasn't that she didn't feel up to it anymore, she told Frannie. She was just tired of people falling asleep while she was talking to them.

Part of me had begun to believe that Mother was going to join this eternal company, too. Her body was crumbling. But her spirit was strong, her calendar full. She could always find the silver lining in the cloud, and get herself to the church on time. That was the way she lived. When Vic and Lee pulled around the little circular drive to the glass front-lobby doors under the portico at Canterbury that Wednesday night, they told the security guard on the desk that they had come for Mother. They waited. When she didn't appear, or answer the phone, the front desk called again, to ask if she was all right.

This time she answered. "No, I'm not," Mother said, the distress in her voice captured by the tape that had come on when she was slow to reach the phone. "I'm terribly ill, and I don't know what's wrong. *Please come*." The security guard phoned the nursing wing and headed for the elevator with a passkey. He would meet the nurse on the second floor, and they would go together to the apartment. Mother had been halfway through the ritual of making herself up, dressing for dinner, when she had staggered to the bathroom, suddenly ill. She had a blinding headache. She was violently nauseated. She was having what she had most feared, what everyone at Canterbury fears. It was exactly what my father had—a massive bleed in the back of her brain.

I t's funny. You have your mother all your life, through your twenties and thirties and into middle age—school, dating, marriage, career, moving, children, all of that. She loves you, fusses over you, dotes and rides herd on you, follows you by phone when you go away, and writes long, newsy letters that always make life at home sound like southern drama, funny stories, and lemon cake. "My Beloved Son," they begin.

In between letters, she sends countless, carefully wrapped, fragrant loaves of home-baked banana nut bread to your summer camps, your college dorm, your army posts and first apartments, so many that you gag at the thought of another loaf of banana nut bread. They pile up in corners like soft sweet bricks, wrapped in cellophane and tied with ribbons. She makes your favorite dishes when you come home. She has parties and dinners and invites your friends. She works to stay close, to get along with your wife, to spend time with her granddaughter. She is thoughtful, supportive, inquiring, opinionated. Solicitous. Persistent. All right, maddening. But she's your mother. The one person in your life who has been unfailingly attentive, available, loving, good-humored, and omnipresent. She structured and textured the whole world you grew up in. And so, without thinking about it, you make these assumptions: that you know her; that you are, in fact, just extensions of each other. That you don't have a choice about it. And that she is never going to disconnect. Then, deep into middle age, you get wobbled by some issues and see a shrink, who says: "Tell me about your parents."

And gradually you realize that you don't know your parents at all. Meaning you don't know their insides. You know only the outside. The Greatest Generation—parents of us dreadfully named boomers—may have been great. But they were also very much into role-playing. They didn't talk about themselves. I realized that I had no idea what my mother and father thought about the lives they'd lived—about their childhoods, or the part of their adulthoods when Melissa and I were children, or later, after we had grown up.

I found I had trouble recalling life with my parents when I was young. I couldn't remember much about my own childhood. I had images in my head, scenes from the neighborhood, the kitchen, and the family room: my dog, Bang, with his rusty freckled nose and waggy tail; my bike; the pup tent that was pitched for me in the back-yard; the games we played after school in the long afternoons; the thunderous summer rainstorms; the leafy forts we built, digging up the damp cool earth and cutting down small trees in nearby woods; the neighborhood boy who bullied me; the afternoon I beat him up; the dinners laid out at dusk on the round pine table in the kitchen, savory pork chops baked with apple rings; hot, feathery bis-cuits; moist, tender rabbit with brown gravy; green beans almandine and rice for the gravy. And Lassie and Disneyland on TV. I could re-member those things. But I couldn't remember the interior of fam-ily life, the scenes from inside the rest of the house, in which my parents and I would have appeared together.

"What was it like?" I asked Nathalie. We had grown up together, two houses away from each other. We had been involved in each other's families all our lives. Her parents, Mary and Wilber Davis, had moved to Canterbury before Mother did.

"What were my parents like?" I said, in all seriousness. "How did they treat me? What kind of relationship did we have?" These are the kinds of questions you bore your friends with when you go into therapy.

Nathalie had looked thoughtfully into the distance, as if she were trying to see the past. We were sitting at lunch in Tampa over bowls of *caldo gallego,* hearty collard greens soup made with rice and chorizo sausage; plates of black beans and rice and chopped fresh white onions; salads of lettuce and tomato, little olive halves and cu-cumber, vinegar and oil; and crusty warm-buttered Cuban bread. There was *flan de leche* for dessert, and *café con leche* to wash it down.

She was quiet for a moment. "Let me get back to you on that," she said.

About ten days later, back home in North Carolina, she called me. "I've been thinking about your question," she said, "and I've decided that we didn't have a relationship with our parents." They were the Grown-ups, she reminded me. We were the children. They made the rules. We followed them. That was our connection.

All right. We didn't have a relationship. And just as you realize that, and start working on what suddenly feels like your first real conversations with your parents, prying to discover the people behind the roles, trying to get them to be direct about things—trying to learn to be direct yourself—they start flaking away. When my father died, he and I were largely done talking about what we felt. We didn't need to say that much to each other. We never had. We weren't that close. He didn't know how to be. His father hadn't been either, and that's the way it was.

But Mother was more complicated. She and I were still in process when I found a message from Melissa on my phone at home in Baltimore from the night before, saying that Mother had had a stroke and was unconscious in the hospital. For some reason, I was stunned. Surely this wasn't it. I had a deadline that day, but I took a plane that evening, a cab straight to the hospital. It was after midnight when I went up the elevator and walked into the intensive care ward. There seemed to be no one around. Mother lay in the shadows, alone and still in a web of tubes and monitoring machines. It was strange, as if she were already on the margin of life. I took her hand.

"Mother?"

Her eyes fluttered open. But she wasn't there. Her eyes had changed. Her beautiful face, her good features and soft flawless skin, her luxuriant silver hair looked the same in the dim light, as if she were resting. But her eyes weren't gray blue, warm and expressive and tinged with gold, as they always were when they looked at me. They weren't looking at me. They weren't eyes. They were dark glittering holes, like wells, filled with the wild, black ghoulish energy I had seen only one other time. It had been just that way with my father, after his stroke seven years before: as if I were looking directly into the wreckage of his brain. But this was too soon.

Her eyes snapped shut. We weren't finished, and Mother was gone.

When you move away from home, the place where you were raised, each return—the long descent and downward circle as the plane comes in to land—is like spiraling back into the past. It has always felt that way to me. There is something about traveling through air that is like traveling through memory, something dreamlike about looking down at the earth from a porthole window in the side of a plane. I know I have been along this route before. If I am returning in sadness and uncertainty, then the journey feels more spiritual. I need to find the meaning. I keep looking out the window. I am in passage, and I need to know where I am.

Coming down from Baltimore or New York, through some part of the lower South, across the central spine of Florida to Tampa Bay, is a long arc over a light blanket of brown polluted haze, with breaks through cloud formations to distant vistas of shining and shadowed water. Endless coves and bays and rivers lie between green fingers of land below, with webs of highway, whitish clusters, and scatterings of cities and suburbs inland, and then smaller towns and settlements, green rumples of hills and low mountains. Isolated little villages and houses rest on the edges of flat fields of crops and orchards and woods, on lakes, swamps, at the ends of tiny threads of road in the middle of forests. The pattern melds and repeats, over and over. It is such a kaleidoscope of altered land and water and built forms that it is not until the pilot announces final approach, and the plane angles down through the lowest vapor cover, that I know I am in the groove, almost home.

The plane drops south through the clouds. The office towers of the city, standing where the thin silver line of the Hillsborough River empties into the bay, are to the right. Just below downtown, across a bridge, the irregular bulk of yellow and tan brick at the end of a green island studded with white is Tampa General Hospital, where my sister and I were born, where she and my mother almost died in 1954 in Melissa's very premature birth, where my father did die in 1991, and where my mother, in days to come, would lie in a coma, awaiting release.

Mother was twenty-nine when she had me there, more than a decade older than her mother had been when she started having children. But a lot of marriages had been delayed by the Depression—and a lot of lovemaking by the war. Mother worked, writing about the domestic side of life as editor of women's activities for the *Tampa Tribune*. There weren't a lot of pregnant women around town, and when she started to show, she bought a dramatically red, very broad-brimmed hat. She convinced herself that if she wore it, people would notice the hat, and not her rounding belly. She wore it all the time, and continued working almost until I was born. Beneath the hat, she had a high 1940s mass of wavy, chocolate black hair, dark eyebrows, high cheekbones, slightly olive skin, and those large, compelling eyes. I know, because her engagement picture, taken two years earlier, sits on a sideboard in my living room. My father was thirty-four. He was lean and muscular and handsome, I think, with slightly wavy auburn hair, rimless glasses, and a square jaw. During World War II he was with the Army Air Corps at Drew Field, near the present airport. He had already been a reporter and an editor for the *Tribune,* and so he was assigned to run the public information section at the field, under the officer in charge. He never had to go overseas. That's how I came to be born in 1944, the year after they married, and a year before most of the other fathers of my generation came home from the war and started making babies.

The plane glides south, along a clublike peninsula of land that hangs to the right in the middle of Tampa Bay, dividing the upper bay into two halves. The western portion is called Old Tampa Bay, the eastern portion, below the mouth of the Hillsborough River, Old Hillsborough Bay. The peninsula holds a part of the city now called South Tampa. It used to be a collection of very different residential neighborhoods that ranged from rich to modest going on poor. It is where my parents and their friends lived, some of them in the big handsome houses along the Bayshore, and some in much more modest ones off it. Palma Ceia, one of those neighborhoods—Spanish for "land of palms"—is where I grew up. Over the last decades, as more people have moved in, the peninsula has become dense and pricey, larded with restaurants, expensive shops, condominium towers, and close-built McMansions. The little prewar wooden houses with their screened porches, almost hidden in the deep shade and hanging moss of live oaks, on dirt lots so shaded that the grass wouldn't grow, are almost all gone.

Many of the big Georgian, Italianate, Spanish, Tudor, plantation, and white clapboard structures along the Bayshore, as the plane follows it south from town down the eastern side of the peninsula, date from the years after World War I and the boom time of the 1920s. That stretch of boulevard—and the neighborhood of brick streets, old trees, and large square houses with deep porches—is called Hyde Park.

Canterbury, standing where two big houses on the Bayshore used to be, comes up on the right about two-thirds of the way down. The Tower is a buff-colored fat cube of a building, fourteen stories tall, hung with balconies and set amid live oaks and palm trees, hedges and green grass, between two much larger towers, across the boulevard from the bay. There is no thirteenth floor—for the same reason, probably, that there are no black cats (at least none that anyone will admit to), although there was once a woman who hid her bad-tempered, beloved cat, pets being prohibited, until she died, and then, by her written instructions, had the cat killed, snuck out of the building, embalmed, and buried in the casket with her, lying on her breast. So the elevator goes from the twelfth floor to the fourteenth, and then to fifteen, the top, which is actually the fourteenth, where I now stay when I am there.

On the south and west sides of the building is the low L-shaped nursing wing of sixty beds where for years my mother was woken and bathed and dressed each day, brushed and fed, salved and bandaged if necessary, kissed, entertained, changed, turned, and finally bedded down each night. We spent hours, she and I, looking at each other, each of us wondering what the other had in mind.

But the apartment tower itself, where Mother first lived after my father died—moving at the age of seventy-nine into the north front corner of the fifth floor, with a view of downtown Tampa across the bay—has just one dining room, one social room, one small auditorium, one lobby, and two elevators for its 125 apartments and 165 residents. There is a modest swimming pool and terrace, a beauty parlor, a little gym, a tiny general store, a library stocked with pleasant books and magazines, the *Wall Street Journal* and *New York Times,* and a nurse's station where at certain hours you can have your blood pressure checked—and talk about what ails you. The whole thing feels rather intimate, like a good apartment hotel, a very adult camp, a tribal quarters, or some kind of club for the elderly, spunky, and vague.

The chunky Tower and its grounds lie at the intersection of Bayshore and El Prado. They take up about a quarter of the block, midway down a line of taller residential towers, most of them condominium buildings, that begin to sprout about a third of the way down the Bayshore from town. The penthouse apartments in the newer, bigger, much taller condominium towers on either side of it go for two to four million dollars—numbers that made some of the older residents on small fixed incomes at Canterbury shudder, and wonder, Who are these people with so much money? Where did they get it? And when did space in Tampa get so expensive?

The cedar-shingle gray and red asphalt roofs of the smaller houses in my boyhood neighborhood are three miles west of Canterbury. From the air I can't pick out the frame house that my parents bought new in 1948—two bedrooms and a bath, a living room and dining room, a little kitchen, screened porch, and single garage—for $12,500, or Wilber and Mary and Nathalie's house either. They've all been added on to, and they're nestled and overhung by the trees that have grown since then. But the buff brick hulk of Henry B. Plant High School, built during the Depression, is visible two blocks south of where we used to live. It's named for the railroad baron who in the 1880s made Tampa a destination by bringing the railroad to it from the north, and beginning a steamship line from Tampa to Havana. It was Henry Plant who imported the workmen and materials to create the enormous, eccentric Moorish-Victorian Tampa Bay Hotel, with its silver minarets and crescent moons and endless carved wooden verandas on the Hillsborough River at the head of the bay, as a winter resort for the robber barons of the late nineteenth century. They could ride down and back in their private cars on his railroad tracks. The hotel is where Teddy Roosevelt and other officers stayed in comfort while their men bivouacked on the grounds before steaming out of Tampa Bay to invade Cuba in the Spanish-American War, in 1898. Now the main building and symbol of the University of Tampa—with a portion operating as a hotel museum—the old hotel is one of the great architectural goofs of Florida, a state of monumental goofery, architecturally speaking, and otherwise.

In the summer of my sixteenth year, I worked at the county courthouse, a gray white marble blob downtown, across the river from the old hotel and east of the main office towers, at the end of the street that runs past the clock tower of the old city hall. The courthouse was built in the 1950s to replace the exotic brick Victorian one, which had awnings and arches, palm trees, a dome, and water troughs for horses. It looked like Plant's hotel. It had been designed by the same architect. The new courthouse was its aesthetic opposite, a soulless blah of a building. I worked for the clerk of courts copying deeds: Open the lid of the machine. Put the deed in facedown. Close the lid. Push the button. Wait for the light to brighten and dim. Open the lid. Take out the deed. Put another one in. The mind drifts. Some days I arrived without shoes because I was always taking them off and walking away and forgetting where I left them. After a time, a childhood friend of Mother's, an Annapolis graduate whose behavior had been kind of funny since his Navy service in the war, came to work at the courthouse, too. He was elected supervisor of elections after years of running for office. He was the town character, and full of zest. He had changed his name, created an organization called the Salvation Navy, which sold old clothes and junk from a decrepit warehouse downtown where he let derelicts sleep, and had a beard and hair like Jesus'. He let the bums sleep between the filing cabinets in the elections office, too, and dead voters pile up in the files. But with him there, the building had a soul.

He called himself Jim Fair, and I used to see him sometimes, down Bayshore Boulevard, at the yacht club. From Canterbury, the boulevard runs another mile and a half south, toward the club, before it shrinks at the edge of what remains of an ancient forest, becoming again a 1920s brick road lined with granite curbstones completely overhung by the gnarled, arching limbs of live oak trees. It continues that way past Ballast Point Park and pier—named for the incoming ships that used to dump their ballast stones so they could navigate the shallows of the upper bay—past the yacht club, a compound of columned white buildings among the oak trees, with a pool and marina on the water, and tennis courts, stables, and a riding ring and pasture across the street. The road then continues down through the trees, just off the shoreline, now jammed with new houses tucked among the oaks, to the gates of MacDill Air Force Base. The base occupies the bottom third of the peninsula. It is there at the tip of the peninsula that planes coming into Tampa begin to bank right, to loop under the base and back north up the west side of the peninsula to land at Tampa International Airport.

It was in the club pool, under the fantails of incoming flights, that the elections supervisor used to swim laps with a woman's rubber bathing cap over his shoulder-length hair on summer evenings, sometimes before coming to our house for a drink at Mother's invitation. It was one of the things she did. She visited or invited people—people who were old, or by themselves, down on their luck, or thought to be charmless, a little cracked, even crooked—because she knew that others ignored them. She always acted as if it were a joy to see them.

It was one of my mother's gifts. Almost everyone who knew her felt a special connection. She and the supervisor, in his rumpled seersucker coat, would talk and laugh over cocktails, while my father sat in a rocking chair, sipping his drink, making the minimal pleasant conversation, tapping a toe as he rocked, knowing that the evening would be over after a while. But I thought the supervisor of elections was the best company in the world. Sometimes, after two or three drinks, he would stand on his head and belt out a song about how he loved a billboard.

> *I love a billboard, I always will*
> *Because a billboard gives me such a thrill.*
> *When I was juh-ust a little child,*
> *A certain billboard drove me WI-I-ILD!!*

Then we would go for dinner to Tony's, a cheap Italian restaurant where the supervisor got free meals because he let them advertise on a billboard on top of his warehouse. All that was before he was removed from office, and before his family committed him to the state madhouse at Chattahoochee, where my aunt Carolyn had been.

Mother thought that was very unjust. If he could have gotten a pass, she would probably have had him back for dinner.

I slept in Mother's apartment when I left the hospital that night, after seeing her in her shadowed room, in a coma. It was a soft, breezy, dark night; a narcotic drive, even in a taxi, from the hospital down the curving, concrete, lamp-lit Bayshore. The broad landscaped boulevard, with its seawall and balustrade, is one of the longest unbroken stretches of waterfront promenade in the world. There is something calming about it, especially at night, with the wind and the lights of islands and ships and distant towers glimmering offshore. The sight of Canterbury coming up on the right gave me a welcome feeling. I knew a lot of the old houses along the boulevard, and the people in them, but it was the pale, off-white stucco cube of Canterbury Tower, its deep windowed dining room and café porch overhanging the thick grass and shrubbery in front, and balconies projecting off all sides, that I now homed in on when I came back. Mother's house was gone, and my feelings had transferred.

The cab turned right onto El Prado, a street still paved with bricks, then immediately left into the crescent driveway and under the portico. It stopped at the lobby doors. The leaves of the foliage atop the low wall along the drive rustled in the night air. The apartment windows above were all dark. No one at Canterbury except the midnight shift and those who can't sleep are up at that hour. The outer glass doors slide back automatically. The guard at the front desk looks through the window on your right, and—if you are expected—signs you in, and opens the second set of electric glass doors into the lobby. There is a mahogany sideboard, flowers in a tall vase, two deep chairs and a cushioned couch facing each other on an oriental rug. The walls are creamy, with halls and doorways ahead and to the right, the space behind the front desk a textured dark wine color, and on the desk are two shaded lamps that cast a low parchment light. The effect is warm, quiet, secure. The elevators are facing you.

It was even more quiet in Mother's apartment, and strange to be there when she was not. Everything looked so much like her. It was even stranger to be in her bed, the old four-poster that had been hers and my father's. There is a guest room for rent at Canterbury. But something made me think I ought to be in the apartment. Not staying there seemed disloyal, as if I didn't want to, or as if she had died. I didn't want to, actually. But she hadn't died—not yet—and I knew she would want me there. She always wanted me there. There was a sofa bed in the den, too, but the mattress was thin. The metal frame was prominent. I woke sore and kinked when I slept in it. So I slept in the bed, fitfully.

It was even stranger waking up in the morning, in the light, to my mother's life—her things, her colors and furnishings, the material sum of her—but not her, making coffee, making her cheerful murmuring morning sounds, trailing the fragrant scent of her various lotions as she moved about, calling out to me.

"Dudley? *Duhd*-leh? Ah you up, dahlin'?"

Well, now, yes.

"Ah want it to be a little Three Thousand Schiller Avenue," she had said when she took the apartment. That was the address of her house, and that's what she had done, with the help of a boyhood friend of mine named Keith, a decorator she liked—made it into a miniature version of the two-story, twelve-room house she loved and didn't want to leave. Because Canterbury had originally been designed as a condominium tower, the apartments were comfortable in size, and so—once Keith and Melissa helped her get rid of a lot of stuff—it worked. There were the same principal pieces of furniture, the rose pink and yellow and soft white upholstered chairs and couches, the mahogany tables, the same gilt-framed wall mirrors and framed photographs and pictures and certificates, the same faint cream and gold wallpaper and pale blue rug.

It had been just right. There were two bedrooms—one of which she turned into a den with bookshelves, the sofa bed, a padded yellow chair that leaned back and swiveled, a small color television, Larkspur, and a white wicker chest to hold videocassettes of favorite films for her grandchildren, Whitney and Christopher. There were two full baths, a closet that hid a stacked washer and dryer, a galley kitchen, a modest separate dining room, and a deep living room with sliding glass doors to a balcony outside. All the rooms looked down the boulevard and over the water.

The balcony was small, but on it she placed some patio furniture from the house, a couple of small garden statues, and some plants. She always surrounded herself with flowers and plants. When she had watered them, Mother would sit in one of the chairs and look down at the neighborhoods where she knew so many people, across the bay she had boated and sailed on and prepared meals from, to the city where her father and husband and she had worked, where she had been married, to the hospital where Melissa and I had been born, and my father had died. Not that she needed to look. The whole south side of the city was a network of familiar faces and places. She knew its social and cultural progression by heart. From birth to death: the hospitals, the neighborhoods, the churches, the temples, the schools and colleges and clubs. She knew its political structure and personalities, its restaurants and businesses and shops, its stores, newspapers, television stations, sports teams, and drugstores, its doctors, funeral homes, and cemeteries. It was her town, and she had worked and volunteered, cooked and clubbed, schlepped and schmoozed, organized and entertained in it from the time she left school until she came to Canterbury.

If you think about it, you can reduce the life of a woman of that era, a woman like my mother, to numbers. It was an era in which men did most of the quantifiable work. But in roughly sixty years of adult life—from the time she was eighteen until she moved into Canterbury—I calculated that she probably cooked more than a hundred fifty thousand meals (many of them for brunches, luncheons, and dinner parties); conducted half a million, a million, or more conversations (most of them effusive); and counted perhaps ten thousand people as acquaintances or friends (qualifying wasn't hard).

A number of the people she knew well, who were still alive, had come to Canterbury. Those who had not didn't live far away. Mother was lucky. She was as well positioned as she could hope for the uncertain years of the New Old Age. She was where she had always been. And her life had always been full.

So she shrank her household, gave away a lot of pots and pans, quit cooking except for light meals—else why move to a building with a dining room?—arranged her family pictures and favorite things, set up the bar, and began to fill her calendar.

It was easy. She was surrounded by old friends and neighbors. They were next door, down the hall, up and down the elevator. People entertained around the building the way they had around the neighborhood when I was a boy, with cocktails and dinner. But no one had to cook the dinner. At least one meal a day was included in the monthly plan they had all signed up for. They had already paid for dinner. So they just had each other for drinks. If they didn't drive anymore, the Canterbury bus went to the drugstore, the grocery store, and the liquor store twice a week. No one had an excuse for running out of whiskey unless they couldn't get on the bus.

It was a perfectly self-contained system. Mother, being Mother, invited new people for drinks to meet the people she already knew. And she went out a lot. She moved into Canterbury in November 1994. I have her calendar for 1995, a wall calendar that Stephen, my other half at the time, made for her. The top part of each month's page is a photograph from her life before. The picture for January 1995 is the front of her old house, in the shade of its trees. Every day of the month below is filled with drinks, dinners, breakfasts, brunches, lunches, bridge, book and garden clubs, church services, cocktail parties, movies, concerts, meetings, parades, boats, museums, birthdays, grandchildren coming for dinner and the night, doctors' appointments, funerals, and visits to my aunts Carolyn and Bessie in the nursing home. Most days have at least two events. Some have three or more.

February was the same. She was eighty years old that month. She didn't feel very good. But every day was full. In that whole year of 1995, there are only fourteen blank days.

Even between things, she seemed always in intellectual or spiritual, if not physical, motion. If I called and found her in, it was usually in the middle of something "marvelous" on the History Channel, or a concert of the Boston Pops, an old Errol Flynn movie, or the chapter of her latest book. Or she was on the phone with someone making plans. Or dressing to go out. Even when she called me—which was often—and got my answering machine, she got interrupted by someone trying to call her as she was leaving me a message.

"Hi, darling, it's Moth-ah—ha, ha—who else?"

Beep. Beep.

"Uhhm, wait just a moment, honey."

Click.

Unclick. "Hello? Hel-lo?" Pause. "Hell-o-o-o-o-o-o?"

Click.

She had never mated well with machines. And as more years passed, and her arthritis got worse, Mother got more out of synch with things.

Like so many people at Canterbury, she had already outlived her own mother, the longest-living member of her family, by almost a decade. "Ah'm gettin' to be an old lady!" she laughed, as if that were just the oddest thing. She was eighty-two. In a building in which the average age was eighty-six, that was not so old, and on her good days—in fact, on almost all days—she still wanted to go out. It was not a casual issue with her. Nothing but hurricanes and broken bones kept her from her calendar, and they didn't always stop her either. And when she couldn't bring me up to date in person, she did it through the answering machine. Even when she had something bad to report, she made a good story out of it.

"Hi, Dudley. It's about . . . uh . . . three thirty. Ah have been to the doctor this mornin' for extensive X-rays because Ah've had difficulty walking and a lot of pain for the last three days, and Ah knew somethin' had happened. And it has. Ah have a fractured pelvis!" she said, as if that was just the most remarkable and interesting thing. "Ah haven't had a fracture for twelve years, which is—you know—*wonderful*. Ah think it must be because Ah stopped taking the hormones, or Ah wouldn't have one now!"

Years ago she had found, to her horror, that the estrogen she took to try to stop the progress of her osteoporosis had reversed menopause, giving her menstrual periods again for the first time in decades. Nonetheless, she had stayed with the hormones all through her seventies and into her early eighties. Part of the battle of old age is the conflict between the good and bad things that medications do. They can help. They can also hurt. In her case, the renewed bleeding was excessive. It made her anemic, which made her faint, which was apparently why she kept falling down the stairs of her house. The falls had threatened to break the very bones she had been trying to preserve. Finally, about the time she moved to Canterbury, she decided to stop taking the hormones.

But now, without them, her bones were fracturing again. The doctor had prescribed a medical corset, rest, and pain medication for the broken pelvis. Mother, following his instructions and also her own star, had driven—a tiny figure, chin uplifted, just seeing over the rim of the steering wheel of her large old car—from the doctor's office to get the corset and then, of course, on to meet friends for lunch. Why not?

She had a very high tolerance for pain. And a very low tolerance for lying about.

"Ah went on out to lunch with Conchita and Gene," she said, finishing her report to me on the answering machine. "Ah'll be home tonight. Ah'm not goin' out. Ah'll have them send up some supper for me. Ah am goin' out to lunch tomorrow. And Ah'm supposed to go for a dinner tomorrow night. And Sunday. And Monday. So we'll just see. Ah think Ah can manage it. It bothers me to drive, but Ah can be picked up. Bye-bye, darlin'. Let me hear from you."

Her calendar for that month of 1995 is full. She didn't cancel a single thing.

Mother believed in dressing well. This kind of living required a lot of clothes. Clothes good enough to disguise the fact that she now had a very strange skeletal shape are expensive, and she was burning through her money. Since I had power of attorney for her—which she was glad for me to have, but of course didn't actually want me to use, not if it interfered with her life—we were having a kind of comical parlor battle for control. I was trying to keep her on a budget, which was silly. I didn't even have myself on a budget. But she kept doing things that struck me as, well, excessive.

Seven months after the pelvic fracture, something else broke. Mother was a little vague on the phone, so I called her doctor. "She has a fracture of the spine," the doctor said. "It's her lower back. A quarter of the way up the right side of the spine. She can't walk. Her right leg hurts very much. Her back hurts. She's on strong pain medication, every three to four hours." She needed a walker, the doctor said.

I flew down and found Mother in a room in the nursing wing, tucked and propped between pillows in bed, hair coiffed and make-up perfect, looking lovely. There was lunch on a tray. Louise Edwards, her maid, had brought china and silver down from the apartment and was sitting on a chair next to the bed. On a rolling table, between them, was Mother's silver ice bucket, with a silver spoon beside it.

"Louise, dahlin'," Mother said, with a sigh, "feed me summah that crushed ice withah spoon."

Louise opened the lid of the bucket, spooned up a shiny little mound of ice, and held it, dripping. Mother smiled at her and opened her mouth, and Louise slid the spoon it. Munch, munch. Mother looked content.

Louise came every day. I started forming a little speech in my mind about limited money and self-indulgence. There was, after all, a whole staff of nurses and certified nursing assistants to see to the patients in the nursing wing. They weren't likely to keep the bucket filled with ice, or to feed it to Mother in a silver spoon. They weren't going to sit with her either, smiling at her patiently, talking to her, fetching what she wanted, keeping her company, the way Louise did. The way, I remembered suddenly, that Mother had when Melissa or I got sick. She would fuss over us, fluff our pillows, bring us hot washcloths, or cold washcloths, books, newspapers, and sandwiches and fresh fruit salad and cold Coca-Colas on a tray. If we had stomach or intestinal flu, she baked egg custards for us. If we had a fever, she fed us cracked ice in a spoon. A silver spoon.

She wanted to be treated and comforted the way she had treated and comforted others. That's all.

I resolved to quit trying to be a disciplinarian, and in a few days Mother went back to her apartment. In a week or two, she began to resume her schedule. She didn't take the pain pills. She didn't get the walker. But she did resume the estrogen. It was her body. She was sure it could be made to work. She had the will. The doctor had the drugs.

It was her mind, I realized, that she was worried about. She was having little blackouts. She would be in her apartment and suddenly realize that she was emerging from a blank space. Her memory, which had always been an encyclopedia of the culture around her, and of everything she had experienced and read, was getting tattered. It felt slow and spotty. "Ah can tell Ah'm slipping," she said. "Ah don't think anyone else can, yet. But Ah can." She looked grave.

I had noticed, too. But I didn't say that. I thought the issue was vanity. She had always had such a good mind. I tried to be reassuring. She actually had far more intelligence and memory than she needed, I thought, particularly now. But I didn't understand what she was really worried about.

What she was worried about was a stroke.

Mother had not regained conciousness. For three days, as we shuffled back and forth from her room at Tampa General to the family waiting room down the hall, unable to sit very long in either place, she sank deeper into a coma. Soon, we knew, that day, or the next, or by the end of the week, with her eyes still closed (like my father in *his* coma), she would expire. The doctors were sure of it. She had suffered a massive bleed in the back of her brain. Could a person come back from that? I asked.

Her physician, Susan Zimmer, who had many older women in her care, looked doubtful. "Very unlikely," she said.

The doctors had suggested that morning that we should begin to think of disconnecting the tubes that nourished her. There was no doubt about her wishes.

"You *know* what I want," Mother had said numerous times, those eyes trained on me like gray blue lasers. And there was the living will, which spelled it out. But it seemed too soon. I needed time, hours, perhaps a day or so, to get comfortable with a decision that had already been made. The room was silent for a while, and then we began telling family funeral stories. Remembering was a way to get into gear. Besides, some of them were funny. Funny helps.

Aunt Virginia was talking about her husband, Baya. My uncle had been a formidable figure, the head of the state university board, a trial and corporate lawyer with his own high-powered firm, a former Army battalion commander of Japanese-American troops in World War II. But he got up at 4:00 a.m. to go to the office. He was a workaholic. He smoked and had heart attacks and by his late fifties was in physical decline. He shrank and grew so weak—sapped by the coronary artery disease that had killed his father at fifty-three, and would kill him, too, at the age of sixty-two—that one afternoon, while he napped in their silent air-conditioned bedroom at home, Virginia slipped his favorite white linen suit out of the closet and took it to a tailor, to be made small enough for him to be buried in. It was hard on her, just hanging around the house. Aunt Virginia liked to plan ahead. When she hung the shrunken suit back in his closet, she felt good about it. Loving and ready.

Then, to her consternation, Uncle Baya began to feel better. His appetite improved. He put on weight. Virginia imagined that she saw the beginning of a twinkle in his eye. Soon, he was going to want to get out of bed.

Oh my God, she thought. *He's going to want to celebrate. He's going to want to go out to dinner. He's going to want to wear that damn suit. It's going to be too small. What am I going to say?*

It was at that moment that the nurse appeared at the door of the family waiting room, her eyes wide and significant.

"Mr. Clendinen," she said in an odd voice, *"I think you need to come here."*

We all looked at her. No one spoke. I stood up. My stomach dropped, and sort of clenched, and I followed her down the hall. She disappeared through the door of Mother's room. I paused outside, heard nothing, and with an effort, looked in. I wasn't ready for this. There was my mother. Not dead. She was sitting up in bed, studying her surroundings with an expression of growing distaste. She had the look of someone who had been deposited in a hotel she had not chosen and did not like.

"This is really *awfully* unattractive," she said aloud, to no one in particular. Her gaze had stopped on a framed piece of generic, nondescript hospital art, hanging on the opposite wall. She glanced over at me, then turned back to the painting, a gauzy, indeterminate thing.

"I'd like that picture *down,*" she said, pointing at it. This was a mother I hadn't experienced before.

The nurse and I looked at each other. We took it down.

"Thank you," Mother said.

She continued her survey, appraising this dreary new space. I excused myself for a moment—she didn't seem that interested in me—and slipped back down the hall to the waiting room. I rounded the corner of the door and stopped. So did conversation in the room. Seven pairs of eyes looked at me.

"She's *back*!" I said.

We looked at one another. None of us knew what to think.

CHAPTER TWO

The Importance of the Moment

1998

Mother kept on living and, in a couple of weeks, went back to Canterbury. So I did, too, and began to experience more of the life she lived.

But there was a change. We didn't know at first that she would never return to her apartment. Her emergence from the coma had been so spectacular that we thought she might get well. For almost a week, in the quiet of her hospital room after she awoke, we had the most unusual conversations. Sometimes she posed me questions.

"How come you know so much about me?" she said one evening. She was propped up in bed, her gaze steady on me. We were holding hands, eyes entwined, each of us trying to plumb the content of the other's mind.

"I just find you fascinating," I said. "I've been studying you all my life."

She gave me a knowing smile, as if that were a nice riposte in whatever game we were playing, but said nothing. She would think about that.

At other times she made cogent observations about things large and small, as if she were seeing with different eyes or had just returned from a long trip to the moon.

"Your *hair* is gettin' thin," she said, her motherly fingers exploring the crown of my head. This mother—the one with so little affection for bad art or thinning hair—was new to me. The one I was accustomed to thought I was wonderful because I was hers. She would have said something more like, "My, what a lovely pink *scalp* you have, darlin'."

The doctors were amazed at her recovery. Practically dumb-struck. Distant, calm, thoughtful, she seemed surrounded by a kind of aura. But as I sat with her in her hospital room the night before I flew back to Baltimore, she made another observation, as if she had decided there was something I should know.

"Ah don't think Ah'm goin' to get well," Mother said, looking at me. Her expression was grave. She seemed pensive, as if her thoughts were elsewhere, perhaps where she'd been—or was about to go.

She was right. A few days after I got home, Dr. Zimmer called to say she thought my mother had had another stroke, a clot this time. She was comfortable, responsive, but her speech and movement were slipping away. I had to be in New York. Over the next two weeks, as I talked by phone to Melissa and Dr. Zimmer, Mother's blood pressure stabilized enough for her to be taken by ambulance to the nursing wing at Canterbury. She seemed to have lost the ability to speak, to walk, to do anything for herself at all. But she was smiling as usual, the nurses said in our daily talks, seemed to know them and to understand. She did not seem distressed.

That's not the way I found her. Perhaps, if I had come a day or a week earlier—or two days or even two hours later, it's impossible to know—the phase would have passed, and I would not have witnessed what I did see, and what I had never seen before: my mother in a state of rage against her life. I was totally unprepared. I turned the corner, expecting to find her sad, perhaps, smiling and subdued, and instead came upon a mad woman, struggling as if she were caught in a net, against the body that had become her cage. She was in a room by herself. There were no nurses or aides present. It was late morning. She was alone, and except for the pants and grunts of exertion, completely silent. She seemed totally furious. Plucking and pulling at her dressing gown with the one hand she could partially use, she turned and heaved in the bed. Thrusting up, she freed

herself of her gown, exposing her shoulders and breasts, and confronted me with a hideous, twisted, triumphant grin of effort just as
I walked in.

"You see? *You see how Ah am?*"

That's how I found my mother. I fled.

I could not imagine what was in her mind. I could hardly think.
I just ran to get a nurse—two nurses—and prayed that my normally
private and immaculate mother would somehow return to herself
and never do that again. The nurses scooted in, full of apologies, re-
dressed and soothed her and tucked her in. It was not their fault.
They could not be with her all the time. I think it was then that we
asked Louise to come back, and in a day or two, as quickly as it had
blown up, the storm in Mother went away. She seemed to settle. She
was bedridden and incontinent. She had to be fed, and she sometimes had difficulty swallowing. But she appeared to have accom-
modated herself to this new state of being.

My willful, complicated mother was much reduced. She was, in
fact, a wreck. Yet she didn't seem further inclined to complain—or
leave. She appeared to be once again herself—to have recovered her
lifelong focus on what joy there was in the moment. I could tell by
the way her eyes and face lit up when I walked into her room. She was
present. I was present. She was glad. We would make the best of it.

I think that may be the credo of the place. Whether in the Tower,
as Mother used to be, or in the nursing wing, where she was now,
Canterbury is filled with people who have come to understand
the importance of living in the present moment with as little
expectation—and as much satisfaction—as they can. Because it just
might be their last. That's the thing about this gift of longer life. No
one knows how long. You just know, when things get creaky, that
you need to be in a caring place. That is the shared need that brings
people of such diverse backgrounds to Canterbury, and probably to
the other tens of thousands of congregate communities across the
nation that house and serve the elderly. They, or their children or
grandchildren—people like me, who nudge and worry about them,

and may be legally responsible for them—are in search of the best last place for them to live and, ultimately, to die.

The result, at Canterbury and places like it, is a kind of national microcosm, a geriatric village in which people have different pasts but a common bond. The inner circle of local people—like my mother and her friends—may have known one another since pigtails and short pants. That is a long time—usually one or two husbands or wives, several children, a thousand dinner parties, long careers, several moves, a few deep sadnesses, and at least some great joys ago. Life evolves. Instead of being down the street or around the corner from one another in the neighborhoods they shared in childhood and middle age, they now are up the elevator or down the hall, still seeing one another after all these decades.

But most of the people in places like Canterbury are meeting one another for the first time, at almost the end of their lives. They come from different places and backgrounds. And so there are teetotalers and drinkers, penny-pinchers and big gamblers, people born on farms and in big cities, husbands and wives who have grown old and sweet together like candies in a box, and couples who can barely tolerate each other. There are spinsters and bachelors, men and women on their third marriages, and couples who aren't married at all who may have found each other one night walking along the bay. There are new widows and widowers, wondering whether they should look again for love, and how, and what they might expect of it. And old widows and widowers for whom romance is firmly a memory, and friends and family are the source of love.

There are southerners and northerners, people from the Midwest and the West, and people born in cultures and countries across the seas: Scotland, Bermuda, Mexico, Poland. There are a few staunch liberals and many conservatives. Fervent Baptists, prim Protestants, blasé agnostics, devout Roman Catholics, serious and nonserious Jews, and one declared atheist. In the building by the bay, there are people who have been a part of history—survivors of the Great Depression, D-day, the Holocaust, and of the American civil rights struggle—and also those who have managed to reach this age of life blissfully and essentially unscarred. Some have children who have been to war. Some had children who died. Some never had children.

Some are merry and some are glum. Some have vacation homes, jam-packed social calendars, and closets stuffed with smart new clothes. A number are rich, many are comfortable, and some barely scrape by. Some of them had money and lost it, and some just never made or married or inherited very much. A few men, in their seventies and eighties, still leave the building each day to go to work, but most residents simply work at the unexpected task of keeping this mysterious last phase of life meaningful and full. Most of them, by a ratio of about three to one, are women. They are not only more numerous than the men at this age but also more colorful and more vivacious and more involved in the Canterbury theater group, the Health Center support group, and other volunteer affairs.

If theirs is a generation in which women were commonly subservient, raising children, making homes and meals and social lives while their husbands worked, it is also a generation in which dominance in older age belongs to the women. Their husbands are mostly retired, or dead, and the men who have survived now pass their time in the amber that has always been the domain of women—the domestic hours. Even the management and most of the support and care staff of Canterbury—and for that matter, of most of the assisted living, life-care, and nursing home facilities around the nation—are women. But the men have their portfolios, and also their moments.

Everyone in the Tower dresses for dinner, and half a dozen widowers, most of them retired businessmen, have formed the Men's Table, where they eat together in the soft blue and white and bronze colors of the dining room on nights they don't have dates, discussing the latest news. Except for one, who keeps a supply of Viagra, they rarely have dates. They are the nightly male equivalent of the Chandelier Ladies, widows who meet for lunch each day at another round table under a large brass Williamsburg light fixture, looking out a big window at the bay. The men gather early, at 5:50, and are usually finished with dinner by 7:00—"So we kin get back upstairs," as Ben

Franklin, a lawyer and widower in his nineties, put it, "and do *nuthin'*."

But whatever their differences in background or perspective—male or female, Christian or Jew, northern or southern, rich or not—given an age range of roughly 72 to 107, what the people at Canterbury had most in common was this: They were older than they ever expected to be, and though the Great Depression had made them thrifty, they had decided to spend some of whatever money they had on a place they would rely on to take care of them—forever.

Two of those couples, Mary and Wilber Davis—Nathalie's parents—and Emily and Ashby Moody, were old, close friends of my parents'. Parts of the three couples had known one another since childhood, more than eighty years before. I had known them all my life. They were constants in the neighborhood when I was a boy. And now they were together to the end.

The Great Depression, bank closings included, had started earlier in Florida than in the rest of the nation. It began in 1926, when the real-estate boom broke, and it lasted a long time. "Some people god ovah id," Mary Davis later said. "Wilbuh nevah did." He was working as an office assistant at Ferman Chevrolet in Tampa when they met, in 1932. But he soon shifted to the office of a local lumber company. He stayed there, and ended up running it for the owner. Wilber was a compulsive manager and doer, as constant and busy as Mary was bellelike and easy. He also had an eye for proportion and a talent for organizing space. And, of course, he got a discount on lumber. Starting in the late 1930s, he and Mary built two houses and then renovated a third, selling each one at a profit. The cumulative profit became their nest egg.

Wilber planned the houses and then landscaped them. He was a constant and careful gardener. He surrounded each house with a green and colored glade of trees, plants and flower beds, and a thick carpet of grass, doing all the hard work himself for decades. He never paid a yardman.

By 1991, however, he was eighty years old, and the joy of mow-
ing and raking and pruning, of dragging around hoses and bags of
fertilizer, was gone. But not the pleasure of stretching a dollar. That
was part of Wilber's game. It was how he and Mary had kept up
through the decades with more affluent friends. When he became
president of the lumber company and was given a company car, they
drove the new company car as their new car, and bought the old one
as their second car. They had a maid six days a week—but just for
half days. They had one child, Nathalie—no more, though Mary always wanted another—because Wilber didn't think he could send a
second child to college. They had an active social and community
life, and many friends. They belonged to the best clubs and had
wonderful parties. Mary was warm and lively and fun. But Wilber
didn't take chances. He also didn't leave lights or fans on, and they
bought clothes and whiskey on sale.

By 1991, their maid, Berta Davis, who had worked for them since
Nathalie was born in 1943—and whose last name was a
coincidence—had begun to feel old. Mary hadn't kept house in almost fifty years. Wilber was tired of doing chores. They needed to
move one more time—to someplace that would last for the rest of
life—and their means were limited. Wilber didn't think they had
enough money for a nursing home if either of them should need it.
Canterbury, which required a lump payment up front but promised
to care for them always, even if they lived so long that their money
ran out, seemed the perfect solution and a good investment, even if
they weren't actually buying an apartment and thus could never sell
it, or leave it to their daughter, Nathalie. The bargain for Nathalie
was that they weren't going to move to High Point, North Carolina,
to live with her and Richard and the children.

So Mary and Wilber signed a contract with Canterbury, sold
their house, and in early 1991 paid $85,000 in cash to secure the
right front apartment on the fifth floor, 501, across from Helen
Hogan Hill in 502. The word at places like Canterbury for what
they did is *endow,* meaning that you don't purchase the apartment.
You pay just enough to endow your use of it. Theirs was a two-

bedroom, two-bath apartment with a small kitchen, a dining room, a living room with sliding glass doors, and a balcony that overlooked the bay. The monthly fee for services—which included all utilities and one meal a day for each of them—was $1,822.04. If one of them needed the extra care of the Health Center for a time, or ended up there for the rest of his or her life, the doctor visits, the medicines and supplies, and extra meals would add hundreds of dollars to their bill each month. But they had Social Security, Wilber's small pension, the income from the remaining $250,000 of their accumulated nest egg, and Medicare for major medical problems. Mary and Wilber calculated that they could afford it and still have some spending money left. The Canterbury board, which reviewed the health and finances of everyone who applied, agreed.

They were accepted.

It was a careful bet, typical of Wilber. He had always been a worrier and a planner, a man who fussed over details. But when Nathalie drove down to help her parents sort through their belongings, to sell off some things and pack what they would take from their last house to the smaller space of the new apartment, she noticed something odd about her normally relentlessly organized daddy.

All Wilber had packed, in two and a half months of supposed preparation, was eleven cases of liquor. One of them, filled with fancy bottles of bourbon, gin, vodka, rye, and Scotch that he and Mary had been given at Christmases and birthdays over the years, had been carefully labeled WHISKEY TOO GOOD TO DRINK. The bar cabinet was almost empty, but the rest of the house was still stuffed with stuff.

In a box on a shelf in the back of one closet, Nathalie found a huge old ball of string, which she recognized as her granny's— Wilber's mother's. It was the kind of frayed, fuzzy, rainy-day oddity that an old lady who had raised a family through the Depression might create. It had been in her apartment when she died, a ball of thrift, dear and comforting and unnecessary. Nathalie sighed and threw it out. The next day, in another closet, she found it again. Every time she heaved it out, along with boxes and bags of other stored and irrelevant odds and ends, it reappeared, tucked in another place.

Wilber was having a hard time parting with his possessions. But that wasn't all. When the sorting and packing were finally done, when the movers trucked Mary and Wilber's shrunken household to Canterbury and rolled the furniture through the lobby and up the elevator to the new apartment overlooking the bay, they found a puzzle. Wilber's carefully drawn diagram, which he had made to show the moving men exactly where to place each piece of furniture in each room, was rendered as if the apartment were on the left side of the hall as you looked at the bay. But it was on the right. The room sketches were all backward, mirror images of the actual space. Wilber walked fretfully from room to room, looking back and forth from the spaces to his drawing, muttering to himself, turning the paper this way and that. He was getting angry. Nothing matched up. He couldn't right the diagrams in his mind.

"He was just undone. I made him lie down, he was so undone," Nathalie said. "I thought he had had some kind of stroke." Then she calmly told the movers where to put the couch and tables and chairs, the lamps and boxes and kitchen goods and cases of whiskey. The box of whiskey that was TOO GOOD TO DRINK and the diagram, she realized later, were the first signs. Others weren't that long in coming. By the time the Moodys moved in across the hall, in October 1992, Wilber was having trouble remembering where he had parked the car. For a while, people sympathized. At Canterbury, everyone has trouble remembering things.

W as I supposed to call you about lunch, or were you going to call me? My memory has just fallen apart," said the Emyfish, in her best faux-drama telephone voice. It was morning, and we were going to her favorite place for gazpacho at noon. Her full name is Emily Maas Winston Moody. She is my "half-ass godmother," but she has always sounded like Bea Arthur. Or maybe, depending on how old she is, Bea Arthur has always sounded like her.

"Ashby is even worse," the Emyfish continued. "It's getting so bad around here, I'm thinking of moving to New York. I'll get a room at the Algonquin," she declared, warming to her theme, "and order room service, and live out my remaining days. Considering the way things have been going, there won't be that many."

The Emyfish had been around since I was born. But we reached an understanding, she says, when my mother, the newspaperwoman, dumped me into Emy's arms one morning and rushed back to work. I was crying.

"*Stop* that," she said. "I don't like crying babies." I stopped.

I started calling her the Emyfish when I was two or three, after she gave me a pink plastic fish whose plump cheeks I thought looked like hers. To get even, perhaps, she started calling me Jughead. We became each other's cartoon characters. The Emyfish and the Jughead. She also became the closest thing in my life to a fairy godmother. She couldn't be my christened godmother because she wasn't Christian, so she became my half-ass godmother. Her description. That way, of course, she could be as she wanted. She was German Jewish, though not serious about it. She's never been serious about religion, and German Jews in the South were very assimilated. She was a department store heiress, an only child born in Tampa—because her mother didn't want a Yankee baby—but raised in New York.

My christened godmother was my aunt Carolyn, my father's oldest sister, raised mostly in Alabama. She was *very* serious about religion. Pathologically serious. I much preferred the Emyfish, who mainly believed in life as theater. That seemed like a lot more fun. Emy had gone to acting school in New York. As a young woman, she tried to make a career on Broadway and, though she played some bit parts, hadn't done it—or didn't stay long enough to discover if she could.

"I couldn't stand the rejection," she said, in self-reproaching tones one day at lunch many decades later. "Isn't that terrible?"

She came back to Tampa—where her grandfather, Abe Maas, had founded the major department store Maas Bros.—worked for

National Airlines, acted for decades in Little Theater productions, and had the first television talk and interview show in town. She married Ashby, a handsome former college boxer and glider pilot from Tampa, after the war. He is as silent as she is vocal. He may also be younger, and at some point—I think perhaps when they began to date about sixty years ago—the Emyfish decided to become ageless. Coming from a household with a German nanny called Dodo, an English bulldog named Bourbon, a father who painted watercolors, played show tunes on the piano, and yelled *"He is riz!"* out the window of their house in New Rochelle, New York, on Easter mornings (and a mother who bought eight dresses at a time, quoted Oscar Wilde, and gradually went insane), agelessness seemed plausible. And smart.

"My mother always said that a woman who tells her age will tell you *anything*," the Emyfish said, in her deep, smoky voice, eyebrows arching under her mop of silver-white hair. She intoned the words as if she were uttering a sacrament. But her dark eyes looked amused. Her mother's and grandmother's bracelets clinked at her wrists. "So Ashby has birthdays. He has one every year. *He* gets older," she finished, dismissively. "*I don't.*"

Besides secrets, she hoarded other things. She still had the blue-chip stocks her grandfather Abe had left her more than sixty years before. In the case of some stocks, that was good. In the case of others, not. She and Ashby also owned a strip of little stores for which he had not raised the rent in years—maybe decades—and an antique shop he had not inventoried since the last millennium. They started it when her mother, Miss Jessie, died, and they cleaned out the big Victorian frame house near the bay, with its sleeping porches furnished with beds and tables, lamps and chairs. It had been her grandparents'. She slept out there on hot summer nights when she was a child, on the side porch on the second floor, with the oak limbs and palm fronds rustling outside, and fireflies winking in the darkness below. It's what people in Florida did before air-conditioning. The Emyfish and Ashby filled the shop with things from that house, named it Grandma's, and sold the house. That was forty years ago.

Now Ashby went to the shop perhaps ten minutes a day. More would be dangerous. "Someone might want to come in and buy something," he said, with a little smile. While he was ringing that sale up, someone else might drop in. Two customers could attract a third. It was an ominous prospect. It could lead to actual business, serious paperwork, regular hours. It didn't interest him anymore. He had become an authority of sorts, and had reason to be out from behind the counter. But the store, with its locked door and stocks of forgotten china and silver, old documents, trays of jewelry, jumbled furniture, and countless geegaws, remained—a dusty, quiet, moldering trove of uninventoried junk, a space that needed to be visited and checked on from time to time, like an old aunt tucked away in a warren of overstuffed, neglected rooms. And so Ashby was gone much of every day, out appraising furniture for divorces, estate valuations, or insurance policies, peering at someone's old maps or books or letters, studying some dented, blackened silver cup under a lamp, or looking in on the store—off on his own doing only he knew what. Following his curious silent nose.

The Emyfish, meanwhile, followed a familiar pattern: playing bridge, reading newspapers to the blind over the local public radio station, having lunch out with friends, shopping, seeing her doctors, arranging their complex social schedule on the phone, getting her hair done.

"He knows where I am twenty-four hours of every day, *and I never know where the hell he is,*" she growled, her dark-brown olive eyes a study in calculated grievance. "Someday I'm going to *kill* him. I really am." It was their routine.

For all her sense of theater—of the dramatic, the irreverent, and the absurd—it was she who was the planner and the scheduler, the caretaker, the worrier, and the stickler for the rules. The Emyfish might adore the stage, but she believed in compound interest. She was a woman who understood that if you take care of the present, the future will take care of itself. And so, at more or less the height of the cold war, she went off to Romania with her friend, our back-door neighbor when I was a boy, the cool, blond, beautiful Jean Kelly, who always wanted a marble mausoleum in her backyard so she could sit in the shade of it on hot afternoons and think cool thoughts. They stayed in a spa and were injected with ground-up sheep ovaries, pancreas, and adrenal glands, a treatment that promised to keep them looking young.

Decades later, they both still looked wonderful. I asked her if she had ever left the spa to poke around, to meet and talk with people in Romania.

"Of *course* not," the Emyfish said, looking at me as if I had turned stupid. "They were *Communists!*"

If part of Ashby's persona was loose shoes, then part of the Emy-fish's was tied laces—not because she thought that keeping them laced would keep her alive, but because at least she wouldn't die prematurely from tripping on them and falling down. Postponing death is half the equation for people at Canterbury. The other half is figuring out how to use the time so that they'll be *glad* they're still alive.

It was the Emyfish who decided that they needed to be at Canterbury. They were living at the time in a stuccoed beige condominium building on the water, on a small peninsula farther west along the bay. It was an apartment that looked out on a marina, an apartment the bay breezes swept straight through and that Ashby loved. They had a grand piano and a pianist friend who was a recovering alcoholic who came some nights and played show tunes while they had drinks. It was swell. But it was the Emyfish, perhaps because she's older (if indeed she is, given that she does not admit to being any age at all), who spent more time worrying about the future than Ashby did (or admitted to, anyway), and there was a time, more than a decade before, when she was sure that he was dying.

That's why they moved to Canterbury in 1992. They hadn't

planned to come then, and Ashby saw no reason why they should. But in the months before, he had started turning yellow. He went to his doctor, and then to a specialist. He ended up in surgery and then in the hospital, recovering, for a very long time—twenty-one days. The problem was unexpected and surprisingly serious. The Emyfish never did understand whether "it was his gallbladder or his liver or which one of those mysterious organs down there that was the problem." She wasn't good at having conversations with doctors. They made her nervous. But when the surgeon came out to the waiting room, he told her that if they were lucky, and the stent he had just put in didn't close up, Ashby might live another year. At least, that's what the Emyfish thought he said.

She never told Ashby that the doctor had told her he was a dying man—and Ashby didn't tell her what *he* had heard the doctor say, which was, if they had found cancer, he would have had only another year. Neither of those versions makes a lot of sense. But that's the way the Emyfish and Ashby sometimes communicate, and after thinking about what she thought the doctor had said, Emy came to a firm conclusion.

"I knew that I didn't have anybody and he didn't have anybody who was going to do anything about taking care of us, and so I decided it was time," the Emyfish said. She had had three miscarriages in the early years of their marriage, and did not become pregnant again. "God knew what he was doing when he didn't give me children," she declared ever after. Freed of the demands of the Little People, she and Ashby had lived a creative but very social and relatively carefree existence—with an emphasis on culture, friends, and fun.

More than a decade before Ashby's surgery, however—not long after Canterbury first opened—the Emyfish had written a check for a thousand dollars to hold a place for them on the waiting list. It was her money. They were getting older. And the Emyfish believed in covering her bets. When she understood the surgeon to say that Ashby was dying, she called to tell Canterbury that they were ready for an apartment when one came vacant. It didn't occur to her that Ashby might recover. Ashby had always liked to drink. Most men of his generation and social circle, in our part of the South, did. Suddenly, however, after his surgery—and surprisingly to the Emyfish—he gave it up. He did it the same way he had quit smoking. Just like that.

Ashby began to feel better. He didn't know the Emyfish saw him as a goner, so he thought her desire to move to Canterbury was a terrible idea. "He fought and screamed and died about it," she said. "He didn't want to move into an old people's home." For the Emyfish, however, whose grandfather Abe Maas had served on the board of the Old People's Home, and whose grandmother Bena had been president of the board of the Children's Home for years, Canterbury made perfect sense. Ashby kept improving, but Emy's mind was made up. Canterbury, however, was full.

If it had stayed full a little longer, things might have been different.

But fate intervened. A cranky, discontent, bibulous couple on the fifth floor, in number 504, just behind Helen Hill and diagonally across from Mary and Wilber, had a huge fight. The husband left. The two had never gotten along, but they were used to being miserable together. The wife soon began to miss her husband and their fights, and when he refused to come back, she moved out to join him in the apartment he had taken in another geriatric tower down the Bayshore. They immediately began to clash again. But before she could change her mind and try to move back, Wilber— the compulsive planner and doer—telephoned the Emyfish and Ashby. If they were quick, he said, they could probably get the apartment.

They did. Or anyway, the Emyfish did.

Ashby discovered that there are advantages to having a security guard at the front door, a nurse on call, a bridge game on Tuesdays and Fridays, a housekeeper and maintenance man to tend to things, and a dining room that serves breakfast, lunch, and dinner just downstairs. He found it was easier for him to maintain a separate schedule from the Emyfish at Canterbury than it had been when they were by themselves in a condominium. She could play bridge. He could do as he wished. He is natty and silver haired, has been tan instead of yellow for more than a decade now. He seems fine.

"He is. He's younger than springtime," the Emyfish says, with her musical chuckle. "He must like his doctors. He has so *many* of them."

CHAPTER THREE

A Place Unto Itself

1998

The days at Canterbury pass with a slow, good-humored dottiness and dignity. But they have an edge of panache, grit, and acceptance—as well as a kind of reserve—that seem peculiar to the place, connected to but apart from the quicker rhythms and more casual emphases of the world beyond. In that way, Canterbury and places like it are villages unto themselves, sheltered and segregated from the surrounding population, their class and cultural differences preserved and protected, so that each becomes a sort of demographic oasis, with its own needs and services, its own set of rules and folkways, and all that implies.

To function efficiently—to work within, and to maintain its difference from the world outside—such a place requires an authority figure, a real one, who understands the need to adhere to its formula and rules, who can control everything with a smile, understand the feelings involved, and manage with a ruthless attention to detail. At Canterbury, that is the dark-eyed, watchful, omnipresent administrator Mrs. Vinas. Caridad Vinas. Fast-moving, attentive, polite, absorbed by the needs and vulnerabilities of the old people she serves, she is forty years younger than the average age of the residents. But in a building in which almost all of the rest of the staff are called by their first names—and in which many of the residents have had long lives of conflict, survival, wealth, and accomplishment—everyone calls her Mrs. Vinas. It is a measure of her seriousness—and of her power over their lives.

She came from Fidel Castro's Cuba as a child of twelve, in 1968, with her parents and older brother. Her father, Isidoro, had a business selling the juice and pulp from sugarcane. He and his wife, Gina, and the children left a three-bedroom cinder-block house in Camaguey, with guava and lime trees in the back, and flew to Miami, where Gina's brother had already gone. Then they moved to New York, to Glen Cove, Long Island, and then, in the 1980s, to Tampa Bay. After community college, Mrs. Vinas began working in the nursing wing, where her workaholic habits, ferocious attention to detail, and obvious organizational talents stood out. She became the protégée of the then director of Canterbury and eventually succeeded him.

She is a perfectionist, warmhearted, all knowing, and tough as nails, and in the year of my mother's strokes, she presided over a primarily white residential population of about two hundred people, nursing wing included, that was sprinkled with a few Asian, Latin American, and European faces—and a black, brown, yellow, olive, and tan staff, many of them émigrés, who spoke with a variety of accents different from the inhabitants' own. Together, they lived and worked in a universe that moved at its own pace, and in its own way. There were cocktail parties where almost everyone sat down. A dinner hour in the Tower that began at five o'clock and ended at eight. Bullfrogs croaking in the (very shallow) swimming pool at night. A charity bazaar in summer at which clothes donated by the residents were sold, but that only employees were allowed to purchase (and never wear inside the building, thus sparing the awkwardness of some forgetful resident looking across the dining room and exclaiming, "She's got on *my* dress!"). And a second bazaar in the fall, at which residents (but *not* employees) could buy each other's cast-off clothes, take them home, wonder why later, and donate them for sale again next year.

There were people still living with the thrifty habits formed in the Great Depression, seventy years before—like rummaging in the trash bins on each floor for a free morning paper or to see what other useful things someone might have thrown away. There were more solemn customs, too, like a memorial service in the assembly room for almost everyone who died, regardless of whether a service was also planned at a church or temple outside. Death, after all, was the motivating reality of their lives. Its imminence was what had prompted many of them to come to Canterbury. Life at such an age meant cherishing the days you had, and honoring those who had no more.

And so, some years before, someone got Mrs. Vinas's permission—*everything* needed Mrs. Vinas's permission—and with donations, and the help of a nursery, started a rose garden for the dead—for the spouses whose deaths had led some of them to move to Canterbury, and for the residents—the friends, mothers, fathers, and grandparents—who had died there. The garden grew to occupy a deep bed along most of a long stucco wall, making a hedge of spindly green outside the chapel/assembly room, perfuming the air of the terrace by the pool.

There were also periodic arrivals of new people. They came with somewhat different accents and habits, each bringing a truckload of their most important possessions from lives left behind. The new arrivals came in the front door. The urgent departures (bound for the funeral home or hospital) went out the back. For the living, there were house rules of conduct. No guests in the apartment while you're away. (Like camp or college, Canterbury is a controlled environment. You don't own your living space, and you can't lend it.) No giving away the assets you listed when you applied to get in. (Inflation raises the fees each year. If you live long, you may need to cash in those stocks and bonds or sell that property.) No tipping the staff (although almost all residents contribute to an employee "Christmas bonus" fund, which is collected and managed by the residents, apportioned by length of service, and amounts annually to about $50,000). And no pets, although there are some. Feathered ones.

"What bird?" Mrs. Vinas would ask, with just the suggestion of a smile. She knew that birds—small birds—were not a problem. Birds live in cages inside apartments. They don't need to go out. A friendly dog jumping up on frail old people who totter around on walkers would be a problem.

There was a code of social etiquette: Coats and ties in the dining room at night, and no wheelchairs. No discussion of politics or religion. And don't ask people how they feel, unless you really want to know.

There were certain basic structures and amenities as well. There was, for example, a kind of club. (The dining room and first-floor social lounge, with its deep couches, upholstered armchairs, and bar, behind which Joyce, the social director, or Linda, the human resources director, or Joe, the portly, genial bus driver, might be pouring the drinks. At Canterbury, staff members often do double duty.) There was a kind of movie theater. (The screen being the big television in the lounge, with its video and CD player. It was a different experience from movies at the mall. If the videos were too sexy, violent, or profane, most of the audience would get up and leave— if they were awake to notice.)

There was a governor-general of the colony (Mrs. Vinas). A president of the local society (Martha Cameron, a retired lieutenant colonel of nurses whose personal cross to bear was that she was so competent as head of the residents' association that she could find no one to replace her). A post office (the mail room, with boxes for each resident). A home for the old and infirm (the nursing wing, which is called the Health Center and, of course, should be called the Un-Health Center). A sort of ladies' auxiliary (the Health Center volunteers, led by the inexhaustibly gregarious Sarah Jane Rubio). A social calendar (published and distributed monthly to the mailboxes, it scrolled daily across a television screen mounted outside the second-floor dining room) and a newspaper (a newsletter, the *Canterbury Tales,* which conspicuously omitted deaths).

There were regular religious services (Episcopalian, conducted by priests and laity from St. John's Church, on Wednesday mornings in the assembly room, and on Sundays in the Health Center). And a police force to protect the residents. (The little security staff, with

Carlos, the bronzed, brisk, trimly whiskered, shined and pressed former drill instructor and first sergeant in the U.S. Army, as its chief. Carlos had left his original homeland, too. He was born in the lush green folds of Puerto Rico in 1948, growing up outside the little town of Laers in the agricultural center of the island. But he left at eighteen for the concrete and tension of New York City, because he could see no future beyond a lifetime of seven-day weeks among the coffee and banana plants, pigs and chickens, and orange trees. "You become a slave when you have a farm," he said. "You do the same thing every day. All my brothers and sisters left." He wanted to be a New York City police officer, but when he applied, "They said, 'You should go into the service,'" and so he had.)

There were, not surprisingly, also certain hazards associated with living at Canterbury (dementia, heart attack, stroke, osteoporosis, Parkinson's disease, hurricane), against most of which Carlos was powerless to protect them. And a whole array of special needs and feelings. In such a place, friendships were very precious. They gave stimulation and pleasure to the day. They gave people—old people feeling as if they were at a strange stage of life—someone to turn to who could listen and understand, and help them laugh. But friendships at that age are as ephemeral as they are precious, and more transient than in the world outside. Among younger populations, external change—a geographic move, a relationship or job change, marriage, the birth of children, success, failure, divorce—can interrupt friendships, or bring them to an end. But in a village like Canterbury, the threat is from internal change. Bones break. Blood vessels rupture. Organs fail. Friends fade. They fall down.

Sometimes friendships end in a flat line on the screen of a monitor at Tampa General or some other hospital. But sometimes they end at Canterbury in a moment of quiet, unplanned ceremony, which begins when a member of the staff—Carlos or Murphy, the maintenance man, or another security guard, perhaps, or someone from the front office, or even Mrs. Vinas—appears on a hall and asks everyone to please go inside and close the door.

Then the door of an apartment in the Tower, or a room in the

Health Center, opens and out glides a human shape in a long zippered bag, strapped to a gurney. Escorted by the solemn, uniformed Carlos, pushed by the funeral home courier who has come to take it—usually a mild-looking, middle-aged man in unlabeled work clothes, or a white shirt and dark tie—the long bagged form on its light metal stretcher rolls silently down the carpeted hall to an elevator Carlos has held for that purpose. If the Tower had been designed and built for this last stage of life, it would have had the kind of elevator that hospitals and nursing homes do—a freight car wide and deep enough for stretchers and gurneys and hospital beds, for the couches and tables and household goods of new arrivals, and the outbound furniture, clothes, pillows, and sheets of the deceased.

But Canterbury Tower had been designed as and built for condominium apartments. For some reason, it doesn't have a freight elevator. And so the dead on their gurneys have to be stood up like mattresses or ironing boards to ride down in the passenger car. Sometimes they descend right side up. And sometimes upside down. Then they are turned horizontal again to roll along the waxed vinyl floor of the rear service hall and out the back door to a waiting, unmarked, windowless van into which they are loaded, locked into place, and driven quietly away.

The next morning, usually, a single long-stemmed rose from the rose garden appears in a slim crystal vase on a small mahogany table placed by the elevator doors in the lobby, along with a framed picture of the departed and whatever is known of the funeral or memorial service to come. That's how the others know for sure that one of them is gone.

The days begin early at Canterbury. As in hospitals or hotels, they don't really end. There are three shifts around the clock, the midnight to 8:30 being the smallest. The first load of newspapers, the *Tampa Tribune,* arrives at the front entrance by 5:00 or 6:00 a.m. to be taken up in the elevator floor by floor and plopped softly at the doors of subscribers. The *St. Petersburg Times, New York Times, Wall Street Journal* follow. A few souls—habitual early risers or insomniacs (old age brings restless sleep)—have already been padding around upstairs by then, among them Lucie Cross, the wary old nurse in 1205, peering under and behind things in her apartment, looking for the diamond ring she hid so the help wouldn't steal it. Born into a German American family on a farm in New Jersey in 1903, trained after high school as a nurse, Lucie had learned thrift and tidiness from early on. Old age had made her suspicious. So if she woke in the middle of the night, she got up and did something useful: She straightened drawers; she looked for the ring. By the time the papers came, she might have had some cottage cheese, a glass of Ovaltine, a piece of toast, and gone back to bed.

Mrs. Vinas often beat the newspapers to the door. She left her husband and children asleep in the dark of their house in the spill of suburbs east of Tampa, forty minutes away, in time to pull through the spiked black metal electric gate of the parking lot— activated by the sensor each car registered at Canterbury has clipped to a sun visor—at 4:30 or 5:00 a.m. She was almost always earlier than anyone. She worked longer than almost everyone. By her own instruction, she was on call twenty-four hours a day. Anything of consequence that happened, she wanted to know about. She never seemed to weary.

Sometimes when she arrived, Mildred Tate, the quiet, white, endlessly attentive director of food services, was already in her office by the swinging doors between the kitchen and dining room in the Tower, supervising the deliveries of food that came by truck, and the breakfast trays that went to the Health Center early in the morning. Mildred was a widow with sandy brown hair and a patient expression, and she looked tired. She had lost her invalid husband slowly, nursing him at home for long years before he died. She worked at Canterbury all the while, going home several times a day to feed and check on him, coming back to plan the menus; order the food; cater special events like picnics, birthday and cocktail parties, and holiday buffets; and supervise the staffs of the kitchen and of the dining rooms in the Tower and nursing wing. She arrived early in the dark of morning, stayed through lunch, and returned home to attend to

her own chores in the afternoon. She came back in the dark of evening. Almost every day. She seemed married to Canterbury.

By 6:30 a.m., as breakfast was moving to the nursing wing, the
certified nursing assistants at the end of the night shift there were
waking and changing and freshening the old people in their beds, or
helping them to the bathroom. By then, Carlos, the security chief,
was finishing his morning run with his big German shepherd, Spike,
through the quiet streets overhung with oak limbs down by MacDill
Air Force Base, where he lived in a tidy concrete-block house with
his wife. They retired there after twenty years in the Army, a career
that had taken him to Berlin, to NATO headquarters in Turkey, and
to the Defense Department's School of the Americas in Columbus,
Georgia, where he trained military forces from Colombia, Brazil,
Ecuador, and the Dominican Republic. In 1990, he had flown into
Saudi Arabia to help prepare the troops massing for the first invasion
of Iraq. Being part of the American military machine at war made
Carlos awed and proud. When he left the service in 1994, he tried
selling real estate in Tampa, but like a good first sergeant, he fussed
too much over the people trying to find a house instead of the people trying to sell one. In 1997 he answered an ad for part-time security work at Canterbury and found a home.

If he was working the morning shift, he would be in by eight to
take control of the front desk in the Tower and with it the building's
office phone and alarm systems, its doors and parking gate. Crisp in
a starched white shirt and dark tie, shiny black belt and shoes, and
pressed green pants, keys jingling, he was full of cheer. And like all
the department heads, he wore a pager and mobile phone to connect him to Mrs. Vinas.

"Ahyessuh [Ahyessum, depending on gender], essa bee-yu-teeful
mornin', suh," Carlos announced as people passed the front desk. He
said that every morning, as if he had personally tested it and found it
good, because he thought the residents should hear something cheerful about the outside world when they came down to start the day.

It was also at eight that the Tower dining room opened for breakfast, the event that officially began the village day. By then, usually, if

he was in town, the thin, balding, intense Dr. Mauricio Rubio, Sarah Jane's psychiatrist husband, would be walking quickly around and around the inside perimeter of the parking lot, head down, arms swinging, not speaking, intent on his exercise. By then, or soon after, Martha Sweet would have turned on the television news in 1501, started the coffee in the percolator, and lit a cigarette. By then, someone was usually pedaling the bicycle or walking the treadmill in the little exercise room on the first floor, off the hallway to the pool. By then, or shortly thereafter, Sarah Jane, in 1504, and Martha Cameron, in 901, would have uncovered and exchanged morning coos and salutations with their respective cockatiels, Pretty Boy and Pepe. Pepe had appeared several years before on the seventeenth-floor balcony of the apartment in the condominium tower on the Bayshore where the Rubios then lived, at about the same time that Bobbie and Bill Faber's bird flew out of the condominium apartment where they lived, in a different building on the Bayshore. The ebullient Sarah Jane took the friendly little gray bird in, bought him a cage, and named him Pepe. It wasn't until the Rubios and the Fabers both moved into Canterbury, and Bobbie Faber was visiting one day, that the mystery of what happened to the Fabers' bird, and where the Rubios' came from, was solved.

"Sarah Jane," Bobbie said, "that's my bird." But by then, Pepe liked the Rubios. They decided on visitation rights.

By 8:00 a.m., the beauty parlor on the first floor, with its chairs and sinks, towels and hair dryers, and stocks of hair color and shampoo, opened for the day. Almost all women of Canterbury age and manners have their hair washed and set by someone else. Many residents—those from Tampa and those who still drove—had their own hairdressers in town. Some of those relationships had lasted longer than marriage. But for those who didn't get out, the beauty parlor was as vital to life as food and water and clothes to wear.

The little general store, with its toiletries and tissues, notepaper, and boxes of cereal and cans of juice, opened about ten. By then, the juice cart was rolling around the Health Center, bringing cartons of juice—vitamins, hydration, and sugar—to the residents there. It was a little break and energizer for the main event of the morning in the nursing wing, which always began at 10:30. On Sundays, it was church; on other days, cooking class with Mildred, music with Arthur (piano), Skippy the Clown, polka music and dance, conversational therapy, music with Dottie (guitar), or Remember When.

By then also, the residents in the Tower had begun flipping the little flags on their mailboxes in the lobby, so that the desk would know that they were up and around—and alive. Some people, of course, forgot. Some were out of town. Some didn't like getting dressed before lunch and asked a friend to do it. Sometimes the friend forgot. By about 2:00 p.m., the little green lights on the ceiling by the elevators on each floor would wink on to signal that the mail was in. If by then the flag on a mailbox wasn't flipped, Carlos would call the apartment and, if necessary, come upstairs with a master key to check on its resident.

If it was Monday, the Canterbury bus went at 9:30 in the morning to the post office, and to a big discount store at 11:00. At night, there was bingo in the assembly room. If it was Tuesday, there were exercise classes or water aerobics in the morning. The Canterbury Lincoln would take people to appointments by reservation at midday. The bus went to the bank in the afternoon. If it was Tuesday or Wednesday or Friday, there were several tables of bridge in the card room in the afternoon, dominated by tough old ladies in their nineties like Lucie Cross and Jessie McKinzie, a retired Tampa school principal who had decided to move to Canterbury when she came home one day and found her husband dead in the bathtub. On Wednesday, there was Scrabble and a film at night. If it was Thursday, the bus went to the grocery in the morning, and the pharmacy and liquor store in the afternoon. It also took those who had signed up to a picnic lunch on Picnic Island. Mildred's kitchen staff packed the lunch. If it was Friday, there was coffee and Danish in the Wedgwood Room, a smaller lounge on the second floor, across from the dining room. On Saturday morning, the bus went to a mall. That night, there was a movie.

And every day, in the dining room, there was breakfast, lunch, and dinner. For those who had no car, no family, no real friends—and there were some—it was possible to be monitored, fed, entertained, and moved about, from chore to chore and function to function, within the schedule and structure of Canterbury, and feel that they had a life.

Most people at Canterbury, especially the ones from Tampa, who had family, social, and cultural connections in town, had their own lives. Some of them, like my mother, had full and even complicated schedules outside the building. But for many who were by themselves, and from elsewhere, Canterbury was a whole universe, and breakfast in the dining room was a way to start the day.

You wan' bagan? Scrambal eggs? Toes?" Chanh asked. She was the senior breakfast waitress, a small, pretty woman of thick, lustrous coal black hair, a serious face, and large dark eyes that looked as if they had seen much trouble. Canterbury is an *Upstairs, Downstairs* culture, and like most of the core staff, Chanh had paid her dues. She was South Vietnamese. In the shadows of her expression, in the life she left behind, lay civil war, the death of a brother in the South Vietnamese Army, the Communist takeover of Saigon, a desperate escape from the country, with her children, hidden in the back of a truck, which took them to a waiting boat, a husband left behind, pirates who stopped and boarded the boat at sea, a long stay in a refugee camp, and the complicated adjustment to a very different new culture. It took more than a year for her husband to make his own escape through the pirates to join her. All this in preparation for more than a decade of waiting on dotty old white people in the cream and blue and soft gold dining room overlooking the bay.

Chanh had worked at a progression of jobs in Tampa before coming to Canterbury in 1989, but it was this one she intended to retire from, and she had become used to the odd habits of the aged clientele she served. Sarah Jane Rubio brought her own little crystal bottles of sea salt and olive oil and vinegar to every meal (and at Christmas, her own china). In the evening, she wanted Grape-Nuts on her frozen yogurt. Each time she ordered them, Yuri, the lawyerly maître d' on the evening shift (who was, in fact, a lawyer in his home country of Bolivia, and whose leftist parents had named him after the famous cosmonaut in the golden age of the Soviet space program), solemnly explained to Sarah Jane that Grape-Nuts was a cereal, and that the kitchen rules required him to charge her for breakfast if she ordered it.

Each time, Sarah Jane insisted the Grape-Nuts were her dessert, not her breakfast; that her husband, Dr. Rubio, was away most of each week, which meant that the two of them had not eaten hundreds of prepaid meals. She should *not* be charged for a sprinkling of Grape-Nuts. But Yuri had his instructions. He had to charge her. Neither side would budge. The issue began to agitate the dining room. Other people got involved. One night, the Emyfish, who was sitting with Sarah Jane, scowled at Yuri and yelled at him. Finally, another resident bought a box of Grape-Nuts, marked it FOR SARAH JANE, and left it in Mildred's office in the kitchen.

Everyone thought that was brilliant.

It wasn't only Sarah Jane, of course. The independent-minded Martha Sweet, who was from Pennsylvania, put salt on her ice cream. The Emyfish and Mary Davis poured Sweet'N Low into their glasses of white wine. Lucie Cross, a Yankee, put sugar on her tomatoes. One person put ketchup on her eggs. A few men and women spoke to no one, and ate alone. Wilber Davis wanted to talk to everybody. Others would sit only at the same table each time. The oldest widows—some of whom, like Jessie McKinzie and Helen Hill, who were approaching a hundred and who had sat near the windows looking out at the bay in decades past—had quit eating dinner downstairs years ago, and now claimed the table nearest the dining room doors each day at lunch. That way, they didn't have to walk the long distance across the dining room to sit at the windows. And they could monitor everyone who came in and out.

Some people came and left every day always at exactly the same time. Others—like Doris Garcia, whose husband's family had owned a cigar factory in Tampa—seemed to have no concept of time, arrived late for lunch, and stayed long beyond the closing hour. And some—women, usually—asked Chanh or Yuri or one of the other waiters for extra rolls, which they carefully wrapped, along with the food they didn't eat, tucked into their purses or the baskets of their walkers, and took with them, even though it was against the rules to take food back to the apartments.

Working at Canterbury was like being on the household staff of a large, sweet, absentminded, slightly privileged, gently eccentric family. The place was full of people of idiosyncratic habits, some of whom broke a rule from time to time because they didn't care—or just sort of lost track of where they were and what they were doing. Or what they weren't supposed to do. One morning, Martha Sweet's large gruff husband, Charles, a retired judge, lit a cigar as he sat in the dining room, reading the *New York Times* after breakfast. In a building with many old people with breathing problems, it was perhaps the next worse thing to absently pulling out a loaded gun. But it didn't panic Chanh. She had come through war and pirates at sea. She was a waitress, not an enforcer. Whatever the problem was, the system at Canterbury would deal with it. There were rules, subbosses, and department heads above her, and all lines of authority led back to Mrs. Vinas, the ultimate enforcer. Being part of such a system, in such a place, gave Chanh back some of the feeling of security that she had lost when she fled Vietnam, where her family had had a bicycle shop and house in Saigon, and a farm outside the city.

And it was not just her. All the principal figures on the staff at Canterbury—Mrs. Vinas, Mildred, Carlos, Chanh, and several others—seemed to have lost some foundation, some important element at an earlier point in their lives, or left it behind and found its replacement at Canterbury. It was the same with Ernestine, Robin, and Murphy.

Ernestine, the ample, loving, unparalleled, coal black singing hostess and chief personality of the Health Center—who took to my mother as she took to all the hurt and crippled and demented souls who were brought to live in the nursing wing—had come in the 1950s as a child with her parents, field workers, from the town of Itta Bena, in the middle of the Mississippi Delta, to a tomato farm near Ruskin, across the bay. Living in a little wooden house in the fields, they had an outdoor toilet and a no. 3 galvanized tub that they filled from buckets to bathe in each night. When she was a girl, in picking season, Ernestine plucked the green tomatoes from the vines and dropped them into red plastic buckets, which she carried to the men waiting in the truck. They gave her a ticket. When she turned in the tickets, she made about $1.25 a day. Ernestine stopped school after the sixth grade and, when she was almost fourteen, married Clifton Burnett on that farm, and started having babies. He was twenty-one. They are married to this day.

The other male figure in her life was Jesus. Ernestine loved to sing the gospel. At a prayerful, singing, shouting celebration at a little country church on another farm one Sunday, at the age of fourteen, she became a preacher. All this occurred on the fertile belt of agricultural land just across the water and south of Canterbury, ten or fifteen miles beyond the factory smokestacks that mark the eastern edge of the bay—not that far, but a cultural world apart.

It was not until decades later, after moving out of the tomato fields to work in federally funded migrant–child care programs, and then in day care programs for the handicapped children of migrant workers—and then in caring programs for the elderly—that Ernestine heard about Canterbury from a friend who worked there as a housekeeper. She made her way around the bay for an interview and, when she walked in, felt "like this was it." She began cleaning apartments in the Tower. That was in 1994.

She had a husband and seven children, six of her own and one she took in to raise. She needed steady, full-time work. But she had always cared more about people than about planting or harvesting crops, or cleaning rooms in buildings. She gravitated to the old and the vulnerable. It was her nature, whether it was her job or not, and after a time, by the nurturing warmth and force of her personality, Ernestine moved from the Tower and became the paid heart and comfort of the nursing wing. There she followed her own instincts, calming the agitated, jollying the depressed, crooning to the ill, sitting death watch with the dying. It was as if she had found her natural work.

"You're home," her husband, Clifton, said, when he brought her to Canterbury each morning before 8:00 a.m.

By 3:30 or 4:00 in the afternoon, when Ernestine left to go home, Robin, the blond, breathless, dressed-to-the-nines marketing director who moved always in a rush of words, a series of high-intensity blinks, and a clackety-clack of high heels down the hall, might be making the last checks with Murphy, the maintenance man, to be sure that the apartment she was about to show was ready. Robin was also from far away, in her case, Australia. She came to Canterbury by way of a career in fashion that had taken her through London and New York, and left her flamed out and on a kind of respite with friends, on the east coast of Florida, staying at the beach. Robin was always slightly mysterious and nonspecific about what she'd done before—she didn't even want her last name mentioned in this book—but it apparently had to do with marketing to the relentless need to stay young and attractive. It had never occurred to her that she might find a different career in selling comfort and security to the old. But she had lost her role and also her desire to stay in the work she'd known. And she had gotten older.

In a newspaper, she saw a notice for a job fair. Robin was a high-energy personality, accustomed to being busy, and she was bored. So she went. Canterbury had a booth and also, as it turned out, a vacancy. She came for an interview, liked the feeling of what she found, and, to her considerable surprise, decided to try marketing a place in which to grow really old. She had the sales office, a two-room suite painted a handsome, clubby sort of British green, furnished with gleaming dark woods and rich, brass-studded leather upholstered chairs. She learned to live with the fact that the thermostat, and the source of the smells that filled her office each day, resided next door—in the beauty salon. The air temperature tended to be warm, so as not to freeze old ladies whose heads were damp.

And the aroma might vary, hour to hour, from sweet mango coconut, to lemon, to papaya, to the nose-curling scent of scorched wet hair.

Still, it was about sales—about what Canterbury offered that people discovered, at a certain age, they needed. Robin adapted, and became a cheerleader.

"They're getting a great restaurant! They're getting life care! They get to be in Florida! And they're saving *hundreds* of thousands of dollars!" she exclaimed in a rush, her eyes bright, blinking intensely. "They get to be on the water, but not the beach, near three hospitals, with downtown five minutes away, the airport fifteen minutes. And all the medical specialists they'll need are here. It *seems irresistible,*" she finished, breathlessly. "And when I get through . . . *it is!*"

Robin liked to show off the building, and its apartments, in the good light of mid or late morning, when there was energy in the halls, or in the golden amber light of late afternoon, when the boulevard beyond the dining room windows pulsed with beautiful young joggers and the towers of downtown Tampa glowed copper and silver in the slanting sun. The location, the boulevard, the cheerful staff could take care of themselves, but it was Murphy who was Robin's unseen partner in marketing, because it was he who got the apartments ready.

Murphy, the droopy, slow-talking, mustachioed maintenance man, with his glasses always riding low on his nose, was a native of the hill country of Illinois. He had retired from MacDill Air Force Base and come at first to work on the custodial staff, cleaning and tending to the building and grounds. But he had stayed on and worked up, graduating to stopping leaks, installing lights, repairing air-conditioning units, and replacing refrigerators and stoves—though not because the residents wore the stoves out by cooking so much. Usually, in fact, they didn't cook, and so often forgot what they had last used the stove for.

They might have put damp, rinsed-out stockings in the oven to dry one morning, turned them on to bake, and wandered off. They might have developed a yearning for frozen chicken pot pie and turned the oven on to preheat, forgetting that they had tucked a stack of old newspapers in there while tidying up the kitchen, and the plastic and Styrofoam containers in which they had brought contraband food from the dining room.

Smolder. Flare. *Foom!*

A day or two after the fire department departed, Murphy would appear either to replace the stove or to remove an element that he could then claim was still on order, no matter how long it might have been on order, or how many times the forgetful resident remembered to ask. The resident could store as many newspapers in the oven as she wished, but not turn the stove on without the missing part. It wouldn't work. The part was on eternal back order. The building was safe. No more *foom*. At least not in that apartment.

When he wasn't not fixing stoves, or installing new fixtures and appliances for Robin, Murphy sometimes drove the yellow Canterbury bus, or the silver gray Canterbury Lincoln. He became a fixture himself—while directors of maintenance, the men who were his bosses, came and went. Mrs. Vinas kept firing and hiring them.

"They *never* believe me when I describe the job to them," she said, shaking her head in wonder at the impenetrable vanity of the male supervisory species. "I tell them they will be on call *twenty-four hours a day*. That they *have* to get in here anytime I need them. They *all* say they understand. That they *want* the job. And then I hire them, and they find out it's true." And when they turned out not to be as available, as efficient, as resilient, quick, or capable as she expected—which so far was almost every previous one of them— she fired them.

But Murphy endured. Like Mrs. Vinas, he was on call seven days a week, twenty-four hours a day. He was the only person on the staff who could fix everything. He liked being indispensable; it suited his temperament. But not his wife's. She moved out. It seemed to leave him more cheerful, and anytime something went awry, in the morning or the afternoon, or the middle of the night, Murphy would appear.

This was the colony that my mother came to inhabit when she moved, in 1994, into 502; across the hall from Mary and Wilber, in 501; and next to the Emyfish and Ashby, in 504. It was as if the circle of old friends had re-formed of its own volition, within the larger core of a population more reflective of the broader world.

Rabbi Karl and Ruth Richter, who had the grim advantage of an extra monthly check of two thousand dollars from the German government—in compensation for the salary Karl had lost when the Nazis dynamited his temple and began murdering nearly all the Jews, just before he and Ruth escaped Germany in 1939—were already in residence up on the eighth floor. They had come in 1991, the same year as Mary and Wilber. The gregarious Sarah Jane and her restless, reticent husband, Dr. Mauricio Rubio, arrived early in 1995, taking 1504, a big apartment that looked down the Bayshore toward town. Within two or three years, Martha Cameron, the retired lieutenant colonel of nurses, who had military and civilian pensions; Judge Charles and Martha Sweet, who had pensions from their separate careers; and the formidable Elizabeth Himes, of Tampa, an old friend of my parents' who had her own money as well as her husband's and his Social Security, all moved in.

When I had started visiting, with so many familiar people there, it felt at first like a different incarnation of the old neighborhood. Some things were different, but others were the same. Instead of streets, there were carpeted halls. Instead of houses, there were apartments filled with the essence of the same stuff they had had in their homes. I saw some of the children I used to play with come and go, visiting their parents. Some, I noticed, were looking way past prime. Some of my parents' friends, on the other hand—like the Emyfish and Ashby, and Elizabeth—seemed almost unchanged. Others were older, slower. Dimmed.

There were other differences, too, the most noticeable being so many new old people—like the Sweets, the Richters, Helen Hill, Lucie Cross, and Martha Cameron—who had lived in so many other places. That was a big change, because now there wasn't a common set of manners or a common past. Now there was only a common condition: The people who lived at Canterbury had all grown old.

One night, coming back into the building after 10:00 p.m. in the months after my mother's strokes, I walked through the electric front doors and there was Wilber. The building is essentially shut down by that time of night. The dining room is closed. The people who were out to dinner are back in. The movie in the social lounge is over. The people in the nursing wing are asleep. Everyone in the Tower is upstairs, most of them in bed.

The day is almost finished.

But Wilber was standing in front of the elevators, tilted a little to the right, peering this way and that. It wasn't just his car that he couldn't find anymore. He was looking for Mary. He'd just left her upstairs, but he didn't realize that. When Wilber looked away, or stepped away, sometimes he didn't remember that Mary was right there—in another room in their apartment up on the fifth floor. He just remembered Mary, and then he missed her. He had begun to go looking. He was looking for the life he'd had.

I had known him since I was a boy of four and he was Nathalie's father, a man of forty. We had lived just one house apart in the old neighborhood, which had begun as a street of new houses, of husbands like him not long back from the war, and their soft, newly (or once again) pregnant wives. And their children—Nathalie and Carla, little T. Paine and me. Wilber had known all the ways in which I was trouble from the day we moved onto that street in 1948 until the last decade, when he began to forget. But his eyes lit up when he saw me coming into the lobby at Canterbury that night, and he blinked, trying to remember who I was and where we were—and just when in his life this night might be.

"How old are you now?" he asked, rocking gently, his bright blue eyes peering at me. His hair had turned silver, and he was shorter and smaller, droopier than he was when he gardened all the time.

"Fifty-three," I said, standing beside him.

Wilber was astounded. In his mind, I think, I was probably still the neighborhood boy, the rebellious teenager, the hell-bent young man whose features he could see behind my softer, fuller, current face.

"Oh com'on," he said, laughing a little. "You're pulling my leg."

No, I assured him. I was fifty-three. He frowned and blinked, and began to calculate.

"Well, then, I must be . . . I must be"—his lips moving, counting numbers—*"I'm over one hundred!"* He gasped, marveling at such a thing. I tried to tell him that he wasn't, that he was eighty-eight, but Wilber had gotten very deaf. He refused to wear his hearing aids, and he was absorbed in his calculations. He stared at the floor and then looked up, eyes agleam. He seemed to have made a great discovery.

"No, no . . . I'm older than that," he declared, pausing as he worked it out. "I'm, I'm—why, I'm a thousand years old!"

He was agog at the realization, and in a way delighted, and then something else, something delicious, occurred to him. He grinned and pulled me close.

"And you know what?" he said, his eyes wildly bright and merry. *"My pecker still gets hard!"*

This seemed potential great news for generations of other aging males, if not for Mary, and I was trying to think of the appropriate response when I heard the night security guard, a man only in his sixties, sigh loudly from behind the front desk. He had been taking in this conversation.

"Better than mine," he said, sorrowfully to himself.

I left the two of them to wherever the conversation was going to go from there, and took the elevator up. This may seem odd. It did to me. But I began to think that night that I had never felt so alive in a way as I did when I was staying at Canterbury, where everyone else was so very old. My mother had been stricken. I was being drawn into a place where many people were diminished. And yet life had never seemed more original or surprising. Or imagination more real. It felt the way Mother had raised me to think of life—as a novel. At Canterbury, I felt as if I were living simultaneously in the future and the past, with possibilities I didn't know existed. I was in the realm of Thousand-Year-Old Men with Erections.

What else was there to know?

CHAPTER FOUR

A Reason to Be Alive

1998–1999

Mother had become mysterious, as silent and beautiful as the Sphinx. It was as if her highly verbal, sociable self, always so engaged, had decided to take a rest, to sit this stage out, leaving her gracious, smiling self in bed in her room in the nursing wing, immaculately dressed and made up as always—attentive, thoughtful, appreciative of company and help, reactive in expression to what you had just said. But her expressions were subtle. Nuanced. It wasn't so much that she had become unknowable. She *looked* knowing. The thing was, I couldn't be sure of what.

She did not seem distressed. She betrayed no irritation, no frustration, no anger or self-pity at the turn life had taken. She was not going to be a bother. It was lovely of you to change her pants, to clean and dress and brush her, and sit her back in her chair. I'm fine now, dear. Thank you. Oh—you're wheeling me in to music with Arthur? The Piano Man. How nice. She remained, in other words—most of the time—in character, as if she had found a level of polite contentment commensurate with her state of being. Her manners were virtually intact. And while she didn't seem to feel any of the negative things, she did seem to feel the positive. She appeared quite distinctly to feel pleasure, and she made you feel, by the way her eyes and face lit up when you walked into her room, that it might be because of you. Meaning me. Melissa. Louise. Christopher. Whitney—when she was home from college. All of us.

Mother appeared to have found a balance. A focus. A reason to be alive. It wasn't simply that she would not let go of life. She wouldn't let go of *us*. In the face of such resolution, as I went back and forth between Tampa and Baltimore, and Tampa and New York that year, sitting and talking with her over a period of months, I began unconsciously to accept that my mother might remain in the realm of the eternal—clouds and mountains, football games, Tampa Bay, and chocolate cake—after all. That she might continue to change physically, to mutate, as it were, in the years ahead, but not actually depart.

And so, without at any point deciding to, I gradually allowed myself to feel, and to behave, as if her smile, that beautiful face, those large, loving, gray blue eyes, would be on me forever.

I began to assume that we had a deal. Mother had reached a new semipermanent condition. She had become a smiling, nuanced, almost teasingly inscrutable presence. Occasionally, she spoke a few words. Mainly, she looked at me expectantly, and waited. I wasn't sure for what. But there seemed to be time enough to know, because she clearly intended to stay. Well, fine. I would look after her. I was legally responsible for her, as I had been for my aunts Carolyn and Bessie. It wasn't hard. And besides, I felt drawn to be there, drawn by this latest, intriguing version of my always complex and seductive mother.

It wasn't hard because I didn't have to do the work. Nathalie and I were lucky that way. Not just lucky. Fortunate. We didn't have to give the care, and so I wasn't the one who turned my mother in bed every two hours to prevent her from developing sores, or who toileted and diapered and dressed her, bathed and weighed her, applied her rouge and lipstick, her eye shadow and eyeliner, snapped her earrings on, lifted her in and out of her chaise longue, wheeled her down the hall to meals or group events, or fed her in small, slow spoonfuls, waiting while she chewed and swallowed, smiling at her, talking to her all the while, letting her take her time. I wasn't the one who took her temperature and pulse and blood pressure, who tucked her pills into applesauce and spooned it to her, who sang to her at church on Sundays, or at sessions with the Piano Man, who salved and bandaged the little tears in her fragile skin, carefully pulled her up when she slid too far down in the chair, or tucked her into bed at night. I wasn't the one who kept checking on her, all through the night, and if she was awake, sometimes sat down and stroked and talked to her quietly, telling her how much they all loved her, everybody did. Her son and daughter would be coming back soon. She was in the care of a system, a kind and relentlessly well-managed system. The certified nursing assistants—Claudia, Meva, Star, and Marcia—and Mother's maid, Louise, did those things.

It was the choice our parents had made. To give someone else the burden. We were fortunate in their choice and lucky they could afford it, even if barely. In most families, it is children like us—usually one child in particular, but sometimes several siblings, or even whole extended families—who give the physical care their parents need when they get old and tottery, or demented, or ill, either because there is no money to allow them to go to someplace like Canterbury, or because family cultural traditions reject the idea of institutional care and place that responsibility on the children. Some people very much want to care for their parents, their grandparents, or their aunts and uncles at home. Or feel they should. Or just despise the idea of their parents being one of a crowd of shuffling, ghostlike souls in some geriatric colony. Carla Kelly, with whom Nathalie and I grew up in the old neighborhood, cannot imagine having her parents, Jean and Paine, at Canterbury, because she cannot imagine being there herself.

"I would rather die *alone in the woods,*" she said one day, shuddering at the thought. She is the eldest child, a Ph.D. psychologist and independent spirit, a woman of beautiful green eyes and blond hair, and cool classical bone structure. Carla is a bit of an introvert. She likes her solitude. The idea of managed communal living gives her the creeps, and so she had always planned to care for her parents herself. She and perhaps her unmarried daughter, Hillary, a nurturing spirit and teacher. She would take a leave from her career or simply retire, Carla said, and move in with them if she needed to. Or Hillary might.

The idea of moving in with Mother gave me the same creeps that moving into Canterbury gave Carla. But I didn't have to. Mother was taken care of. She was down the elevator, down a hall and through three doors from the Tower full of old and new friends, in the Health Center, all dressed and fresh, ready for company. And the company came, at first, but many people, even old friends, had trouble relating.

"Yoah Mothah duzzen know me *from Adam*," Mary Davis said, in her languid, certain way, after she and Wilber went to visit. "She duzzen havah *clue.*"

I thought she probably did. But we couldn't be sure of that, of course. Mother didn't talk to Mary. She rarely spoke at all, and then only to say "Thank you" or "Yes" or something else simple to the staff. Usually, she remained silent, lovely and mysterious, a serene presence whose eyes seemed always to be watching. She didn't say what she thought or felt—about herself, or me, or Mary, or the rest of life. It was almost as if she was enjoying the role. But that was the way she had always dealt with life. She made you think she was enjoying it. That attitude—and the other traits and pieces of personality that seemed still intact—had begun to make me feel that our relationship had in fact survived. Enough that was familiar remained, so that we *could* understand each other. I was becoming sure of it. It was just a matter of focus and form. Once I forgot about the silenced voice, once I focused on her eyes and her face—her marvelously expressive face, which had always seemed capable of a thousand shades and gradients of emotion (like a trained actress, a very good oil painting, or, in her case, a consummate hostess), once I settled into the habit of just talking to her—talking with my eyes as well as voice—and watching her eyes and face, letting them guide me, I became convinced that it was just our way of communicating that had changed. As the flow of words between us had diminished with each stroke, our expressions of thought and feeling had become purer, I told myself. Less cluttered by words.

More intense.

It was, after fifty-four years, as if we had refined the complex, still-conflicted, in some ways willfully unresolved relationship that existed between mother and son to the bare essentials. For most people, the relationships with our mothers are the longest ones of our lives. Mine with my mother had seemed to get more complicated as we got older. In addition to being a woman of great empathy, energy, charm, and good works—who worked constantly at the task of making life seem graceful and effortless for the rest of us—she was also calculating, relentless, and stubborn. The more she aged, the more infirmities she attempted to conceal, the more help I thought she needed, the less control she was willing to relinquish (and the less I was willing to be manipulated or to humor her), the more delicate and multifaceted our relationship became. We needed lawyers and psychologists to help us talk to each other.

In middle age, when it had finally begun to dawn on me what a controlling personality she was, I had arranged for a joint therapy session with my mother and father, with the therapist who was leading me through a thunderous midlife blowup. We actually had two sessions, which seemed more like debates argued to a draw than anything else, mostly between mother and the shrink. When they were over and my parents had left Atlanta to go back home, I asked the shrink what she thought of Mother.

She looked at me in silence for a moment. "Margaret Thatcher," she finally said.

And so some part of me, I think, was secretly glad for my mother's reduction. It seemed simpler now to know where we stood. If I said something that amused her, Mother would laugh, her mouth opening in wide merriment, her eyes hilarious, even a little mad, and I could take that to mean that she was happy. So I tried to think of funny things to tell her.

If she smiled, and seemed relaxed, I could take that as contentment. So I tried to talk about things that would warm and comfort and relax her. What warmed her most, I found, was to hear me say I loved her, and so I always told her that. It was true. It was the beginning and end of all our conversations.

But if she looked grave, or distant, if her gaze seemed uncertain, then I was at a loss. I had no way to know whether she was troubled by some thought or feeling I couldn't guess at, or simply frustrated by her brain-damaged remove from life—by some formless sensation or thing she didn't understand, didn't know how to think about, much less express. I realized that I had no idea how her mind worked anymore, or whether she still had what she and I would have considered a mind. She had always had such an interesting mind before—strong, thoughtful, curious, retentive. She seemed to know everything about everyone in the world in which I grew up—all their relationships and histories, their strengths and weaknesses and needs.

She had been in charge of women's and family coverage and then of food for the *Tampa Tribune* in the 1940s and 1950s, a time when food and families and houses were the common daily work and main means of expression in women's lives. Especially in the South. With Mother in the kitchen—or Allene, our maid, when Mother was at the paper—the little house my parents bought after the war, and added on to when Melissa was born, became an aromatic wonderland. Mother seemed always to be cooking or writing, entertaining, supervising my childhood, or flying off to food writers' conventions in places like Chicago, New Orleans, San Francisco, or New York. The ones in New York were at the Waldorf. The women in the photographs she brought back all wore big hats and smiled. It was the 1950s, a boom time, and people were working hard and celebrating.

The great rituals of the decade, aside from football and politics, were church and cocktails. Followed by dinner. Not serially, of course. Church was on Sunday morning; cocktails and dinner were every night.

Religion, I think, was the link to the past, and also the consecration of the families my parents and their friends were all building after the war. It was all part of a continuum. Next to stained glass, organs, and silver crosses, worshipful women have always been the chief adornment of churches, and my mother looked wonderful in a pew. In church or out, she always carried herself as if she had a little private chapel, with the choir singing "Oh, Happy Morning," tucked between her breastbone and her spine. She loved the feeling of communion. I knew that, because as a child I knew how much she loved dragging my father and me to church for it. It was important to her. We were southern, after all. Florida southern, and Sunday mornings were a ritual: grapefruits plucked from the tree behind the kitchen of our house in Tampa, cut in half and broiled with brown sugar, and served on the old brick patio with country ham, cheese grits and egg casserole, tomatoes baked with Parmesan, and baskets of biscuits with the consistency of warm buttered clouds. It was a sublimely tactile and sensual meal ruined, from my point of view, by an abrupt rush to St. Mary's, as Mother and all the other women in her tribe hauled their husbands and children out of the home station like so many family taxis, to get them to the church on time.

It was a penance of bells and hymns, prayers and lessons, solemn sermons and soulful expressions. The kneeling and the sermon and the sharp, interrogating look that the plump, perspiring Father Mangrum gave as he grabbed me with a viselike hand on my way out the door each Sunday—"How *are* you?" he always asked, bending close to search my guilty adolescent soul with his flashlight eyes— were the price of the ham and biscuits we'd left behind. I knew that. And I didn't want to pay. Church didn't seem spiritual to me. It seemed like a place invented so preachers could torture boys like me, a place where women who wore white gloves and hats could greet each other with expressions of elaborate joy and piety, admire each other's smiling husbands, and pat each other's captive children on the head. Life's appearances had held together for another week, and the prospects were good for Monday.

I think that helps explain the way that Mother dealt with Aunt Carolyn. Carolyn was sort of strange. Jesus was the only man she ever really loved. She was so fervent about it that she had been committed to the Florida State Asylum for the Insane at Chattahoochee as a religious nut (if you can imagine how obsessed with Jesus you'd have to be, in the South in the early 1920s, to be considered a religious nut) when she was not quite twenty years old. Chattahoochee sounds like a town name Faulkner might have invented to hold a southern madhouse, but like much else in Florida, it is an Indian name. It's in the rural Panhandle, northwest of Tallahassee, hard against the Georgia line. Mother told me (after my father died) that he had driven Carolyn up there in a Ford Model A when he was about sixteen. Mother seemed to think that Chattahoochee had calmed Carolyn down. Jesus was clearly still the biggest thing in her life when she came out, but she was quieter about it.

It had to have been Mother's idea to make Carolyn my godmother. It was completely irrational, and typical of her lifelong faith in the possibility of making silk purses out of sows' ears. She was, I suppose, a Jane Austen social romantic, and her thinking went something like this: Dear Carolyn is (a) always trying to bring people to Jesus, which is (b) a problem; so why not (c) make her an Episcopalian godmother, which will (d) convert her fundamentalist energy into (e) a more acceptable form. Episcopalians don't go around trying to convert people. This will (f) benefit Dudley by giving him a godmother who actually cares about God, (g) tame and please Carolyn by giving her a role, and thus (h) make everyone happy.

Except me. For a godmother, for the next fifty-five years, I had a quietly cracked, obsessive fundamentalist whose life mission was to bring me to Jesus.

I much preferred the real communion, which occurred on Sunday evening and, in larger or smaller form, most evenings of the week. Adult life, so far as I could tell, centered on the cocktail hour. I think it was the ritual the generation of the Great Depression and World War II had adopted to reward itself for escaping the jaws of misery, deprivation, and war. Life after work could be self-indulgent. Entertaining. Fun.

My parents and many of their friends had started out with very little. The South—west central Florida included—had been in economic low gear for a long time. But as middle-class families grew more affluent and social habits relaxed in the years after the war, and window air conditioners began to be manufactured at affordable prices, family life in neighborhoods across the South moved off the porch in the evenings, away from the more formal living rooms in the front part of every house, and into new rooms built on to the back. Elsewhere, in the idiom of new suburbia, these were called family rooms. In Florida, they were Florida rooms, and just as Nathalie and Carla and her brother, T. Paine, and I sailed toy boats and caught tadpoles in the open ditches that carried water from our neighborhood after thunderstorms on summer afternoons, so our parents—the Grown-ups—often gathered late in the day in chairs in the cool of someone's backyard, if it was spring or fall, or at our house, or in Mary and Wilber Davis's deep, pine-paneled Florida room, with its broad brick fireplace and hearth, its comfortable couches and captain's chairs, to celebrate the cocktail hour.

To us children, outside the circle, it seemed so jolly. The Grown-ups laughed and talked of politics and sports and business, of friends and children and family things. They ate plump, fresh Gulf shrimp with rich, red, horseradishy cocktail sauce; moist, dark smoked mullet on crackers; pickled artichokes; and salted pecans. They drank vodka and bourbon and gin, with lots of ice. Bloody Marys. Gin and tonics. Old-fashioneds, Manhattans, and martinis. The food was the preserve of women. But it was men who controlled the bar, and when their glasses were empty, the women raised them above the backs of the couches upholstered in floral prints in the Davises' Florida room and waved them, laughing, their graceful arms moving like tall stemmed flowers in a garden breeze. And Wilber came and plucked them and mounted the steps to his lighted bar, which was like a pulpit in a church, and filled them back up to water the merriment of the night.

They had all come from harder times, and they were determined to do well and enjoy themselves. I never heard the men—Nathalie's uncle Bill, who had built our house, and Wilber and Mary's, and several others on our street; or Wilber, whose lumberyard sold the lumber for them; or Ashby, who helped run a barge and tugboat company that brought in coal for the power plants; or Carla's father, Paine, a trial lawyer who represented automobile dealers and a railroad; or my father, who was writing editorials arguing for new voting laws to end the rural domination of the state legislature— talk about what happened to them in the Depression or the war. Our fathers didn't talk to us children much at all. About anything. They were busy at work, building and changing the culture we lived in. They came home late. They had no interest in passing on the history of before. They wanted to leave it behind.

The men all seemed so solid in middle age when we were children. So enduring. Even the things that changed only added to the impression of permanence. The houses and cars in the neighborhood grew larger as the years went by. The lawns got thicker, the trees taller, the flower beds and parties bigger, the clothes and rugs and furniture better. Even the people themselves—like their lives, their families, their businesses, their churches and temples and clubs—grew visually more substantial. They got larger. Grayer. Heartier. The women seemed to get bigger bosoms, plumper cheeks. The men, bigger faces, bigger noses, bigger laughs. A few of them did divorce early on. But the women seemed to stay in place and find work, or new husbands. The old husbands seemed to marry new wives and move them into new houses in the old neighborhoods.

Some of the men in my family and their circle of friends, smokers and hard workers and drinkers, did begin to die of heart attacks in their late fifties and early sixties. My uncle Baya, who went to his law office every morning around 5:00 a.m., was one. But divorcées and widows always seemed included in the things my parents' circle of friends did. Part of that was my mother, who was always on the lookout for strays, people in need of care and company. Some of the widows achieved marriage again by pursuing—or agreeing to marry—men they knew, whose wives—friends of theirs—had died. Or they found men elsewhere and brought them back to Tampa, to our part of town. Hardly anyone seemed to go away. Instead, the world around me grew and evolved and changed in place: the family, the neighborhood, the city culture, all the hundreds of people who were connected to one another in my mind by their relationships with my parents. It was like a great garden, year by year growing, some things dying or being uprooted, but the garden growing and filling in. Sometimes I felt like a plant, and later like a young tree, growing in a garden wood.

C anterbury felt that way to me when Mother described life in the Tower on the phone after she first moved in. It was full of people from town and the old neighborhood, and some of the personalities and emphases seemed the same.

Far more than in the world outside, life at Canterbury is centered on food. Many people in the Tower still have cocktails. Everyone dresses for dinner, even if they do nothing else that day, and some evenings, it is only manners and good clothes that seem to hold life together. The line between independence (the Tower) and dependence (the nursing wing) is fiercely maintained, and for that reason, wheelchairs aren't allowed in the Tower dining room.

"Oh dear, *noooo*," the Emyfish said once, with a look that indicated that it was simply out of the question. Too depressing. "I think if they were, I'd have to move to another place."

It is one of the iron rules at Canterbury—one that Mrs. Vinas always insists comes from the residents themselves. The residents, on the other hand, either think of it as Mrs. Vinas's rule or have been convinced by her that it is theirs. Whichever, it is a way of guarding the border between the worlds of the mainly well and the mainly unwell, and it was a fight over that rule that Mother, before her strokes, called to tell me about one morning.

"*Ooooh*," she said, with relish, "we had *quite* a row in the dining room last night. A real knock-down-drag-out."

That night, as Mother's old friend Elizabeth Himes looked up from her plate and her glass of white wine, she spotted another elegant old sack of bones being hoisted, she thought, from her wheelchair into a chair at a nearby table. Elizabeth knew immediately what was afoot. The woman was being moved so that the visually offending wheelchair could be whisked away. It was a sore issue with her, and her blood pressure began to rise. In fact, the woman had already had her drinks and dinner. She was being lifted back into the wheelchair so she could leave. But Elizabeth—blond, perfumy, wealthy, opinionated, and somewhat hampered in her perceptions by trifocals and degenerating vision—felt stirred to battle. She was the president of the Canterbury residents' association that year. She had been the first woman elected to public office in Hillsborough County, the chairman of the county's library and welfare boards, a leader of many groups. She liked martinis and she cared about social issues. A major street was named for the father of her late husband, John, a former judge and prominent attorney. (When John died, Elizabeth had gone out for a time with another lawyer, a widower she found unresponsive. She didn't care much for passive men. So she bought him a book entitled something like *Sex After Sixty*. When he proved a slow learner—or recollector—she dropped him.)

Elizabeth was, along with the Emyfish, the curmudgeonly Judge Charles Sweet, and a few others, one of the most assertive personalities in the building. She was also dying of liver cancer and declining treatment. She had recovered from a broken hip and from eye surgery, but you had to know where to draw the line, she said firmly. If she had chemotherapy for the cancer and lived, she'd just go blind from macular degeneration and be crippled by neuropathy, both of which were already eating at her. What was the point of that? Her plan was to expire in her fifteenth-floor apartment, among her own good rugs, antiques, and oil paintings, cheered by her red walls, faux fireplace, and glued-on white moldings, with a supply laid in of chilled chardonnay and Chunky Monkey ice cream, just in case she still wanted either.

Meanwhile, there were causes to be fought, and life to be lived.

"What are you *doing*?" Elizabeth blazed, her blue eyes getting huge behind her trifocals when she saw the woman suspended above her wheelchair. She thought the policy against wheelchairs was deeply demeaning.

"Moving her. You know the rule," said the Emyfish, with a frosty look. The woman was her guest.

"That's a violation of the Americans with Disabilities Act!" Elizabeth snapped. She knew her law.

"It's not your table!" growled the Emyfish, in her deep smoky voice.

This infuriated Elizabeth, who felt she was raising an issue of human rights. It didn't matter whose damn table it was. "You're an *ageist!*" Elizabeth yelled, standing up in fury.

"You've had too much *to drink!*" the Emyfish boomed in return. Eyes glittering, scowling and furious, the two women stared across the room at each other.

"Everything stopped," Mother said with satisfaction on the phone, marveling even as she painted the scene to me. "You could hear them all over the dining room."

Still, something seemed missing. "Who was the woman in the wheelchair?" I asked.

"Millie Griffin," Mother replied. I knew Millie; I knew her sons, Gordy and Don. And her younger sister, Marguerite Dressler, lived in the Tower. But that seemed odd. The Millie Griffin I remembered was a tall, good-looking, strong-minded woman with magnetic dark eyes, big eyebrows, and sterling silver hair. She drank bourbon and rode horses western saddle at her ranch. Her first husband, a pilot, had been killed in the war, and with two boys to raise, she'd had the good sense and adaptive chemistry to marry an older bachelor who was chairman of one of the city's two biggest banks. When he died, Millie took a lot of long Arthur Murray dance cruises on ships at sea. She liked men, and she'd never been at a loss for words in her life. So where was her voice in this story?

"What'd Millie have to say?" I asked.

There was a long, thoughtful pause. "Well, you know," Mother said, after a moment, "Millie doesn't hear that well anymore."

She had missed the whole thing.

There was no way to know, once Mother left the Tower and the old neighborhood and social friends behind and moved to the nursing wing, what she herself could hear, or see, or feel about things. After the second stroke, when she was released back to Canterbury, the speech and physical and occupational therapists who came to the nursing wing had made no difference. Mother could still swallow, though sometimes with difficulty. She could eat when fed. But that was all. She was totally dependent on the staff of nurses and assistants for everything else. She was in precisely the condition she had most feared, and wanted to avoid. In conversations and in her living will, she had always made her desires clear. If she had a stroke and went into a coma, she didn't want to wake. If she was mentally damaged, she wanted food and water withdrawn. Her wishes. Our responsibility.

But she was fed. She ate. She lived. And she took an interest in life. So long as she ate, and nothing else happened, she would continue to live. We had no election in the matter. If she could swallow, we could not refuse to feed her. It was against the law. Only if she ceased to be able to swallow, and had to be fed and watered by tube, would we have a choice. We didn't have to tube her. And we weren't going to. Until then, there was nothing to do but be there. As I sat with her, talking to her, watching as others approached her and spoke, she plainly recognized people—some people, anyway. Or at least she wanted them to think she did. It was plain, too, that she remembered things, and could understand what was said. I tried to tell her stories about people she knew, and one day, telling her the latest story about Mary and Wilber, it occurred to me that maybe I shouldn't assume she really knew who I was talking about.

"You remember them, Mother?" I said, teasingly, I hoped. I didn't want to offend her. I thought she might just nod—or shake her head to indicate she didn't—in which case I would remind her who they were.

Instead, she looked at me with an expression of outright indignation, as if she were astonished at the question. I must have lost my mind.

"Of *course*," she said, her eyebrows arched at me. She was offended.

I was stunned. So she *had* known Mary and Wilber when they came to visit her in the Health Center. Mary had been wrong. From that moment on, I decided to treat my mother as a full person, someone who was mute by choice, as if to test the rest of us.

But how long could this state last?

Mother remained in bed and in her chaise longue, bright eyed and imperishable, for the remainder of that year, and through the next one. I didn't tell her when Elizabeth died in May 1999, in her own apartment, as she had wished to, with a nurse companion that Mrs. Vinas had found for her, or that Mrs. Vinas had taken Elizabeth down the elevator in her wheelchair late one afternoon and wheeled her right into the Tower dining room, to a table by the window, where they had had a last glass of wine together, with Elizabeth sitting in the wheelchair, in smug violation of the rule, just about a week before she died. She reacted happily to my sister, Melissa, when she visited, and to me when I came down from Baltimore or New York, but increasingly, I thought, it was to her maid and companion, Louise Edwards, who attended her, fed her, and kept her company three days a week, that Mother was most responsive.

"Louise loves you, Mama," Louise said, looking into my mother's eyes, holding her hand. "Louise loves you." The look in my mother's eyes—the feeling she gave back—was unmistakable.

Some of her old friends who came to see her felt she knew them, but gradually, whether they lived just next door in the Tower or in the town beyond, their visits dropped off. Most of them ceased to come. They found it too painful. Those who live at Canterbury try to dwell in the present, not the past.

The old Episcopal priest, the Reverend Bridges, always stopped to say hello, patting her with a large soft hand. He was in the Health Center for most of every day to be with his wife, a stroke victim, too. But another person who did come to see Mother that year, and kept coming, was a new friend, one she had made after moving to Canterbury—Rabbi Karl Richter. He had been one of the last rabbis remaining in Nazi Germany when he was able to get out with his wife, Ruth, and little daughter in April 1939. They left with a lifesaving U.S. immigration visa procured for them by Senator

Harry S. Truman, acting for a Jewish congregation in Springfield, Missouri.

Karl Richter was only twenty-eight then, a young man, sensitive and learned, just a few years out of seminary. But his synagogue in Mannheim had been blown up and burned, the chapel in the Jewish cemetery dynamited. The sealed coffins were already arriving back from Buchenwald and Dachau, from the first forty thousand Jews to be arrested, when he and Ruth and Esther escaped.

After a career serving temples in Missouri, North Dakota, and Indiana, the Richters had retired to Sarasota to a condominium apartment on the beach, and then, at the insistence of their son, David, and his family, who lived in Tampa and wanted them closer, they moved to Canterbury. Karl Richter was eighty-one when they came. Of all the people who had come to pass the final years of their lives in the little sugar-cube high-rise on Tampa Bay, Rabbi Richter was probably the most different from the southern core, and as I discovered, as time passed, perhaps the most cherished. He was warm and witty and wise. The old WASPs called him the Archrabbi of Canterbury. He had always been the first to extend a hand, and there was something that happened, in the fall of 1999, that made me glad I had decided to spend this time at Canterbury. It is a story that represents the best of the ecumenical spirit that can occur when people come together late in life, in places like this.

When Martha Sweet's husband, the tall, cantankerous former judge Charles M. Sweet of Pennsylvania, stopped breathing one day after months of decline in the nursing wing, Rabbi Richter went immediately up the elevator to the Sweets' apartment on the fifteenth floor. Martha was chain-smoking cigarettes, looking out over the water from her living room balcony. It was Saturday, October 30, 1999. The day before Halloween. Martha was perhaps the youngest person in the building, only seventy-one then, and the rest of life seemed suddenly very long. She had adored Charles. He was her third husband, and the great passion of her life. They argued and laughed and made arcane lists—"Can you think of twelve other women who had been famous in Europe by the time of Joan of

Arc?"—and had a great lust for each other, until Alzheimer's had suddenly begun dismantling him, about four years before.

That is why they had moved into Canterbury. And although the dementia had seemed to make Charles even more obstreperous, getting them into conflicts with other residents, the staff, and even Mrs. Vinas—"I'm bored," he declared loudly one night, when my mother invited them to her apartment to meet some other residents over drinks, and the conversation turned to old Tampa things—Martha could not imagine living through each day without him. She was wishing that she were not such an atheist when Karl Richter knocked at her door. If she believed in heaven, if she thought Charles was up there waiting for her with a glint in his eye and his big soft lips, Martha Sweet would have pushed her short self up on the railing of the balcony and jumped off. It would have been so simple, she thought, if she just had faith.

The rabbi looked at her with his long seamed face, which had seen so much. "Would you like to say a prayer for Charles?" he asked. It was just an offer. He knew her feelings.

"Oh, Karl," Martha said, her round face red and her blue eyes grainy and swollen from cigarettes and tears, "I'm sorry. I'm not much of a believer. I wouldn't know who to pray to."

"Well," the Archrabbi of Canterbury had said, with a wrinkly smile, taking her hand in his cool old paws, "we can pray To Whom It May Concern."

CHAPTER FIVE

The Cocktail Hour

SUMMER 1999

I t is 5:30 in the afternoon, cocktail hour in the cool, quiet apartments of the Tower. The sun, hanging in the west, is still bright, but the front of the building, facing east on the bay, is in shade, and the people who live on that end, freed from the light that dazzles them in the morning, can stand behind their windows or sliding glass doors or even outside on their balconies—if the hot breeze doesn't wilt them—and drink in the deep, changing view that nature and the city have laid at their feet. The view, and the Health Center, are two reasons many of them have come from near and far to spend the rest of their lives here, however long that may be.

Sitting in a comfortable chair in an apartment, surrounded by familiar old things, with the air-conditioning whispering through the vents, Carlos in control of the security desk at the front door, dinner waiting to be served by Chanh and Yuri in the dining room downstairs, a nurse on call to take one's blood pressure if needed, and Ernestine available for hugs and comfort (or to sing at one's funeral), a person can sip something cold and slightly intoxicating from a glass and feel that he or she has found the perfect perch for the end of life.

Below the front balcony lie beds of plantings, clipped green hedges and lawn, and beyond its grassy edge the broad, bayside boulevard and promenade, with streams of cars and people passing back and forth, from before daybreak until late at night. Then the concrete balustrade of the promenade atop the seawall, which stretches for miles to the left and right, holding back the restless, darkening water of Old Hillsborough Bay, which flows on the outgoing tide into the greater estuary of Tampa Bay, then through the barrier islands that form the beach towns between Clearwater and St. Petersburg, into the Gulf of Mexico.

To the left, at the head of the bay, the bridges and buildings of downtown Tampa form a cluster of lines and curves, concrete and glittering glass, less than three miles away. Straight ahead, perhaps half a mile across the water, are the private docks and houses of Davis Islands. To the right, farther out where the harbor channel leads down toward the Gulf, sailboats and freighters, tankers and cruise ships move slowly up and down; and beyond them lies the bay's eastern shore, a distant, clumped line of farms and coal-burning power plants and phosphate factories. The plumes of smoke from their tall stacks make windsocks on the horizon, and above it—overlaying Canterbury and all it surveys—is the great air painting of cloud and light and deepening color that forms the evening sky.

More than the cool Atlantic Ocean off the east coast, the warm waters of the Gulf charge the atmosphere over the west coast of Florida with great circulating clouds of moisture. The sky is unstable, often boiling with energy, and Tampa Bay, midway down the Florida Gulf Coast, is a meteorological bull's-eye, one of the great magnets for thunderstorms in the world. The weather has begun to be unpredictable. But the sky often turns dark on summer afternoons, as it always did. The lightning sizzles and flashes, the thunder cracks and booms, and the rain falls in silver torrents. The torn and drifting cloud formations that linger afterward can make spectacular sunsets to the west, illuminating the eastern sky with a dimmer but lovely, soft, reflected light. It is nature's theater. It gives life here an edge, imparting a sense of drama and energy to what otherwise would be the waning years. It is great entertainment. It is also threatening, and so Canterbury at cocktail hour stands as a kind of vertical viewing platform, its roof and parapets bristling with more than fifty lightning rods, its back-up generators and auxilliary pump motors at the ready.

For people so well served, in a building so apparently secure, the days can seem easy on the surface. There are no chores unless one chooses to create them, no responsibilities. For some, there are not even basic bills to pay. That is what we children are for. But there is not much control left either. Or, to put it another way, competence. For the residents, nothing, beginning with their bodies, feels the same.

"Your nose grows, your ears get bigger, your eyes get smaller, your hair gets thin—I hate it," the Emyfish growled. *"This is for the birds."*

Everyone is shorter than he or she used to be. And all the senses—sight, hearing, taste, smell, touch, balance, the perception of heat and cold—that connect a person to the world are weakened. When sensations fade, so do felt relationships with objects, surfaces, machines, and tools, not to mention other people. As Jim Cardwell said one day, smiling through his trifocals at Carlyss, his wife of so many decades, "Every night we climb into bed, take out our hearing aids, yell at each other, . . . and go to sleep."

And then there are those changes in that other sphere—the brain. The things that were once the basic instruments, conveniences, and comforts of life—cars, stoves, checkbooks, writing pens, telephones, television remote controls, social calendars, clothes (this was not the computer and cell phone generation)—can become obstacles to the simple task of passing unimpeded through the day.

There is still pleasure in growth and change for some, and stimulation in new things. But for others, particularly for those who feel themselves slipping, the most elemental need of old age—to feel a comfortable relationship with one's own life—can depend utterly on the ability to hold close to old patterns, old friends, and old ways. To just hold on. That is why so many of them hate change.

This had always been Mary and Wilber Davis's favorite time of day, and as Wilber stood at the end of their living room on the fifth floor, looking over the balcony rail, the vodka and the glasses and the bottles of mixer waited on the counter in the kitchen by the sink. Wilber stayed where he was, his back to the lamp glow, the family pictures and familiar furniture of the room behind him absorbed by the world outside. He didn't know what time it was, exactly, but he was dressed for the evening—for drinks and dinner, and the company he hoped was coming—in a shirt and tie and his favorite tan cotton-and-polyester pants, the ones he kept putting on, with the spots on them. His sport coat hung in the closet, a place he found increasingly elusive, as if it had taken to hiding from him.

His blue eyes and square face, under the thin white hair, looked bright and eager and a little puzzled as he gazed down at the traffic, and out at the water, and then to the left, where the city rose at the mouth of the river in an almost-perfect arc of colored towers: rose and pale green, cool blue and lustrous glass, bronze and creamy stone. Wilber could watch the view for hours, and sometimes did. The sweating young men and women, running endlessly up and down the broad sidewalk along the boulevard. The women's breasts jiggling. And the cars. So many unfamiliar shapes whooshing by, big boxy ones and middle-size and little ones, like blobs. So smooth and shiny. So expensive. He tried again to remember where he had parked his own car. He couldn't.

Sometimes he thought he recognized a Ford, a Chevrolet, or a Cadillac passing below. But the shapes all looked the same now, especially from above. Mainly, he wondered where they all came from, and where they were going. They fascinated him, the volume of them, the constant colored stream of them on the boulevard, a long, curving crescent from town past Canterbury, south to the Tampa Yacht & Country Club, and then to the front gate of MacDill

Air Force Base. For most of the distance it was a divided highway, two or three lanes on the near side of a middle island of grass and trees, and two or three on the far side. Then the sidewalk, and the people running and jogging and speed-walking up and down, some of them with dogs and some puffing along behind wheeled baby carts.

It was all so different now. There had been trolley tracks running down the middle of the boulevard when Wilber was a boy growing up in this neighborhood. That was how he and Mary met, when he was a young man, sixty-six years before. She was standing one morning in a light cotton dress on the corner of Bayshore and Bay Villa, just a few blocks south, waiting to take the trolley downtown to work at the business association, where she filed account notes about people who couldn't pay their bills. That's when he drove up and decided to stop. She was just nineteen, slim and big breasted, with curly dark hair and freckles, and brown eyes that sparkled at him when he pulled up beside her. Wilber thought he would remember the excitement of that soft morning until the day he died, but he was wrong. Like so many other memories, it had dissolved into blurry fragments and gradually disappeared.

W il-buh?" Mary spoke slowly, in the languid southern accent that people from Florida used to have. Her movements in the last twenty years had become as slow and deliberate as her speech. She carried herself as carefully as she would a tray of glasses, and now she stood still as a statue, holding the back of a chair for balance, watching Wilber as he looked out over the balcony at the traffic below. She was dressed for cocktails and dinner in good white slacks and a silk pastel overblouse, which fit well around the shoulders and fell in a straight line from her ample bosom to the beginning of her pant legs.

"*Wil*-buh!"

He didn't hear her. His hearing aids weren't in. He wouldn't wear them. He was looking toward the city, trying to recognize things, but memory kept eluding him. He couldn't keep the thread.

He sometimes sat with the morning paper for two hours, turning from page to page, picking the sections up and putting them down, and couldn't remember what he'd read. He couldn't follow a film or television program either. Couldn't hear them, and couldn't track who the people were or what the movie was about. It was like trying to recollect a dream. Every time some thought or vision began to form in his mind, he would get the edge of it, maybe the next piece toward the middle, and a vague impression of the rest—and then the whole thing would slip and dissolve away. That's when he would turn to Mary. For whatever he couldn't remember. Whatever he didn't know.

"Where did we park the car last night?" he wanted to know in the morning, as if it had just slipped his mind. "I don't remember."

"What are we doing here?" he asked in the afternoons, frowning as if he were in strange surroundings.

"Where are we going?" he said at night.

"Downst*ayahs,*" she'd reply. It would take two or three repetitions for him to hear.

"Why are we going downstairs?" he asked.

"For *dinnah,*" she said, frowning at him.

He didn't understand. Usually they had people in for drinks and then they went *out* for dinner somewhere. Not downstairs.

"Are we going somewhere later?" he asked. "When are the others coming over?" He always wanted to be going somewhere. He always wanted to have people over.

"He duzzen understayand why no one asks us foah drinks and dinnah anymoah," Mary said. "He duzzen understayand why no one wants to come heah anymoah." He didn't understand that he was the reason, that people were tired of hearing him talk about the car he couldn't find, tired of his asking them the same questions over and over, tired of having to wait for the drinks he insisted on making for them. He would get their orders mixed up as he rattled around the kitchen, and have to ask again and again, and sometimes, when he got them made, would drink them himself and then come back out to ask them if they would like a drink.

That cut down the return guest list in a hurry. But there was no way of explaining this to Wilber. There was no way of making him understand that he—who had been the most gregarious man in the building, dressing up to play Santa Claus, undressing to appear as the diapered baby of the New Year—that he, who had always loved parties and club memberships, loved being with people more than anything else, had finally become a pariah. He had lost his mind, and overstayed his welcome in the Tower.

Almost everyone thought he should long ago have been taken down the hall and put in the Health Center, with all the others who had lost their health or grip on reality. That was the bargain they all had made. When a person couldn't function independently anymore, he or she disappeared into the Health Center. It had to be that way. Otherwise, the Tower, a place inhabited by people who wanted to feel healthy, would start feeling like the Health Center, a place littered with broken bodies and minds. But Mary would not or could not let him go, and so the people who would have been glad to be with her looked across the room at the two of them, now sitting alone. There was no way of explaining this to Wilber. There was no explaining anything. He couldn't hear. Mary would answer him and he would ask her again, and she would end up speaking in a loud voice to him, just short of a shout, which ladies, after all, didn't do. But he couldn't remember what she'd just said when he did hear her answer. And so the questions would start all over again. It never seemed to end.

"Nathalie sayed, 'Mothah, you talk to him too much.' But how can Ah not talk to him?" Mary asked, her dark eyes pained. "Ah've been talkin' to him for sixty-five yeahs."

She could see no way out, and so she took naps in the morning after breakfast, and for hours after lunch, and still felt angry most of the time when she was awake. She honestly didn't know whether she loved or hated him anymore. All she knew was that he couldn't drive them anywhere anymore. He had gotten lost, ending up in St. Petersburg instead of picking her up at the beauty parlor west of Canterbury where she had gone for forty years, and so, on one of her trips down from North Carolina, Nathalie—who was as decisive as her mother was passive—had finally given away the car. She didn't do it lightly. She consulted with one old friend who owned automobile dealerships, and with an old boyfriend, a senior lawyer in town. They both told her she had to take the car away. When she was about to leave High Point to drive down to Tampa, her husband, Richard, was even more emphatic. "Don't come back," he told her, until the car was gone.

"Honest to God," she sighed wearily after the deed was done, wondering at the psychology of southern males of her father's age, "you would have thought I'd *castrated* him."

Then Mrs. Vinas had barred Mary and Wilber from riding the Canterbury bus as a couple because the other residents had gotten fed up with the shouting back and forth. Which meant that they couldn't go together on the Canterbury picnics to the parks on the Hillsborough River, or on the outings to the museums or symphony, or even on the twice-weekly shopping trips. Mary hated going by herself. She was unsteady on her feet. And it wasn't easy to just leave Wilber and go off alone, because he got confused when she wasn't there. He went looking for her.

She felt trapped. They couldn't even go in peace to the dining room. Wilber had been barred from the line at the salad bar because someone reported that he had picked up an olive from the vegetable tray, bitten it, and put it back down.

"*Ah* told Mrs. Vinas, 'we have become prisonahs in owah own apawtmahnt,'" Mary said. She sat in her accustomed place in the yellow wing chair in the corner, erect and stoic, her body thick, her eyes grim, her hair thin. Her face was an expressionless mask.

"Ah doan dare cry," she had confided one night by the elevator. "If Ah started, Ah would nevah stop." Mary had had an operation on her back three years before, and a heart valve had been replaced a year later, after Nathalie and Wilber had come back up from the dining room one evening and found her unconscious in bed. Mary had said she was fine when they left to go downstairs that night. She just wasn't hungry; she would stay in and read.

"Mother has never been very in touch with her own body," Nathalie observed afterward.

Nathalie had pulled every emergency cord in the apartment when they entered and found Mary unconscious. The nurse and security man had come running, with the ambulance crew not long behind. Mary had almost died, but the experience didn't change her languid habits. She did nothing she didn't have to do, and took no exercise, even to walk down the hall. She'd since had one or two spells. She sometimes fell down. Berta, who had finally quit working for them in 1996, at the age of eighty-seven, had expired at ninety-one. And now Wilber was falling apart.

Still, Mary held on, instructing him, answering him, correcting him, trying to keep him in the pattern they had shared so long, because she didn't know what else to do. Wilber had essentially stopped bathing. He didn't remember that he needed to, or how to. "We have to have someone heah to bathe him three times ah week," she said. "Nathalie says it cost two hundred thirty dollars las' month."

Mary could scarcely believe it. It seemed an astronomical expense to someone who had lived frugally all her life. But she didn't know what else to do. She didn't think the nursing staff could keep Wilber confined in the Health Center if she and Nathalie decided to put him there. If he couldn't be kept, she might have to send him someplace else, which they couldn't really afford. And if the Health Center staff did manage to keep him, she didn't see how she could live without him. She didn't have the will to act, and she couldn't see the end of it. Except for his right shoulder joint, which was worn out, Wilber was in great shape from the neck down, the doctor said. He could live to be one hundred. And that wasn't even the worst part.

The worst part was that sometimes he thought she wasn't Mary, that Mary and his child were somewhere outside, out there where they lived, where they had always lived, waiting for him. With all their friends. It was the life he had always had. He wanted to get back to it, and some people were coming by this evening to pick him up and take him there. That was the fantasy. It would often seize him at sundown, which had always been their favorite hour, the cocktail hour. But it was also, as Mary discovered, a time when Alzheimer's patients can become particularly disoriented and agitated, and so all she knew to do was to try to hold on, and to hope that tonight would be different. That it would be all right. The cocktail hour was the one time of day that she still looked forward to, the one hour that offered her both comfort and release.

And so she refused to take the responsibility of making the drinks. "Ah haven't in fifty yeahs, and ah'm not goan tuh staht *now*," she said. Instead, she sat in her wing chair in the corner, waiting to be served. They had managed one drink on an evening I was with them, and now she raised her glass and shook it. The ice rattled. It was what a lady did in the South in the 1950s and 1960s. Men were supposed to pay attention. It was bad form for her to say out loud that she wanted another drink. But Wilber didn't hear. He was looking at me, trying to recall what he knew about me.

"I see you've still got all your hair," he said. "Did you get married yet?" I had been married almost thirty years before, and divorced ten years ago, but he had forgotten that.

"Wilbuh!" Mary said. He didn't hear.

"Wil-*buh*!" He turned toward her, and Mary raised the glass straight up as if she were leading a charge to the bar, and rattled it again.

"Oh." He rocked to his feet, holding his own glass, a little crookedly. "Can I get you a drink?" he said solicitously. "What are you having?"

She nodded, looking slightly annoyed that he should have to ask, and held out her glass. "Thuh same thing," she replied.

He blinked, and shook his head. "What was it?" he said.

"Vodka," she said grimly, as if she had drunk anything else in forty years.

"Are you having something with it?' he asked politely.

"Wahtah," she answered, her jaw set. She always had water with it.

Wilber thought a minute, swaying slightly. "I don't think we have any vodka," he said.

"Yea-yus, we *do*. Thea'hs some left. You juss used it."

"What?"

"You juss used it!"

"Oh," he said, amiably, nodding. Then he made a little frown. "Where is it?"

"In thah *kitchen!*" she said, exasperated.

He headed that way.

"Wil-BUH!"

He stopped and did a half turn.

"Mah *gla-yuss,*" she said, holding it up.

"Oh," he said. He came back and collected it and moved down the room again, turning left toward the bedrooms.

"*Wil*-buh!"

He stopped and swiveled around, looking at Mary.

"*That* way!" she said, pointing.

"Oh," he said again.

He disappeared, rocking sideways in his tilted gait, through the kitchen door. Mary gave a deep sigh and turned toward me with the expression of one who has just summoned the patience of Job.

"You see how it ea-yuhs?" she said. "Ah have to tell him ever-ahthang. All the rehsponsabiladies now fall oa'n me. And it's moa'h than Ah can handle. It rally eas. Ah doan' know whut we're go'wan-tuh do. Foah example," she said, indignation beginning to fire her dark brown eyes, "hea-ah it is—Monday! We'ah almos' outta vodka. And the bus foah the liquor stoah duzzen go agayin"—she paused, calculating—"till *Thuhs*-day!"

She fell silent, looking at me in grim exhaustion. How, her expression said, was she supposed to cope?

CHAPTER SIX

Last Communion

2000

I began to spend more time at Canterbury. One afternoon, as I took the Tower elevator down, a white-haired woman with glasses got on. Almost all women at Canterbury have gray or white hair and wear glasses. She smiled. We said hello and began to descend. Then the elevator stopped again. A mild, white-haired man with glasses got on. Almost all men at Canterbury have white hair, spare hair, or no hair, and wear glasses. The men sometimes complain that they can't tell the old ladies apart because they all have white hair and glasses. The women sometimes say the same thing about the men, but not so often, because there are fewer of them, and the added feature of male baldness helps to sort them out.

"Well, nice to see you, Fred," the woman said, in a neighborly way. He smiled. She paused, then asked, "How's Helen?"

He blinked, and continued to smile, but didn't answer. He appeared to be thinking about something. She waited. Not everyone at Canterbury hears well.

"How's Helen, Fred?" she asked again, a little louder, as the elevator dropped slowly down.

He looked uncertain, as if preoccupied by some other question.

She tried a bright smile and more projection. "I was asking about your wife, *Helen*," she said, propelling the words as she leaned toward him.

He was silent a moment, and then quietly—with an expression that suggested he found this uncomfortable—replied, "That's not her name."

"Oh, I'm *sorry,*" she said, recoiling with a small gasp and a rueful look. "I've gotten so bad with names, Fred. Forgive me. What is her name?"

He looked at her absently, as if he were trying to make up his mind about something. The elevator was descending. She glanced up at the floor numbers flashing above them—4, 3, 2. She wanted desperately to get the name right next time, and they were almost at the lobby.

"Your wife, Fred. What's her name?"

The doors opened.

"I'm *thinking,*" he said.

On a different day, I headed into the elevator in shorts and a T-shirt for a long fast walk along the sidewalk by the bay. (I used to run for miles down that concrete, which is probably what happened to my knees. Now I walk.) I heard steps coming down the hall, so I held the elevator door and the Duchess came in. It is an earned title. In the funny nomenclature of Canterbury, the residents are "inmates," a name they give themselves in acknowledgment of the fact that once paid in, they probably will never leave. It would cost them money. But they also give each other nicknames, and the Duchess is what her inmate friends called Marguerite Dressler, formerly of Virginia, in honor of her sense of style.

The Duchess had an eye for things, and as she stood next to me that morning—a tall glossy vision in black and white, with her big signature earrings glinting boldly at the neck—she was eyeing me. "You stay in good shape," she said approvingly, her large dark eyes roaming beneath arched, dramatic eyebrows. "You look real fit. You exercise, don't you?"

I felt, under her gaze, sort of like a lamb chop. It felt nice. "Well, I try," I said.

"I thought so," she replied, her long fingers and lacquered nails

sliding over her silver-headed cane, the eyes still moving up and
down. "You're nice and lean. You've got curves in all the right
places."

I have male friends who would kill to start their days like this.

"Thanks," I said with rising feeling. "You're looking pretty
smashing yourself." With her mass of silver hair, her long cheekbones and good skin and big sexy jewelry, she did, especially for a
dame in her early eighties with a weak heart and osteoporosis. We
stood there a moment, warming in mutual regard. Then the elevator
hit her floor. She threw me a wink and sashayed out, leaving us both
feeling better—foxier, more desirable—than before.

Some months later, as Ms. Dressler reclined in a chair in a nearby
salon, having her toenails cut and polished and painted to comple-
ment her shoes, the pedicurist looked up and realized that her client
had departed. The Duchess's inquiring but tired heart had stopped.
Things then got very busy. This was Florida. It was a good salon.
The pedicurist had training in cardiopulmonary resuscitation. She
started mouth-to-mouth. Someone called 911. An ambulance came
screaming to the door. For two weeks, lying in a stationary hospital
bed with monitors beeping and an oxygen tube up her nose, the
Duchess made no sense.

"This ship isn't moving," she declared, when her Canterbury
neighbor, Martha Cameron, then eighty-three, went to see her. "We
must be in the Arctic Circle." She had been there on a cruise ship with
her sister Millie, the widow of a bank chairman. But Ms. Cameron,
the nurse, one of the first women ashore at Utah Beach after D-day,
knew that her friend was reacting to the cold oxygen flowing up her
nose. The Duchess thought she was stuck in an ice floe.

Ms. Dressler still doesn't remember the events of that day. But
gradually, with therapy and care in Canterbury's nursing wing, her
strength, and the twinkle in her eye, returned. She moved back into
her apartment, and one night, at dinner at a table looking out over
the bay, after cocktails upstairs at her friend Colonel Cameron's, she
sat in a long black sheath with a slit up the left leg and a huge red
silk rose from Saks Fifth Avenue at her breast, and said that she had

made a decision: "I always saved for later on," she said, a true child of the Depression. "But later on is now!"

So it is. And sometimes, now is later on. I thought Mother had already made that passage. We had been through the issue of dying or not, and she had come to rest in the interim—the long, silent in-between. So, when I flew down for another visit one bright January morning, I wasn't prepared for the ambiguity in her gaze. We had a plan. She was going to live. I was going to visit. I arrived midmorning feeling illuminated, happy in our mother-son conspiracy. And then it dawned on me that my mother might be on a different plan. She was going to die.

Now?

I was stunned. Well, not right away. When I walked in, she was tucked among pillows and an afghan in her padded chaise longue, looking frail, of course, but beautiful. She gave me a loving, wistful, ambivalent smile, as if she were of two minds about something, and coughed. She had always been a woman of many layers, the outer of which was usually constructed for the benefit of those around her. Her silence the last two years made it that much harder to divine her feelings, and I didn't realize at first that the cough was meaningful. I had slipped so far back into the old habit of thinking of my mother as indestructible that I wasn't alert for signs of passage. I mean, we had been through this already. She was going to die, but then she didn't. She was. She wasn't.

It wasn't an issue, and I was on a schedule, and behind. The plane had run late. I had a meeting to go to, and so I swooped into Mother's room with other things on my mind.

"Hello, Mother!" I said, coming through the door. It was our routine: the cheerful hello, the bended knee, the smile, the kiss, the held hand, the long gaze, and usually, the glad, loving look in return. I told her I loved her. I told her what was new with me. Well, not all of what was new with me. But the things I thought she'd like. I told her stories. I told her how long I'd be there, who I was going to see, what I was going to do, when I was going to leave. I told her how long I could stay at the moment. I told her when I'd be back—later that day, the next morning. And when I left—always—I could feel her large eyes watching me go. Again. Gone again.

I always left feeling selfish, and returned in guilt. But this day I was busy. I had appointments, things to accomplish. It wasn't until I came back at lunch, in the dining room of the nursing wing, and later, after her nap, that I noticed the cough.

By the next day, the cough seemed to have descended into her chest, and I got concerned. It had a deep, phlegmy sound. I got the nurse to listen. By afternoon, it sounded deeper, moister, more congested. The nurse called Dr. Zimmer, who ordered an X-ray, which meant that Mother would have to leave the nursing wing and go by ambulance, in January, to someplace with an X-ray machine, or the machine would have to come to her. A portable machine and a technician came up the elevator that night. My sister, Melissa, lives just up the Bayshore, and the next day we had a conversation with the doctor—the conversation I had so dreaded in the first months after her strokes, and then had forgotten to worry about.

"It does show that she has what we call an infiltration on the right side, developing into pneumonia," Dr. Zimmer said. "Aspiration pneumonia."

My choky mother had inhaled something, probably food during one of her meals, and it had created an infection in her lung. Everything prepared for her at Canterbury—pot roast, baked chicken, mashed Idaho or sweet potatoes, carrots, green beans, broccoli—was pureed, like smooth applesauce, to make it easier for her to swallow. Her meal plates were palettes of unidentifiable greens, browns, creams, oranges, and yellows. But her swallowing reflex was so poor that sometimes she choked on even her own saliva.

Now Susan Zimmer talked quietly to us, choosing her words carefully. She is a tall dark-haired woman with striking features, large understanding eyes, and a soft, clear way of speaking, so when she turns solemn, she seems very grave indeed.

"Many times, an antibiotic by mouth is used to fight an aspiration pneumonia," she said, looking at Melissa and me, studying our reactions as she spoke. We all knew that we had decided not to give Mother an antibiotic. But Dr. Zimmer was waiting to see if we might change our minds.

"If we were to keep her comfortable, our goal would be to keep her fever down," she continued quietly. "If we were to treat the cough, we would use one of the cough suppressants. Then morphine as needed. And oxygen."

She stopped and looked at us, waiting.

"How long do you think it could be?" I asked.

"If this progresses, and it's an aspiration pneumonia," she said, her voice very even, "it would probably be within two weeks. If it were not your mother"—here she smiled slightly—"I would say seven to ten days."

Ah, yes. Our resilient, maddeningly deceptive, unpredictable mother.

Melissa and I thanked her. There was nothing more to be said, nothing to decide. We already had. Melissa felt strongly that the mother she knew was already gone, and should now be allowed to die. If I changed the instructions, and ordered antibiotics to save her life, would I be doing it so that she could live and I could write about her—or would I be doing it for her? Or from some revised calculation of what I thought she might want now? We couldn't start down that road. If we reopened the issue at every turn, there would be no end to it. I couldn't flip-flop that way.

The decision had to stand.

Still, I found myself feeling ambushed, unprepared, floodingly sad. It was only in sitting with Mother, in one nook or another of the nursing wing where we could be alone in between her meals and naps and daily activities, that I began to feel focused, at one with her, embarked on the passage. That night, after dinner, we were together, she in her bed, I in the chair, in the dimness of her room where the television seemed always on. The look she had greeted me with when

I arrived—what I now thought of as a slightly worried, slightly guilty look of "Sorry, darling"—was gone.

It may have been only the projection of my wish, but Mother seemed happy in that moment, as if the uncertainty was over. I felt cozy and content. There was an adventure travelogue on a cable channel, a nature show, with monkeys and wildcats and barking deer, nosing through the ruins of a temple complex—in Thailand, I think. It is the kind of thing Mother used to love to watch after having dinner downstairs at Canterbury, sitting in her favorite padded yellow silk barrel chair in the den of her apartment. That was before the strokes.

"Look, Mother," I said. "This is interesting. Monkeys. Tigers. Temple ruins." She didn't look at the screen. She was staring at me, her large eyes fixed on me in fond, motherly fascination, as if I had just said the most adorable thing.

"You don't care about the monkeys, do you?" I said, smiling back at her. "You just want to look at me."

She laughed.

We passed a quiet hour, settling in. After a time, it was enough. Mother was in a semiprivate double room in the nursing wing. I got up to leave, and I put my head past the dividing curtain to say good-night to her roommate, a nice white-haired Baptist lady who seemed vague and a little childlike. She brought me back to reality.

"You going to have the funeral at one of the churches?" she asked brightly.

Days passed. My mother's eyes grew dull. Her blood oxygen level dropped.

"What does that mean?" I asked at the nursing desk.

I got a studied look. It meant less oxygen was passing from her lungs into her blood.

"Why?" I asked.

"Her lungs are filling up," the head nurse on the day shift said, staring at me solemnly. This seemed to be having an effect on her.

More time passed. Mother seemed less present. She shrank into her bed. Her disposable pants, for which she was billed at so many pair per month, and which were usually wet with urine several times a day, now stayed dry.

"What does that mean?" I asked.

"Her kidneys are shutting down," the nurse answered. Her eyes were damp and sad. This no-medication policy was my decision, and while the nurses and certified nursing assistants respected it, their work is to support life. They were fond of Mother. Some of them were deeply attached. They are warm, compassionate people, which is why they do what they do. They didn't want her to die. They remembered her from years before when she was well, from all her visits to sick and dying friends in the Health Center. She was the Florence Nightingale of visiting friends. It was one of her chosen roles.

For decades, Mother had been a legend around town for her faithful attendance at the bedsides of friends—or close acquaintances, or even fond familiar figures like the yardman, the shoe man, or anyone else to whom she felt some connection, and who struck her as in need of sympathy and comfort. In those days, all the businesses—the dry cleaners, the drugstore, the banks, the automobile dealerships, the upholstery shop, the fish and meat markets, the clothing and furniture stores, the gas stations—were locally owned and run. She knew everyone, and they all knew her. When someone died, she fried chicken, or baked a cake or a casserole for the family. Melissa is that way, too. When people got sick, Mother arrived at their door with a tray of egg custards, fresh from her oven. A pale, creamy yellow, they were silky and warm—easy to swallow for people who didn't feel like eating much of anything—slightly sweet, and full of energizing proteins, vitamins, and sugar.

But there was something else. Mother never seemed sick herself, or unable to function. Except for that one period of tortured agitation when she was brought back to the nursing wing from the hospital—when she heaved and tore at her gown as if she were trying to escape from the prison of her damaged body—I had never known her to call attention to her own needs. Once she settled down to live out the rest of her life in the clean, quiet, self-contained series of rooms that form the nursing wing, she never again complained, or acted as if she were angry at her lot or sorry for herself. She didn't believe in it. She had always been the iron magnolia. She smiled at people, and they smiled back.

But now her smile was faint. She ate little. Slept a lot. I decided to stop asking questions. There didn't seem to be much point, and it was painful. Melissa is a busy Realtor, with a husband, Brad, a son, Christopher, and a household to manage. Together and separately, we sniffled and dripped, fell into silences, made lists and tended to chores, moving through days that felt like fog. We consulted with the priests at St. John's Episcopal Church. We picked out hymns. We would offer Holy Communion at the funeral service. Then Melissa reminded me that Mother would want her own while she was still alive.

Of course.

And so, two days later, on a Thursday afternoon at four, Melissa and Christopher and Louise and I gathered for a last Communion at her bed. As the priest unpacked and set out the little crystal containers of water and wine and the canistered wafers, moving them about with soft clicking and clinking sounds, I noticed that Mother seemed attentive. For a woman dying of pneumonia, I thought, she actually looked quite lovely. That was Mother. Always up to the moment. It gave me a warm feeling. The nursing staff had sent her down to the beauty parlor for a wash and set. Dead or alive, they knew, pneumonia or no pneumonia, my mother would want her hair done. She was not alone. There are women at Canterbury who have permanent appointments with their hairdressers for a wash and set after they die, so that they will look at least as good in open caskets as they would at a cocktail party. And why not? It's the last time they'll be out in public.

Louise had dressed her, fastened on her earrings and fake pearls, brushed her luxuriant silver gray hair, and applied her lipstick and powder, her rouge and favorite faintly violet eye shadow and eyeliner, to accentuate her gray blue and sometimes still-greenish eyes. Bathed and lotioned, powdered, fluffed, and painted, Mother seemed poised and content as she sat up in bed. She was nodding and smiling at Father Martin.

This is nice, I thought. It was almost as if she was enjoying the occasion, instead of dying, as we gathered around her. I leaned down to take her hand and gave it a squeeze. The hand felt warmer.

"Look at you, Mother. You're bright eyed and bushy tailed," I said. "I think you're having a good time." I meant to tease her a little.

She gave me back a gay look. I studied her more closely. She *was* having a good time. It was then that Louise pulled my arm. Through the decades, she and Mother had come to know all that was worth knowing of each other's families, hearts, and minds. They had been especially intimate since my father died, and in the nursing wing, Louise watched Mother like a loving hawk.

"Psssst," Louise said, nudging me again with her elbow. I turned toward her. She gave me a significant look and leaned in to whisper in my ear.

"Doctor put that little thang on her finger, and say her blood be better."

Better? I snapped around, to stare at my mother. She *did* look better. In fact, she looked wonderful. She didn't look as if she was going to die at all. Christ, she didn't even look sick. I slipped away from the little cluster around her bed and crossed the hall to the nurses' station.

"Did you take another blood oxygen reading on my mother?"

The nurse beamed, radiant as an angel with good news. "This afternoon," she said, eyes shining. "It's ninety-six. That's almost normal."

I crossed the hall, back through the door, to stand at the foot of Mother's bed. She turned her gaze from the priest to me. She was unperturbed, as gracious and happy as if Father Martin had just arrived for drinks and dinner.

I was dumbfounded.

Yes, dear, her expression said. *I do feel better. Isn't it lovely?*

And with that, she smiled her motherly, reassuring smile, the one I knew so well. It was her confident smile, her "Everything's just fine, darlin' " smile.

It looked as if it could last for years.

CHAPTER SEVEN

The Dining Room Waltz

JANUARY–FEBRUARY 2000

Each night in the early months of 2000, as the men and women in the dining room turned their heads to watch the latest chapter in the drama of Mary and Wilber unfold, Wilber did a little dance step coming through the doors. It was always to the same tune, one that only he could hear. There was no music in the dining room. Sometimes, usually on Saturday nights, a little combo played in the big, comfortable social room on the first floor at the cocktail hour. For years—in the period when Mary and Wilber first moved to Canterbury, and still later, when Charles and Martha Sweet came—the staff laid down a portable dance floor of polished wood on Saturday evenings, and an actual dance band played so that the residents who still felt like it could twirl each other around. But dancing at Canterbury ended the memorable night in 1996 that Charles Sweet lost his balance while doing the jitterbug, tilted, turned slowly—like a blimp floating loose from its mooring—and fell with a great, soft whomp and crash atop a bony, elegant woman who had been sitting in a chair at the edge of the dance floor.

"Demolished her chair. That ton of blubber," Martha Sweet said in her gravelly voice, shaking her head at the memory. "And not a scratch on her. Not hurt at all." She paused, exhaling a cloud of cigarette smoke while she marveled at the thought. "It's the closest thing to a miracle I've ever seen."

The person who seemed least affected by the removal of the dance floor was Wilber. Which was odd, because for him the fun in life started as the sun went down. Wilber loved to dance, loved being the life of the party. But when the dance floor disappeared, he just kept on dancing. Every night when he and Mary came down for dinner after drinks in their apartment, he did his little three-step, sashaying into the room like a cabaret performer opening his act, stopping at each table to laugh and talk, patting people on the hands and shoulders, grinning and chuckling as if he had a joke and a story for everyone.

He was the prince of good feeling, the bringer of cheer. Start the party—Wilber is here. What he said, however, amid all the jollity, made no sense at all. He just started talking—which is what he had always done—and then couldn't finish his sentences, because he didn't actually know what he was talking about, or to whom.

Each night as he entered the room, it looked as if he might just carry it off. If he had been the star of a silent film, he would have been fine. The time of day, the room, the faces of the people were all familiar to him. The outline of the moment, the body movements, the surface emotions were all rote. He just couldn't fill in the verbal blanks. He couldn't think. Whether he realized it or not, no one could tell. What was obvious was that he wanted life to still be fun, and for a while, people at the other tables humored him. They squeezed his hand when he came up, patted his elbow, threw their heads back and laughed as if he'd just said something clever, or reminded them of an old story they'd always loved. As if they were still all in the warm conspiracy of friendship and memory together, jollying each other, teasing old age for all it was worth. Their generation, after all, had been through much together. They could put up with a little more.

But even after most people got tired of him and quit playing along ("He should be in the Health Center," Martha Cameron said, sitting in the dining room. "It's what we all agreed to, you know."), some of the other women understood why Mary continued to hold on to him. This was not, after all—with the exception of strong personalities like Sarah Jane Rubio and Martha Sweet, who had each divorced two husbands, and Martha Cameron, who divorced the same husband twice—a generation of women prone to give up on their men. They didn't in war. ("The reason none of us divorced was because we were separated from our husbands for three years," one of my mother's old Tampa friends, Eleanor, said. "We were just glad to see them back.") They didn't let go emotionally in the long, difficult periods of marriage that often followed either—or even, sometimes decades later, when their husbands died. So it wasn't surprising that the women who still had their men would hold on to them, even as creeping dementia changed them more each day.

Whether the men were dead and gone or still around, many of the women continued to save and treasure their letters, their pictures, their awards and plaques. They kept them around—on the walls and in desk and bureau drawers—even if their husbands had been gone for decades. Sometimes even if the women had remarried and were living now with other men. And even if *those* men were dead and gone.

Some of the women who were still with their original husbands—men who had gone from virile youth to middle age, to older age, to the very extended age they were now in—wouldn't exactly claim to still love them after all this time. But they were *used* to them. They were the balance of each other's days.

"He's mah company," Mary said of Wilber. "He's thuh only company Ah have. Ah need him. Ah rally do."

Some of them fussed and fumed at their old husbands, pretending not to love them, even though they really did. "Poah Ashby," Sarah Jane said one night, chuckling because poor Ashby was having to squire her to dinner, along with the Emyfish and Martha Cameron. Mauricio was out of town.

" 'Poor Ashby,' my foot!" the Emyfish snorted, almost spilling the iced bourbon and water she had just mixed in one of her grandmother's gold-rimmed goblets. "There's nothing poor about *him*. I'm so tired of people saying 'Poor Ashby'! He's the most spoiled-rotten person there ever *was!*" And with that, and a glare, she shoved the drink at Sarah Jane.

"Ooooh, deah." Sarah Jane laughed, nervously, reaching for the glass. "Ah don't think Ah'll say *that* agyun."

Others plainly still adored their old husbands, even if they were reduced to dry husks of their former youthful selves.

"My lover *emeritus,*" Ruth Richter said one morning with a smile, her sly, knowing old blue eyes teasing the rabbi, who was sitting across the breakfast table from her. They were eating German pancakes at Schiller's, a little restaurant up El Prado Boulevard from Canterbury, where they went the first Monday of each month. She was eighty-three, and a little stout, with thick beautiful white hair, an ample bosom, handsome features, and behind her glasses, those sharp, playful, piercing blue eyes. He was ninety, as solemn and seamed and thoughtful in expression as a basset hound, with a bald pate and large dark eyes that appeared to see and understand everything, the sadness and comedy of life. He always had a joke. He was always the wisest man around. They had been married for sixty-five years, longer than any couple at Canterbury, longer by eight months than even Mary and Wilber. So each night, when they sat at their accustomed table in the dining room and watched Wilber come grinning and shuffling through the door—Mary trailing stonily behind—they understood the drama they were seeing.

They knew it well.

"I hope I go first," Ruth told Karl some days, looking at him tenderly as they sat in their apartment. "I don't want to live without you."

Each time she said that, he heard the voice in his own heart, saying the same thing in reverse: "I don't want to live *without you.*"

And yet Karl Richter could not hope to be that selfish. For one, he and Ruth both knew that his great-grandfather had lived to be the oldest man in Austria, or so people said. He was 110. For another, he knew that his good wife, whom he had loved almost from the moment he met her on the stairs of the Jewish Theological Seminary in Breslau, when she was a slim and beautiful flaxen-haired girl of sixteen, was beginning to fail. It was not just that she had high blood pressure and arthritis, which made it difficult for her to walk. Her mind was starting to wander, something Karl told no one. But he had become watchful. Ruth would sometimes go out in the hall, and then be there by herself, without knowing why.

So when they saw Mary and Wilber Davis come through the doors of the dining room in the evening, Karl watching thoughtfully, Ruth with her calculating, practical gaze, they understood the tie that bound the other couple—the need for each other, the feeling that life could not exist in any meaningful way without the other person there to define and share it.

Culturally speaking, the Richters had little in common with Mary and Wilber Davis—nothing really, except for almost seven decades of life together, and the inability to imagine themselves apart. But it bonded them at the core, that feeling, even though they hardly spoke. It was intense for Karl and Ruth because they had almost lost each other, long ago, in the first years of their marriage—the last years in the lives of almost all the Jews of Europe. And it was Ruth, Karl always said, who saved them.

They were in Mannheim, where Karl was the twenty-eight-year-old rabbi of the main synagogue in the fall of 1938, when the order was given and the destruction of the Jewish temples—the horror of *Kristallnacht,* the "Night of Broken Glass"—began. The Richters, along with the rest of the Jewish population, had lost the rights and protections of German citizenship three years before, with the passage of the Nuremberg laws. Life in Nazi Germany had grown steadily more ominous and abusive since. On October 27, all men of Polish ancestry had suddenly been summoned to the main train station, where they were torn from their wives and children and forced into trains, to be deported to the border of Poland, most of them never to be seen again. Then on the night of November 10, the terror took a new form. The Gestapo began invading synagogues, cemeteries, houses, and apartments of Jews across the nation, smashing up the interiors, throwing furniture and china out the windows, burning and dynamiting, arresting thousands of Jewish men and taking them away.

Karl had first been interrogated by the Gestapo, and threatened with imprisonment, almost three years before, and as terrified members of his congregation began coming to his door and telephoning him at home to report what was happening that night, he became certain that this time he would be taken away. He sat at his desk, waiting. It was Ruth, holding Esther, their two-year-old daughter, who insisted that they should not wait. They should take refuge in the Jewish hospital across the park. And so they hurried through the bare, dark trees and shadows, the autumn leaves crunching underfoot, to the hospital and old people's home.

The nurses there bundled them into the hospital's isolation ward. If the Gestapo came, the nurses said, they would tell them that the section was quarantined, that it contained patients with highly contagious scarlet fever. Perhaps the Nazis would be afraid to search. It was a traumatic night, with wounded and bleeding Jewish men arriving for emergency treatment, and open trucks bringing loads of terrified, half-dressed old people. The old age home in Neustadt had been burned. Karl and Ruth and Esther spent long, fitful hours in the dark of an empty room, listening to the muffled sounds of violence in the night. Halfway through, they heard a large explosion. The Nazis had blown up the chapel of the Jewish cemetery and—as they would discover—Karl's synagogue.

In the morning, Karl's father, who had come from Stuttgart to look for them, found them in the hospital and insisted on taking them back home with him. It would be safer there, he said. No one had been arrested yet. He knew of a taxi driver, a Communist who hated the Nazis, who picked them up and took them to the train station. They boarded a train, holding National Socialist Party newspapers in front of their faces as they rode to Stuttgart, and for three days hid in the attic in the house of a Jewish couple, family friends there.

When it seemed safe, they went back to Mannheim. But the Gestapo beat on the door, looking for Karl. This time he was in his own attic, and it was Ruth—so pale, so light haired and blue eyed, so Aryan looking to the Nazis that it always threw them—who opened the door. "I don't know where he is," she said, as tight lipped as if they were adding insult to her injury. "*You* took him off the street. *You* should know where he is. I don't know."

Deceived, unsure that their mission hadn't already been accomplished and that the fabled Nazi record-keeping system hadn't somehow gone awry, the jackboots went away.

More than sixty years later, sitting in the dining room at Canterbury, where the drama of Mary and Wilber was playing out, Ruth turned the eyes of a survivor on me with a look both tender and grim. "You will always find that women can handle the situation better than men," she said. "We have survived many situations in which men have perished. But I think that an experience like that changes a person forever. And men do not understand that women suffer this much more than men."

Karl Richter knew, when the Gestapo left the door of his house that day, that if they could not somehow escape Germany, they would die. Still, when a telegram came from the president of a Jewish congregation in Springfield, Missouri—alerted by a friend who had already emigrated to the presence of this brilliant, scholarly young rabbi in Mannheim, who could play the violin; read in Latin, Greek, French, and English; and preach from a deep knowledge of Judaic culture and Western philosophy—Karl could not bring himself to tell the simple lie that might save their lives.

The congregation of Temple Israel was looking for a rabbi. The telegram offered the hope of escape from Germany, and it posed one crucial question: "How is your English?"

Karl wrote in reply, on a telegram form, that he could speak a little but was studying to improve, which was as much as he thought he could stretch the truth. He really spoke no English. Then he gave the paper to Ruth, his Aryan-looking wife, to take to the telegraph office.

She was far more practical. As the telegraph operator waited, she crossed out Karl's answer. ENGLISH IS PERFECT, she wrote instead, and sent the telegram to Missouri.

She could see what needed to be done if they were to survive. When the time finally came to get the precious passports that would allow them to leave, the functionary at the police station who was in charge of issuing them looked at the jeweled watch pinned to the lapel of her dress—the fashion of the time—and smugly asked what it was worth. Ruth did not hesitate.

"You can have it if you like," she said. She took it off. She already had money palmed in her hand. She put the watch with the money, and shook hands with the corrupt clerk. He palmed the contents of her hand. And gave her the passports.

That was more than sixty years ago, and still she had nightmares. Still she was watchful, observing everything, noticing everything, calculating the odds of risks large and small.

"Your nose doesn't look too good," she said, eyeing me as she might a too-ripe tomato at the market. The three of us were sitting together in the dining room at lunch, looking out on the bright summer day. "You should be careful of the sun."

Martha Sweet wasn't close to Mary Davis. She had no interest in domestic arts, and none in domestic women. (She particularly loathed, in fact, that *other* Martha, the one on television—Martha Stewart. "She represents everything I despise in women," Martha growled.)

Martha Sweet wasn't southern, like Mary Davis. She wasn't drawn to children. She had never met an animal she liked. She wasn't trained to the niceties of the cocktail hour or dinner parties, the obligations of small talk, or in general a life constructed around the adornment of men. She was of German stock, from the mountains and valleys of Pennsylvania coal-mining country. She was romantic but hard minded. As a senior in high school, she had won the state prize in oratory. She was proud not of being pretty, but of being smart. She liked history. Literature. Politics. Theater. Public affairs. Books. *Men.* Smart, big-spirited, testosterone-charged, funny, sensual, lovemaking *men!*

But she also understood why Mary was hanging on to Wilber, because Martha Sweet absolutely adored her husband, Charles, the large, learned, imperious former Marine Corps officer and judge, and was hanging on to him, too—the difference being that Charles was dead.

He had died the year before—in October 1999—the year in which Wilber had gone from being still sort of amusing (if you didn't have to live with him) to being mainly annoying. He had now become a serious, constantly irritating problem. He would soon be maddening. It worried his daughter, Nathalie. She didn't exactly know what to do about her daddy. Like Mary, she sometimes fell into the trap of trying to reason with him. But she couldn't love him in the way that Mary did; she didn't depend on him or need him, and so she had less patience. There were times, in fact, when she didn't think she liked him much at all. Wilber had always embarrassed her with his insistence on being the life of the party, and now, when she drove down from North Carolina to see her parents and stayed in the second bedroom of their apartment, he had begun appearing by her bed in the middle of the night. He had been like that when she was growing up—"the Night Patrol," she called him—coming in to turn off the fan by her bed, to cover her up, to make sure she was all right; a fussy, solicitous daddy. But now she wasn't sure that he knew who she was. It made her feel weird. It made her uncomfortable. When she started locking the door to discourage him, she could hear the doorknob rattle in the night.

All Wilber's comments and questions had become repetitive, part of a pattern, and when he told Nathalie—as he had Mary—that he was so frustrated, he felt like throwing himself off the balcony, Nathalie took his arm and walked him across the living room carpet, through the sliding glass doors, out onto the balcony.

"Look down there, Daddy," she said, pointing over the railing. "You see? That's somebody's terrace two floors below. It's not far enough. If you jump from here, you'll just break your legs." (He had always been proud of his strong, shapely legs.) "You need to be higher," Nathalie said. *"You need to go up on the roof."*

Wilber gave his daughter, his only child, a dazed look, trying to gather his thoughts. *"I don't think I remember how to get there,"* he said.

Nathalie and Mary didn't really believe it was in Wilber to kill himself. They also wondered, separately, without voicing it to each other, if it would not be better if he did. They didn't know what to do about him. At Canterbury, of course, they were not the first family to have such a problem, and one day Nathalie asked Martha Sweet what she had done about Charles.

Charles had become maddening, too. He and Martha had great fights, but then everything about Charles was great. His size, his personality, his intellect, his passions. They had had, by Martha's way of reckoning, the perfect grown-up marriage, and almost thirty years of bliss. They argued, they made love, they made lists, they took long vacation trips to far distant countries, they went to a million political events in the decades he was in politics. It suited her to a T. She loved to argue, she loved making lists ("Name fifty women who lived in the fifteenth century," "Name fifty rivers in the world"), she loved to travel, she was passionate about politics. As the tall, glowering president judge of Washington County, Pennsylvania, a man who suffered no fools in his courtroom, who could—and did—break into long passages of Latin on impulse at any public occasion, who loved to talk and drink beer, Charles loomed over the political and cultural life of the town. And even with his big belly, he had this gusto, this animal sexiness about him. Martha loved his big, rubbery lips. She thought she was the luckiest woman in the world.

"We could drive all the way to Miami arguing about the Crusades," she said. "I thought they were xenophobic and barbaric. He thought they expanded trade."

They both had retentive minds, nearly photographic memories. They both had memorized banks of verse. (It was one of her fears, that when she and the last of her generation were gone, there would be no one left in America who learned to memorize poetry as a child, and who could still quote it, on an instant, out of love.)

"Probably Charles and I could have gotten in the car here and driven to New York City and quoted poetry the entire way," she said, sitting one day at lunchtime under the banana leaves in the patio of Mad Dog's Saloon, a restaurant owned by the son of the actor Robert Morley, near Canterbury.

"Really?"

"Yeah. If you count Shakespeare, we could have probably made it to Montreal."

And that is what had made it so difficult when Charles's great mind began to fail. They had moved to Canterbury from their first retirement home, a condominium apartment on the Hillsborough River, above the city, where they had been for eight years when Charles had begun to forget things—like where he was going in the car. It was Martha who made the choice. She had been the director of benefits for a division of a national manufacturer of electrical transformers. She was accustomed to dealing with health issues and bureaucratic systems. She knew how to get things done, and when she came to see Canterbury, she loved the location, the view. She knew, soon enough, that he would need the nursing wing and, when he did, that he would be just down the elevator and down a hall. She could see him every day.

When the specialist they saw diagnosed dementia, Charles had resigned himself to move, and within two months Martha had them in Canterbury. But it was not uneventful. First, when the *New York Times* did not appear outside their apartment door one morning, Charles went down to the lobby to look for it. In the elevator. In his robe. Which was *untied*. Charles was six feet four, weighed 260 pounds at the time, and was not a modest man. That exposure earned them a trip to Mrs. Vinas's office for a conversation about the decorum necessary in the public spaces of a building primarily populated by widows and some spinsters. Then, in the dining room after consuming a large breakfast brought to him one morning by Chanh, Charles leaned back contentedly in his chair, reading something in the *Times,* and lit one of the small Tampa-made cigars that he always carried. It was his after-breakfast pleasure. It was also strictly forbidden.

When they came back to their apartment from *that* trip to Mrs. Vinas's office—he had not only smoked the cigar, he had responded with an epithet when told he couldn't—Charles Sweet was in a foul humor. Frustrated. It was like being called before the principal, something that hadn't happened to him in more than sixty years. He was seventy-eight years old and not penitent. He was a judge, accustomed to giving the lecture, not hearing it, and so he and Martha had a huge argument. This time it wasn't in fun. She knew if he did not behave, he would have to go to the Health Center, or they would have to leave Canterbury. They argued about the cigars. He had to give them up.

He rumbled and refused. He would not give them up. He would *not!*

But she was as determined as he was. And quicker. They were shouting at each other in the living room. Before them was the balcony, and the view over the bay she loved. They could be happy at Canterbury; they could make it work for whatever time Charles had left, Martha thought. He could be safe there if they could just hold on. And so she grabbed the box of Phillies Panatella cigars, which he loved and would not relinquish, and stepped to the balcony, yelling back to him that he could not—*could not!*—smoke those damn cigars at Canterbury, and hurled the box over the railing, as far out as she could. The lid flipped open. The long, slim, sweetly malodorous cylinders spilled into the air. They floated off from the box, light brown sticks turning slowly where seagulls fly, and sailed down to where the lawn mowers mow, and the joggers jog, and the traffic flows, far below.

The two of them stared at each other, flushed and furious, each of them stunned at the moment. Exhausted. Then Charles, the judge, the Marine, sank into the deep leather couch, glum and beaten.

"*OK,*" he said, in his deep solemn voice. "*You win.*"

It was not an argument she had wanted to have, much less win. But it was like that, off and on, for their remaining time at Canterbury. Each week, each month, he was less the man he'd been. But only in reality. Never in her mind. For Martha, Charles Sweet was all the things about men that she loved and hadn't known existed before she met him. That's the way he would always be to her, and she wasn't about to let him go.

As she told Nathalie, the time did come when Charles left the apartment for the Health Center, but Martha was lucky. She didn't have to make the choice. He was taken to the hospital for prostate surgery. When he returned to Canterbury, he was brought to the Health Center to convalesce. But he didn't recover. Instead, he declined. Three times a day—morning, afternoon, and night—Martha went to see him. One night she was there with him again—they had even danced a little together in the afternoon—and early the next morning, he was gone.

Martha knew, when it happened, that she was more fortunate than some widows. She was only seventy-two. She had interests. She was a silver master in duplicate bridge and still played each week. She helped to write and act in the skits and comedies that the Canterbury Players produced. She gave docent tours of the University of Tampa's old hotel museum, in the huge old brick building with its Moorish arches, its silver minarets, and its Victorian verandas on the river. She read voraciously, two books or more a week. She watched the History Channel. CNN news. Movies on television. She even reread the Bible. She took to eating dinner every night with the men at the Men's Table. At first they didn't object because they knew Charles had just died and she was lonely. And then they got accustomed to her being there. She was the only woman at the table, and she became the energy of the evening. She liked men.

"I miss the sex," she said one day, surprised at herself that it should be the keenest loss.

That part of missing him she could not change. But Martha didn't have to let him go. Even if she had wanted to, he was all around—the oversize couches and chairs she had bought for him, his books, his plaques and certificates and photographs on the wall. Her sassy, plain-spoken daughter, Meredith, the child of her first marriage, called those things "the shrine."

"Take down the goddamn shrine, Mother," she would say, in another few months, on the phone from New York.

But Martha had already decided that she would rather keep the memory of her beloved Charles alive. She would never find anyone his equal. So why let him go? Besides, she didn't feel she had a

choice. She loved him. And so at 11:45 each night, she had a routine. After watching Jay Leno's monologue—the end of a day as
filled as she could fill it—she stood on the balcony for a long moment, looking out at the dark bay and the vast glittering night,
thinking how lucky she was to be at Canterbury. And then she
locked the apartment door, put on her nightgown, put out her last
cigarette, crawled into bed, and turned out the light. It was the same
each night.

"I put my arms around him," she said. "And I go to sleep."

CHAPTER EIGHT

In Case of Fire

FEBRUARY, MARCH, APRIL 2000

I t was just after noon, and Mother was at lunch, propped up in her chaise longue at her usual place at a table for four in the dining room of the Health Center. A spoonful of something gloppy and green (peas? beans? broccoli? brussels sprouts?) hovered in front of her mouth, pureed so she could swallow it without choking. Claudia, who was feeding her this day, waved the spoon gently, waiting for her to open up. But Mother's head was turned away. She was staring, wide-eyed, at the new person sitting on her right—a woman of faded red hair and ferocious smile—just arrived, I think, from Arkansas. She was in the middle of a breathless peroration.

> *Tackza*
> *Jackza*
> *Lackza*

"Lambda!" she shouted, gasping with excitement. Mother thought this was hilarious. No one had talked like this at lunch before— or been so fervent about it. All the other diners (except the sleepiest, and the most demented) swung their heads around to look. The red-haired woman switched into cadence. With an ecstatic look, she began to beat a fist rhythmically on the table, her voice rising with each line.

And my MONEY
And my Uhh-ney
Mid my any—
And my mother
And Liza—

"Lie! LIE! *LIE!*" she sang out. She beat the table even harder, thrilled with her own articulation.

And my mother
And my money
And my money
And my Liza
And my taxi
And my Laxie
And my Liza

"And my LI-ZER!" She rocked in her chair, a glow of blissed-out creation on her face, and began the windup.

Pfizer!
Lizer!
Jackza!

"*LACKZA!*" she yelled, arms outflung. It was her joyful last line, at least for the moment. The red-haired woman fell back in her chair, breathing heavily, grinning at the ceiling—waiting, perhaps, to see if her message had been received. At the other tables—which had been mostly silent, riveted by her performance—people continued to gape at her, as if a monkey had just ridden a bear into the room and left it there, and they were waiting to see what the bear would do.

Around the room, the certified nursing assistants smiled and rolled their eyes at one another, and began to murmur to their old charges.

"Miz Clen-*dinen*," Claudia said, nudging Mother's lips with the spoon. My mother didn't turn toward her, or take her eyes off her new companion. She didn't want to miss anything. But she opened her mouth. Claudia is strong and beautiful, like a woman athlete, and she was fast. Her wrist and hand moved sideways like a piston. The spoon slid into Mother's mouth and out, leaving behind most of its small, pudding load of . . .

Who knew? It was on a menu somewhere, but no one ever looked. Mother began chewing absently, her bright eyes still fixed expectantly on the red-haired woman, who was still grinning at the ceiling. Claudia dipped the spoon into another section of the luncheon tray, which held a dark brown pudding (Salisbury steak? meat loaf? roast beef and gravy?). She brought it up under Mother's nose. And waited.

This was not like the old days, when Elizabeth Himes and the Emyfish stood up and roared at each other across tables of white wine and baked grouper in the dining room of the Tower, scandalizing and titillating all the dressed-up old ladies and old men in their jackets and ties. But it would do. Lunch was off to a good start. Someone had actually had something to say. If anyone at the table had a memory, this would go down as a memorable day.

On another day in February, in the evening, the cocktail hour came round again. Mary and Wilber were in the living room. He was in his usual corner of the couch, peering at a framed pastel painting on the other wall, as if he had just noticed it. It was Elizabeth, their granddaughter, blond and delicate, at the adorable age of four. They had had the picture for more than twenty years.

"Who's that?" Wilber asked, nodding toward it.

"She used to be his shinin' laht," Mary said quietly. He couldn't hear, though she had come to stand by him.

Wilber glanced up at her, and the watch on her wrist caught his eye—an old-fashioned woman's watch in a silver setting.

"Is that my watch?" he asked, reaching for it.

"No," she answered. Her expression was resigned. "He gave it tuh me," she said, with a sad, sideways look. Decades ago.

Mary began to try to make conversation, but Wilber couldn't hear her and interrupted.

"Where are we?" he said, speaking loud enough to hear himself. "Do you know?" He had lost his hearing aids.

"In ouah apahrtmahnt in Tampah, Florida," she told him. For the thousandth time.

"On a ship?"

"In ouah apahrtmahnt."

He looked puzzled. "Where are all our clothes?" he said.

"In the clahset."

He frowned. "How long have they been there?"

She frowned back at him. *"Youah talkin' too loud,"* she said, raising her voice so he could hear.

"A *lot?*" he asked. He was practically yelling.

"Too LAHYOUD."

"Where?" he said.

"HEAH!"

Wilber paused a moment, thinking. "But I wasn't here," he said, speaking in a quieter voice.

Exchanges like this made Mary feel her head was going to explode.

"Weah goan *to eat,*" she declared, as if that would make a difference. She put her drink glass down. "Go get yoah coat."

"OK." Wilber wobbled to his feet and headed toward the back of the apartment.

"Here?" he called out, a few moments later, his voice coming from down the hall.

"No, Wilbuh. Youah in *thuh* BAATH-*room.*"

Mary stared at the hallway door for a long moment, then turned to me. "Las' naht, he asked me whut wuz wroang with him. An' foah thuh furst time, ah tole him he had Alzheimer's. Ah had nevah use' thuh wuhd befoah."

She paused, looking stricken. It had to have been an effort. She had refused to acknowledge it to herself for years. Then for more years, after the doctor told her and Nathalie that it was almost certainly what Wilber had, she had avoided using the word with Wilber. Finally, she had told him.

"An' it didn' mean a *thang* tuh him," Mary said, looking at me as if she could scarcely believe it. "In five minutes, he had foahgotten aawl about it."

The next day, Nathalie drove in from North Carolina. I spent an hour with Mother in the afternoon, before her dinner, which is at 5:00 p.m. in the nursing wing, and then went with Mary and Wilber and Nathalie at 5:30 for drinks at Carroll Boden's apartment. Carroll—platinum haired, crooked, immaculate, widowed—was another old friend from the decades when our parents were all in their fifties and sixties and seventies, and were still couples, with their own houses and functioning husbands and regular lives.

Wilber and I sat on the couch and began to talk genial nonsense. The three women settled into comfortable chairs across from us, holding their glasses. They chatted about this and that, and the conversation soon turned to the elephant in the room—Wilber, who couldn't hear them. Carroll, who had a three-wheeled walker and paid companions to keep her from falling, day and night, couldn't hear very well either. As the conversation wandered, Nathalie kept giving her father long, somber looks.

Wilber noticed.

"Tell me," he said, leaning toward me. *"Who is that woman over there?"* He pointed at Nathalie. "That woman sitting there."

I kept my face to him and tried not to change expression, as if we were just making small talk about something in the apartment he was trying to identify. At first, he had thought that Carroll's wheeled walker, standing across from him—outfitted with a horn, a bouquet of plastic flowers, and a sign that said ROLLS-ROYCE—was another person. But we weren't talking about the trolley. And it is hard to quietly explain to a deaf, demented, persistent old man that the woman he is asking about, only eight feet away, is his daughter and only child. At least not without being overheard. I slid a sideways glance at Nathalie's face. She had heard.

I could almost see what was going through her mind. She had always had mixed feelings about her father. She and I both had issues about our parents. Who doesn't? They are all flawed—like us children—and the older they get, the bigger the cracks and quirks become. But she had loved him. He was her doting daddy. He adored her. And now he didn't know her. He didn't know where he was. He didn't always even know who Mary was.

What were they going to do?

Wilber was already as far gone as Charles Sweet became *after* Charles moved to the Health Center. Wilber was already as demented as many people who were already *in* the Health Center and had been there for some time. Mary and Nathalie knew that. Everyone knew that. He had become a Canterbury legend. The question was what to do about him. Or rather, how and when to do it. Unlike Charles Sweet, Wilber had no physical condition that needed hospital treatment—and that might then bring him into the Health Center for a convalescence that could become permanent as he became accustomed to the place. If he didn't have a surgery or a broken bone to recover from, Wilber wouldn't understand why he was *in* the Health Center. And Nathalie and Mary didn't think his dementia had yet made him docile enough to accept being kept there.

But it wasn't simply that he was driving Mary crazy. There were real physical problems involved in keeping him in the apartment.

"Ah will keep him up heah until he becomes incontinent," Mary had said. "But Ah cannot handle *that*." In fact, they had crossed that line. Wilber had been dribbling and trickling for months. Nathalie had bought a moisture-proof mattress cover for his bed, but they could figure no way to moisture-proof Wilber. He knew he was leaking—he was stuffing his pants with washcloths, paper towels, and Kleenex tissues, leaving a trail of damp paper bits and the scent of ammonia behind him wherever he went. But he would not wear the adult diapers that Nathalie bought. He got angry when Mary or Nathalie suggested it.

It had helped when Mrs. Vinas started sending someone up to give him a shower three times a week. It also helped that Mary had a talent for disconnecting from the moment. It was a survival skill. But it made deciding anything more difficult. Numbed and distracted as she was, sleeping as much as she did during the day, it was hard to think clearly what to do about her life. It was all she could do to live it. And that is what she did. There were plenty of other people at Canterbury doing much the same, either because they preferred to be absentminded about their problems or because they *were* absentminded—whether they preferred it or not. Time passed, and when Mary heard that Dr. Eric Pfeiffer, a psychiatrist on the University of South Florida Medical School faculty who specialized in geriatric issues, was coming to Canterbury to talk about Alzheimer's disease, she decided to go. Maybe it would show her a way.

She almost forgot about his talk. She was late coming into the social room that morning. The blue-carpeted room, with its upholstered sofas and wing chairs, and rows of little straight chairs set up for the meeting, was practically full. No other issue affects as many people of Canterbury age as dementia, and most of the other residents of the Tower were already there, hoping to learn something about symptoms or treatment that could help them, or the spouse or friend they were worried about. Mary spotted an empty seat and made her way slowly down the row while Dr. Pfeiffer spoke. He was white haired and balding, a little round in the shoulders, standing at a lectern in front of the residents.

He didn't seem to have anything new to say about Alzheimer's, but he showed a video about who got it and when, about symptoms and progression, and what could be done, which wasn't much. He talked about the drug Aricept. And he asked them to take part in a survey. He wanted to use the residents at Canterbury as a kind of sample. He had a sheaf of information forms for them to read, with phone numbers for them to call in order to take a memory test. He said he would leave the forms behind. When he finished, Martha Cameron, president of the residents' association, presented him with a bottle of wine and thanked him for coming.

Dr. Pfeiffer left, forgetting the wine. Someone caught him at the door and gave it to him again. But he also forgot the video he had brought, which they found afterward and had to mail to him. Martha Cameron at first forgot about the survey forms he had left, and then when she did find and distribute them, a lot of people meant to call the phone numbers at the medical school to ask about the test.

But they forgot. Some, like Sarah Jane Rubio, did call and arrange to take the memory test by phone. But when she was in the middle of trying to repeat the list of words the survey taker had just read to her, Sarah Jane—who has dozens of enthusiastic conversations every day—heard the beep on the line that meant she was getting another call. She took it, of course, and when she got back to the surveyor, forgot the rest of the answer she had been giving.

Another resident, a former secretary used to taking dictation, did better. She forgot it was a memory test and wrote the words down as the surveyor read them out, and then read them back over the phone, perfectly. The surveyor was impressed by her memory. It didn't occur to Mary Davis to take the test, to find out about herself. She was there because of Wilber. But when she got back to her apartment, she couldn't remember hearing anything that gave her an idea of what to do about him.

I t was Wilber who ended the stalemate. He didn't intend to, of course. Almost all his effects on other people were unintended. As late February turned to March, March to April, and April to May, he slept more and more during the day. But at night, after dinner, his restlessness—the feeling that someone was waiting downstairs to take him to where Mary and their friends were waiting—grew more acute. He and Mary went back upstairs to their apartment at eight o'clock each night when the dining room closed, and sometimes had another drink. Mary was often asleep by ten, but she couldn't always quiet Wilber, or get him to go to bed and stay there. He lay down in his clothes, and if he got up and wandered into another room, he wouldn't remember what time it was, or that he ought to be in bed. And if he didn't see Mary, he might go looking outside the apartment.

It is at ten o'clock each night that the guard on the security desk at the front door goes on rounds, checking all the public rooms on the first two floors, the entrances and exits to the building, and the parking lots and electrically controlled perimeter gates. By that hour, whatever film was shown on the big television screen in the social room is usually finished. The dining room and kitchen staff has gone home. The social life of the building is over for the day. And by ten, the residents who have gone out for the evening are usually back in. Everyone in the Tower is upstairs, most of them in bed, asleep. For ten or fifteen minutes, the lobby is empty, the desk unattended, the glass front doors locked.

It was just after ten, one night in mid-May, that Wilber came off the elevator into the lobby. Carlos, who was working the evening shift, had just left to make his rounds. The lobby was empty. Wilber may have tried to go outside, to look for Mary, or for the friends he thought were coming to pick him up, but the doors were locked. Without an electronic card key, he couldn't get out any of the exit doors. They were all controlled from the security desk. The social room, the assembly room, the gym, the little general store, the card room, the beauty parlor, and the offices on the first floor were already dark. Wilber couldn't see anything in those rooms. He didn't know how to turn on the lights. And so he stood at the front desk in the vacant lobby. There were usually people there—he couldn't remember who. Maybe they would come back. Wilber could see the flicker of images on the television monitors behind the desk. He leaned over the counter, looking closer. He may have watched the video screens for a moment, but he noticed the sign. There was nothing wrong with his eyesight, and he could still read. He got the first part of it.

It said PULL HERE. And so Wilber reached over and pulled the red lever.

IN CASE OF FIRE was what the rest of it said.

The alarm bells and automatic fire evacuation announcements on the speaker system went off on every floor throughout the building, and the high-priority fire-at-a-nursing-home signal went into the Tampa Fire Department. Firemen in different firehouses jumped up and began pulling on their overalls and fire hats and running for their trucks.

On the television monitors behind the desk, which look through video cameras down the hallways on all fourteen floors of Canterbury, at the areas beyond all the building's doors, and at the fenced parking lots outside, the screens showed worried old heads peering out of apartment doors, looking up and down the halls for smoke—and Carlos running across a parking lot with the end of his tie flipping up and down against his starched white shirt, his tobacco pipe held tight in one pumping fist, a frozen expression on his face.

M ary wasn't sure why she woke, but when she looked across at Wilber's bed, he wasn't there. He didn't seem to be in the apartment, and so she walked out onto the living room balcony to see what the commotion was below. Her neighbor was standing on the balcony next door, gazing down at the tangle of flashing lights and fire engines. There were six of them, nosing the base of the building like large, shiny red beetles.

The neighbor looked across at Mary. "Where's Wilber?" she asked.

"Ah doan know. He's not heah," Mary said, placidly, shaking her head.

The neighbor looked down at the engines again, and back at Mary. "Do you think it was him?" she asked.

Mary, who rarely took the trouble to connect the dots unless someone else connected them for her, felt a sudden breathlessness at the question.

Oh, damn. Just then, behind her, the telephone rang. It was Carlos.

"Ah, Missus Davis, ahyou com-ah down ah-here *right now!*" he said.

CHAPTER NINE

Going Home

MAY–EARLY JUNE 2000

It was the month of May, the bright drought before the heavy mid-summer rains began on the Gulf Coast of Florida. To the west, on the other side of Tampa Bay, a Learjet rose from the runway at dozy St. Petersburg–Clearwater International Airport, flashed up into the flame-blue sky, and turned north toward New York. It carried a determined Mary Chase Tommaney; her faintly breathing husband, John, who was on a hospital gurney; their son, Peter; and a hired nurse and aide.

The Tommaneys had spent the winter in their apartment in a tall building on the barrier island of Sand Key, across a bridge and channel from Clearwater Beach, with a high terrace looking west over the Gulf of Mexico. They loved to linger there over breakfast, watching the panorama of gulf and sky as the seagulls wheeled around them in the mornings. They repeated the ceremony over cocktails at five with a growing feeling of reverence for the splendors of creation spread all around them. It was on one of those evenings, as she and John sat with their drinks, and the red ball of the sun bled into the water before them, that Mary felt the whole earth turning for the first time in her life, and herself turning on it.

The terrace gave their mornings and evenings an almost spiritual dimension. But the building's cold, echoing lobby seemed always barren and empty when they came through. They knew no one, and after a while, although they were good company for each other, lively and intelligent, worldly and comfortable, the view paled on a man dying of leukemia. John was a New Yorker. The blood transfusions were no longer working. The stent leaked onto the carpet. He longed for Manhattan.

"Mary," he whispered, over the soft hiss of the oxygen, "get me back to New York. I don't want to die in Florida." He closed his eyes.

"Hang on, sweetie," she said, putting her arms around him. "I'll do my best."

It took her some time, but she had the carpets cleaned, arranged for hospice care, the medical team, the chartered jet—which would fly up from Miami—and ambulances on both ends. In the last days of the week before they were to leave, she thought, *Oh, God—he's not going to make it. He's sinking so fast.*

He was still alive the morning of the flight, but his color was draining. Mary was terrified he would expire in the air, over someplace like Pennsylvania, and they would have to land. *They'll have to come down, and I'll have this body. That's going to freak me out,* she thought. It was why her son, Peter, had flown down from New York to make the trip back north with them. She needed him to lean on. John seemed barely present as they took off. But soon they were flying like an arrow above the clouds, up the spine of Florida, over Georgia, the Carolinas, Virginia, Maryland, Pennsylvania, New Jersey. She sat by her husband, squeezing his pale, cooling hand.

"Hold on, John," she said, moving to peer out the window, then turning back, bringing her face close to him. "We're over the Hudson River."

His eyes remained closed, but Mary thought she could see around his mouth a softening, the flicker of a smile. He was a big man, and he had always been so smart, so strong. She felt certain that in some part of his great, disciplined lawyer's brain John had registered the information and calculated that there was still time. He would make it. They did. As they touched down at the private airfield in Teterboro, New Jersey, he was still breathing. The hired ambulance was waiting. John Tommaney was rushed to Beth Israel Medical Center in New York City, carried up the elevator into a waiting room, and placed in a bed.

And then he died.

"Wait," he said, as a nurse and an aide started to undress him. Just that word. Then he was gone.

Within a week, his remains—ashes and shards of bone—were interred in the hushed baronial columbarium beneath the Byzantine stone pile of St. Bartholomew's Episcopal Church, on Park Avenue, just as Mary had arranged. It delighted her. There, for generations, centuries perhaps, her beloved John would shiver to the chords of the magnificent organ above, and the rumble of the Lexington Avenue subway below. He was a lucky man. He would have one of the great postmortem experiences of New York.

"Honey," she said, standing before him in his new resting place, her hand on his tablet, speaking to the cool stone that now enclosed him: "You're home. You're in Mecca."

Jack Tommaney had been a silk-stocking estate lawyer, with American and French clients rich enough for him and Mary to acquire houses in New York City and the Berkshires of western Massachusetts, and apartments in Paris and in Florida. St. Bart's was not his church. It was Mary's. Jack was a drifted Irish Roman Catholic. But his professional life had been spent in planning for perpetuity. His law office had been in a building across the street. *He ought to be pleased,* she thought. Besides, *she* was the survivor, and she was Episcopalian. It was her choice to make, and she wanted to feel her husband's presence when she was in the city on a Sunday morning, kneeling in a pew above.

With the service over and her husband at rest, Mary flew back to Tampa. She liked having a place in Florida in which to spend the winter months. But she was alone now. Her children and grandchildren were in the North, and she wanted a different kind of space, more like a good apartment hotel, someplace where she would know people and be known, feel cared for and at home. She began to look around, and when she came to see Canterbury, and Robin, the marketing director, gave her a tour, the personality of the place—the small size and creamy color of the building, its feeling of intimacy and order, its small, loyal, idiosyncratic staff—reminded her of one of her favorite hotels in New York.

She decided to call it the Tampa Stanhope.

Mary Tommaney, with her chic, short auburn hair, her bright eyes and smile, her energy and edge, clothes and art, would make a splash when she moved into an apartment at Canterbury in the fall. But at the moment, as she headed back north, the talk in the building was about Wilber, who was about to go on a much shorter—and irreversible—trip.

D addy's *packing!*" Nathalie said. She was on the phone from North Carolina, speaking in the "Wait till you hear *this!*" voice with which we kept each other posted on the latest events in our parents' eccentric, extended, interminable lives. It was May 21, and she had just talked with her mother.

"He's going *home,*" she said. "Every day, he packs two suitcases. And every day, Mother unpacks him. In the middle of the night, he wanders downstairs because someone is coming to pick him up . . . and take him home."

Wilber's wanderlust had grown, and Mary could not contain him. The uproar he caused on the Night of the Fire Alarm had not affected him in the least. Wilber didn't worry about things like that. He didn't remember them. It was Mary—and Nathalie, once her mother called and told her what had happened—who dreaded that the six-engine alarm might be the straw that broke the camel's back. They feared Mrs. Vinas would feel the time had come. That Wilber had to go to live in the Health Center. That he was too disruptive to stay in the Tower. Too dangerous to himself and others.

But the phone call from the front office didn't come. Nathalie had the feeling that Mrs. V. was giving them a little slack, one last chance to decide on their own. Wilber was *their* husband and father. He was their responsibility. They would deal better with the decision to put Wilber in the Health Center nursing wing if they made it themselves. They all knew, of course, without saying so, that the decision had already been made. Wilber had made it for them. They simply had to find the emotional strength to accept it.

But first, Mary and Nathalie each had a fear to confront. Mary's was that if Wilber went to live in the Health Center, she would have to go and see him all the time. She hated to lose him. He was her other half, the foundation of her life. But if she *did* let go, she didn't want to feel obligated to walk down the hall to the nursing wing every day to find him again. She couldn't stand the idea of sending him away and then going to look for him. That would only keep alive the insanity she was trying to find some way to end.

Nathalie's fear was different. "I had visions of Daddy beating up on some nurse," she said. "Tearing up the Health Center." She was afraid it wouldn't work.

All over Canterbury, people wondered the same thing. "I don't know that they're going to be able to keep him," Carroll Boden said confidentially out of one side of her mouth, arching her eyebrows as she glanced across her living room at Wilber one evening. It was about ten days after the fire engines came. She had asked the Davises up for cocktails again—something Carroll much preferred to having cocktails *with them*. When she was at their apartment, Wilber always wanted to make the drinks. Sometimes he drank hers.

"He's slippery, you know," Carroll said, continuing to look appraisingly at Wilber. She had asked the Emyfish and Ashby up, too. And Nathalie and me. We all studied Wilber, who was squinting at Carroll's walker again as if it were someone he knew from somewhere before.

"You know what I like about Canterbury?" the Emyfish said, in her deep, smoky, amused voice, smiling at Wilber over her glass as her bracelets made music for the drinking hour. "It's like that old *New Yorker* cartoon, where one man is saying to the other, 'You know what I like about you, Charlie? You're fatter than I am.'"

Everyone laughed. Wilber held his drink and grinned back at us.

Then something occurred to him. "Is our car still where we were?" he asked.

"*Stop* talking about your *car!*" Carroll snapped, glaring at him.

Mary broke the awkward silence that followed. Nathalie had taken it away, she reminded Carroll, more than three years before, "when Wilbuh was suppos' to pick me up at thuh beaudy pahluh wheah he'd picked me up foah forty *yeahs,* an' ended ub *in Saint PETAHSBUG* insteayud."

"Really?" someone asked. "Forty years at the same beauty parlor?"

"Oh yay-yus," Mary said. "Wilbuh had the sayum bahbuh foah thuhty yeahs. He cut Wilbuh's haiyuh, an' then his *son* cut Wilbuh's haiyuh."

"The son won the Florida lottery," Nathalie finished, smiling, "and he *still* cut Daddy's hair."

That got Wilber's attention.

"His son won the library?" he said, quizzically.

"The *laah-dahry,*" Mary said, looking sternly at him.

"The liberty?" Wilber asked, innocently.

"THE LOTTERY!" we all shouted.

"The lazury?"

"Oh, *nevah mine!*" Mary growled.

It was time to go to dinner.

I told Mother a couple of days later that her old friend Wilber might be coming to join her. We were sitting at lunch in the Health Center. I think she understood. She stopped chewing (not chewing so much as swishing), gave me a madcap sort of *c'est la vie* look, and ground her teeth. Grind. *Grind.* She had been doing that so much lately, I had begun to wonder if it was her idea of communicating—the only noise she could make now. It may have been a year since I had heard her speak.

"Mother, you're grinding your teeth," I said with a wink, as if I were on to her.

That seemed to amuse her. She gave me a mad smile and really ground her teeth.

Ah. So we were playing a game. I gave her a "You're doing that thing I just told you about" look and what I hoped was a teasing smile, wagging my finger at her for good measure.

For good measure, Mother flared her nostrils, bared her incisors, and made a face like a wolf. Then, eyes gleaming maniacally, she ground her teeth. *So there.*

This was getting strange. It was also making it difficult for Claudia, watching with some concern, to feed her. I tried to shift the focus.

"What's for lunch?" I said to Claudia. "Can you tell?"

The tray, as usual, held puddles and clumps of green, cream, and brown. For Mother, there was also thickened, silvery gray water in a glass, and a little carton of syrupy cranberry juice. Claudia has chocolate skin; large, calm, observant eyes; strong arms; and wonderfully glossy, curly hair. She peered at one of the puddles, spooned some of the brown glop, and held it up, considering. Then she studied the tray.

"Looks like green beans, mashed potatoes, and Salisbury steak," she said. "That's what it looks like to me."

She offered the spoon of brown stuff to Mother, who bit the spoon, held on, and shook her head like a terrier. Brown stuff flew in all directions.

I had not seen my mother act so bizarrely since the early days after her second stroke. I wanted to go. Maybe if I left, this weirdness would leave, too. I could come back later, at dinner, and see how she was. But after I told her I was going, that I would be back, and began to thread my way through the other tables of decrepit old souls, heading for the door, I could hear, behind me, the ever-louder grinding of teeth. Mother has always had strong teeth, and she was grinding them for all she was worth.

The grating sound cut through the other noise in the dining room, trailing me through the door, growing quieter in the hall. As I left the dining room behind, it became a soft edge of sound, like a memory—and carried me back, unexpectedly, to the sound the cicadas made in the twilight when I was a boy. I could hear them on summer evenings as I sat with my nose against the screen on the porch in the years before air-conditioning, watching the fireflies glow like little pieces of phosphorus in the dusk. The song of the cicadas came out of the darkness, from somewhere in the grass and shrubs and trees. I don't think I ever saw one of them, but I could hear the sharp, haunting, oddly melodic chords they made by grinding their tiny limbs together as I ate the tender white rabbit that my mother, or Allene, had baked and served with a savory brown gravy, and baked apples, and green beans, and biscuits still warm from the oven. I hadn't thought of that in a long time.

It was a brown and green and cream-colored meal, too.

I had lunch in the Tower that day with Lucie Cross, the tough old nurse who had come to Canterbury from New Jersey as a widow's companion when the Tower first opened and, when the widow died, had stayed on in her apartment. That had been almost twenty years ago. Lucie's own husband had been dead nearly forty years. But Lucie was a survivor, and she had been watching like a hawk as the drama of Wilber and Mary and Nathalie and Mrs. Vinas played on.

She had long ago become a guerrilla fighter in the war against her two greatest enemies—the disintegration of her body and the Canterbury administration. At least, that's how she saw it. Lucie was always between heart attacks, or surgeries, or cradling some newly broken bone. Her medical history was epic. She had had colon cancer, a stent implanted in a coronary artery, a pacemaker, and by her count, six or eight heart attacks—in the building, at her son's house on a lake in northern New Hampshire, and on a cruise ship coming through the Panama Canal. Almost every time I saw her, she was leaning on a cane, or had an arm in a sling, or some new splint on her wrist or hand.

When her son, a silver-haired, seventy-one-year-old retired commercial airline pilot, told a neighbor of his in New Hampshire that he was going down to Florida for his mother's birthday, the neighbor's eyes got wide.

"And how the hell old is *she*?" he asked.

She was ninety-seven and scrappy. The year before, when no one came after Lucie pressed the call button beside her bed in the Health Center—where she was recovering from one of her operations (she was having angina pain and wanted a nitroglycerin tablet)—she picked up the phone, punched 911, and demanded an ambulance.

"I need help and I can't *get* it here," she rasped to the paramedics, when they arrived. *"I want you to take me to the hospital."* They took her.

Mrs. Vinas was furious. It was a breach of protocol—a mortal insult to Canterbury. When someone fell ill, she wanted to know about it *before* an ambulance was called. Mrs. Vinas had been planning ever since, Lucie was convinced, to use Lucie's innumerable health issues to force her out of the Tower, where she had been for twenty-two years (for most of them in a second, smaller apartment), into permanent care in the Health Center. Then Canterbury could market her apartment to someone else. Lucie was dead sure that was Mrs. Vinas's intent, and she was determined to stay right where she was.

Other residents became infirm, declined, and at some point shuffled off to the nursing wing. But Lucie kept on playing bridge. She kept eating bananas and peanut butter and crackers between meals and drinking a glass of Ovaltine when she woke and felt hungry in the middle of the night. She kept looking for the sapphire and diamond ring she had hidden somewhere in the apartment to keep it from being stolen by the housekeeping staff (and then couldn't find). She kept booking passage on her beloved cruise ships. She refused to admit defeat.

"If Mrs. Vinas tries to speak to you," her son, Chick, counseled her, "just tell her to call and speak with your attorney."

"I don't trust that woman any farther than I could sling a cat," Lucy hissed at lunch. Her old blue eyes were hard and resentful—and wary, in case the devil should appear. She ate carefully. One index finger, which had begun curling again of its own accord after surgery to correct the problem, was in a splint she had made from a pair of bobbie pins wrapped in surgical tape. She couldn't use the finger, wrapped up that way. But at least the damn thing was straight.

F inally, on the morning of June 2, Mary and Nathalie decided they had had enough. The moment of realization came when Nathalie walked into the apartment, discovered that Wilber had had a bowel movement in her parents' bathroom, missing the toilet entirely, and had gone back to bed. Aghast, Nathalie rushed to get a mop and bucket and returned to find her slow, unsteady mother reaching tentatively toward the lumps and smears with a Kleenex tissue.

"*Mother!*" Nathalie exclaimed, horrified. "*That's* not the way you clean a bathroom!"

Mary raised her head toward Nathalie, and straightened up with slow, furious, dignity. She looked her daughter dead in the eye.

"Ah have *ne-vah,*" she declared, spitting the words out, "cleaned a *bayath-room!*"

Nathalie was astounded. "Well, *who* cleaned them the first eight years of your marriage, before Berta came to work for you?" she asked.

"Yoah *fah-thah* did," Mary said. "Ah washed the shirts, in the bayathtub."

For a moment they stared at each other, and then turned and slowly walked into the living room and sat down. He had to go. They both knew it. Nathalie, who had power of attorney for her father, called the Health Center. They got Wilber up, and dressed, and walked him—slowly, protesting, halting, questioning all the way— out the door, down the hall to the elevator, down to the second floor, out the elevator, down the hall, and through the four successive doors that lead into the nursing wing.

Mrs. Jordan, the head nurse, was waiting. She took Wilber's arm with a smile.

"Let's go see your apartment," she said. Her heavy face and voice were pleasant, but firm.

"My *apartment?*" Wilber looked panicked. "Oh . . . *no,*" he said.

He was trying to pull away from her. But he was ninety years old, and shrunken. Mrs. Jordan was bigger, and she was not letting go.

"Yes, you have a new apartment," she said matter-of-factly, beginning to pull him toward a hallway of rooms.

He turned frightened eyes toward Mary, standing mutely just inside the Health Center door. She looked stricken. Tears were popping down her cheeks. Nathalie was behind, pressing backward against the door.

"What about *my wife?*" Wilber sputtered. He kept jerking and tugging, trying to pull away. He might as well have been tied to a truck.

"*Mrs.* Davis doesn't *have* a place here," Mrs. Jordan told him calmly. "Now give her a kiss good-bye."

With that, Mary stepped forward. Wilber was scared. And confused. Mary was unsteady, her vision blurred by tears. They managed a kind of glancing, clumsy half embrace, he still reaching, she withdrawing.

She turned toward the exit door, walking blindly, tissues clutched in both hands to her eyes.

Wilber started after her, his feet slapping at the floor. But Mrs. Jordan was stronger. He could get no traction.

"*Noooh,* Mr. Davis. You're not going with her," she said soothingly, beginning to draw him up the hall. "Why don't you and I go have some coffee and talk?"

Wilber, cradled awkwardly in her embrace, looked up at her in alarm. "I *never* drink coffee," he answered.

"Well, how about some juice?" she said, blandly.

"Well . . . where has Mary gone?" Wilber asked, swiveling around. She had disappeared.

"Mary has gone back up to the apartment," Mrs. Jordan declared, marching him steadily away. She looked like a mother with a large, unruly child in tow. "You're going to live with us now."

"What are you all *doing with me?*" Wilber bleated, flapping vainly against her grip. "*I don't understand what's going on!*" They were almost at the end of the hallway.

"You're going to live with us," Mrs. Jordan said evenly. "We're going to take *good* care of you." And with that, they disappeared around
the corner. He was nearly home.

Almost an hour later, Nathalie and Mary came down the elevator. Nathalie's hand was on her mother's arm, holding and
steadying her almost the way the nurse had steadied Wilber.
They moved numbly through the open dining room doors, toward a
table in a far corner of the room, closest to the water.

Considering that all its connections are so old and frayed, the gossip tree at Canterbury is, in fact, remarkably fast and efficient. Everyone in the dining room seemed to know that Mary and Nathalie had
just—finally—put Wilber away. Men and women looked up sympa-
thetically, some reaching out to touch or pat them as they moved
slowly by. No one ventured the standard cheery greetings, or tried to
engage them in small talk.

They were left alone at their table, to begin a silent, snuffling
lunch of acceptance. Wilber would not be in the apartment when
Mary went back to it this afternoon. He would not be there for
cocktails this evening, or down for dinner with her tonight, or in the
bed next to hers when she went to sleep, or when she woke up in
the morning. He would not be padding around after her all of tomorrow, asking his endless repetitive questions, making it impossible
for her to have a separate moment, an undisturbed thought, any time
or experience of her own at all. He would not wander away again
while she failed to notice, and then pop up as if he had been looking for her all the time.

Mary's time would be her own. She would not have to constantly worry, respond, or try in vain to control him anymore. She
was free. Lunch was the beginning. Mary and Nathalie had a glass
of wine. Mary looked tragic, drinking and eating mechanically,
dripping tears—when she forgot to use the tissue—on her plate.
She did not look up. She and Nathalie did not talk. But she was getting through the moment. It was going well enough. Everyone
watching them knew that this was hard, but that it would get

better—it could only get better, couldn't it?—when outside the dining room, the door at the end of the hall (the door leading to the Health Center) banged open.

Wilber, eyes excited, wobbled through. He was tottering along at full speed, heading straight for the entrance of the dining room. He had escaped. The open double doors beckoned. On the other side, he knew, was food, their friends—and maybe Mary. It was lunchtime. She would be inside, so glad to see him.

He was almost there, bobbing along like a top, when the elevator doors directly across from the dining room entrance opened and out slid Mrs. Jordan. For a substantial woman in middle age she was surprisingly fast. She moved to grab him, just as Wilber reached the threshold of the dining room. He had never needed eyeglasses. His vision had always been sharp. His eyes were already on the far table. He did not see Mrs. Jordan closing on him from behind, and when her arms encircled him, Wilber was caught by surprise. For just a moment, in the doorway, they swayed, an awkward, teetering scuffle, her pull against his frail momentum, and then her gravity and leverage prevailed.

Mary and Nathalie, sitting glumly at their table, eyes on their plates, missed the drama in the doorway. It lasted a bare moment. Mrs. Jordan had a grip. She pulled Wilber, off balance, toward the hall. In a flash, he was out of sight of the corner table. Ten seconds more, and they were through the first door. Three more doors to go, but Wilber was gone.

Home, this time, to stay.

CHAPTER TEN

The Plumbing Problem

It was mid-June. Wilber had been in the Health Center two weeks, and Nathalie, back home in North Carolina, has called to check on him.

"How's my daddy?" she asked the Health Center nurse.

"Well, he has good days and bad days," the nurse said.

"What's a bad day?"

Pause. "He gets up at night," the nurse said, "and urinates in his roommate's closet."

This didn't seem to bother Wilber's roommate, Howard Gill, who was mostly silent and in a wheelchair. Howard was pretty detached. He also wasn't the one who got his clothes out of the closet. His wife, Helen, did, and it was driving her crazy that Wilber kept peeing there. If they had been strangers to each other, she might have stomped her foot about it and demanded that Wilber be moved to some other room. Not that complaining would do her any good. Shifting rooms in the Health Center is not as easy as doing it in a hotel. The director of nursing has to agree that you need to move, and usually she doesn't. But Helen felt constrained. Almost seventy years ago, when they were young, she and Howard and Mary and Wilber were friendly as couples. It was from Howard's sister-in-law's family that Mary and Wilber had bought the lot on which they built their first house. Now Helen, who lived in the Tower but spent every morning and afternoon in the nursing wing with Howard, found herself trapped, as if she were double-dating with Mary and Wilber again—the difference being that this time two of the four didn't recognize the others, they couldn't actually go anywhere, Mary was often missing from the date, and Wilber was peeing in Howard's closet.

The social dynamic had changed. But even Helen, who was beside herself at the idea that she and Howard might be tormented every day for the rest of their lives by the hapless Wilber, understood that it was not his fault, that he wasn't alone in becoming a human sprinkling system, and that they weren't the only families having to deal with such a problem. The damp truth was that how the human plumbing works—or doesn't work—is one of the great common issues of the New Old Age—just as it was, to some extent, of the old old age. It is just more common now that more people have grown to be more old, and thus more impaired and demented.

The ability to pee and poop in polite ways probably separates the dependent from the independent as much as any other behavior. It is the reason that someone like Wilber has to move out of his home and into institutional care. But whether it emerges as the first big issue of old age or later on, there is invariably a moment—tender, ghastly, and abrupt—that comes to everyone who lives long enough. It is life-changing not just for our parents, when it happens, but for us children as well, because we are as unprepared as they—and as helpless to the need.

It came to Aunt Carolyn, my Jesus-obsessed godmother, one night in the nursing home room she shared with Aunt Bessie. Carolyn woke and realized she had to go to the bathroom. She may have been eighty-eight and demented, but she was still a private, modest, straitlaced Christian lady. To my knowledge, she had been with only one man in her life, her husband, Raymond. When I asked, she told me she had been attracted to him because he was a fine Christian man, and because he didn't smoke, drink, or swear. (He may not have done anything else, either. He was eighty-six when he married him, and died six months later. But you never know about these things.)

Anyway, Carolyn would not have wanted to call for help—not for something so personal. She had managed her own toilet since the outhouse of her childhood, eighty-five years before. Besides, the aide on duty at that hour might have been a man. She would take care of herself. But she lost her bearings. She climbed out of bed, slowly but urgently, and then couldn't find the toilet. So she mounted a trash can—one not designed to be straddled by tottery old women, unbalanced by darkness—and crashed to the floor.

The fall hurt her knee. It would have hurt her pride even more if she had remembered doing it, once the night aide found her and cleaned her up and put her back to bed. From then on, the staff put her in adult diapers and tried to keep her confined to bed. Forced into incontinence this way, Aunt Carolyn receded rapidly. What she had lost was not just her way in the dark. It was what remained of her dignity and privacy—the feeling of being an adult, no matter how impaired.

It is our ability to live and function at a personal remove from others, able to tend to our own private needs, that gives us the sense of being sovereign in our own space. Learning the toilet is perhaps the first grown-up ability we gain as children, and the last we relinquish to age. I was sitting with my mother—my elegant, strong-willed, dignified mother—in the week after she woke from the coma of her first stroke. We were in a private hospital room, talking carefully, quietly, when suddenly she stopped.

"Darling, I need you to help me to the bathroom," she said.

Uh-oh.

"Let me call a nurse," I answered. Mother had changed and bathed and diapered me. She had cared for me when I was sick. She was my mother. But I had never done those things for her. I had never helped her to the bathroom—much less *in* it. She had never asked. Mother's maid, Louise, gave her that kind of help. My sister, Melissa, might have—or my daughter, Whitney, as she got older—if Mother needed help when they were there.

The bathroom was ten feet away. It might as well have been a mile. I reached for the call button dangling on its cord by the bed, pulled it, and yelled *"Nurse!"* toward the hallway door. *Not loud enough,* I thought, when I heard my voice.

"That will take too long," Mother said firmly, struggling to rise. "Just help me up."

Do it! a voice in my head said. *Just lift her up.*

How? another asked. *She's weak. She's had a stroke. Some of her body doesn't work. I don't know if she can walk at all.* I was paralyzed, caught between my mother's lifelong, paramount sense of dignity, and the urgency of the moment. What if I dropped her? What if we fell? Her bones were brittle as glass.

"Mother, I don't think we should do this," I said. If I was able to get her into the bathroom, I didn't know what to do next. I couldn't just plump her on the toilet and leave so that she could proceed in private. She might fall off. And I knew if I left the hospital room to try to find a nurse or an aide, she'd try to walk—and crash. All my strongest instincts said: *Stop!*

Wait.

But there was that other voice. *You wimp!* it snarled. *Move! You can't let this happen to her!*

"I *can do this!*" Mother said, trembling in her effort to rise. Her eyes, fixed on the bathroom door, blazed with determination.

"Mother, please . . ." I started to say.

And then the moment was lost. Nature moved. The air between us turned suddenly pungent. My mother froze, her eyes staring fixedly at the opposite wall, and began to sink imperceptibly back toward the bed.

"I'll get the nurse," I mumbled, heading for the door. I did, and as I waited in the hall, a failure to the moment, aimless and mortified, she went in and shut the door. When she emerged, some long minutes later, with a solemn "she's ready now" look, I walked quietly back in. My mother was propped up in bed, wearing a fresh gown and a blank expression. She seemed distant. Something had been taken from her, and she had retreated. She seemed more remote after that.

If I had helped her to avoid incontinence that afternoon—if she

had retained her independence at least one more day—she still
would have lost it at some other moment, some hour, some day soon
after, when neither the nurse, nor Louise, nor Melissa, nor Whitney,
nor her grandson, Christopher, was there. Or perhaps even if they
were, because they would have been in the same predicament that I
was. I know that. But it was me who was there. It was a moment no
one prepares us for, and that comes to all of our parents, if they live
long enough. It transformed my mother's sense of herself, and her
place in the world. It is a moment I cannot forget or—no matter
how many times I relive it—improve. I think it will stay with me
until I get very old and lose my mind. And start peeing in the closet.

It is that breaking down of the person—the loss of memory, co-
herence, physical competence, speech, personality, and eventually
even expression—that makes it so hard on the family and friends
of those whose individuality is melting away. The people we love
become like abandoned houses, a haunting reminder of the life that
once was there.

It is painful to witness. And it poses a problem. What do the rest
of us do? We may know how to relate to people in the big stages—
when they are well, or sick, or newly dead. But partially gone is
hard. Do we keep acting the way we did when the whole person
was there? Or do we deal with the fraction that is left? The whole
person would miss us if we didn't visit. The fraction might not
know the difference. How much *is* left? How do we know?

The Emyfish had a policy. She avoided people who had fallen
into the two conditions she was most determined to avoid—illness
and death. "I'm a *terrible* friend," she declared in a deep, reproachful
voice one night, when she and Mary and Nathalie and I were having drinks, talking about life and friendship, funny stories and dra-
mas past. Her mother, Miss Jessie, had been a champion complainer
in her last years—grumpy, accusatory, unappreciative, plagued and
obsessed by phantom undiagnosed pain. The Emyfish's funny, puck-
ish father, Punk—who drove an old blue Cadillac convertible,
smoked unfiltered Camels, and poured gin into his martini shaker at

five each day—was dead of lung cancer. Without him, Miss Jessie had become impossible to appease. When Nat, her long-suffering houseman and driver, finally refused to work for her anymore no matter *how* much the Emyfish promised to pay him, Emy gave up and put Miss Jessie in a nursing home. Then she and Ashby got on a plane and flew away.

"When Ashby and I went to Mexico," the Emyfish said, "it was *your* mother who organized all our friends—Mary and Sophie and Conchita and Patty and Maida—so that *somebody* went to see my mother every day. Your mother went, and she made sure everyone else went. And now *she's* in the Health Center, and I don't go to see her. I'm *not* a good person." She shook her head sorrowfully over her vodka and Sprite, then looked at me with rueful eyes.

Whatareyougonnado? her expression said.

So I know for a certainty how relieved, though sad, she and Mary and all the others were to hear that Mother had finally—abruptly— died. It happened just as Wilber was about to come join her in the nursing wing.

It was Mary Davis who heard it first, and in the chatty, neighborly way that women of her generation had always tended to these things, she immediately sat down and started telephoning to make sure that the old circle of friends were all aware. First she called the Emyfish, who was leaving with Ashby in the morning on the *QE2*. It meant that Emy would miss Mother's funeral service, but the Emyfish had an aversion to funeral services, anyway—"Especially my own," she had noted, in that mournful voice. Other people's deaths reminded her of mortality, and mortality was no friend of hers.

Then Mary started calling some of their other old friends. After her long claustrophobic siege with Wilber, it felt good to be doing something assertive and helpful—and to be involved in a drama that was not, for a change, her own.

I don't remember now who first called me. It wasn't Mary, of course. She assumed I knew. It would normally have been someone at Canterbury, probably Mrs. Vinas, or Susan Conley, the director of nursing. But I think in this case it was Nathalie.

"I don't know exactly how to say this," she began, when I picked up the phone, "but did you know that my mother has been telling people that your mother is dead?"

Well, no. Especially because, so far as I knew, Mother was alive, watching Lawrence Welk most mornings on the big television set in the Health Center activity room.

"I thought Lawrence Welk was dead," I said, when I walked in and found him bubbling away on the screen one day. "Not at Canterbury," Joyce Mitchell, the director of social services and activities, replied, shuffling her videotapes to see who else she might get to perform that morning from the realm beyond.

On the phone, Nathalie sighed, trying to explain. "Mother's not sure how it happened," she said. "She claims someone called up from downstairs to tell her."

That didn't seem likely. At Canterbury, where gossip is the chief recreation, death is always lurking just down the hall. False reports are rife, and it is verboten for the staff to entertain themselves by calling up friends and residents to chat about who just died, or seemed as if they were nearly about to.

Just to be certain that I hadn't somehow missed the news ("Well, we *tried* to reach you"), I called Susan Conley, the head of nursing, who had been training for years as Mrs. Vinas's deputy. Or perhaps she called me. I'm not sure. But Miss Conley was not amused.

Supposedly, some nurse in the Health Center had told Mary, she said, a chill edge to her voice. But she had just interrogated her staff, and found that there had been no such report.

"My nursing staff know they will be *terminated* if they give out information," she said flatly. "They're not at liberty to tell anyone *anything*."

She paused. In places like Canterbury, where the residents are all old, and often dotty, odd things can happen, and frequently do. "Sometimes residents get confused," Miss Conley said, pausing again. "Sometimes they have too much to drink."

Well, yes. And given the number of times my mother had been expected to die, and probably reported in gossip as having passed away (Person A: *Ring, ring.* "Hey—did someone die in the Health Center yesterday? Was it Bobbie Clendinen?" *Pause.* Person B: "Well, I'm trying to remember. Have we had this conversation before?"), it would not be difficult for residents at Canterbury to get the memory of an anticipated event confused with the memory of an actual one.

But it didn't matter. One more report of Mother's death, I decided, wasn't going to kill her. It might not even hurt. To begin with, she wouldn't know. Confirmation that she was, in fact, alive might remind some of her friends to visit. And it would give Mary something to think about besides where Wilber was peeing.

It was, actually, the kind of story that Mother, when she was lucid, would have absolutely loved. A Canterbury tale. She would have thought it hilarious. She still might, if I could figure some way to tell her. Musing along in this way, I was beginning to get fond of the story. But Mary, after discovering that Mother was alive, was suffering from a bad case of remorse.

"Ah did somethin' *terr-i-bul* the othah day," she said, calling to confess. "Ah had called down tuh find out abouht thuh guest room foah Nath-a-lie. And somebody downstayahs called back tuh say that yoah mothah had *died*. Ah doan know *who* it was. So I immediately called Emy to tell *huh*, because it was the night befoah huh trip."

Good work. The Emyfish and Ashby were now mourning in the middle of the Atlantic, and no one knew how to reach them. She would be upset, I knew, when she got back to discover that she hadn't missed the funeral.

I told Mary not to worry about it. Really. It was a funny story. We could talk about it over a drink when I came back down.

The next month, sitting in her apartment before dinner, with the bright clear day fading to deep gauzy colors over the bay outside, I looked over at the bar table, and noticed a different label on the vodka bottle. No Wolfschmidt this time. "You're drinking a better brand of vodka," I said.

"*Yea*-yuh." She nodded affirmatively, raising her glass. "Wilbuh's *goan.*"

"You're *drinking* the whiskey that was 'too good to drink'?"

"Ah *ayam*," she replied, with a satisfied smile, smacking her lips. She looked entitled, and content. "Ah'm drinkin' it *all* up."

I f Mary was feeling better by late June—and she certainly seemed to be ("She has *blossomed*," Nathalie reported, pleased that people were inviting her mother for drinks and dinner again, now that they didn't have to listen to Wilber talk about his car. "I think she has turned into a social butterfly. She's flitting all over the place.")— my mother, though now officially confirmed among the living, seemed actually in decline. She was grinding her teeth relentlessly, and—more ominously—shunning her food.

I hated the grinding. It was the most disturbing noise I had heard since the gurgling sounds my father made almost a decade earlier as he lay in a coma, trying to breathe through the mucus and saliva that collected in his throat. He had lost the ability to swallow. That, I realized, must be the death rattle I had always heard of but never heard. Mother's grinding was a harsher noise—fierce, like pottery and china being crushed under a stone. She had always had a beautiful smile. She had had one cavity in her entire life. One. Now she was turning her teeth into rubble, staring at the nursing assistants, at Louise, at me while she was doing it, as if this were a game—her way to make teasing conversation.

The sound affected everyone. "She's grinding her teeth *so* badly," the nurse on duty said worriedly, when I called one Monday morning. "I just hope she doesn't break one of them off and choke on it."

That did it. My worst fear was that my mother, with her impaired swallowing, would gag on something when none of the rest of us were around, and choke to death. My next worst fear was that she would do it when I was there. Then what would I do? The prospect haunted me. I called her dentist, a family friend, Charles Martin, and asked if he could examine her and tell me what he thought. I was thankful to have him to call. Transporting someone like Mother to a dentist's or doctor's office for examination isn't practical. It requires a hospital gurney, paramedics, and an ambulance. But getting dentists and doctors to come to a nursing home to examine and treat patients they don't know isn't easy either. Most of them would rather not. It's time-consuming. It doesn't pay well. It's difficult or impossible to communicate with patients like my mother. And you can't really make them better.

When I was trying—long distance—to monitor the care my aunts Carolyn and Bessie were getting in a much cheaper, for-profit nursing home in Tampa, where they lived their last years and died, their bills mostly paid by Medicaid, I kept running into an odd, and then maddening, problem. I was responsible for my aunts and their care, but Bessie and Carolyn couldn't tell me whether the doctors who were supposed to be looking in on them actually were—and whether they were attentive or not.

And when I tried to call the doctors who were their physicians of record to discuss their care, I discovered that those doctors didn't actually come to the nursing home. Their "associates," often recently emigrated doctors from third world countries, were the ones who came and saw my aunts, under the aegis of the doctors of record—who never came, because it wasn't worth their time. And none of them, the doctors of record or their associates, ever wanted to call me back.

When I got mad and fired one, and tried to find another, I discovered that all the available doctors on the list maintained by the home seemed to operate the same way. And when once I did reach a doctor by phone, to take exception to his treatment and give different instructions, his English was so poor that I wasn't sure we understood each other. The next time I called the nursing desk, I found that he had dropped my aunt. He didn't seem to want a patient with a monitoring, meddling, difficult guardian.

But Canterbury, which operated under Mrs. Vinas's relentless drive for quality control, had an assortment of specialists—an internist, a podiatrist, a dentist, technicians—who did actually make visits. And Charley Martin, that sweetheart, shortly called back.

He had already been to see my mother. "She hardly knew I was there," he said, but he had examined her, and he didn't think the grinding was a problem. "At her stage, it's just a nervous habit that's built in," he reassured me. "I've been going over there for fifteen years, and usually at that stage of life, their teeth are the least of their health concerns. Most of the people up there have teeth broken off at the gum line—with the root just sitting there exposed—and they go on their merry way. It's almost as if nature does its own root canal. The nerve retreats almost faster than she can grind the tooth down.

"She has a couple that are broken off at the gum line, but there wasn't anything that was sharp or cutting her lip," he said. "I think I would just leave it alone, and hope that her teeth will go the distance."

I was relieved. It's unnerving—excruciating, actually—to watch someone you love disintegrate in front of you. Because of the grinding, and her tendency to choke, I had come to regard Mother's meals as life-threatening experiences. She had to be fed. But I had stopped feeding her when I came to visit—which suited the management at Canterbury fine. Family members like me aren't trained to handle demented people, and loving them doesn't make us good at it. Neither does any of the other emotions we feel. I didn't trust myself. That was why I was so grateful for the certified nursing assistants who fed her every day—Meva and Claudia, Star and Marcia. Ernestine. And especially Louise, who sat with her and talked to her, stroked her hand, dressed her, put on her makeup, and fed her lunch, three days a week.

Each nurse assistant in the Health Center feeds dozens of meals a week, spoonful by spoonful, to resident after resident. They are patient and observant and kind. But it was Louise who fussed and watched over just Mother, and called to tell me how she was. She knew my mother's funny moods, her idiosyncrasies, her shades of lipstick, her favorite foods. It was Louise who bought most of her clothes. She had developed an eye for the right colors and designs. She knew Mother was good in blues and greens, creamy whites and lavenders. And she bought loosely fitted blouses and housedresses that didn't bind her as she lay in bed or in her chair, and that didn't have to be pulled on and off over her head. Mother's arms, which were stiff and drawn from arthritis and lack of use, couldn't be raised without hurting her. They could hardly be raised at all. Louise knew that. She was different from the rest of us, I think. She was with Mother not because we paid her, not because she thought she ought to be, but because she wanted to be. She paid attention to all the details of choice remaining in my mother's tiny, restricted life.

"This is that Oil o' Olay she uses foah huh face," she said to me one morning, pulling Mother's shrunken supply of cosmetics out of the bedside drawer. "Look, Mama." She smiled, holding up a tube and uncapping it so Mother could see. "Got some *pretty* lipstick."

The two women had been looking out for each other—and each other's families—for more than twenty years. Louise tended to have a sunny view of life. ("She ate real *good,* today," she usually said.) But she was also practical, and by the end of June, her report had turned glum.

Mother wasn't eating. "She done los' a lotta weight. She real light now." Louise frowned, giving me a dead serious look before turning back to smile at Mother. I had just come in from the airport, and we were sitting in my mother's room in the late morning, before lunch. I was in front of her, Louise at her side, holding her hand. Mother was looking at us as we talked, but listlessly, with an expression that seemed sort of blank.

"The girls yesserday said she not urinating," Louise related, her eyes dark with concern. "Huh panties was dry. An' huh bowels hardly movin'. Ah know when they stop eatin', they be ready to give up. An' she stop eatin'."

She gave me a final sharp look and turned back to my mother.

Maybe she was right, I thought. I watched the two of them, sitting together. There had been so many times when Mother seemed to be departing—and then didn't—that I had stopped looking for new patterns, for signs of decline. Whatever happened, she just seemed to float along, as if she were on some broad, invisible river of strange eddies, long meanders, and sudden treacherous currents. She drifted. She lurched. She sank. She rose.

If she should go now, I thought, watching Mother as she stared back at me with dull, unblinking eyes, *she and Louise will have been together twenty-one years. They are so different and so much the same: my silent, omnipresent old mother, now frail as an infant, all eyes and weak limbs and impervious spirit, still kept elegant by Louise. And Louise, so handsome and determined and dark and strong. They are so close.* While my mother often still seemed excited when I walked into her room, I was usually not there. I came and went, and while I might be in Tampa for a week or ten days or even two weeks at a time, I never stayed long at her side, not more than an hour. When I ran out of things to say, I left.

It was Louise who sat with her, hour after hour, brushing her hair, applying her makeup, feeding her lunch, wiping her mouth. It was Louise who played her bingo letters for her on bingo days, who pushed her down the halls, sang hymns as she sat with her in church on Sundays, or the old tunes that the Piano Man played on Wednesdays. Or just sat and talked to Mother. It was Louise who knew how to just *be* with her.

"Louise loves you, Mama," she always said. "Louise *loves* you."

The most important, the most caring and intimate relationship in my mother's life, I knew, was not with me or Melissa, with Whitney or Christopher or Brad. It was with Louise. For however long my mother lived, I hoped they would be together.

"How would you want me to describe your relationship?" I had asked her. It seemed a funny question to ask someone you love, and have known more than half your adult life. Someone whose family you know all about, and who knows all about yours. But personal and cultural understandings change. I didn't want to make assumptions. Did she prefer the more professional, less intimate and subservient term popular now—*housekeeper*—to the old traditional one—*maid*?

"*No!*" Louise said, flaring. She gave me a scowl of displeasure, as if I'd said something offensive. She turned to my mother, then back to me, still holding Mother's hand.

"Ah is yo' mothuh's *maid*!" she said. "This is puss-onal." She stared at me, unblinking. "We is *family*."

I agree. It's what I feel. It's what everyone in my family feels. Some of us—at least some of the time—like Louise more than we like one another. But in a larger sense, what Louise said is simply what many of us at Canterbury—the residents, us children, the staff— have come to feel about the whole experience of being here. At a certain point, especially in the nursing wing, you realize that you have shared so many painful, funny, awkward, exhausting, intimate moments with one another, intentionally or not, that it all just feels like family. We're all together, until the end.

"There he goes again," Sally, the nurse on duty, sighed later that week, watching Wilber wobble by. "I need one of those retractable cords."

Chin in hand, she leaned wearily on the counter of the nurses' station, her eyes following Wilber. Sporty as usual in a yellow cardigan sweater, tan pants, and white shoes, he was in hot pursuit. Eyes lit with excitement, he was bobbing along like a mechanical man, hands and arms outstretched for better balance, heading straight into my mother's room.

"Mr. Davis, that's *not your room*!" Sally called out, as Wilber sailed past Mother, who was parked in her chair outside the door. He was aimed at her roommate, Mrs. Fleming, who was in the far bed under the window, watching his approach with widening eyes.

"*But I just found my wife!*" Wilber yelled, over his shoulder. He sounded happy.

"*No*, Mr. Davis," Sally said, heading after him, "that's not your wife."

"She was *yesterday*!" he yelled, now deep inside the room.

"*No*, Mr. Davis," Sally said, patiently, disappearing into the room. In a moment, she emerged, leading him by the hand.

"He thinks a lot of the women here are his wife," she explained. The day before, Wilber had spent hours pushing Mrs. Jensen, a glamorous 104, with her dark glasses perched on top of her thick silver hair, up and down the hall in her wheelchair. He thought she was Mary, Sally said.

"How did Mrs. Jensen feel about that?" I asked the nurse who had been on duty then.

"She liked it," the nurse said. "She likes to be entertained. And he felt needed. It made them both happy."

Different people, of course, feel different ways. And not everyone was happy. One morning, as Nathalie waited on the second floor for the elevator, she saw through an open door that Helen Gill, into whose husband's closet Wilber had been peeing, was seated across from the nurse in the assistance-in-living office. Helen was having her blood pressure checked. It was only the end of June, and summer already seemed very long. She was feeling tense, she explained.

The nurse pumped up the arm sleeve—*squish, squish*—and as the air hissed out, read Helen the numbers.

"That's pretty good for as much stress as I'm under," Helen said tiredly.

"What stress are you under?" the nurse asked, unwrapping the sleeve.

"His name is Wilber," Helen sighed.

CHAPTER ELEVEN

Meanwhile, Back in the Tower

JULY, AUGUST, SEPTEMBER 2000

The annual dry spell of spring and early summer had become a drought. The air was a smoky white, the grass scorched brown. The live oak trees, with their great canopies of limp, dusty leaves, stood as still and spent as stunned wrinkled old women holding parasols against the sun. The residents of Canterbury peered through their tinted windows at the seared land outside, came in gasping from the short trip between their air-conditioned cars and the front or back door, and talked about how oppressive it was. Heat and blinding glare are hard on old hearts and eyes. And on the environment. The water table had receded. The reservoirs had shrunk. The local government had imposed a watering ban in daylight hours. When a valve got stuck (or someone forgot), and the sprinkler system in front of the Tower stayed on one morning—spraying precious water out in silvered, pointless arcs across the grass to evaporate in the blazing air—a couple in an apartment above telephoned to report Canterbury to the water-rationing police. People who came through the Great Depression, and World War II, take waste seriously.

They also take it personally. Each week, Sarah Jane—that southern blossom, that aging, colorful, wilting good heart—loaded up a shopping cart with the bottles and jars of her hard-won conservation efforts and pushed it, bouncing and jingling, across the parking lot toward the tiny St. Francis of Assisi Park at the far end. It was a slow process. She wasn't steady, and she ached. Her legs and back were a rusty, Goldbergian assembly of worn cartilage, mended brittle bones, and aging artificial joints. If she hadn't been pushing the cart, she would have had to use her walker. And the cart was heavy. Halfway across the parking lot one morning, her rosy, powdered, bouffant self had begun to dissolve in little drips and trickles that began at her hairline, snaked down her rouged cheeks, her lotioned neck and shoulders, and disappeared inside her bright, flowing flowered housecoat. But Sarah Jane's spirit was strong, her smile serene. She had been in pain for half a century, and she had long ago mastered the art of behaving as if life were a privilege, with joy in the doing.

"These," she said, pointing to some mason jars in the bottom of the cart that were filled with water that had been left in glasses at the tables where she had sat in the dining room. "You knowah, thuh stayaff isn't suh'ving water unless people ask foah it, but they ask foah it, and then they doan' drink it awul," she said, "an' it gets throwan ouwat."

As always, Sarah Jane brought her own little jars and beakers of condiments and oils to the dining room each day, but she had also started bringing larger, empty containers, in the big purse she hung on her walker. It was she who had been the chief inspiration and force behind the creation of the little triangle of green shade in the back corner of the parking lot, with its three-quarter-size statue of St. Francis. She saw it as a place where residents of the Health Center could gather for picnics, or be wheeled out for a quiet moment with family. Sarah Jane was the long-term president of the volunteers, and the plants and the lone, drooping tree that they had planted to shade the cement figure of the saint were not going to die because of *her* neglect.

"This one," she said, adjusting her large, softly blue-tinted glasses, which had begun slipping down her dewy nose and reaching into the cart to tap a milk jug that was filled with the water that flowed from the hot water faucets in the kitchen and bathroom before it got hot.

"Ayund these," she said, pointing at a cluster of former juice bottles that were filled with pot water left over from cooking beans or broccoli or asparagus (Sarah Jane was one of the few women in the building who still cooked), or with water dipped out of the sink in which she washed her face in the morning (she had stopped letting the water simply run down the drain), or from the tub in which she bathed, or the pan in which she had soaked her aching feet. Sarah Jane believed in confronting life's problems. Gracefully, of course. She was southern, and those were the manners she was raised with.

But she had saved it all, and when she reached the little park—which also served to give the Tower residents a safe destination to walk to in the afternoon, and a shady concrete bench to sit on if they wished a private moment—she adjusted her glasses again, patted her perspiring brow with a handkerchief, and began to pull the bottles, one by one, from her cart. She poured each of them at the feet of St. Francis, or on the roots of the sunstruck plants. It was only late morning, and the atmosphere was already incandescent. There were seven fearsome hours of sun still to come. Her laboriously conserved and assembled jars and jugs of water would be vaporized in no time flat.

Still, a person did what she could. In that, Sarah Jane was following her upbringing, the dictates of her own warm heart, and the caring tradition that had so impressed her years before, when she was recovering from knee surgery in the Health Center. Ever gregarious and empathetic, she had dragged herself on crutches down the hall to a little memorial service for a woman she had barely met, but who seemed to have no one to care about her. It was conducted by the Reverend Ralph Bridges, a large, soft, white-haired Episcopal priest who lived at Canterbury. In talking to him afterward, she realized that he performed such services for anyone who would otherwise die uncelebrated.

Since coming from New Orleans with his wife, Pat, in 1979, Father Bridges had treated the place as his unofficial parish. He kept a log, faithfully noting every new arrival—and all departures and deaths as well. Usually, of course, the last two were the same. It was his hobby, and his last calling. He didn't have a church anymore, so Canterbury had become his mission. Sarah Jane was touched by his ecumenical devotion, and by the fact that *every* need at Canterbury should be so well attended, right to the very end. She was very southern and feminine—"The girliest girl I ever met," Nathalie said, after she got to know her. Like my mother, Sarah Jane had been raised to appreciate—and perpetuate—the social and religious rituals. Form and ceremony. Good whiskey, white linen, good food, and good china. And laughter. Because life is a mixed blessing.

On the surface, Sarah Jane was always sunny and bright. But she had dealt with hard things from early on. Her left leg and right arm had been smashed by a drunk driver when she was in her late twenties. She had been married to two southern playboys in a row. The first was an alcoholic who kept guns, threatened to shoot her, and after their divorce, drank himself to death at thirty-three. Her second marriage, to a man who liked sex as much as the first one had whiskey, gave Sarah Jane the children she longed for. But she counted herself lucky to get out of that one, too—especially after she found, in therapy afterward, her long-lasting third husband, the disciplined, hardworking, empathetic Mexican American Dr. Mauricio Rubio. She didn't have to look far. He was her psychiatrist.

"He cudden' curah me," Sarah Jane liked to purr, looking cozy as a cat, "so he had tah marrah me."

Sarah Jane was only sixty-seven when she attended the little memorial service conducted by Father Bridges on that day in 1994. But she had had six major bone surgeries by then, three on the leg and three on the arm, to correct the damage done to her by the car. She suffered from very painful arthritis in her legs and arms, neck and back. She knew she was going to need care as she aged. And so, within a couple of years, sooner than Mauricio had wished, she prevailed on him to sell their house on Davis Islands, just across the water from Canterbury, and move into an apartment on the fifteenth floor—across the hall and one door down from Charles and Martha Sweet.

Once in residence, they discovered that certain people at Canterbury took on special roles, some self-appointed, and some not. Their character became defined by their roles, which they took seriously. For Reverend Bridges, who specialized in log keeping and good-byes, the time came when he had to consider himself.

"I want you to take care of my best girl," he told Marcia, the Jamaica-born nursing assistant, before he was taken to the hospital. Mrs. Bridges had had a stroke. The old priest had been at his wife's side in the Health Center every day. But now he was failing, and he had seen how compassionate Marcia was.

"*Ahhh,* Mistah Brid-ghes," Marcia said, in her lilting voice, her big warm smile and eyes shining down on him, "you'll be baaack."

"No, I won't," he said, in his soft rumble, shaking his head gently at her from the pillow. He was right.

Marcia fed and tended to Mrs. Bridges as often as she could after that, and with a few other nursing assistants—Meva and Claudia and Star—became noticed and appreciated by the Tower residents who felt sure that someday they would end up in the Health Center, too.

"Ah hope yoah heah when *my* turn comes," my mother told her when she looked in one afternoon on a beloved but demented old friend, Heebie, for whom Marcia was caring. Now Mother sat at the same table with Mrs. Bridges, and Marcia fed her, too.

In a building full of WASPs and Roman Catholics, evangelicals and agnostics, Karl Richter became loved and respected not so much for his rabbinical decree, but for his great knowledge, his warmth, and his wisdom and wit.

"I saw a hearse at the front door this morning," Margot Trautman, who had come to Canterbury from Wisconsin, said to him over German pancakes one day. It was July, and Margot and the rabbi, his wife, Ruth, and Martha Sweet were having their monthly breakfast at Schiller's delicatessen, not far from Canterbury. "I don't think that can be good, seeing a hearse in the morning," she said, looking inquiringly at Karl.

"Good if you weren't in it," he replied serenely, cutting up a pancake.

Without seeking it, Martha Cameron, the retired lieutenant colonel of nurses, had become the unofficial camp nurse. Canterbury, of course, is like a very senior camp, but there was also something about Martha that seemed to bring her together with people who needed care. It had been true all her life. She grew up in New Jersey in the 1920s, before most of modern medicine was conceived. People still walked the streets with large goiters on their necks, she remembered—from lack of iodine—and died of simple things. President and Mrs. Calvin Coolidge lost a son to an infection that started with a blister on his foot that he got from playing tennis, spread into his bloodstream, and killed him within weeks. All the power of the White House couldn't save him. There were no antibiotics then. Just a decade later, one of President Franklin Delano Roosevelt's sons barely averted the same death, from the same improbable cause. Sulfa drugs had been developed.

Martha Cameron had known illness all her life. She had almost died of rheumatic fever as a young girl in 1930. Her only sister, crippled by cerebral palsy, needed the same care and attention as a six-week-old baby. It was Martha and her mother who had to give it, until the sister was institutionalized at eighteen, when the mother became terminally ill. And it was then, at the age of twelve, that Martha became her mother's nurse. It was she who had to learn to feed and change and comfort her—and to give her shots of morphine—as her mother died a slow and painful death from metastatic breast cancer at home. Nursing wasn't such respectable work for women then, but the responsibilities that came to her so early made Martha Cameron realize it was what she wanted to do.

She became a nurse, and then one of the early nurse anesthetists, trained to administer anesthesia during surgery. By the time she came to Canterbury—after a long career assisting in operations on soldiers during battle and on civilians in peace, after running departments of nursing in civilian hospitals, after marrying a doctor she met and was charmed by in England during the war (and whom she later realized was an alcoholic, and divorced, and then, when he entreated her, married him again, only to divorce him again)—Martha Cameron had acquired a handsome beauty, an unmistakable aura of authority and calm. She had a direct way of speaking, an amused,

appraising, practical mind, and a skeptical, slightly mischievous understanding of life. It drew people to her. And because she was so capable and organized—a compulsive doer—she developed a dual role as
the producer and director of most of the Canterbury Players' theatrical productions and as the friend that other women turned to as
a first check on their latest symptoms.

It wasn't that residents of Canterbury lacked for professional
medical care outside the building or within. But they reached first
for the comfort and convenience of one another's experience. No
matter what the subject, there was almost always someone else in the
building who was familiar with it. Although divorce was a rare and
socially shameful event during the earlier lives of the oldest residents
(Helen Hogan Hill, for instance, *never* spoke of what happened to
Mr. Hogan), there were certainly a number of onetime divorcées in
the building who could talk about divorce. Two-husband divorcées,
like Sarah Jane and Martha Sweet, formed a more elite group. They
preferred to talk about divorce only to each other—unless, of course,
a conversation with someone else became cross-referential, as when
it began being about one thing and overlapped into another.

At Canterbury, almost all conversations are cross-referential.

Sarah Jane was sitting at lunch one day with Judy Drake, who had
moved back to Tampa from South Carolina after her husband died.
Judy had sold her house on Pawley's Island, given most of the
money to her two daughters, and taken a small studio apartment at
Canterbury. Judy was a hoarder of things, old family things, but also
all kinds of stuff, including newspaper and magazine articles and intriguing discards she found by poking in the trash rooms on each
floor. It had been years since she had allowed anyone into her apartment. Other people conjectured it as a labyrinth of towering, can-
tilevered piles, navigated by a warren of rabbit paths that only Judy
knew. She was a tiny woman. Only a little more than five feet tall as
an adult, in recent years she had shrunk six inches from the skeletal
collapse of osteoporosis, and had developed asthma. Her allergies
and asthma, compounded by her constricted lung space, made it
hard for her to breathe sometimes.

She was telling Sarah Jane that it affected the kinds of places she could go. For instance, she now went only to the afternoon matinee of the Canterbury Players' annual show, when women in the audience didn't wear as much perfume as they did at night. Judy had become allergic to the scent of perfumes and colognes. For the same reason, she now ate in the dining room only at lunch.

"*Ohh, Ah knowah,*" the ever-empathetic Sarah Jane exclaimed. "Mah eyes teah so badleh from parfumes, and chemical thangs." She was always being ambushed by smells, she said, and began to tell about the day she was standing in the aisle of a grocery store, having divorced her second husband with as much drama as the first, and having then married Mauricio. She was leaning on the grocery cart, wiping her eyes, which had begun to react to the scent of all the chemical preservatives and cleansers around her, when an old friend rolled up the aisle with a cart and saw the tears dribbling down Sarah Jane's cheeks.

"Oh, *Sarah Jane,*" she wailed, "*not anothah divorce?*"

There were, of course, many widows available to talk to one another about widowhood—which usually meant talking about their late husbands. This was almost always a subject the talker enjoyed more than the listener. Most widows came to realize, after a while, that other people, by and large, didn't find their dead husbands that interesting. (Most of them had dead husbands of their own, after all.) Once they realized that, they moved on to other topics.

Diseases and maladies, for instance. There were breast cancer survivors, like the Emyfish, to serve as examples to those newly diagnosed, and prostate cancer survivors to commiserate about prostate cancer—although the men at Canterbury were now so old that some of their sons were getting prostate cancer, and, in fact had their own club, which met for lunch at the yacht club once a week.

There were stroke survivors to talk about strokes, and a long list of residents with macular degeneration who peered at one another as they made their way carefully through hallways and rooms that were gradually going dim. Rabbi Richter no longer made notes to put on the lectern when he delivered long, erudite sermons at temple, or authoritative speeches about German history and the Holocaust. He could no longer see the notes. So he composed the sermons and speeches in his head, and delivered them from memory, in elegant, nuanced, grammatically perfect sentences and paragraphs.

Those who had learned to live with congestive heart failure, atrial fibrillation, blocked arteries, leaky valves, stents, angioplasties, or pacemakers formed such a large group that they were almost a club unto themselves. And then, of course, there were the survivors of assorted other surgeries: bladder, brain, colon, skin, esophagus, eye, open heart, hip, intestine, knee, liver, lung, ovary, testicle, uterus—the whole repertory of the surgical suite.

"*Organ* recitals," the Emyfish declared, chuckling in deep amusement. "That's what Punk [her father] used to call them when old people talked about their operations—'*organ* recitals.'"

Not everyone, of course, liked listening to organ recitals, and the more discriminating learned to be careful in their greetings, especially in the elevators. "Therhr ahrrh only two elevatorrrs," Winnie Quindry, the tiny Scots lady who had taught gymnasium classes generations ago at Miss Hewitt's, on the East Side of Manhattan, explained one day as the summer ripened, describing how life at Canterbury worked. "You get to know everrrrybody," she said, still softly burring her *r*'s after half a century. "At first, I said, 'Hello, how ahrrh you?' But you soon find out, you don't do that. You just say, 'What a prrrretty dress.' You don't ask them how they *ahrrrh*."

But some subjects are irresistible. At Canterbury, one is never far from mind.

Sarah Jane, whose life was a vast calendar of plans, causes, and social appointments, resolved with some of her old Tampa friends over snapper *alicante* at a Spanish restaurant one midday that they should all write their obituaries in advance. Then they would edit each other's narratives over a series of jolly, life-reviewing, wine-wet lunches—so that when they died, the published accounts of their lives would read the way they wanted them to. Or thought they were. Or wished they had been.

She found herself thinking about things like that a lot. One afternoon in early August, coming back from St. Joseph's Hospital, where she had visited a family member who was dying, Sarah Jane remembered that she still needed to shop for dinner. She stopped at her favorite market, Whaley's—where she knew the butcher, the manager, the cashiers, the fragrant fresh fruit and vegetable bins, and the location of such piquant native or transplanted Florida specialties as calamondin conserve, guava and red pepper jellies, and Key lime salad dressing—to get some filets mignons for herself and Mauricio. She hauled her aching bones and little grocery bags back to the car and drove on to Canterbury, to drag herself upstairs to her kitchen. "Suddenly the light went on, and I thought—*'That's what I need.* I need a *wife!* Someone who will fix *me* steak *salteado* because she knows I would love it. I need a *wife!'* " Sarah Jane said, the realization dawning on her with great clarity. *"All I've ever had is husbands!"*

In a day or two, when Mauricio left to drive back down to Sebring, where he spent most of each week in a hospital emergency room, counseling violently injured and suicidal migrant workers— many of whom were illegal aliens, depressed by the trapped lives they lived—her thoughts turned over again. *If Mauricio was around when something serious happened to me,* Sarah Jane thought, *he would do what I ask—I know he would.* She could trust him to respect her wishes. He would make sure no heroic measures were taken to save her, if there was no point.

"But now that he's spending so much time in Sebring, what if something happens while he's gone?" she asked. What then?

Sarah Jane was only seventy-three, but she'd had a lot of wear and tear. If some vital part of her interior blew out or broke down, she didn't want to be carted off by the paramedics and automatically hooked up to a machine. Strokes and dementia are perhaps the things that people at Canterbury fear most, and no one wanted to end up like my mother.

That, I had begun to realize, was one reason people always asked about her.

"How's your mother?" they'd say.

Some days, Mother seemed content to be in her limbo, and some days she did not. Sometimes she looked wonderful. And sometimes she did not. On Wednesday, the week before Sarah Jane's rumination about what turn her life might take while Mauricio was away, I had walked into Mother's room in the Health Center and found her looking glorious. She was radiant. Regal. She was also down to 84.3 pounds. She had lost a quarter of her body weight since her strokes, two years before. All her curves and contours and muscle tissue were gone. But her dark silver hair was brushed to perfection, her skin still beautiful, her makeup applied just right. Her eyes looked warm and alive.

In the recreation room, however, three days later, as Ernestine crooned and hummed her way through "Abide with Me," Mother seemed different, lying in her wheeled chaise longue. She seemed sunken and sad. Ernestine looked at her, and tried something else.

"I got a feeling," she sang, clapping her hands and beaming right into my mother's eyes, "that everything is gonna be all right!" Mother didn't look so sure. She had a pale, creamy yellow pallor, and didn't seem to be much present

Four days after that, I came into her room to find Louise yelling at her. Mother appeared to be asleep.

"*Mama, Mama! This is Louise!*" Louise said loudly. She kept patting Mother's cheeks, as if she were trying to make biscuits out of them. But Mother wasn't waking up. Louise looked worriedly at me. "Usually Ah can touch huh cheek, an' she respons," she said. "But she not respondin'."

I leaned down. "Mother? *Mother?*"

Nothing. I went to find Sally, the blond, warm, ever-attentive nurse. She came back to check. Mother was on three medications—Clonidine, Lopressor, and Prinivil—to regulate her blood pressure. Even so, the upper, systolic number still ricocheted up and down, from a low of 90 or 100 to as high as 210 or 230. Now, as Sally took it, her pressure was 116 over 80, her heart rate a slow forty-four beats a minute.

Sally sat beside her, watching. After a few minutes, Mother opened her eyes, and Sally smiled. "I think she has so little food intake now, that her body is compensating," she said quietly to me. "It's like she just shut down for a little while."

I had also come to realize that many residents at Canterbury felt sure that there must have been some instruction my mother could have included in her living will, or something that my sister, Melissa, or I could have done—or not done, or still do—that would have prevented Mother from being trapped in this endless state of irresolution. They were always trying to imagine how to keep it from happening to them. That was what Sarah Jane had on her mind.

There had to be some way that a woman could have her DO NOT RESUSCITATE instructions inscribed on a piece of jewelry, Sarah Jane said at lunch one day—something she could wear, so that if something happened and she fell unconscious, the instruction would be found around her wrist or neck, and her wishes would be known.

"It's *got* tuh be somethin' you weh-yah," she said. And it had to be jewelry good enough for a woman to *want to wear*, "Because if you take it oaff an' fall in thuh bayathtub, it does no good!"

She thought about it, staring off for a moment through her lavender blue lenses, and sighed. "It's gettin' moah and moah difficult to die with dignity, and thass whut we aw want," she said. *"To die with dignity."*

Actually, that is not what all residents want. Some, like the Emyfish, preferred not to die at all. They don't want to think about it. They would rather celebrate life.

Life.

LIFE.

And so in September, there was a birthday party for Ashby. At eighty, he was full haired, chiseled, and handsome; a natty dresser; and a silver fox. He was also given to small acts of help and kindness. In the company of so many women, he had become a cherished male, and one of his presents that night was the Rylstone and District Women's Institute Calendar, composed of tasteful nude shots of the members of a spirited ladies' club in England, women in their forties to sixties, each of them dressed only in a hat and pearls, a smile—and skin. The naked ladies got passed around, and as the drinks went down, the jolly birthday crowd in a mirrored, white-upholstered apartment on the fifteenth floor warmed to an inspired idea: They could do something even more daring, something that would strike a blow for geriatric feminism, panache, and wit—a nude calendar of Canterbury women, average age eighty-six.

Before the night ended, nine women, from their mid-seventies to God only knows, had signed up to pose—including the soft-spoken Jean Wilson, a University of Chicago graduate and the Canterbury librarian; Martha Cameron; Winnie Quindry; Sarah Jane; and (to her own surprise) the Emyfish. I think it was the lure of the greasepaint, the remembered roar of the crowd.

It was Sarah Jane, with her ash blond hair, her blue-hued trifocals, and rainbow wardrobe—which make her look, morning, afternoon, and night, like a southern garden in bloom—who shamed them into it.

"*Ah'll* do it!" she said, looking around the room, a Cheshire smile spreading across her large soft cheeks. "Ah'll start it oaff bah bein' the fuhst to volunteah." It was, in a way, her prerogative. They were sitting in her apartment. She had invited them all—six women and two men—for cocktails, for Ashby's birthday. The serious Mauricio, a tie-your-laces man, was conveniently away in Sebring, counseling migrants.

His absence invariably left Sarah Jane feeling unleashed, and so when no one else jumped to follow her lead, she rose up like a giant daffodil and made a little speech about the importance of women having a sense of self-worth at their age. Everyone else clutched their glasses, sitting on her white couches, and looked askance.

"Ah thank we ought tuh be *juss* as proud an' happy with ouah physical selves nowah," Sarah Jane said, in her breathy voice, "as we use' tuh be when we had *figures.*"

"*Ohhh, how* can you *say* that?" groaned the Emyfish, her hand over her eyes. But by the time they all got downstairs to dinner, and drank the complimentary glasses of Canterbury house wine, she relented. When the Emyfish signed on, becoming the second name on the list, the others followed. They all knew she had lost a breast to cancer. If she was going to pose, how could they refuse? Soon, giddy at the prospect, drunk with their own sexiness and daring, they were eyeing nearby tables, scouting the dining room to see which other old dames might want to bare all, for the sheer verve and adventure of it. Their excitement became contagious. It spread throughout the building like a conspiracy, and out through the town.

Almost immediately, they had a choice of photographers. The first was a friend of some of the women who had been at drinks that night, Helen Davis, a silver-haired beauty, a rich old Southern Baptist of about eighty-four who gave money to many causes, including the Children's Home and the public school system, and lived in a penthouse down the Bayshore. Her husband, Sam, a former football player at the University of Florida, had made a fortune developing subdivisions, as well as owning pieces of the local horse track, a shipyard, and a chain of Burger Kings. Helen came every day to Canterbury to see her sister-in-law, Ida King, the widow of the late Hollywood film director Henry King, who lived in the Health Center since suffering a stroke.

Helen was stone deaf but statuesque and strong willed. She was used to turning heads. Also to being in charge, and the idea of the calendar appealed to her.

"Listen," the Emyfish said, in her throaty contralto, "Helen is a *very* good photographer. And if you want these old dames to take their clothes off, it's gotta be somebody they know."

The second possibility, to their amazement, turned out to be the iron-clad administrator of Canterbury, Caridad Vinas herself. Fiercely protective of the old people in her care, Mrs. Vinas was so swept up by the statement of glamour and nerve the calendar could make—when the Emyfish, Martha Cameron, and Sarah Jane took her to lunch at the yacht club to announce the plan—that she informed them that she was a photographer herself. *She* would take the pictures, if they wanted.

They were stunned. They had known they had to tell her. Can-

terbury is an independent facility, and the indefatigable Mrs. Vinas
ran it for the board of trustees as if she were captain of the ship. Disciplined, determined, obsessed with the quality of the place, she was,
by her own choice, either on deck or on call at all hours of the day.
Nothing occurred that she didn't approve of—or find out about,
sooner or later. Usually sooner. There also seemed to be nothing she
wouldn't pitch in to do if she thought it needed to get done—and
no one she wouldn't fire for breaking the rules, or not doing their
jobs. She sometimes took the midnight shift herself, if the staff was
short a security guard, and occasionally slipped into the building at
3:00 a.m.—through a door the security desk video monitors
couldn't see—to make sure the nursing staff in the Health Center
wasn't napping in the middle of the night.

Not surprisingly, her husband and children worried about her.
Some of the residents—the ones who were bossy themselves—
weren't so crazy about her, either. But everyone at Canterbury knew
she was the Boss. After Mrs. Vinas volunteered to take the nude photographs at lunch that day, the excited Calendar Girls went back to
their apartments to share the glad news. It was then that their remaining husbands realized this was getting serious.

Back from Sebring, Mauricio, the psychiatrist, listened as Sarah
Jane, the ringleader, described the project. Then he told her what he
thought. "He said if I wanted to do it, it was all right with him,"
Sarah Jane sighed, "but he thought I was experiencing 'a severe senile derangement of judgment.' "

When Mauricio left the room, Sarah Jane took a good look in the
mirror. "You know, you may not realize this," she said later, explaining her reaction to the image she saw that day, "but most of us don't
really look at ourselves in the mirror anymore. We don't realize how
much we've changed. We think we still look the way we did ten or
twenty years ago." Some of the others had a good look, too. And
their feet began to cool. They stopped talking about the calendar. It
went on hold, and after a while, she and the other Calendar Girls
turned their energies in a different direction.

The new in-house project became the manufacture of something that was the Emyfish's own conception—the Glamour Bib, elegant at the throat as well as washable, for ladies of her years and station who have good jewelry and silk blouses but also the drips and dribbles at dinner time. After countless planning sessions and scouting trips to fabric stores, the Emyfish, Martha Cameron, and Sarah Jane began making bibs out of stylish sequined cloth and selling them for $29.95 apiece, tax included. They glittered softly through the dining room in the evenings, and began appearing around town.

The bibs were a different kind of project from the calendar, a statement not so much about remaining youth as about advancing age. But this was a village of people who were learning to live with one another and also with time—learning to find energy, friendship, and entertainment where they could. What was important—whatever the project, the current gossip, or the crisis—was what Sarah Jane had learned when she first came to the Health Center more than fifteen years ago to recover from having her knees replaced. After attending the memorial service for the woman she thought of as having died alone in the nursing wing, Sarah Jane, ever sentimental, had hobbled over to thank Father Bridges.

"Whut a shame she didn' havah family," she said to him.

The old priest turned his fleshy, solemn face to hers, fixed his old brown eyes on her, and squeezed her hand. "She *had* a family," he rumbled comfortingly. "She had all of us."

Sarah Jane had never forgotten that. *How true,* she thought. *We do have each other. We all care for each other.* It became her creed at Canterbury.

CHAPTER TWELVE

Looking for a Man

OCTOBER 2000

Doris Garcia, who is opinionated but a little vague about things, stood surveying the litter in her overstuffed apartment at Canterbury one day in October. She had just had dozens of people in for a political coffee—something Mrs. Vinas had written to tell her she shouldn't do; partisan political events are discouraged at Canterbury—for her friend Jan Platt, who was running for reelection to the county commission.

"You *know*," Doris said languidly, blinking her blue eyes—which always looked a little distant and perhaps amused, as if she might actually be thinking of something else—"I'm not very bright. She uses such *complicated* language, I thought she was saying I *could* have it." She smiled. Misunderstandings can be so useful in life, a negotiation in which Doris usually did what she wanted. She fingered her necklace and turned her wondering eyes toward the mess in her apartment, a collection of nineteenth-century-ancestor portraits, antique furniture, brass and silver, and sheaves of paper stuffed here and there. The rooms had a mellow, rich glow. Doris's line was English, and she rather looked it—a redhead gone silver, a woman of slightly uncombed elegance who moved through the days with the distracted manner of someone anchored in another time.

"I've been spacey all my life," she said one day, batting her eyes. She smiled her inscrutable smile. "I don't know why."

She was arch and a little craggy, liked to talk about castles in the family past, and was famously and imperturbably late or absent for almost everything. She sailed serenely into places just as everyone else was leaving, including the dining room staff. (She might keep the waitress and busboy waiting for two hours after the doors closed and service was supposedly over while she finished a leisurely lunch.) She was a little better, though not much, at making rehearsals of the Canterbury Players.

Strictly speaking, it wasn't always her fault. Out for a walk one day, she was picked up by the Tampa police, who were looking for a demented old woman who had wandered away from a nearby nursing home. Listening to Doris, the officers thought they had found her. Only when they took her to the other nursing facility—which informed them that they had the wrong old lady—did they bring her back to Canterbury.

Doris is a sport, and tells these stories on herself with what might be a deadpan sense of humor. No one can be sure. But the leading lights of the Canterbury Players—Martha Cameron, Martha Sweet, the Emyfish, and Sarah Jane—marveled at her sense of theater. When Doris appeared at the little swimming pool one morning, dressed for the aquatic exercise class in a black rubber frogman's suit (which girdled her from neck to toes, doing a spectacular job of elevating her bosom and flattening her stomach), Martha Cameron and Sarah Jane rushed excitedly to the diving shop where Doris told them she got it, only to discover that she had bought the last one. Still, they wouldn't give her a leading role in any skit the players put on, for fear that when the curtain went up, Doris wouldn't be there.

Manuel, her husband, had been her anchor. Short and balding, with thick glasses, an impatient, patriarchal manner, and a large cigar, Manuel Garcia had run the old cigar factory that was the source of the family's affluence. Cigar manufacturing had been Tampa's first great industry. The owners of the cigar companies were often Spanish, the cigar makers Cuban or Italian. The men and women who worked for Manuel sat at benches rolling Perfecto Garcia cigars by hand in the old-fashioned way, in a nineteenth-century brick building whose tall open windows looked out on the old brick streets, the wooden worker houses, and Italian and Spanish and Cuban clubs and restaurants of Ybor City. Bolita tickets, chances based on the drawings of the Cuban national lottery in Havana, could be bought in Ybor City and other places around town. It was illegal gambling, but it was available, as it had been for generations, run by the local Mafia family, the Trafficantes. Manuel Garcia had intended to be an investment banker in New York. It was what he had schooled for, the life he wanted. But the family had needed him to stay and run the business, and so he did. He never looked very happy about it, even if Perfecto Garcia was a historic cultural and economic symbol of the old Tampa. But it kept them in Cadillacs, good clothes, and clubs.

It was also a handy stage set. At four-year intervals, during the Florida primary election campaigns, the motorcade of one or another of the men running for president of the United States might pull up at the Perfecto Garcia building in a snarl of cars and police motorcycles and television crews. The candidate would clump up the wooden stairs to the factory floor, and walk up and down the rows of workers, smiling and shaking hands for the cameras. Whenever this happened, Manuel put on his coat, quick-stepped down the back stairs to his parking space, hopped into his green Cadillac Eldorado, and roared away. He had political interests, but little patience, and he was nobody's prop. He and Doris lived in a low, spreading house on an old brick street in South Tampa. Their lives embraced both the city's old Latin and WASP cultures, large parts of which were married to each other, just as they were. They raised and married off three daughters from that house, about a block away, as it happened, from Santo Trafficante Jr., the Tampa Mafia don, and his family. Life was an accumulation of circumstance and choice.

But Manuel was dead. He had died at ninety-four of congestive heart failure, about two years after he and Doris had moved to Canterbury—though not fast enough for him, once he was nearly blind from macular degeneration and other things started shutting down.

"What's *taking* so long?" he had rasped to Doris.

Doris turned her vague blue eyes toward me. "I didn't get out in time," she said, smiling her disconnected smile. "I came here with Manuel, and then he died and I got trapped."

She had held on to her mother's old two-story frame house, nestled among oak trees on a brick street off the Bayshore toward downtown. She rented rooms and little apartments in it by the month to odd characters—some of whom she relied on for slapdash maintenance—and liked to collect the rents in person, which gave her reason to be out of the Tower. It was also sometimes her excuse for being late to rehearsal. Doris liked to say that she had seventeen cousins in seventeen states, and she was often gone, to England, or to visit grandchildren, or some of those cousins, anything to get away. But mostly she was at Canterbury, and she found life there wanting.

Death is not really the main preoccupation of life at Canterbury. Life is, and Doris sometimes found herself wondering what many of the residents—the women especially—wondered, which is where and how they might try one more time for companionship, or love.

She paused, fingering the necklace. "What I need is a nice little old man to live in my other bedroom and take care of things," she sighed, looking around the apartment. "Louise Timm found hers, you know—at her high school reunion. And he came right down."

Doris turned back again. "But I don't *go* to reunions," she said serenely. She blinked, and smiled her enigmatic smile.

And there—just as Doris had articulated it—was the problem.

If a woman in her eighties gets to feeling untended, or incomplete, where does she go to find a nice man—for general housekeeping, or romance, or sex—if she doesn't go to high school reunions?

A college reunion, perhaps. Which is actually where Louise Timm found Bob Nelson, though she wasn't looking for him. It was Bob who was looking. Louise, who now, in the fall of 2000, was living quite happily with Bob in number 803, had gone to the reunion with another man.

"The man I was with, I had known for many years," she said. He was a retired doctor, and they had enjoyed taking trips together and keeping company for much of the decade after Louise's husband died, in 1989, of cancer. But by the fall of 1998, the doctor "was dying of cancer, too," she said, and so she made one last trip with him, to be his comfort and companion, the lovely woman on his arm, at the sixtieth reunion of his class at Colorado College, in Colorado Springs.

Louise Timm was still beautiful then at seventy-eight, as she is now, a woman of pale, clear skin; aquiline features, large, glowing, expressive eyes; and rich, wavy red brown hair. She had been a model, a reservationist for Braniff Airlines, the only child of an adoring mother and a successful corporate executive. She had lived in the Philippines, in France, and all across the United States with her husband, an Air Force officer. They came to Tampa in 1963, when he was assigned to MacDill Air Force Base, the new headquarters of the Strike Command bomber force. Louise was a sophisticated woman, and she liked men.

But it wasn't her class reunion that she went to that year. She had graduated from Colorado College, too, but three years later. She was class of 1941. So she went to only one reunion event, the first luncheon. And as it happened, the man who sat on one side of her, the man with pale skin, gentle brown eyes, a soft, full white mustache, and a head of thick, fluffy, snow white hair—who kept looking sideways at her—was Bob Nelson. It *was* his reunion. He was the class of 1938. And in that last academic year, when he was a senior and Louise a freshman, they had had one class together, in French, at eight o'clock in the morning.

She was Louise White then, carefree and privileged. Her father did not die until two years later, at the age of forty, stunning Louise and leaving her mother, who had been very much in love with her husband, a solitary widow for the rest of her life—unable to imagine being with another man. Bob Nelson was attracted to Louise his senior year at Colorado, but he was a poor boy then, and she seemed beyond his reach. He had a scholarship of $37.50, which paid half the semester's tuition. To earn the rest, he washed dishes in the women's dorms, monitored attendance at assembly and chapel, got up at 5:00 a.m. to fire the furnace in the house of a ninety-five-year-old widow who gave him a room in return, and clerked afternoons and weekends at a sporting goods store.

Bob had joined the officer's training program and, like the man Louise went on to marry, he made a career of the military when he graduated, retiring as a colonel after thirty years in the Army. He had a second, shorter career as a budget officer for the University of Colorado at Denver, and worked for years without pay as an administrative aide to the minority leader of the Colorado House of Representatives, because it interested him. He found time to get a master's degree in business, too, from the Wharton School.

Bob liked being involved, and he was reliable. He was married a long time, and at the end, he nursed his wife, who had emphysema, for five years, until she died in 1994. He kept his mother at home, too, feeding and caring for her until she died at 103, asleep on the chaise longue after a lunch of tomato soup and a grilled cheese sandwich that he had brought to her on a tray.

"You've been so good to me," she said, before she closed her eyes for a nap.

Like Louise Timm and her husband, Bob Nelson and his wife had raised two children. Like Louise and her husband, they had lived for a time in France. But at his sixtieth reunion, he was alone. And as he sat there at lunch in 1998, a man of eighty-one, looking at a woman he had not seen since 1938, a woman who looked as lovely to him now as she had in youth, Bob kept thinking, *What can I say to her?*

As the luncheon ended and the crowd eddied out, he caught up to her in the foyer. He said something in French. Louise smiled at him, and said something back. "And then she disappeared," Bob said, looking across the living room at Louise as she sat in an armchair, listening to his version of the story. "I spent the next three days at the reunion walking all over the campus looking for her, to every event." But he couldn't find her.

Louise flew home to Tampa with the doctor, her companion. He died that Christmas. On New Year's Day, Bob called. He had found her address and number through the college alumni office. They talked. He called again. She called him. They talked back and forth, discovering that they had many things in common. The same college. Decades spent in the extended family of the American military officer corps. Years living in France.

Louise had seen a little something of another man, a Canterbury resident, a recent widower named Lou Magid. But they didn't have much in common, and she found herself very drawn to Bob.

"We liked the same music, the same books, the same food," Louise said. "We're both sentimentalists." There were two big differences, however. He was Roman Catholic, she Episcopalian. He was a Democrat, she a Republican.

"We can both read the same article in the *New York Times*." He smiled. "She thinks it's appalling, and I think it's a great idea." They agreed not to talk about politics.

He flew to see her in April, the first time he had ever been to Tampa—the first time they had spent together in sixty years. The first meaningful time ever. He came again in May. She flew back to Colorado to see him in July. Bob took her to the best restaurant he knew in his home city, Boulder, on her birthday in July. They were having a wonderful time, and they both knew it. Their phone bills showed that they had talked for twenty-seven hundred minutes in the month before she came to Colorado. On July 15, as the time for her return flight to Tampa drew close, Louise looked at Bob.

"Have you ever thought about moving to Florida?" she asked.

"Yes." He smiled.

"When?" she asked.

"Let's go," he said.

They both thought it was important that they live in a space neither of their former spouses had inhabited. Louise's husband had not lived at Canterbury. Louise had moved there after he died, after she lost a kidney and her gall bladder to cancer, and had convalesced in the Health Center. She had been impressed by the care.

But they had to decide whether or not to marry. And they had to find out if Canterbury would take them as a couple if they didn't. They thought carefully about the consequences of marriage. "It would have been stupid for me," Louise said, "because I would lose a lot." Her surviving widow's membership in the Palma Ceia Golf and Country Club, for one thing. Rejoining would be expensive. And they would both lose income.

"We figured we'd probably lose forty thousand dollars a year," she said, "and that's not to be sneezed at."

Finally, they decided against marriage. "But it took us a while to reach that conclusion," Louise said, smiling across the room at Bob, her nonhusband. "We weren't raised to do this." They applied to live together in Canterbury as an unmarried couple. No one else in the building had done that. The board agreed to take them if Bob would pay half the endowment price of an apartment—even though Louise had already paid the full single price for her two-bedroom, two-bath apartment, which was big enough for her grandchildren to stay in overnight.

Bob agreed. Louise flew out to Boulder so they could drive back from Colorado to Florida together, and arrive at Canterbury together. Their coming caused a great flurry.

"For two weeks, it was all anyone could talk about," Martha Sweet said of their arrival. "And then other stuff happened, and everybody sort of forgot about it and accepted it. That's the way it is at Canterbury. There's a huge fuss for two weeks, and then everybody forgets about it."

Louise and Bob's grown children were happy for them and supportive, but when Louise's daughter told her eight-year-old son, Michael, that Bob was coming to live with his grandmother, Michael looked troubled.

"Mom," he said, after a moment, "can I ask you something? Is Bob going to sleep with Grandma?"

Oh, dear, she thought.

"Yes," she said.

"Oh, *good,*" Michael said, relieved. "That means he's not going to take my bed!"

In November 1999, they took up residence at Canterbury together, as Louise Timm and Bob Nelson, and began to share their lives. He cooked breakfast. She made lunch or dinner. They used the same doctor, the same dentist, the same optometrist, the same manicurist. It felt right. It felt complete. It made Louise think again of her mother, who had been widowed so early, and lived for so long without other men.

"I'd say, 'You ought to remarry, Mother.'

"But she'd say, 'I can't imagine looking at him over the breakfast table.'

"I used to tell her, 'You'll never find what you *had*. You should look for companionship.' " But her mother couldn't conceive of it.

Once, she said, her mother did go out on a dinner date and afterward said, "Oh, Louise, can you imagine? *He had gravy on his tie.*" She died a chaste widow at sixty-five.

Louise Timm and Bob Nelson don't know how much longer they might have together. Her remaining kidney is quixotic and sometimes shuts down. But they decided that they did not want to simply live together and then expire, with no record or product of the happiness they had found together. And so they decided to establish the Louise White Timm and Robert K. Nelson Scholarship, at Colorado College, where they had met so long ago and—more important—so recently.

"We wanted to have our names forever together," she said, looking at Bob. Bob smiled, and thought perhaps he should say one other thing. They fund the scholarship, he said, with the forty thousand dollars a year that they would have lost if they had married.

Of course, not everyone goes to college reunions. But some people like to walk. The long, curving sidewalk on the Bayshore stretches for miles along the water, and it was there, just down the seawall toward town from Canterbury, that Lucile Foster, that jolly, warmhearted Christian widow, found Louis Magid, who became the third love of her life. Or rather, he found her.

Neither one of them would have guessed it. He was small and

balding, dry and mild and thin, a retired research pharmacist, a Jew of Russian descent, reserved and precise. She was all effervescent humor and voluble, bosomy warmth, with curly highlighted walnut brown hair, bright liquid brown eyes, sweeping eyelashes, and soft, constantly moving lips.

Lucile was a toucher and a hugger, a forceful personality, passionate about the Lord, a devoted member of Bible study at the First Baptist Church, a woman of such pell-mell spirit, she said, that "When I go out, I have to pray to God to put his arm around my shoulder, and his hand over my mouth." She was ever amused, and ever earnest—someone to whom God came in dreams to tell her what to do. Louis was cautious, empirical, and pragmatic, a man of clinically exact speech—a gifted laboratory scientist whose pharmaceutical research had enabled the development and production of Librium and Dalmane, and the manufacture of Valium in tablet form.

Louis didn't trust in God to keep him safe. He relied on what he knew of human biology, disease transmission, and modern pharmacy. His lungs were weak—they had been since a chlorine gas explosion in a chemical warfare research project in which he worked during World War II—and as he grew older and more frequently ill, he became more controlling of his own universe. He would soon stop shaking hands with anyone, sitting close to anyone but Lucile, touching doorknobs or elevator buttons with his bare hands, or even leaving Canterbury to go out. He isolated himself physically in order to avoid the germs and viruses he feared. Louis hated hospitals. He thought they were dangerous to his health.

Louis was fourteen years older than Lucile. He was eighty-six, and he had spent his adult life in New Jersey, not Tampa, where Lucile was from. There seemed nothing to recommend them to each other, and nothing about Louis to suggest him as Boyfriend of the Month. Still, he had an eye. There was a beautiful widow at Canterbury whom he had noticed—Louise Timm.

Louis and Louise weren't exactly right for each other, but Louis could not help himself. And though he had promised his wife when she was dying that there would never be anyone else, it was he, not

Lucile, who spoke when they encountered each other that morning on the Bayshore.

"You're walking too fast for me," he said. "I can't keep up."

This man is telling me how to walk? Lucile thought. She looked back. She had never seen the small, mild-looking old man behind her. Louis had grown up in a different part of Tampa than she, left more than sixty years before, and had just moved back to be near his sister after his wife died.

It was five days before Christmas 1997. Lucile Foster was seventy-two. She had slept with only one man in her whole life—her husband, Bob—the big, cheerful, gregarious co-owner of a substantial furniture manufacturing business in Tampa. He was a man's man, with male appetites. "Ours was not a perfect marriage," she said, her dark eyes aware and accepting, "but we were determined—just determined—to make it work." Mainly, *she* was determined. Lucile's father had died in a car accident when she was seven. Her mother had married and divorced several more times, but Lucile never felt that she had a father's love and attention again. She was not about to create that loss for her own four children by pushing Bob out of the nest.

"There is *nothing* he could have done to make me divorce him," she said, with the satisfaction of a woman who had made her decision. When life gave Lucile lemons, she made lemonade. To her way of thinking, it worked. "We had a wonderful, happy marriage," she said, emphatically. "We lived an exciting life. We lived in a beautiful house on the golf course." That was the way she saw it. And so what happened in the moment after she and Bob came home from the reunion of the 1941 basketball team he had captained at the Virginia Military Institute was a terrible shock to her. They walked into the condominium apartment into which they had moved from the golf course, and put down their bags. Bob picked up the mail from a table, said, "I feel strange," and fell dead of a massive heart attack in front of her. Lucile was stunned. And brokenhearted.

"I would have died of grief if I didn't have such faith," she said. "But I knew where he was. And I knew someday I'd be there. And we'd be back together."

That was just before Christmas 1996. Because Bob was six years older, they had talked about what she would do if he died first. They had already moved to the condominium building, the Monte Carlo, about a mile north of Canterbury on the Bayshore. Lucile knew that she would move to Canterbury eventually, but she wasn't ready yet. She didn't feel old.

Almost a year passed, and then the phone rang. It was the film and television director Fielder Cook. He had been her first love, a Tampa boy. They had dated in their college years, before Fielder left Washington and Lee College to join the navy. Lucile had been in love. She was sure he was, too, but when Fielder gave her a black silk nightgown, and Lucile's mother saw it, that was the end.

"You two are getting too serious," her mother said. "You have to break up with him."

"But we're going to *get married*!" Lucile protested.

"*No, you're not,*" said her mother, who had married four times.

"But *I love him,*" Lucile said.

"*No, you don't,*" her mother said. "You're just in puppy love."

Lucile was crushed. But she was an obedient daughter, and she obeyed. She knew nothing about men. Or sex. All her mother had ever said to her about that was "Don't let anybody kiss you too hard." That was in 1944.

But by the end of 1997, the tall, urbane Fielder, a man of silver hair, ascots, and tweeds, was in between wives and girlfriends in Los Angeles. Lucile was newly widowed in Tampa. Bob was in heaven. Fielder came to visit his sister and brother-in-law, Mary Ellen and John Germany. For a whole week, he and Lucile went out.

"We had such a good time," she said with a sigh.

Then Fielder left. The next morning, feeling blue that he was gone, Lucile walked down the Bayshore, looking at the water and the birds, and mainly at the pavement, thinking about their time together. And that is when she encountered Louis, coming her way. They passed, she paying no attention, and then he turned and started following her, and she heard a voice behind.

"You're walking too fast for me," he said.

She slowed and turned to look at him. They walked for a way together, and when they came opposite Canterbury, Louis stopped. "This is as far as I go," he said, with the slight smile he seemed to wear. She stopped, too, and they faced each other.

"I'm Dr. Magid," he said, looking at her.

"I'm Lucile Foster," she replied, her warm eyes looking amused and curious.

When he got back to his apartment in the Tower, Louis wrote down her name. And then he lost it. (I should say here that Louis probably had more to tell about his side of this story, and I would know it if he had allowed me to interview him. But, of course, I carry germs and bacteria. I might have viruses. And so he wouldn't talk to me. He didn't want to be near me. Louis talked to Lucile, and then Lucile talked to me. But he wasn't interested in talking about himself. "Remember," she said Louis told her, "this isn't about me. This is about us—and our love affair.")

At Bible study class one day, Lucile mentioned to her old friend Margaret Meloy, who lived at Canterbury, that she had met an interesting man on the Bayshore, who said he lived in her building.

"Oh, I know *him*," Margaret said. Louis was considered kind of a flirt, and had been linked in talk with several women at Canterbury, one of them Louise Timm.

In the Canterbury dining room one night, Margaret managed to sit next to Louis and mentioned that she'd heard he had met a friend of hers, Lucile Foster.

"Yes," he said, brightening. "I'd like to see her again."

Like Lucile, Margaret was southern, devout, gregarious, and social. She saw her opening.

"I'll have a party," she said. They could meet each other again there.

At Canterbury, this was cause for major gossip.

"Everybody was waiting to see us meet each other." Lucile laughed. "And all these women kept coming up to me, saying, 'I was his *first* girlfriend.' 'I was his *second* girlfriend.' 'I was his *third*'—one after the other.

" *'Well, I'm going to be his last,'* I said. I was getting tired of that."

She began coming to Canterbury to have dinner with Louis. They did crossword puzzles. Watched movies on videotape. Talked. He was so intelligent, she thought. So different in experience and knowledge from her own background, and Bob's. Louis's parents were Russian Jews who emigrated through Montreal around 1900. They came to Tampa when Louis was only two. They had both died by the time he was fourteen. But he was smart and driven. He went to college early, and earned his doctorate in 1934, the first year that Ph.D.'s were awarded by the University of Florida. He was the youngest person ever licensed as a pharmacist by the state. Lucile found him fascinating.

But the more time she spent with him, the more she began to worry. At the Second Coming, when Jesus came back to take her and all good Christians up to heaven, she thought Louis was going to miss the bus. It was such a waste. But he wasn't concerned. He wasn't even interested.

"I don't care to discuss that at the present time," he would say in his dry, precise way when she tried to bring it up. And that was that. Lucile had a warm, embracing spirit. She found herself getting more and more fond of him.

One day, she recalled, her daughter Bonnie said, "Mother, what have you not asked God for that you really want?"

Lucile thought about it. "I don't know of anything I don't have that I want," she replied.

"Yes, you do," her daughter said. "You want a loving companion."

"Boom," Lucile said. There it was. "It was so unexpected. Here is a man fourteen years older than I am. And he is in poor health, and a different religion. But he is such a sweetheart. We just enjoy just being with each other."

Fielder Cook, however—the charming, worldly, handsome, seductive Fielder, her first love—was still telephoning. He had suggested that they meet in Paris. The idea was so romantic. Lucile was torn. And then the Lord intervened.

"God said to me in a dream, 'Louis is your sanctuary.' "

Exit Fielder.

But Louis—sweet Louis—didn't think he should be her sanctuary. Lucile's evenings with him at Canterbury had become her whole social life, because Louis wouldn't leave the building. He had even taken to punching the elevator buttons with various objects in order to keep from touching them—and their billions of germs—with his fingers. A sign went up. PLEASE DO NOT USE CANES, KEYS, AND SHARP IMPLEMENTS TO PRESS THE ELEVATOR BUTTONS. Louis started using his elbows.

"You need to go out. You need to see people," he urged Lucile. "I'm not enough for you."

But the Lord was determined, and Lucile had another dream. In it, "God said, 'I want you to move to Canterbury.' And I said, 'All right, God.' "

She told Louis that since he couldn't come to her, she was coming to him. "I knew I was going to move here *someday*," she explained, sitting in the living room of her apartment at Canterbury. "And I was lonely—I was *so* lonely over there at the Monte Carlo. Here, we could have dinner every night. We could play bridge. He could come to my apartment."

She moved into Canterbury, taking an apartment on the seventh floor, making it warm and comfortable. There was a guest room next door.

"Louis started getting sick," Lucile said. He had asthma. He began to get respiratory infections, pneumonia. She worried about him. She wanted to take care of him. "He asked Mrs. Vinas, could he move into the guest room next door?" It would mean one less room Canterbury could rent to guests, but one more paid-up resident apartment. And it was a caring solution.

The answer came back, *Yes.*

It was also, of course, even more major gossip, especially because Lucile and Louis's arrangement, and Louise and Bob's, came on the heels of each other.

"Everybody talked like mad about both couples for a while," Martha Sweet said, "and then it all died away."

Lucile and Louis didn't care about that anyway. They had each other—even though Louis had never dreamed he would love another woman. He had had one love in college, and then his wife, and he had thought that would be it.

"Which of my friends would you want to marry?" his wife had asked him, as she lay dying of cancer. She didn't really want him to remarry. She was checking on him.

"None of them!" he had protested. "I'll take a shotgun to anyone who comes near me!"

"I think it was such a shock to him," Lucile said, "to fall in love again."

Yet there they were. Louis was so feeble by then that intercourse was out of the question. But they didn't have to make love, Lucile said, to have love.

"Hugging and kissing at any age is wonderful," she said. "We hug and kiss so much that we don't even need to hold hands to feel close. It's just the intimacy of knowing that you love each other."

She was sitting on the couch where they sit together when he is with her in her apartment in the evenings, and her dark eyes were loving and merry as she thought about him.

"He stays here and watches TV, and goes home about nine thirty or ten every night," she said. "And I call him every morning, to see if he's still alive."

CHAPTER THIRTEEN

Sex and Satisfaction

OCTOBER 2000

Sexy, irreverent, liberal spirit that she was, Martha Sweet was fascinated by the new couplings of Louise and Bob, Lucile and Louis. And glad. In a building stuffed with so many traditional WASPs and southern Christian Republicans, the arrival of Bob Nelson was a plus for her side.

"I *like* him," she said, curled up in a contented ball in a corner of her oversize couch, smiling through the smoke from her cigarette. "He's one of the few Democrats in the joint. There are not many of us, you know. We mostly have to huddle together for warmth."

"How many of us do you think there are?" Bob had asked her, she said, when the two first realized they shared the same politics.

"Oh, out of a hundred fifty people in the building, I think maybe fifteen or twenty," Martha told him.

"Well," he said with a twinkle, "that makes us intellectually equal."

"I *knew* I was going to like you!" Martha roared.

She also felt a personal stake in the choices the two couples had made. "I've been married three times and engaged about five," she reminded me. But it had taken finding Judge Charles Sweet, the former marine and Harvard Law alumnus, to make her believe in the possibility of happiness. After meeting and falling in love with him, waiting years for him to be divorced and free, and then marrying him and feeling absolutely right about it for thirty-three years, Martha had become convinced that new love was possible for almost anyone.

Anyone but her. She had had hers. For Martha, the day she met Charles was the difference between B.C. and A.C. "Everything I did before I met him was wrong," she said. "I didn't know men like him existed."

She had fallen into such a slough of despair after his death that one day, the thin, intense Dr. Mauricio Rubio appeared at Martha's door: It was his nature to comfort and counsel. When he had first retired—before the collective idleness of life at Canterbury drove him back into practice—Mauricio had offered to treat residents who were troubled without charge, an offer so generous that Mrs. Vinas had given him a vacant studio apartment on the second floor to use as an office.

"Mauricio, I'm OK," Martha said with a wan smile, trying to reassure him as they sat in her apartment. "I just had a little bad patch because I made a stupid mistake. I read his love letters. And that was a stupid thing to do." Her face crumpled. She looked as if she were about to fall apart, just thinking of them.

Mauricio smiled and shook his head, as if that were not the least bit stupid. Then he gave her a serious look. "Get them out and read them again," he ordered. "Just keep reading them. And talk about it—talk to people about it and you'll get over it a lot faster than if you keep it in."

Martha took his advice, and kept on talking. But something different happened. She didn't get over Charles. Instead, she turned him into a verbal monument. She kept him alive by talking about him. She thought he had been so much the perfect husband, that she—like Louise Timm's widowed mother—had no interest in another man. None that she knew of and none she could imagine. She had already had the best of men.

So she wasn't prepared to discover, as she admitted when a few months had gone by, that "I still have an interest in sex. I am a more sexual person than I realized I was."

It came as a surprise, "because in Charles's declining years," she said, "that stopped. The sexual magic went. And I didn't care." But now that the living, breathing Charles was gone, she realized what she missed the most was not the cultural life they'd shared, or the political passion, or his earthy, sardonic sense of humor, or even his encyclopedic knowledge of things. What she missed the most was the sexual intimacy.

She had no idea what to do with the feelings. It was a physical void, and it wouldn't go away. "There's one of the guys in the building that's eyeing me up," Martha said. "But I think I will avoid *that*. It could get complicated."

And then, a few months shy of the first anniversary of Charles's death, she got a call from the other side of the state. For decades, she and Charles had spent a long weekend each year at the beach, in a group of condominiums taken by a large Italian family who vacationed on Cocoa Beach. The patriarch of the family—let's call him Mario—a resistance fighter against the Nazis in Italy in World War II, had immigrated to the United States after the war. He had had a problem getting a license to practice law, and Charles, before he became a judge, had found a legal way to resolve it. The two men and their families had become close, and once a year they celebrated their friendship together in Florida, on the Atlantic coast.

Martha, if she thought about it at all, had assumed that the annual reunions were over—just one more pleasure that had died with Charles. But one of Mario's sons, on the phone, told her that his mother had died as well. They missed her. They were sorry about Charles. But they all expected Martha to come. They wanted to see her and would be disappointed if she didn't come. It would do his father good, he said, and her, too. Martha was touched. She said she'd think about it. And then Mario called. They commiserated with each other. The two couples had been so close, Mario said. They had shared so much. Please come.

The old resistance fighter—who had lost a leg in the war, and now had lost his wife—was eighty but full of life. He didn't want to give up on things. Martha could feel the energy, the insistence on living to the brim—and also, perhaps, an undercurrent of something else. It reached through her doldrums, and she thought, *Oh, what the hell.* It would be nice, and maybe even fun, to see them all again, to talk about what they'd lost and what they had. She decided to see if her friend Martha Cameron—so calm and savvy and good humored about life—could go with her, for company and, *uhmm,* chaperonage. She could. The two of them went in late summer. They all got along. And it was good to be with Mario again.

But there was still this funny feeling of something else. When Mario phoned after the weekend, and continued calling, inviting Martha to come back by herself in October, she began to wonder if the old bird wasn't trying to bed her. She found it amusing to think about, and she called her daughter, Meredith, in New York, who had inherited her mother's Tom Jones sense of humor.

"If he tries anything, I'm pretty sure I can outrun him," Martha said, roaring over the phone at the thought of Mario chasing her around the beach apartment on his artificial leg.

"I'm sure you can, Mother," Meredith responded, a smile in her voice. "The question is, *Can he outrun you?*"

They both howled. But Martha found herself intrigued. She told Mario she would come.

So Martha drove across the state to spend the weekend with Mario at his condominium at the beach, this time alone. May and October are perhaps the loveliest months on the Florida coasts. The days are bright and crisp and warm, the nights and mornings just a little cool, the sand just a little empty, the crowds of tourists with children gone back home.

They did not run from each other.

The morning after her arrival, Martha got up early and went down to the beach in her housecoat. She plunked herself down in the sand, looking at the glimmering eastern sky and the gray rolling ocean, and smoked a cigarette in the soft moist air. She looked down at her toes, grinned, and shook her head, and began laughing as she replayed the night just ended.

Well, whaddayuhknow? her expression said.

Later in the month, back at Canterbury, we had lunch. "So," I said, "did you jump in the sack?"

Martha looked thoughtful—and a little self-conscious—like a cat caught digesting a canary while someone watched. She rolled her eyes.

"Yes," she said, with a sheepish grin.

"Was it fun?"

"Yes!" she said, beginning to laugh, looking at the table.

Forgive me, God. There was one more question I wanted to ask.

"Did he take off his leg?"

"YES!" she yelled. And she threw back her head and roared.

As soon as she had arrived in Cocoa Beach, Martha said, she discovered that she would be sharing an apartment with Mario.

It surprised me to hear her say that. I had assumed, without thinking about it, that the ritual of courtship and seduction between men and women in their seventies and eighties would be more cautious. Slow. Uncertain. Tentative.

Martha shook her head. "There were no preliminaries," she said with a calm smile. "It just happened."

And why not? Who knows better than people of that age that there's no time like the present? I felt foolish. But Martha shook her head again. She had assumed the same thing.

"One has the attitude that people this age don't do that anymore," she said, "until it happens to you. I used to think that people over fifty didn't do that." She looked at me and shrugged.

Live and learn, her eyes said.

"I think the reason I like men so well is that I had a wonderful father," she continued quietly. "You know, it's wonderful to have a man put his arm around you, and care about you. That's what a woman wants. But I don't want any more than that."

She paused, thinking about her life with Charles, and her weekend with Mario. She looked at me again.

"I don't want this to have a future," she said.

M artha wasn't the only one at Canterbury who missed the intimacy of marriage. There were probably others, but one man in particular felt the same way. It was lonely in his apartment with his wife gone, and just a nurse's aide tending to him after surgery. He had been married from the time he was a young man, and he and his wife had had intercourse until the very last years of their marriage, he said. She had never refused him sex when he wanted it. Not once.

He missed that, but it was awkward to try to find a relationship among the women at Canterbury. Most of them weren't interested, and the ones who were, were too obvious. The building was too gossipy, too small. There was a woman in another retirement and resort city on the west coast of Florida who was a possibility, he thought. She and her husband, and he and his wife—the two couples—had been friends in the North. They had visited back and forth in Florida. Now her husband, and his wife, were both gone.

She had invited him to come for a weekend. More than once. Be good for them, she said. It might just be a friendly reach, from one lonesome old friend to another.

It also might be an opportunity. Neither one of them had a lot of opportunities at this point. But he couldn't know that, and he also didn't know whether he could perform at his age, with someone new. He hadn't made love with anyone else but his wife, he said, in more than half a century. And he was over eighty. It was hard to know what options he really had, or even how to identify them, or where to find them. He was in his apartment convalescing much more of the day than he was accustomed to, and the nurse's aide, a young dark-skinned woman, was much better company than he had thought he might be stuck with. She was pretty and relaxed, personable and easy to be with. She was there to change his dressings, to help him bathe and dress, and to do whatever else he might need. But there was a lot of idle time.

Home care relationships, when there is one person who needs care, and mainly one person giving it, can become very close and trusting, even emotionally intimate. When there is a great difference in age, with such different experiences of the world, the young can find the experiences of the old extremely interesting, and vice versa. And if they are of different genders, there is a natural chemistry that may still exist, which can be harmless or not, but helps to make the time go by.

The man and the nurse's aide were both talkers. They talked about his late wife. About her boyfriend. About relationships between men and women. About feelings and sexual attitudes. They both liked to flirt. The nurse's aide one day said something about oral sex. His eyes got bright. Smiling, she told him how much she and her boyfriend enjoyed it. Oh yes.

He was fascinated.

She was really talented, she said, proudly. She liked doing it, and she was good. Her boyfriend loved it. The man had never had sex with anyone but his wife, he told her. And he had never had a blow job. He thought most men his age had not.

"You know," he confided, looking at me later, "my generation didn't do that."

Mostly, men his age died without having experienced it. Traditional wives and girlfriends didn't perform oral sex, the man said to the nurse's aide, and he had never strayed with prostitutes, or slept with younger women. He was raised with strong religious beliefs. He just didn't live that way. She looked at him with veiled eyes, and smiled.

It occurred to the man that this could be an opportunity, a new beginning. And, in fact, it was. She was a nurse's assistant, accustomed to other people's bodies, relaxed about life, skilled at what she did. She had a warm heart. He had needs, and money. And he was grateful. It was not such a reach—from helping him to the bathroom, helping him bathe, helping him dress, massaging him to help with circulation—to helping him feel sexual again. She began to give him blow jobs.

"She was *fantastic,*" he said dreamily, his eyes shining. He paid her. It made them both happy. It resolved, for the time, at least, his dilemma about how and where to find intimacy at his age, and with whom. And it was extra income for her. Nursing assistants didn't make much more than ten dollars an hour. Some made less.

But after a while, for that reason, she and her boyfriend decided to move to another city so that she could go to a vocational beauty school. It made the man sad. It was less than two hours away, but she had a school schedule now. And convalescences don't last forever. He didn't really need the care anymore. He was getting around pretty well on his own. Alone again, with just the usual schedule at Canterbury, he had plenty of time to think about how much he missed being intimate—now even more.

Then, one day, the nurse's aide's boyfriend called, which surprised him. It made him a little nervous. But the boyfriend simply said she had left a sweater and something else behind. He was coming to Tampa, and she wanted him to pick them up. She said to tell him hello, and asked how he was getting along. The nurse's aide had, in fact, left the things. The man knew that, and when the boyfriend came, he told the attendant on the security desk to send him up.

When he opened the door, the boyfriend was as easy and confident as the nurse's aide had been, and good-looking, too, like her.

"I know what you and my girlfriend were doing," the boyfriend said, when he was inside the man's apartment, holding the clothes he had come for, standing there in the man's living room, looking at him. The boyfriend was taller and strong, and at least fifty years younger, and he didn't act as if he was ready to leave.

Uhh-oh, the man thought.

"She's really good, isn't she?" the boyfriend said, with a suggestive look and a little smile. He didn't seem angry.

"Uh—*yeh,*" the man said, allowing himself to smile a little. He hadn't expected this. And he wasn't sure where it was going.

"I know," the boyfriend said, with a bigger smile. "I taught her."
The man felt his stomach clench.

"I'm better than she is," the boyfriend said, grinning at him, his eyes dancing a little.

It occurred to the man that this might be the second chance of a lifetime, that the first was past, and that he didn't know when—if ever—the third was going to come along.

They had some more conversation. They came to terms. The boyfriend stayed, and gave him a blow job.

"He was better *than she was,"* the man said, his eyes wide. He looked as if he still found it incredible. He had been telling this story, increment by increment. Now he stared at me as if he was about to say something important.

"It was the best sex *I ever had,*" he said.

But the boyfriend wasn't a therapist. He wasn't a nurse's aide. There was no good reason for him to be coming to the man's apartment. And he now lived in another city. So the man was again left alone, missing the possibility of sex more now than he had ever imagined. He called his cardiologist and asked if perhaps he could have a prescription for Viagra. The doctor gave him one. He tried the twenty-five milligram, but the littlest blue pill didn't seem to make a difference. He took two, but the results were so-so. He asked the doctor if he could risk taking the big pill, the one hundred milligram. The doctor said yes. Then he called his old friend, the widow in the distant city, and told her that he would like to come for a weekend. After the nurse's aide, and the boyfriend, it seemed an easier decision to make.

When he arrived at her building and came up the elevator from the front desk, she was waiting for him. Her eyes were bright. She gave him a kiss and a smile, and said she would show him where to put his bag.

"You know," the man said, with a chuckle, pausing in his story, "at our age, there aren't a lot of preliminaries. We don't have a lot of time." It was the same thing Martha Sweet had said.

He followed her down a hall. She was tanned and coiffed,

lotioned and moistened and made up to perfection, in a blouse and silk pants, trailing good perfume. She showed him a guest bedroom.

"You can stay in here if you like," she said, with a wave of her hand, and then led him farther down the hall, to her bedroom. "Or you can stay in here with me."

It was different from being with the nurse's aide, or with her boyfriend. Those were just blow jobs. This was the old way—a man and a woman in bed. Together. When they lay down, after he took the big Viagra, he found himself excited, after all these years, by another woman's breasts. He had an erection. A real one. He buried his head in her breasts, covered them with his mouth. And he was stunned, as old and bony, as soft and wrinkled as the two of them were, by how aroused she was. But they were bathed and shaved, brushed and combed and manicured, perfumed and powdered, cologned and hungry, missing the experience they had each been wanting. They weren't just ready. They were avid.

"You know," the man said, grinning at the memory, marveling at the whole progression of discovery, "she came even before I entered her."

CHAPTER FOURTEEN

"Laugh, Even If Your Heart Is Breaking"

OCTOBER–NOVEMBER 2000

One night in late September, while Doris Garcia was planning her forbidden political coffee, my sister's husband, Brad, who loves animals, plants, dirt, and nature in all its forms except cold, had wheeled my mother out onto the screened porch at the east end of the nursing wing, overlooking the bay. It was a squally evening, the air dark and damp and blowing through the screens, the lightning flashing over the water. Brad hates closed windows and air-conditioning. He sleeps out on the deck by his pool at night. The still, vacuumed, chemically scented atmosphere of the Health Center was stifling to him, and he wanted to spend some quiet, soulful time with Mother. She wasn't eating well. Her blood pressure was rocketing up and down. So he took her out in the elements, where he was most natural, and where he could tell her how he felt.

How to talk with her, of course—and what she might hear when we did—was the great mystery for us all. We couldn't know what she understood. But if his mother-in-law was dying, Brad thought, there was something he needed to tell her. Meaningful conversation between Mother and Brad had always meant bridging a certain cultural divide. My mother was an immaculate southern Episcopalian, a woman who took seriously her identity as a "lady." She believed in cocktail and dinner parties, good wallpaper, good upholstery, lead crystal, and good manners, just as much as she did in God and good works. Or so it seemed to me. Brad was a prep school boy from Connecticut, but also a joyful pagan with a beard, living in the woods with a flock of animals when he and Melissa began to date. I think he liked my mother for her warm heart—and vice versa.

But they had very different boundaries. Brad had an earth-moving business, and sometimes, on impulse, after he and Melissa married, would stop by my parents' house on the way home from a job site just to say hello. The living room might be full of friends, old southern WASPs in for cocktails, dressed up the way my parents' generation always dressed. The doorbell would ring, the door swing open, and there would be Brad, standing in a cloud of dust and dirt in his work boots on Mother's pale blue carpet, his dump truck parked at the curb.

"Hi," he'd say, a big white smile flashing in his dirt-grimed face. He and Mother had a long way to go.

But they had both worked at it, and Brad wanted to tell her that he was sorry he hadn't appreciated who she was and what she did for them all when he first came into the family. He parked her big, padded, wheeled chaise longue on the porch, and with the damp wind playing around them, sat close by her side. They were alone in the dim light that fell through the glass doors from the hall. Mother, an afghan over her knees, looked questioningly at him. Brad told her he was sorry he had tracked dirt into the house. Sorry he hadn't liked her wonderful dinners. He loved cheeseburgers. He always wanted cheeseburgers, and she gave him hot crab and artichoke dip, little slivers of Smithfield ham with melted bleu cheese and green pepper jelly on toasted halves of homemade biscuits, tomato aspic, braised asparagus, and veal piccata.

How could a guy eat stuff like that?

But moving earth had given Brad back problems, and alternative medicine had taught him a new appreciation for diet and stretching and exercise. He had become much more informed and careful now about what he ate and drank, he told Mother, as the damp night billowed around them. Lots of water. No more soft drinks. No more double bacon cheeseburgers. Fish and fowl, vitamins, veal and vegetables. Mother's eyes grew wide and she seemed to stir as she listened to him. He thought about all those wonderful meals he hadn't enjoyed, he told her, years and years of them, and how much he would like them now. Now he could appreciate her cooking. Now he appreciated the many ways she had tried to make life warm and beautiful. He held her hand and leaned in close and told her he just wanted her to know that. Brad said my mother's eyes glistened and swam with feeling, and she smiled and moved her mouth as if she was trying to tell him something.

It might have been *Damnit, Brad. Get me off this porch. I'm getting wet.* She did not share his love for being out in the primal elements. But Brad felt that Mother had understood him that stormy night. He was convinced that they had reached a state of communion in the dark, and it left him feeling happy, and unburdened. I could picture the two of them as he told me the story, and it stayed in my mind, because I was beginning to wonder if there wasn't something I should try to do about my mother's life.

It seemed so downhill. What made it confusing were the upswings along the way. She had started eating more regularly again in August, and gained back two pounds. The nursing staff tracked her weight, which wasn't easy. Mother couldn't just step on a scale. The staff had to lift her out of her chair and put her in a kind of sling, suspended from a hook and line that pulled on the weights of a scale. It is much the way large animals are weighed. Given her severe arthritis, her osteoporosis, and her increasingly fragile skin, which bruised and split at any pull or pressure, all that lifting and handling had to hurt—if her damaged nervous system still registered and transmitted pain. No one knew.

Bathing her every two days involved the same risks. She was gently washed in bed each morning, and cleaned each time her diaper needed to be changed. But in order to be bathed in the shower, Mother had to be taken to the shower room, lifted out of her chair, undressed, lowered onto a vinyl shower chair shaped something like a toilet seat with an open laddered back—so that the soft spray of water and soapy gloved hands and sponges could reach all parts of her—and then carefully blown and patted dry, re-dressed, and lifted back into her chair. Frequently, after one of those sessions, I would get a call in Baltimore from Canterbury Tower.

"Ahyessuh, howahyousuh, iszthuh secura-de desgattah Cannaberry ahcallin', Carlos ahspeaking. The nurse wouldlikah to speaka to you about chore mothah." And then he would transfer me to the nurse on duty—Sally, or Lucia, or Mrs. Jordan, or whomever, who would inform me that my mother had developed another small skin tear on her arm or leg or back. The evidence of the care she got from the nurses and the certified nursing assistants—the way they salved and bandaged her, gently dressed and undressed her, and turned her every hour or two in bed or in her chair, to relieve the pressure on any one area of skin—was that none of those skin tears ever developed into a bedsore.

That is what tends to happen in inferior nursing homes—usually for-profit ones that are understaffed and loosely managed. Residents, especially those who are chair and bed bound, aren't changed and bathed and salved and lotioned frequently enough. They aren't turned and inspected often enough. They're handled too quickly and roughly. Their skin rips and splits. The small tears aren't properly treated; they get infected, become bedsores, aren't cleaned and medicated, and begin to grow, eating like gangrene into the body of the patient, devouring flesh and infecting the bloodstream. Old people die that way, painfully and redolently—from neglect and sepsis.

Mother's appetite, or perhaps her ability to swallow, had improved after she reached the low weight of 84.3 pounds in August 2000. She seemed better for a while, and then in September stopped eating much again. That continued for a week, which is when Brad decided to take her out onto the porch, and when I got another call from Canterbury, this time from Susan Conley, the cool, blond, efficient director of nursing. Like Mrs. Vinas, Ms. Conley seemed always aware and omnipresent, if not in sight, then just around the corner or down the hall. She told me that my mother was getting very little nourishment, and seemed to be shutting down.

A healthy maintenance diet for someone like her, eighty-five years old and unable to move at all—or perhaps, to worry, or feel anger, or any kind of stress—is different from what a younger, active, feeling person needs. Mother expended less energy, and required fewer calories. The menus for the Tower and Health Center dining rooms are all planned in advance by Mildred, who runs the kitchen and food service, with individual attention given to what each person is allergic to or in particular need of. Mother's three daily meals were designed to provide two thousand to twenty-one hundred calories, more than enough, if she ate it all. By Mildred's estimate, Mother probably needed to digest and absorb the equivalent of only a thousand to twelve hundred calories a day.

Some residents of the Health Center, who ate everything on their plates, gained weight and got plump, even fat. Wilber, for instance. But if, like Mother, they ate even less than their very limited lives required—and if their digestive systems were no longer efficient at absorbing nourishment from the food—then their flesh and remaining musculature became fuel for the energy needs of their cardiovascular and respiratory systems. Their bodies began to consume themselves. There is a point at which a body has very little left to give, and life becomes endangered. Mother seemed only a few pounds away.

"She is having a very difficult time taking in fluids," Ms. Conley reported. "We are very concerned. She is hardly ever swallowing her food. She is pocketing it in her mouth. Holding it. I don't know if she's having a swallowing problem, or refusing it." But Dr. Zimmer had been in that day, she said, and "felt that comfort measures were in order, and that we should stop weighing her."

I hadn't forgotten what *comfort measures* meant. Mother was in dying mode again. Maybe she was tired of living in such a state of indecision.

"She doesn't seem to be in pain," Ms. Conley assured me. "But she's becoming more and more lethargic. The last time we really saw her eat anything, one of the nursing assistants got her to eat some oatmeal. Out of a bowl. And now, every time we give her anything, she's coughing, as if it's getting into her lungs." At this point, she said, Mother was just eating the little plastic cups of food supplement, which are like soft puddings, and contain about four ounces of concentrated protein and sugar and vitamins. They provide some nourishment, and slow the breakdown of skin from lack of protein. But they aren't enough to sustain life.

"Pretty soon," Ms. Conley finished, "I think we won't be getting her up but once a day."

I called the airline to book a ticket, and stayed in touch with the nursing desk. Two weeks passed. Mother ate a little. Hardly ate. Ate a little more. Didn't eat. The staff decided to weigh her again. When I flew back to Canterbury, the first week in October, she was down to 81.7 pounds. Her blood pressure, in a ten-day period, ranged from 140/78 to 210/98. She had lost thirty pounds since her strokes, two and a half years before. She seemed moderately glad to see me when I arrived. But mainly she looked sort of blank, and listless.

My mother's life, so limited in every way, wasn't even physically stable. I had come to accept her existence as tolerable because it didn't seem to anguish her the way it did us. If she was content the way she was, then I had to be. But that rationale was breaking down, and on Thursday, October 5—the afternoon of the annual Canterbury Players matinee performance for the residents of the Health Center—it fell apart.

It was the same show the players would put on for the Tower residents on Friday night, and for the public on Saturday afternoon—a home-grown cabaret and musical comedy they had been developing and rehearsing since August. This was the show that was supposed to be funny, and that the Emyfish had warned was such a groaner.

"Laugh," she had commanded me, grumpy at the idea of being involved in such an unintended farce. "Laugh"—she chuckled, beginning to be amused at herself—"even if your heart is breaking."

She was right. It was a groaner. But that wasn't the worst part.

My mother had already been rolled over to the Tower from the Health Center and was parked in a line of wheeled chairs in the front row when I came into the assembly room, where the players perform. She didn't seem to notice as I squeezed a straight chair in beside her. She was staring at the little stage, where the women who had been her friends—when she had a real life—were beginning to appear.

Martha Sweet came out in a long, flowing black dress, tanned from her daily exercise routine in the pool all summer, her blond hair shining, her blue eyes amused and grave. She was the emcee and first act. The matinee was a medley of things. There was some short poetry that Martha began to read in her gravelly, sure, commanding voice, a couple of solo acts by two male residents who had been dragooned to perform (an old fighter pilot in his mid-eighties had brought the house down the year before when he emerged in a black bikini), and then a skit, written by Martha Cameron and performed by a very gussied-up troupe of the players—Sarah Jane, the Emyfish, Mary Davis, the Duchess, and a few other of Mother's old friends.

The last poem Martha Sweet had chosen to read was "Richard Cory," by Edward Arlington Robinson, a work known to almost everyone of her generation. Slowly, with clear emphasis, she read the first two quatrains, and then began the last dramatic two, about Cory, the handsome principal figure in his small town, so envied for his privileged life.

> *And he was rich—yes, richer than a king—*
> *And admirably schooled in every grace:*
> *In fine, we thought that he was everything*
> *To make us wish that we were in his place.*

> *So on we worked, and waited for the light,*
> *And went without the meat, and cursed the bread;*
> *And Richard Cory, one calm summer night,*
> *Went home and put a bullet through his head.*

I looked to my right, at Mother. I was wedged in a little behind, so that what I could see was her profile. She looked still, and sad.

The skit began. I cannot remember the intended story line, but it was supposed to be campy and amusing, a sort of soap opera about life at Canterbury. There was laughter, and prancing, and some tottery conga-line dancing, all of it about ten feet in front of Mother. When her energy was up, I could sometimes get my mother to laugh by telling her a story or something that I knew would tickle her. But she wasn't laughing now. Her head didn't move. The houselights were down, and when I looked toward her again, there was another line in her expression, which I didn't recognize at first. And then I realized that the illuminated crease in her face was a tear, moving down her left cheek. She was trapped. And so was I. I couldn't turn her. I couldn't, because of the angle of our chairs and the arm on hers, reach to embrace her. She had no ability to move or turn herself away. She was pointed at the stage, and there she sat. There we both sat. Hemmed in by other old people in wheelchairs, unable to move, or leave.

For perhaps another twenty minutes or half an hour—the players' productions aren't long, but this one seemed eternal—we stayed that way, my inert, brain-damaged mother silently crying while her old friends performed with all the vitality they could muster, her son cringing beside her. She made no sound. She just looked tragic, staring at the creaky, carousing players, while the tears coursed down her cheeks.

And that still wasn't the worst part.

When the show was over and the lights went up, Mary Davis and the Emyfish and two or three others came up to say hello and stood talking—to me. Ignoring Mother. Or pretending that by talking to me, they were including her. They had all been friends for generations, from childhood until now. They had been together literally thousands of times. Mother and Mary had lived two houses apart, raised us children together. They had been the same size, worn each other's blouses, skirts, and dresses. Mother and the Emyfish had been close, personally and socially, for sixty years. They had shared all the fun and sad and intimate things of life. The Emyfish smiled in Mother's direction, and edged away. But Mary lingered, saying something to me.

"Say hello to Mother," I suggested, nodding to my right. Mary was standing two feet away from her.

"Ohh . . . she dudden recognahze *me*," Mary declared, in her exaggerated drawl, hardly glancing over. "She dudden knoah me from *Adam*." It had become her mantra about Mother.

I don't know how to describe the look I thought I saw on my mother's face. I am not a camera. I see through an emotional filter. But it could have been the expression of a proud, brain-damaged old woman who understood the moment well enough to feel it, and was trying, very hard, to look as if she didn't.

When we got back to the Health Center, I stopped at the nursing desk and told them, out of Mother's hearing, to enter a new instruction in her chart. She was never, *ever*, to be taken to the Tower again.

For nine months, I had been renting a guest room at Canterbury, or the vacant small studio apartment on the second floor in which Mauricio had given free counseling to other residents when he and Sarah Jane first moved in. In the studio, I slept on an old hospital bed Mrs. Vinas had found, which occasionally began to hum in the middle of the night, and then slowly to fold up on me. The bed in the guest room was a conventional mattress, a twin, but there was an emergency pull cord at its head, as in all apartments at Canterbury, and one night I was roused from a sound sleep—with my hand tangled in the cord—by the vision of a tall white figure who looked like Nurse Ratched striding through the opened hall door, followed by a security guard aiming a bright flashlight at me in the dark.

"Mrs. Harris, are you all right?" the nurse called out, as she descended on me. I lay there in my Jockey shorts, transfixed by the flashlight beam.

"Mrs. Harris? *Mrs. Harris?*"

Jesus, I thought. *I'm practically naked. Do I look like Mrs. Harris?*

They had confused the glowing emergency light on the signal board downstairs with that of another apartment—Mrs. Harris's, of course. All of this went into a growing pile of notes about life at Canterbury—all of which, so far as I was concerned, centered around Mother.

I was her son. My first responsibility and reason for being there was as her power of attorney and trustee—her legal voice, conscience, and defender in all events. I represented her person and property. But that presumed the existence of a person. From the time of her first stroke and coma, and in the months following the second stroke, when its huge effect became evident, my sister and I had felt differently about Mother. Melissa looked at the face and form propped in the bed or chair and saw the shell of her mother, who was gone. I looked at the same face and form and saw the remains of my mother, looking back expectantly at me. For Melissa, who is as small and lovely, as warm and intense, as highly driven as Mother—and who came almost daily in the first year or so—being with the woman in Mother's bed was excruciating because she could see only what was lost. I could see only what still was there.

It is like that with people in my mother's condition. Everyone who is with someone like her sees something different, but by my next trip down, in late October, after the deterioration of the previous few months, and the performance of the Canterbury Players on the previous visit, my feeling had changed. My mother's existence now seemed so painful and wretched to me—both in the eyes of other people and in daily fact—that it had become hard to justify or support. When she was eating, when her blood pressure was in the normal range, she could seem calm, present, warm, and even comprehending. But I realized I hadn't seen her like that in a while. When she wasn't eating, when her blood pressure was too high—or too low—she was more likely to appear sunken, agitated, vacant, or asleep. Her personality—if that was the word—had grown variable and bizarre. Sometimes, I realized, her look and behavior were so strange, they frightened me—as if she were inhabited by demons. In earlier times, I suppose, people would have thought she was.

She simply wasn't like herself. Whatever state Mother was in now seemed tortured and cruel to me. I began to feel guilty for not trying to find a way to help her end it. If she had been on life support, I could have withdrawn it. But, of course, she wasn't.

And yet, in a way, she was. There were those three medications she took each day to control her blood pressure. Even with the restraining effect of all the drugs, the pressure level in her cardiovascular system bobbed up and down like a cork, and seemed to be growing more erratic. If I withdrew the medications, her blood pressure might shoot up uncontrollably. She could have a heart attack, or another stroke—a big bleed. And die.

On the other hand, she might suffer a heart attack or stroke, endure even more damage—and not die. That possibility was almost too horrible to contemplate. But given her perverse medical history—and what I thought of as my mother's sometimes serenely irrational way of reacting to things—it was not unlikely. Yet even that might still be a way out. If her neurological system was further damaged, she would almost certainly lose her already fluttering ability to swallow. If she couldn't swallow, we would not allow the implantation of a feeding tube. That had already been decided. If she wasn't fed, she would die.

Whatever the outcome, withdrawing the medications was all I could do. The more I had thought about it, in the two weeks I was away from Canterbury, the more it seemed the right thing to do. The problem was, I couldn't stop thinking of it as *killing* Mother.

The first day back offered no relief.

"She's not eating again," Mrs. Jordan, the head nurse, said, when I walked into the Health Center on the last Wednesday in October. She guessed Mother now weighed less than eighty-one pounds. "I expect it's lower than that," she said somberly, "but it hurts her so much to be put on the scale, I haven't done it."

The head nurse's expression, always concerned, downshifted

into More Bad News. "You know," she said, looking at me inquiringly, "she has this lump on her spine—scoliosis. She's always had
it." I remembered. It was like a Ping-Pong ball under the skin, on
one side of her spinal column. "The skin is wearing off," Mrs. Jordan said. "The first layer is off. I was very upset to discover this."
The abrasion, she explained, came from the hours Mother spent sitting up in the wheeled chair with her backbone, curved from osteoporosis, rubbing against the back of the chair.

"So we can't let her sit up as long. We'll put her back to bed. Turn
her and change her every hour." She sighed, glancing at me, then settled her gaze on the door of Mother's room. She was a ruddy, handsome woman with red brown hair and a worn expression, chewing
the inside of her lip. "I think basically she's got a strong heart," she
said finally, "and that's why we're still looking at her."

I thanked Mrs. Jordan for her report and started toward Mother's
room. Mother had been gone earlier, taken to the whirlpool, so the
warm swirling water could soothe the raw place on her back. But
she was now back in her room, with a new roommate who seemed
to be moaning a lot. I was wearing a white shirt with a collar, and
a black pullover sweater. A tall, rail-thin woman—a retired beautician, a Scottish spinster with no family and large, watchful eyes—
was sitting in her wheelchair by Mother's door, and smiled to see
me coming.

"Hello, Father!" she hailed.

"He's not a priest," Mrs. Jordan told her from the nursing desk,
behind us.

"I don't know *what* he is!" Mrs. McMullen sniffed, as if it were
suddenly of no interest to her. "That's *his* problem."

Mrs. Vinas had found other uses for the small studio with the
Venus flytrap bed. There were only two guest rooms for
family members to rent at Canterbury. They weren't always
available. I needed reliable space, if I was going to be in Tampa almost half the time, and so I had leased an apartment a few blocks

away the month before. Late that afternoon, sitting outside in the garden as a southerly breeze began to stir toward the bay, rustling the big leaves of an old magnolia tree behind us, Melissa and I talked about withdrawing Mother's medications. If we were going to do it—if I was going to order it—the question was when. It had to be when I was in town and could stay for a while. I couldn't just cut her off and fly away. If I was going to make the change, I ought to be present for the consequences.

How much longer was I going to be around this trip? Melissa asked. She always appeared tanned and athletic and stylishly sensual— Florida glamorous—but she was pensive, looking at me. About ten more days, I said—through most of the first week in November. I might not be back for that long again until January, because I was going to Rome in two weeks to see Whitney, my daughter, who was spending the first semester of her junior year there. Melissa thought about that for a moment. She is ten years younger, which means that we had different childhoods. It gives us different perspectives on our parents, and so we often serve as checks on each other. She is also better organized.

"If you're here for ten more days—why not do it now?" she said, staring softly at me. "Otherwise, it won't be until sometime after the New Year, and we'll all be miserable until then." Melissa had been ready to withdraw the medications all along. She thought it was what Mother would want. I hadn't agreed earlier, but now I thought she was right. I knew she was right. I just didn't want to act on it. But if we had made the decision, it would be irresponsible to wait any longer. Procrastination was cowardice, not love.

Melissa, her son, Christopher, and I had dinner that night at the yacht club, Mother's favorite place, and talked about it some more. Whitney was away in college. Christopher was still in high school and close to his grandmother. We all thought we should each have a last conversation with Mother.

The next morning, a Thursday, I called Susan Zimmer, her doctor, from my rented apartment. Two of the medications could be stopped immediately, she said. The other had to be tapered off. If I was ready, she would call the nursing desk at Canterbury and give the order. The withdrawal process would take three or four days, but the effect, she thought, would come soon.

I asked her to make the call. When I hung up, the old, pine-paneled apartment felt very strange and quiet and isolated. I didn't know what to do with myself. I couldn't just go and sit in Mother's room until something happened. It could take a few days, a week— I had no idea. But I couldn't stay away, either. There was no point. I couldn't concentrate on anything else. So I went to see my mother. It was lunchtime, but no matter how Claudia talked to her, holding the spoon before her lips, Mother didn't seem interested. She just kept looking at me with this solemn, doubtful expression. It made me very uncomfortable.

She didn't know what I had done. Did she? How could she?

I had to leave.

I couldn't just sit there, having decided to kill my mother, and make small talk with her. I hadn't tried to discuss it with her. That wouldn't have been fair, even though it was her life. She wasn't in-tellectually or emotionally capable. She couldn't comprehend all the issues involved, and the uncertainties, or tell me how she felt, or what she wanted me to do. And if she tried, I didn't think I could understand her. This was *my* responsibility. That's why she had given me power of attorney. But having made the decision, I thought, now I had to try to tell her what I'd done, and what was coming. I had to find a way to talk to her about this.

The way that Brad had.

I went to a meeting that night, a 12-step meeting, the kind that those of us who attend aren't supposed to talk and write about in public, because no one speaks for the organization. But it's a great gift to have group therapy sessions available to drop in to almost anytime and anyplace, always with people who have the same faults you do in the room. I talked about my mother. We all have mothers, and lots of people think that's reason enough to drink. Everybody told mother stories, and we all felt a lot better. Then I went to an old-fashioned barbecue place off the bay, with tables on a wooden porch out under some moss-hung live oak trees, and ate baby back ribs and fresh coleslaw, baked beans and corn bread and Key lime pie. I went alone. I didn't want to make small talk in the dining room at Canterbury. Everyone there always asked me about Mother.

At almost midnight, I went again to see her. It was the first time Mother had gone to bed in years without two of her three blood pressure medications. Sometimes, at night, when I checked on her, she would be awake, just lying in bed, her eyes open, as if waiting for someone to look at. But now she was asleep on her left side, carefully tucked and folded into her clean pillows and sheets and blankets. She coughed once, lightly, in her sleep. Meva, the most senior nursing assistant, who had come to Canterbury almost twenty years before from New York, and from the Philippines before that, sat in a chair in a corner of the room, silently watching. She gave me a slight smile, and said nothing.

They all know, I thought. *And they don't like me for this decision, because they all like Mother. Tomorrow, somehow, I have to tell her.*

On Friday morning, I had a long walk and talk with my old friend Carla Kelly, who had grown up in the neighborhood with Nathalie and me. We have known each other since we were four and six. She had become a shrink, a Ph.D. psychologist, and we always talk to each other about our romantic lives, our siblings, and our parents. I don't know what she gets from it. But it is very helpful to me, and when we were done, I went to see Mother. She was asleep again on her left side, her head on one pillow, another wedged behind, and a white cotton glove embroidered with climbing roses on her left hand—the one she could still move—to keep her from scratching herself. She had started doing that again.

I sat for a while and looked at her, and at the old woman in the other bed. She was new to me, the latest in a long line of roommates who appeared and disappeared in the bed next to Mother. They stayed awhile, and either improved and were moved to some other room, or died. Mother was in a semiprivate room right across from the nurses' station, where she could be easily monitored, since she couldn't call out or pull the emergency cord if she got into trouble. Her roommates were usually people who needed watching, too, and this woman seemed to be doing a lot of gasping and moaning. She was very pale and ghostly. I thought she might have congestive heart failure.

I went back to the apartment, and in the days that followed, without consciously making the choice, began to fill the time with things that needed to be done but didn't require much thought. That day and the next, I arranged for a FedEx delivery. Took my thirdhand computer to the thirdhand computer shop to be fixed. Did my laundry. Wrote late birthday notes and wrapped presents and sent them off to two young cousins. Sent expense receipts to the *New York Times,* where I had a part-time seat on the editorial board. Went to the store to buy Drano. Drove the car through the car wash.

And thought more about Brad's conversation with Mother. I'm no good at not talking about what's on my mind, so that night I decided to eat alone again, away from Canterbury—at La Fonda, a little Cuban place nearby where I could get black beans and yellow rice with chopped onions and olive oil; a salad of lettuces, tomatoes, onions, and olives, with oil and vinegar; hot, buttered Cuban bread; baked plantains; stuffed *boliche* roast; and iced tea. With a flan for dessert and espresso coffee. Comfort food. I ate early, and then went to see Mother after her dinner, before she was put back to bed.

It was a good time. She was still awake, parked in her chair in the hall in front of the nurse's station, looking sort of dull. She raised her eyes, coughed, and gazed at me wearily, as if reserving judgment. I got behind her chair and pushed her down the long hall toward the porch. Except for the people who had money enough for private rooms, finding somewhere in the nursing wing to be alone was always a challenge. But we were in luck. The porch was in deep twilight and empty, the bay a glimmering dark space through the windows, the city a glow of copper and silver to the left, the boulevard a rich platinum flow of headlights, with joggers dancing down the sidewalk beyond. I could never tell if Mother looked at any of those things, but I always faced her toward the water. The bay in front, and the Gulf of Mexico behind, were the points of our compass. She had been born and had made her life on this peninsula. She and my father had developed many friends and connections around the country, but their lives were always based here, in this city and its southern-, European-, and Cuban-inflected culture, by these waters.

She had shaped my whole life, I said, drawing closer to her in the dark. Did she realize that? It was she who had given life texture and structure and feeling, she who gave me a sense of identity—and obligation. It was Mother who made me think of life as warm and funny and fond, at least in its private moments. She was an impossible romantic, and she had not prepared me at all for the greed, the meanness, the naked aggression, and conflict in life, or for all the people in the world who would take advantage of you if you were nice. That should have been my father's job. He, of course, was never home. Or interested. Her romantic insistence on my being good had also left me feeling guilty about all those times when, of course, I wasn't. But this was no time to quibble.

"You have been so loving, Mother," I said. "So giving. You have been so thoughtful and done so much. There are so many people who love you. Wherever I go, everyone asks about you."

Her face was shadowed, but in place of the blankness, there was a rise of feeling. She was listening to what I was saying, and her expression had begun to turn grateful and tender. I began naming all the people who loved her: Melissa and me, Christopher and Whitney, Brad, Louise, her nephew and nieces Baya and Ginger and Lynn, and their children, a long list of family and friends. I could see well enough in the dimness to tell that Mother looked sad but happy. She was feeling acknowledged. A lot of those people, of course, were in heaven now, I said. I told her I thought she might be taking a long trip soon, herself.

"I think you may be going to heaven, too, Mother."

The porch had grown darker, but I thought I saw a change in my Mother's face. I realized she was making sounds. Low sounds. I wasn't sure how long she had been doing that.

I began naming all the people she loved who were already in heaven, waiting for her. I started with my father. I went all through the family, and pretty deep into friends, and Mother was still making those sounds, as if she was trying hard to say something. The light had gotten very dim, but her face looked different—urgent. Maybe even alarmed. I paused, wondering how to navigate this change of feeling when the door from the hall swung open and a nursing assistant pushed someone in a wheelchair through.

It was Wilber, in a white shirt and yellow cardigan sweater, and his tan pants. The aide was going on about how nice it was out here on the porch, and let's just sit over here by the windows, but it was lost on Wilber.

"Where are we?" he said, confused. "I don't understand."

She smiled indulgently, steering him into position on the other side, and then glanced in our direction. Her gaze lingered.

"Are we interrupting you?" she asked.

Well, yes. But I wasn't sure what to do next, anyway. "Look, Mother," I said, "there's your old friend Wilber." There was no way or place to continue the conversation after that. So I didn't try.

I went to another 12-step meeting that night, and talked some more about my mother. She had looked unsettled when I left, I thought. I was going to have to try again.

I don't remember what I did on Saturday. It's a complete blank. But on Sunday I went to watch the Tampa Bay Buccaneers play the St. Louis Rams, with the Emyfish and Ashby. It was the furthest thing I could imagine from the nursing wing, and besides, I liked the woman who had invited us. Joy McCann Culverhouse had been the women's golfing champion of Alabama, and years later, of Florida. She was past eighty, and a sport. She was passionate about what she believed, read the New York Times every morning, had some really big diamonds, and minced no words. She and her husband, Hugh, had owned the Bucs. They lived down the Bayshore in a huge penthouse apartment with a smaller one underneath, not far from Canterbury, and she thought she knew her husband very well, until 1994, when he died, leaving an estate of $380 million. Then she discovered that Hugh had gotten her to sign away control of the team, of the Culverhouse Foundation, and of much of their fortune, which became lodged in a trust. Worse, he had had affairs with and showered money and gifts on a number of women, some of them younger, some in Tampa and some not. Like the television commentator David Brinkley's wife.

She was so mad at Hugh, Joy told a reporter, "I'd love to dig him up out of his grave—so I could shoot him." Joy liked guns. Given that she kept a loaded revolver in every room and every car, Hugh was probably lucky to already be dead. So, instead of shooting him, Joy Culverhouse sued and, in a settlement, won back substantial money and income from the trust Hugh had created, and control of the foundation. They had sold the Bucs, but it was her skybox we were going to see the game in. I thought she was a pistol.

I rode out to the stadium with the Emyfish and Ashby. He drove, and the Emyfish talked. She was feeling pretty good about herself. Susan Zimmer, who was her doctor, too, had told her to perform tai chi five times a week. The Emyfish was taking an instruction video downstairs to play on the VCR in the exercise room at Canterbury every weekday morning.

"I can't do it in the apartment," she said. "I'd trample the orchids." She had pots of them on an oriental carpet in the living room, like an indoor garden. She turned her attention to Ashby, who was parking the car at the stadium in a way that she thought could be improved upon. She told him how. He ignored her.

"You *never* do what I say," she said, giving him a look. "And I'm *always* right."

That afternoon, Mother was asleep when I looked in, so I asked Luisa, the nurse on duty, about the woman in the other bed, the one that I thought had congestive heart failure.

Oh no, Luisa said. That woman had the flu, which had gone into pneumonia. That's why she was in the room with Mother. She needed watching. There had been a lot of flu in the Health Center that month.

The *flu*?

I felt ambushed. Also stupid. For five days, I had let my mother lie next to a woman infected with a flu virus, and perhaps viral pneumonia, too. I was prepared for Mother to die of a stroke because I had taken away her medicines—but *not* from pneumonia because I wasn't paying attention. I was supposed to protect her from threats like this. I told Luisa I thought the woman ought to be moved. Ms. Conley made those decisions, she said. "Well, please ask her," I said, "and ask her to let me know."

On Monday, my cell phone rang. It was Susan Conley, and her voice was cool. The other woman needed to be close to the nurses' station, she said, so she could be watched. But my mother could be moved. (Oh, I see. She no longer needs to be watched?) Anyway, she said—after a pause, to let that sink in—the other woman just had a cold, and she was getting better.

I had thought the woman was dying of congestive heart failure, I said, trying to be restrained. When I realized that she had the flu, and that my mother had been coughing, it made me think we were exposing Mother to a flu virus—and the possibility of pneumonia.

The temperature of Ms. Conley's voice dropped several more degrees. No, she said, rather deliberately, my mother was actually much closer to death from high blood pressure than her roommate was from the respiratory infection. My mother's blood pressure had spiked last night, she said icily. They were watching it closely.

This was making *my* blood pressure rise. I didn't know Mother's pressure had spiked last night. No one had mentioned it. It sounded to me as if the director of nursing was suggesting that her staff was having to cope with the consequences of *my* indifference to my mother, when I thought I was complaining about *theirs*. The whole conversation suddenly seemed petty and defensive, as if we were bickering about who was endangering Mother most. I felt off balance. *I've gone weird,* I thought. *I'm bearing down too much. Maybe I'm overreacting out of guilt.*

I said good-bye and hung up. I felt as if I had set my mother up to be assassinated. And what was I to do now? Keep going out to dinner and the ball game? Sit home in sackcloth and thorns? Nothing felt right.

The next day was Halloween. When I popped in to see how Mother was, she was propped in her chair in her room in a dark royal blue blouse, all lipsticked and made up. She was staring at Louise, sitting next to her, as if she were someone she didn't know. Louise had on a Carol Burnett wig.

"Why you givin' me a mean look?" Louise asked, smiling at her. She reached up to pat her wig, then reached over to pat Mother's shoulder, and her cheek. Pat, pat, pat. "This is *Louise*. You ain't sure this is Louise? This is Louise, right on."

Mother kept giving her a hard stare.

"This is *yoah Louise*," Louise said, putting her face close to Mother's. Mother's eyes got wide. "Got onah wig," Louise said. "Got onah flowered shirt, because it's Halloween." She stopped, looking at Mother, then turned to me. "See? She ain't sure o' somethin'. She not smilin', thass for sure. She wudden even eat fo' me today."

She turned back to Mother. "It's yoah *Louise*," she said. "Doan you worry. You doan like the wig? You woan see id fo' a long, long time—aftah today."

Mother looked as if she had no idea who this strange woman was, or what she was talking about. On the other hand, she *did look alert*. I decided to leave.

In the hallway, the old Scottish beautician was waiting in her wheelchair. She had begun feeling very needy lately.

"*Help, help, help!*" she said, sort of in the tune of "Hip, hip, hooray." Then she spotted Wilber, wobbling toward her.

"Would you help me to get *out* of here?" she called.

Wilber stopped, and looked perplexed. "I don't know *how* to get out of here," he said.

That evening, the Emyfish and Ashby had a cocktail party in the social room of the Tower, for their anniversary and Halloween. They were married on Halloween. Ashby, as always, was costumed and had made himself up as Emmett Kelly, the sad clown. Winnie

Quindry, the little Scots lady, came as a penguin. The Emyfish had some Cleopatra thing on her head.

I went back to see Mother.

She was lying in her bed, after dinner. I had lost track, but either that day or the day before had been her first day without all three drugs. She looked at me, and I sat down on the floor beside her, and decided to try again. I told her how much I loved her, how she'd shaped all my sensibilities about life, how she was in my bones and always would be, even after she was gone.

Her eyes got tender. She was liking this. I told her again how much everybody loved her because she was so warm, so thoughtful, so giving, always. "Melissa loves you, and Christopher, and Whitney, and Brad," I said, holding her hand, "and Ginger and Lynn and Tony and Little Ginger and Rusty, and Baya and Barbara, and their children, little Baya, and Lucy, and Nathan Dudley, and Louise—and even Aunt Virginia." Mother had looked all smiley and crumpled and warm and moist until I got to Aunt Virginia, and then she laughed hilariously. She made no sound other than a kind of hiss, but her mouth opened wide and her eyes got wild, as if I had said something insanely funny. She and Aunt Virginia, Uncle Baya's widow, had feuded and fussed for two generations.

I knew then that she was with me, every word. "I wish I knew what you wanted, Mother," I said. "I wish I could help you. I wish I could wave a magic wand and make life sparkle for you again the way it used to."

I know you do. I know you would. I know you wish you could, her eyes said back to me. If she could have, Mother would have reached over and touched me.

"I can't do that," I said.

She nodded.

"But," I said, "I think maybe I can help you get to heaven. You know, Jobie is there, and Nana is there, and your brother, Baya, and Louise and Nicki-Nat are there. . . ." I kept on with the list, name after name.

Her face had begun to change.

I soldiered on. "You know, so many of your friends are there now, Mother—Heebie, and Elizabeth, and Pattie, and Frank, and Dave, and . . ."

My mother was staring at me with this very strange expression—as if she was looking at someone who might be a danger to her.

Wait a minute, her eyes said. *We were just talking about how everybody loves me. Loves me right here. I like lying here listening to how people love me. I like people taking care of me. What is all this stuff about* heaven? *Do I look like I want to go to heaven?"*

It was exactly the way she had begun to react the last time. I just hadn't recognized it, in the dark.

Oh no, I thought. *It doesn't matter how well I try to say it. She's not with me on this.* She doesn't agree. Whatever Mother thought when she was herself, before her strokes, before she ground her teeth into bits and started dying every third month, she doesn't think now. She doesn't feel that way anymore. She doesn't want to go to heaven. It doesn't matter that we think her tiny life is pointless and pathetic. She doesn't want to leave it. Not one bit.

And I can't change anything now. It's too late. *Oh shit.*

For two days, I stayed away. I had some excuse. I had a lunch engagement and a lecture to give at the University of South Florida one day, and other work to finish the next.

Finally, on Friday evening, November 3, I went in to see Mother. I couldn't wait any longer for something to happen, and there was nothing more I could do. I was leaving in the morning. The evening shift change had just occurred when I entered the building, and as I walked by the nursing station, April, the nurse who had just come on, saw me and smiled.

"Isn't it amazing about your mother?" she said, holding a patient chart. "Luisa said her blood pressure has been more stable without the medications than ever before."

"*Really?*" I said, stopping in my tracks.

"Oh yes," April said, looking at the chart. Her blood pressure had been 170/88 last night, and 160/80 the night before. "And she ate a hundred percent of her meals today," she said. April looked happy, marveling at the numbers on the chart. Her patient was better. She was a nurse.

We had known that Mother might not die. We had talked about that. But it had never occurred to us that she might *improve*. I told April about my conversation with Mother about going to heaven, and her reaction.

"I just wish I knew what she had in mind," I said glumly.

April looked at me. "Some things are not for us to know," she said softly.

I guess not.

I went in to see my mother. She was on her right side this time, all bathed and brushed, clear eyed and serene, as if she were waiting there for me. She watched me come in, and I could swear she had a little smile. I looked at her. She looked back at me. She was waiting for me to speak.

A little gold plastic tiara, a leftover from Halloween, glinted dimly on her bedside table. I picked it up and put it on. I have a big head, a lot of silver-black hair—like my mother—and horn-rim glasses. It didn't fit.

"Do you think it's good on me?" I asked, watching her reaction.

Mother looked at me as if that were a ridiculous, goofball idea. Just silly. Her eyes grew merry. Her mouth opened in a happy, silent laugh, and gradually closed, leaving her looking faintly amused—and fond. She seemed absolutely present. I took the tiara off, knelt down beside her, and took her hand. We studied each other.

"Well, Mother, the nurse tells me your blood pressure has stabilized," I said. "You seem to be sailing along just fine without your blood pressure medications. And you're eating everything." For just a moment, her smile seemed a little—what—smug?

Yes, I know, her eyes said. She looked content.

"So I guess you're going to live awhile longer. I guess you're going to be here when I get back. Aren't you?"

Her eyes appraised me. *Yes, darling, I think so.* She seemed pleasantly tired now.

Have a nice trip, her expression said. *We'll talk about heaven some other time.*

"OK, Mother," I said. I kissed her cheek. "Good night."

CHAPTER FIFTEEN

Sleeping with the Sweetso

2001

Morning at Canterbury Tower. Early 2001. A Saturday, maybe. Or Wednesday. It doesn't matter. It was the beginning of another day in the village, and all over the building, people were waking to discover that they were still alive. In the apartment on the right front, at the very top, the Sweetso and I were stirring. Even with the curtains drawn, with the room still dim and slumberous and my face in the pillow, I could feel the heat of the sun on the window by my bed. My door was closed, but there were sounds of life down the hall.

In the kitchen, the coffeepot was chuffing. In the living room, the large television in the corner was announcing the morning's news. Mostly it failed to surprise, although sometimes it did. When the 8:30 segment ended, I knew, a solemn-looking lawyer would appear and offer to sue any nursing home that might have abused my old loved ones. He would seem certain some nursing home had. Then he would give an 800 number to call. He did that every morning. And every morning, after the lawyer faded from the screen, a very different persona materialized: Martha Stewart, looking cool, composed, and somehow chic in her loose, flowing kitchen and garden clothes. But she no more than began to describe the terribly clever domestic things she was about to do, when she was interrupted— every morning—by a cry of alarm. It was the Sweetso, erupting from her favorite corner of the couch, in frantic search of the remote control.

"*Aawwkkk! It's that dreadful Martha Stewart!*" Zap. She was gone. Sigh of relief. "I cannot *abide* that woman," the Sweetso growled.

This was Florida after all, and some things are reliable. Seagulls float and cry to one another on the morning breeze. Mullet jump in wet gray arcs and plop back into the shallow water near the seawall. Farther out, porpoise and shark fins cut the surface of the bay. And on the horizon, jetliners angle down through the clouds to circle south past Canterbury, around MacDill Air Force Base at the end of the South Tampa peninsula, and then back north to land at Tampa International Airport, with more loads of people from all points of the globe.

It was a constant, ever-changing vista, and from the front of the apartment, facing over the bay, tobacco smoke—dry, irritating, defiant, and regular as the dawn—was drifting back toward my bedroom. The Sweetso—one of the last joyfully compulsive smokers of her generation, a woman who courted death by tar and nicotine when all around her were doing their feeble best to stay healthy and alive—was standing on the balcony in her housecoat, a short round figure surveying the world from her last perch on life, poisoning the atmosphere with a grin of serene and righteous bliss.

It delighted her to be on the highest floor, because there was no balcony above to box her in, or put a ceiling on her view. In her previous life, in the mountains of her native western Pennsylvania, the ridgelines running north and south pocketed the rising and setting sun, hiding the beginning and end of each day through all her decades there. And so the Sweetso loved the flatness of Florida, the vast open horizons of sky and water, which give to people in tall buildings on the coast the sense of being able to see almost to the ends of the world. The great painterly sunrises and sunsets, which occur east and west of the Tower, were a daily intoxication. Every morning she stood out on the balcony, and as the breeze whispered over the character lines and wrinkles in her face, ruffling her mop of blond hair, she held her cigarette and stared in avid blue-eyed plea-

sure all around her, at the towering layers of darkly luminous clouds
not yet thinned toward evaporation by the sun, at the boats and ships
and islands in the glittering mist-wreathed bay, at the legs of the
morning runners dancing down the shadowed boulevard below—
and three miles to the north, the city of Tampa, shining copper and
platinum in the orange morning light. This was the Gulf Coast,
where the Toronto Blue Jays, certain butterflies, mallards and pintail
ducks, and various economic and social classes of people all spend
the winter, and where septuagenarians, octogenarians, and nonage-
narians with an eye to the future looked for their very last home.

"I am *so* lucky to be here!" the Sweetso roared in satisfaction, her
voice gravelly and tobacco-cured, arms outflung. She did not exactly mean with me.

I am not her boyfriend—although she had one, sort of. I'm not really a resident of Canterbury. I don't qualify. I'm not sixty-two,
the minimum age for admission. Most people at Canterbury, of
course, are a lot older than that. Many of them were born before
passenger airplanes, or indoor plumbing, or electricity in their houses.
Almost all were born before air-conditioning and television at
home. Most of them were citizens before women had the vote.
Many, if not most, were born *in* their houses, at times and in places
where births occurred at home. There are men and women at Canterbury born when most of the world was still ruled by kings, queens,
and emperors. There was a woman born before the manufacture of
automobiles and radios; before Florida became a tourist state; before
Teddy Roosevelt and the rest of the U.S. Army Expeditionary Force
embarked from Tampa to invade and conquer Cuba, in 1898; after
the battleship *Maine,* only three years old, blew up and sank in Havana harbor—igniting the Spanish-American War. That is seriously,
culturally, politically *old*.

But I liked it. I felt at home there, almost like a boy again, and I
found that waking and sleeping in the apartment I had rented
nearby—the bottom half of an old frame duplex, nestled in some
trees a block off the Bayshore—made me feel oddly separated from

the life that drew me to Canterbury. For a year, since first suggesting it early in 2000, Martha Sweet had made it clear that I was welcome to stay in her spare bedroom and bath.

"I rarely have use for it," she said, shrugging. "You could come and go as you please. I'd be glad for the company."

"Oh no. Thank you. I can't do that," I said.

But I was intrigued. She was good company—smart, funny, totally candid, a keen observer with an irreverent take on her own stage of life. Every so often, as we talked over lunch or dinner, or occasionally breakfast, she repeated the offer. "Why not?" she said.

After almost a year, I thought, *Well, why not? She volunteered. It costs her nothing more if I stay there, and if I do, I can live the life of Canterbury.*

She asked only that I spell her name right. "Oh, and make me tall, thin, and blond," she said laughing. Well, she's blond. I call her the Sweetso. I can do that because she has a sense of humor. And because Charles, the Marine, the Judge, the big, blunt grump, is dead. I think she wanted to have a man around again. Someone to talk to. The Sweetso talks thoughtfully, amusingly, unendingly—mostly about Charles, and their life together. Listening is the rent I pay.

I would have liked him, Martha says. He would have liked me.

I'm not so sure about that last part. But I think I would have liked him. And I'm damn sure I wouldn't have wanted to live with him. Lastly and mostly, however, I call his widow the Sweetso because—for all her tart, blustering, witty, literate, profane, grumpy, and opinionated ways—she is, underneath it all, sweet. But tidy. Oh yes. Tidy.

She sometimes calls me "darling." I kind of like it. But then, she calls a lot of people darling. More often, she calls me something that more resembles *Ahem.* Not the word, exactly. More like the slight clearing-of-the-throat sound a person makes just prior to asking a disapproving question.

As in, "*Ahem.* Do you know anything about these shoes on my living room couch?" Or "*Ahem,* were you planning to do something with that pile of newspapers on the dining room table?" Or

"*Ahem*, I don't suppose you would know what all these Styrofoam boxes with congealed disgusting leftover food in them are doing in my refrigerator. *Do you?*"

Ooops, I say. Sorry, I say. Forgot. Can't help it. I was born that way, I say. But I am getting better, I tell her. I may get neat before I die. Some slobs do. I also might get rich. I think I'd rather be rich.

More than the litter I create, we talk about important things— politics, love, art, literature, history, relationships, our children, our finances, our sex lives, our divorces, the economy, our health, religion. About the differences between the values of her generation and mine. Between her generation and the one before. Between Republicans and Democrats. Liberals and conservatives. Gay men and straight ones. Between people who have loved and people who have not. Between people who have married and people who have not. Between people who read books and people who do not. Between people who have children and people who do not.

Often, one subject overlaps another. "I told my kids," she said one day, with a grumpy set to her jaw, "that if they bitch anymore about my smoking, I'm cutting them out of my will."

For years, after discovering the existence of a Seminole Indian reservation across town—on which the Indians had established a drive-in, tax-free, cigarettes-by-the-carton business—the Sweetso bought all her cigarettes there. Owing to a three-carton limit per person, Martha always brought a nonsmoking friend with her. When they drove up to the window of the cigarette shack, Martha paid for six cartons for the two of them, and drove off. Then the friend would take the wheel, drive back to the window, and hand over some more of Martha's money for six more cartons of cigarettes. Eventually, however, the Sweetso wearied of driving across town. She quit doing it when she discovered that she could order in bulk from Brown & Williamson for twenty dollars a carton. Now she gets six at a time by mail. She says they last about six weeks. I think they go faster. There's a lot of smoke in 1501.

"You know," she said, telling the story, "I have never once—in all the years I went there—seen an Indian."

It is a contrarian experience, having these conversations across generational and gender lines. But then the Sweetso is a contrary woman.

"I am in *much* better shape than you," she will say, her blue eyes squinting at me appraisingly through her cloud of cigarette smoke. This from a woman of almost seventy-three, whose favorite food group is starch, whose favorite nonsexual exercise is turning the pages of the large books she is always reading curled up in her corner of the soft leather couch, and whose nightly before-bed snack is a bowl of Belgian chocolate ice cream.

"You *wish*," I say.

I, who go to gyms in Baltimore and Tampa. I, who gave up cigarettes at forty-two, alcohol and women in bed at forty-four. I, who love fruit and salads and spinach and protein shakes; I, who spurn all junk food except fried chicken, barbecued ribs, desserts two or three times a day, and free Belgian chocolate ice cream at 11:30 p.m. That is just before the Jay Leno monologue—which we watch, laughing and eating Belgian chocolate ice cream as we lounge on her pillowed leather couches, and then turn in. (*Oh well,* I think. *Why make her eat a dish alone?*)

The days of 2001 have come to have a certain structure. They begin with the coffeepot, the solemn lawyer, the drifting cigarette smoke, and the brief, evaporating appearance of Martha Stewart, followed by a greenish protein shake (mine), four slices of buttered raisin toast (ours), and the first blood-sugar-level test of the day (hers—the Sweetso is diabetic).

Oh well, I think, munching and beginning to scribble as she talks. *What harm can some raisin toast do?*

There is no full breakfast unless I have a breakfast date, or unless I drop downstairs to get some milk and orange juice for the protein shake, and succumb to the charms of Chanh. "You wan sit down?" she asks, with her serious face, pointing to a vacant table. "You wan bagan? Scrambal eggs? Toes?"

Canterbury has very good bacon. Warm. Crunchy. Kissed by grease.

Oh well, I think sometimes. *Why not? I never have breakfast at home. Besides, I haven't talked to that person sitting over there.* The same thing happens at lunch and dinner. It's like being on a cruise ship. You eat your way through the day. "It's terrible," Sarah Jane says, one evening at dinner. "We were all raised in the Depression. So we hate to waste anything. Besides, we've already paid for these meals. I've gained twelve pounds!"

There is no morning newspaper at the Sweetso's. (It was Charles who devoured newspapers. She grazes on books and television.) So I have a choice. I can rummage for a copy of the *Tampa Tribune* or the *St. Petersburg Times* from the trash room down the hall. (Everyone at Canterbury is tidy as hell. The wire basket is deep in papers by 9:00 a.m.) Or wait for Martha Cameron, five floors below, to finish her *New York Times* so I can borrow it. Or get in the car and go buy one.

This is when the day begins to get complicated. I have to decide whether (*a*) to go walk the Bayshore, or go to the gym to wear off last night's ice cream and this morning's breakfast; (*b*) to go find the *Times* and then try to read it while the Sweetso keeps talking to me; or (*c*) to give up on being fit and informed, and just stay in the apartment, talking to her. After all, I am there to live the life. Besides, pretty soon I have to go to see Mother.

There are basically two good times a day to do that: late morning (after she is woken, changed, bathed, dressed, fed, and taken to the morning recreation, therapy, or music hour, but before lunch) and late afternoon (after lunch, her nap, and being woken, changed, bathed, re-dressed, and placed in her chair again). Mother was almost always fresher in the morning. But she had also been generally better lately—more aware and focused—since she'd been off the medications. On good days, she seemed relaxed and more alert, the way she was a year or so ago. It was nice. It made me feel almost as if I had my mother back.

On a breezy, bright green, cheerful morning late in January, I took her out on the porch after breakfast. It had become our routine. I would hold her hand and talk. She would look at me, grind

her teeth, and seem happy. Talk, grind. Smile, talk, grind. Smile—as
if we were having a leisurely conversation, with the traffic passing
on the boulevard outside as accompaniment in the background:
Whiz. Whoosh. Whoosh. Whiz.

Her moving hand, I noticed, was encased in the heavy cotton
gardening glove I had bought at the hardware store some months
before. If the nurse's aide had put it on, Mother must be scratching
again. And for the first time, as we looked at each other, I noticed a
continual slight movement of her eyes back and forth, left to right,
almost at the rate of a slow heartbeat. Something had changed.

Everyone, in fact, seemed just a little different as the New Year
began. Lucie Cross had broken the big bone in her arm—the left
arm this time. She had it in a sling and was trying to be careful, because she was booked to leave on another cruise from Tampa down
through the Panama Canal. This time, she hoped, with her new
pacemaker, she wouldn't have a heart attack on the boat. Last time,
she said, "They wanted to put me off in Costa Rica."

Her blue eyes were fierce. "I said, 'You can throw me *overboard*
before I'll get off this ship.'"

At lunch in the dining room, Mary Davis and Judy Drake, who
had known each other since the third grade, eighty years before, sat
discussing alcohol and their noses. Mary had a glass of wine and
looked cheerful. The case of whiskey that Wilber packed because it
was "too good to drink," she reported, was all gone.

"After he went to the Health Center," she said, "I used it *all* up!"
She seemed very pleased. Happier than before.

Judy, the pale tiny Episcopalian with large eyeglasses and a silver ponytail, had given up drinking years ago. She sat looking
wanly at Mary, dabbing a tissue at her nose. Everything made her
nose drip now.

"That's why I don't drink alcohol anymore," she said. Dab, dab.
"One of my daughters said, 'Mother, you'd seem a lot more interesting if you'd say you don't drink because you're a recovering alcoholic than because your nose drips.'" She sighed. "But I have to
carry a Kleenex all the time—especially at the communion rail."

"So she duzzen *drip* inta thuh communion wine," Mary said helpfully, with a big smile.

Judy nodded and dabbed. "It runs *all* the time," she observed. "Soon as I put anything into my mouth. Even a toothbrush."

Back in the apartment, the Sweetso seemed preoccupied. She was sitting in one of the swivel chairs at the heavy, wine-red vinyl dining table, chin in hand, staring up at the Charles shrine. She looked glum. This time of year, when it's too chilly outside to do her afternoon exercises in the pool, she gets grumpy. But she was pondering. Her daughter, Meredith, in New York—the child of her first marriage, and a chip off the Martha block—was trying to get her to loosen her grip on Charles, who had now been dead almost eighteen months.

"Take down the goddamn shrine, Mother," Meredith had said on the phone.

There was also, on the Atlantic coast of Florida, the issue of Mario, the would-be boyfriend. Every few weeks now, for several months—ever since their erotic weekend on the east coast—he had been coming to Tampa to see Martha. Each time, he took her to Bern's Steak House for dinner, and then they came back to Canterbury and went to bed. The next day, he drove back home. Now he wanted to take her to Brazil.

"He called and asked me if I wanted to go to Brazil for a *month*," the Sweetso said, her face a mask of bewilderment, "and I said, 'Are you out of your mind? Why would I want to go to Brazil for a month?' "

That had seemed to discourage him.

Her daughter weighed in. "Mother, why didn't you say, 'A month is way too long—but I could come for a week'?" Meredith scolded. (We children are so much smarter about these things.)

"Well, because I didn't think of it," the Sweetso replied. She shook her head and rolled her eyes. *Dumb me,* the expression said.

But the real reason she didn't want to go away to Brazil with the would-be boyfriend is that she didn't want to have to think of creating a new life—one that might take her away from Canterbury. This was her life now, she said, this building, and what's inside it.

"When you get to be my age, isn't this just what you want— friends and activities, and people to take care of you who aren't your friends?"

Every morning, out on the balcony, smoking one of her endless mail-order cigarettes, the Sweetso gave pagan thanks for Canterbury, for the life she has here, and for the chance to die in a place that—however different and far away it may be—reminded her of her childhood, a time that seemed somehow increasingly near.

"I grew up in a little town in southwest Pennsylvania called Charleroi, on the Monongahela River," she said, her eyes distant, seeing again what she saw then. "I could look out the window and see the water. And I kind of want to die the way I lived—looking at the water."

CHAPTER SIXTEEN

When They Were Children

JANUARY 2001

Ever wondered why I'm peculiar?" the Emyfish asked one day over a bowl of fresh, chilled, chunky gazpacho at 42nd Street Bistro. The ceiling fans were whirring, and high up, all around, were murals of Broadway scenes. The restaurant was her preferred out-of-the-Tower spot for lunch. But the question surprised me. I had never thought of her as peculiar. She just seemed like Auntie Mame to me. She had played the role in Little Theater, in the decades before there was anything else in Tampa. There was a portrait of her as Mame on her living room wall, with a cigarette holder and feather boa. It sort of matched her personality, which was arch and opinionated, in a funny, privileged, don't-fuck-with-me sort of way.

"Emy will only do what Emy wants to do," the Sweetso observed, between blissful bites of eggs Benedict, her favorite breakfast, one bright, mild Sunday morning in January. "You can't shove her into doing things she doesn't want to do. She doesn't shove. I just adore her," she said. "You always know *right* where you stand with her."

The Emyfish was different in that way from southern women such as my mother and Sarah Jane Rubio, who were brought up to please. They were tough in their way, but elaborately complimentary and polite. The Emyfish, however, was raised mainly in New York. She expected to *be* pleased—and she said what she thought.

"I don't know why people are polite," she told me once, as if it was a mystery to her. "I really don't."

It was only after she began talking about her childhood a little, for the first time I could remember, that I realized something. She, like the Sweetso growing up on the Monongahela—perhaps like all the old people in Canterbury—were still shaped by what had happened to them when they were young, seventy or eighty or ninety years ago. *Well, of course they were.* Why wouldn't they be? But I had never seen pictures of my parents as children, or of the Emyfish, or Mary and Wilber, or the Sweetso—or of the world they had inhabited as children. Perhaps they didn't have pictures, or lost them, or just didn't care about showing them. I had never heard them talk about that time either. I had no idea what growing up was like for them. I didn't think of them as ever having been children.

When people talk about childhood, their stories are often illuminated by events and pictures of the era in which they were young. The horses. The stable. The first car. The outhouse. Gas lamps. The ice box. The brother who died in the First World War. A popular song. A Broadway show. The first dress. The president on the radio. They make a visual calendar of the time. But not the Emyfish. She never spoke of what else was happening when she was a child, because that might give away her age. She never spoke about growing up in a way that connected it to time or events. But it was clearly a childhood that she remembered and that was still alive to her, even as she tried to repress and edit it, because it began to emerge as we spent more time together: a story at lunch, another over drinks or dinner, something mentioned in the car.

Her parents had hired a nurse to care for her when she was a baby, a sturdy young German girl with plump pink cheeks whom Emy adored and called Dodo, who stayed on and became her nanny and protector through most of her childhood. (There must have been a tradition of young German nannies in New York, along with Dodo as a nickname. It was what Gloria Vanderbilt called her nanny, too.) Much later on, there was a black houseman and chauffeur named Nat, and the family bulldog, Bourbon. Emy's father, Jules Winston, whom everyone called Punk, was apparently a man of twinkle and charm, and a certain eccentric pizzazz. He wore a gold signet ring, drank gin martinis from a cocktail shaker, and smoked unfiltered cigarettes that he took from an engraved sterling silver case on formal evenings. He also played Broadway show tunes on the piano, and painted little landscapes in watercolors. But hers was a childhood rich—or different—in other ways, too.

It was split between New York and Tampa at different times of year, and the Emyfish had respiratory ailments when she was little. "When I moved north, I got the mustard plasters. And when I moved south, I got the goose grease. It was also very good on rye bread," she recalled, her musical chuckle welling up at the memory, "seasoned with garlic."

She was a privileged only child and grandchild, and life with her mother, Jessie Maas Winston, sometimes had a fairy-tale quality. When they went together into Manhattan, to buy for her grandparents' department store, Maas Bros., in Tampa, her mother might order eight dresses for herself as well, and six for Emy. Indulged by her parents, loved by Dodo, she sometimes felt like a princess. But her mother's personality was changeable, and she could be cruel.

"My, you're really an ugly little thing, aren't you?" Jessie Winston said one night when Emy was about twelve, an awkward age, especially for a plump girl. That is the Emyfish's memory, and it has lasted all these years. Dodo, her protector, was gone. Her mother had walked into her bedroom after dinner. It was the hour when a parent tucks a child in, talks quietly, kisses her, and says good night. But her mother just stood there, staring coldly down at Emy, as if she were eyeing some piece of clothing that had been brought out for her inspection, and that she was about to send back. Then she made the cutting comment, turned, and walked out.

Miss Jessie, as the servants and Emy's friends called her, was later diagnosed as a manic-depressive. She had shock treatments as she got older, but they did no good. She just got worse. And the knife stayed in.

Helen Hogan Hill, who was living happily in 502 when the Emyfish and Ashby first moved into 504 at Canterbury, had a very different mother and father and childhood from what Emy had—as different as middle Georgia was from New York City. But it had made her assertive, too, in a more southern kind of way. And she didn't mind talking about it. She had begun to be proud of being so old.

Helen was born in 1905 on her parents' plantation near Fayetteville, Georgia, a cotton farm of two thousand acres, part of which predated the Civil War. She was a curious, observant little girl, and in her world nature prevailed. If the rain and sun and temperature cooperated, the crops were good. Men rode horses. They hunted squirrels and possums, which in Helen's house were roasted with sweet potatoes in the oven of the big, wood-burning Majestic range in the kitchen. Her father's tenants worked the land with mules and plows. Water came from streams and wells, light from wood fires or kerosene lamps, and news from newspapers that arrived by mail from Atlanta—several days old. There was no radio. Children learned in a wood-floored, one-room schoolhouse, and the mailman—like Helen's mother, known as Miss Bouncie, and Dr. Camp, the local physician—drove a horse and buggy. The mailman, the doctor, and an occasional peddler with his cart were the only visitors who clip-clopped up the unpaved road from the world beyond, to stop at the old frame house. It was two rooms on either side of a central hall, with a kitchen, dining room, and porch across the back. The tenants' shacks were down the road. Behind the house were five hundred acres of untamed woods and marsh, which held deer and fox, birds and possum, moonshiners and moonshine stills. And danger.

Helen's father, who had taught her not to cower in the house when lightning flashed but to walk down off the back porch into the storm at night—to prove to the lightning that she was not afraid, and to herself that lightning did not strike brave little girls, but lit the night so she could see—forgot some rule of the gun one day, and shot himself to death climbing a fence while hunting in the woods. She was four years old. It was an accident. That was the decision of the sheriff and coroner after his body was found and they investigated. Not suicide, they said. Or murder. That is Helen's memory. But after that, it was her mother, a young new widow with only a grade-school education, who had to keep the books and run the farm, overseeing the planting and the harvesting, supplying and paying the seven or eight tenant families. All Miss Bouncie had known of the farm's business before was the little money she got from selling butter and eggs and, occasionally, turkeys and goose feathers. But she learned soon enough. Each week, on Friday, she drove into Fayetteville in her buggy to get money from the bank. Each week, when she got home, she put the money in the family Bible. On Saturday, as Helen sat beside her mother at the desk on the porch, the tenants lined up to be paid for what they had done that week.

It was plantation life, secure in its rhythms, but also lonely—and not safe. Their mother kept a low-burning lamp lit at night if she felt uneasy. When three men who had passed by on the road several times one day crossed the fence in their horse and buggy and rode up to the front porch of the house at almost midnight, she woke Helen's twelve-year-old brother, Billy, and told him to fetch and load the double-barreled shotgun—the one his father had killed himself with.

"You cock the gun. You stand there and hold it," Miss Bouncie said. Then she stepped out onto the porch.

"You take one more step," she told the men, "this gun is trained on you. And he will pull the trigger." Sitting in their buggy in the darkness, the three men looked at her a moment, and then the driver flicked the reins. They turned and drove away.

After four more years—after Helen had cut the end off her curious right index finger by sticking it into the cider mill, after she and Billy survived a case of measles that killed the neighbor from whom they got it (and after her mother was forced to take her first ride in an automobile when an ambulance came from Atlanta to take her back to a hospital, thus saving her life from the blood infection that had swollen and blackened her right leg)—Miss Bouncie sold the farm and moved her children into town. But from family and country life, Helen had learned the importance of being self-reliant, of making decisions for yourself, in times when you are alone. Women had few choices other than marriage then. She finished school and a degree in home economics, but the only job she could find at first was teaching a roomful of first and second graders in the small town of Mansfield, Georgia. She boarded with the family of a member of the school board. It was not joyful.

"I spent the daytimes teaching, and the nighttimes on my knees praying that it wouldn't go on much longer," she said. It didn't. At the end of the year, she found a job as a home economist, teaching poor mountain women in north Georgia how to bake angel food cake in wood-burning stoves, and to can fruits and vegetables from their gardens in order to get through the winter. She drove the rocky dirt mountain roads in her own car, a Ford that her mother, by then a convert to the wonders of internal combustion, had bought for her.

She was only twenty years old. One day her boss, the county ordinary, called her in.

"I want to ask you to do something," he said.

"Well, what?" Helen said.

"I want you to start carrying a gun, and I want it to be known." Helen was floored. *"Why?"* she asked.

"You're young and pretty and you're driving through the mountains alone," he said, his eyes serious. "I've heard someone might try to stop you. You don't have to keep it loaded if you don't want— but let people see that you have it."

Her mother let her have a revolver, and Helen loaded it and began carrying it. Months went by, and she received a more specific warning. The postmaster pulled Helen aside one morning when she came in to check for mail, and told her he had overheard some of the local boys planning to ambush her on the road back from a dance in the next town that Saturday night.

They did, Helen remembered. They jumped from the shadows, from both sides of a narrow dark place in the road, going uphill, some of them in front, trying to block her. But she didn't brake. She aimed the Ford right at one of them and gunned it. He jumped back. She barely missed him. The others scattered, and she got away.

The next day, in town, she saw the boy who had been in her headlamps.

"You near ran over me last night," he said, giving her a mean, scared look. She stared straight back at him.

"You try it again"—she smiled—"*and I'll be faster.*"

Helen married and divorced, settled in Marietta, Georgia, north of Atlanta, worked for decades as director of food services for the county schools to take care of herself and her two boys, and then, pretty late in life, married a nice man who died not long after.

"I didn't get to know him long enough," she said softly.

But she kept her spirit. And so, when a friend in Marietta asked why she didn't just marry again, instead of selling her house and leaving the state where she'd always lived to move to Tampa, to a place called Canterbury Tower, Helen answered her the same way she had the boy she'd almost run down more than fifty years before.

"Because I'd rather be a widow than wish I were one," she said, giving her friend a level smile. She couldn't trust in fate or husbands, she had learned. She had to trust herself.

A cross the Atlantic, at just about the time that Miss Bouncie, Helen, and Billy left the farm and the lurking moonshiners, and moved into town, a little boy and his mother were walking down a street in Stuttgart, the capital of Württemberg, a German kingdom that has long since vanished. They slowed, and the boy felt himself being tugged gently to the side. His mother had recognized the bearded older man walking toward them with two poodles. It was 1913.

"Look, Karl," she said, leaning down, "*it's the king.*"

Karl Richter stared. He was just three years old. A solemn, precocious little boy, interested in everything, he was at the sunny age of childhood, innocent of the complex, unresolved history of the region in which he lived, the horrors that awaited him, or the fact that the education he would begin in a classic Latin school in three more years was a privilege of access only recently granted by the government to Jews. So tenderhearted that he carefully unstuck flies from flypaper, it was just as well that Karl was too young to sense the political tensions growing again in central Europe, which would shortly explode and bring the whole ancient, unwieldy, incompetent structure of government down. The boy knew some things, though. He knew he lived in a kingdom, with a king. He knew where the king lived, in a castle of some 360 rooms in the park, in the center of the lovely old city, with a promenade where people walked all day. He knew, from listening to his great-grandfather, the pride of the family—who was amazingly old, 106 even then—that there had once been a French emperor named Napoleon, who had conquered all of that region but whose great army had been destroyed by the Russians and the Russian winter. Karl's great-grandfather, born in 1807, had seen the pitiful remnants of that army, shrunken and ragged and pale, dragging back toward Paris in 1812, when he was a little boy like Karl.

Many of the small kingdoms, principalities, and duchies in that part of Europe had been created by Napoleon. The strategic creations of conquering ambition, imperial ego, and war, brought into being by the stroke of a pen, they would disappear from the map just as quickly, for the same reasons—and soon. This was the twilight. Karl's father, a reservist in the army, would shortly go to war, fighting on the Russian and Italian fronts for the German kaiser, Wilhelm II. He was luckier than many. He would eventually return. But in five more years, the Austro-Hungarian, German, and Russian emperors would all be gone, along with the complicated presumptions and security arrangements of the world into which Karl had been born.

In the moment that his mother smiled and whispered into his ear, however, that day and that part of the old city of Stuttgart were bright and beautiful, and the elegant whiskered man approaching them was the kindly, mythic, central figure of the world the little boy knew. He was also frequently visible on the streets, a popular icon.

"Hello, Mr. King!" Karl piped, smiling up at the man whose throne would dissolve in the Great War about to begin.

He was a little boy whose ancient world of castles and kings was about to change, affecting him in ways that neither he nor anyone could imagine then. His sister would die, struck down by an automobile on the street. His father would put on a uniform, go off to war, and disappear for years, while Karl began to go to school and learn. He was a funny little boy but an ideal pupil, scholarly and deeply serious about his studies, even when he was young. When Karl's father finally came home, haggard, proud of his service, if not of the war, he returned feeling himself a German. For a Jew to feel himself a proven patriot, a countryman like other men of his country—even in defeat—was enormously reassuring.

But the political culture had collapsed. The economy was in ruins. The postwar decade of the 1920s in Germany would be volatile—radical and liberating and then regressive—as a runaway inflation destroyed the value of money and everything else, making the population angry and frantic, feeding a Fascist movement on the rise. The bright, serious little boy would become an idealistic, brilliant young man, a Jewish rabbi, graduated from the best seminary to begin his work just as the new Nazi Germany condemned him for what he was. His parents would have to leave, emigrating to Tel Aviv. His maternal grandmother, two uncles, and many other members of his family would be murdered. He would almost not survive the country that Germany would next become.

L ike Helen Hill—indeed, like most of the population of the United States in the decade before World War I—Lucie Cross lived as a child in the country, but in the Northeast. She grew up on an old apple farm in New Jersey. Her father was an undertaker. He prepared bodies for burial in the basement of the old farmhouse where they lived. Lucie hated coming home from school when there were dead people in the basement. And then, in 1917, just as she reached the awkward age, the United States entered the war, and her older brother, John, went off to fight in France.

At first he wrote to them. And then he ceased to write—and disappeared. Every day, Lucie's mother pored over the casualty list in the newspapers, but John's name was never on it. They had no report, no explanation, no way to inquire. They didn't know that he was alive but horribly injured.

"He had volunteered to take a message to the front," Lucie said, sitting in the dining room at Canterbury with lunch in front of her—a plate of tomatoes, a peach, a little mound of cottage cheese, a deviled egg. Outside the dining room windows, the winter day was as bright and crisp and vivid as the food on her plate. But Lucie was imagining again a bleak, cold, misty day, blasted and dangerous, far away.

"He had to crawl under barbed wire through a field. The field was saturated with mustard gas. He was burned over his entire body," she said. She and her parents had no way to know that. They had no idea whether John was dead or alive, injured or well. Or where. They couldn't understand, if something was wrong, why no message had been sent. Finally, after almost four months, a nurse cabled from a military hospital in Germany.

"She said, 'Your son is here,'" Lucie remembered. "'Today, for the first time, he has seen light. He has been blind. If he was blind, he was never going to tell you. He was going to let you think that he was dead.'" It was several more months before John was brought home. His skin was scarred, his sight and lungs and hearing affected. He was prone to infections. He would not have a long or healthy life.

Lucie's face was hard. She blinked, looked down, and spooned some sugar on her tomatoes. "Yankee custom," she said curtly, stabbing a fork at her plate.

Tough stories, most of them—even the stories of how the Sweetso and Charles grew up. Charles's father was a medieval scholar, a professor at Washington & Jefferson College, not far from Pittsburgh, Pennsylvania. His attitude about child rearing had been shaped by *his* father, the grandfather for whom Charles was named, the sternly formidable Episcopal bishop of Japan. When Charles's father was twelve—in 1902, before the opening of the Panama Canal in 1914 shortened such journeys—Bishop Sweet and his wife put the boy on a ship that took him all the way from Japan, across the Pacific, around South America, and up the Atlantic coast to a boarding school in Maine.

"He did not see his parents again until he had graduated from college," the Sweetso said, her blue eyes angry at the very thought of it. Ten years. "He was *twenty-two years old!*

"That was Charles's father. So he was a very serious man—serious as a scholar, serious as a churchman. When Charles was a boy, his parents would sit at the table on Sunday after church, a tablet in front of them. And they would write down everything he had done wrong all week. And they'd sit there, and they'd say, 'Well—now God gave us this child, and we must say something good about it.' They'd try really hard to think of something good, and finally they would decide—'Well, he's dog loving.' So they would write that on the other side. It was *that* bad."

The Sweetso was luckier, in a way. Martha loved her father, Ralph Gossard. She thought he was wonderful. But he was not the man who had fathered her. Her actual parents had been rich in children—but poor in fact. She was the newest and, being sickly, would be the most expensive to care for. When she was still a baby, in 1928, her grandfather, the patriarch of her German American family (and apparently a stern autocrat, much like Charles's grandfather), proposed that her parents give her to an aunt and uncle who were childless—but successful. They could afford Martha. They would love and raise her. They could also afford to give some money to her birth parents. And that is what was done.

"I was sold for thirty pieces of silver," the Sweetso said, staring through a plume of cigarette smoke at nothing in particular.

She ever after had conflicted feelings, resentful at being bartered, but also crazy about her adoptive father—a big, warm, outgoing, capable man. He was an electrical engineer who sat down each evening at the upright piano in the bay window of the dining room at home, and played for an hour after dinner. The neighbors brought chairs and sat outside, listening. Ralph Gossard taught Martha how to swim at the family's house on a lake in the summers, and showered her with affection.

It was his wife, Inez—Martha's adoptive mother, a cold, Germanic personality, a disciplinarian and perfectionist like the grandfather—who made the Sweetso feel unloved. Inez Gossard showed no affection. At least Martha felt none. She seemed to have no desire or need for closeness. But she did seem driven to correct all the flaws and mistakes in the world around her, most especially her adoptive daughter's. Or so it seemed to Martha.

"*I wish I was dead!*" Martha yelled once, in a pubescent fury at being so picked on.

"*Were,* Martha," Inez corrected, looking at her coolly. "*Were.*"

I t wasn't easy being a girl. In a silver frame, on a table just inside the door of Martha Cameron's apartment at Canterbury, is a faded photograph of a serious young woman in a quiet, almost romantic pose. There is something affecting about her. She was the aunt who killed herself by drinking bleach. It may have been the only thing she had at hand that she knew to be poison.

"Awful," Martha said, sitting on her couch, looking grimly at the ghostly image.

Hard to imagine someone doing that—or to conceive of what bleach would do to soft esophageal and stomach and intestinal tissue. Her aunt was pregnant, Martha guessed, though she couldn't be sure. Families didn't talk about such things to children then. But she was apparently driven by a terrible self-judgment, and had no one to talk to, no one to give her sympathy, or understanding, or other choices. The state of medicine—particularly the new fields of psychiatry and psychology—was primitive then. Martha was born two months before the end of the Great War, in September 1918, so it would have been in the early or mid-1920s that her aunt died such a terrible death. It was a time of peace—but still, a period of extravagant waste of life.

"Children died right and left," Martha said, her face reflective, remembering. "In my third-grade class, this little girl we all liked got sick, and the next thing we heard, she died. I got double pneumonia," she added, looking thoughtful, "and almost died."

If she closed her eyes, Martha could still revisit the out-of-body experience she had at the time. It was the sort of vision people are reputed to have in the moment of passage. She was floating upward, free and peaceful, like a soul, looking down on her own slack, fevered, semiconscious young body, which was lying under an oxygen tent, burning with a temperature of 106. There was a vase of red roses on a table by her side. In the next hour, Martha's temperature fell dramatically. Her soul returned to her body, and she survived.

A year later, she got appendicitis. When her father took her to be examined by the school physician, he told her she was getting her period. The next day, her appendix burst. She almost died again.

But Martha didn't have the luxury of worrying about herself. There was her mother's cancer to contend with. And before that— every day from the day of Martha's birth until the day her mother, Vashti (actually, Martha Vashti, but she was always called Vashti), finally gave up and put her daughter Anne in an institution in New Jersey when Martha was twelve—there was her older sister. Anne had been born with cerebral palsy. She could only laugh and cry. Everything else had to be done for her, by Martha and her mother, and her mother gave Anne up only after getting cancer and her doctor insisted on it.

"Mother thought it was a disgrace to put a child away," Martha said solemnly. Vashti had been determined to keep Anne. She was resourceful. She did beautiful needlework, constantly hand-embroidering linen handkerchiefs, smoothing and working the fabric on Anne's back as she held her, selling the elegant handkerchiefs for $1.25 each—even in the Depression—to wealthy women. But Vashti was a long way from home, and she was not a happy woman. She had married Earle Cameron, from Nova Scotia, who became a manager in a DuPont factory in New Jersey that made insoles for men's shoes. Vashti was from a large, prominent business and political family in Columbus, Georgia, the Murrahs, a vastly different background. She was always homesick in Arlington, New Jersey, where she lived near the factory with her husband, and Martha and Anne.

"So we were on the train going back and forth all the time," Martha said, traveling from the North, where they lived, to the South her mother missed. It took two nights by rail from Newark to Columbus. They traveled in a drawing room, the largest Pullman compartment, for space and privacy, because they had to take Anne with them, in her specially built carriage. Anne had beautiful dark brown hair and eyes, Martha said, and delicate pale skin, but her body was limp and atrophied, and Vashti couldn't stand the way people stared at her if they rode in coach.

In Columbus, in Uncle John's big house, with family and servants to help, Vashti was happier. She and her children sometimes stayed for months. But eventually, always, they had to go back to New Jersey, and then the fights between Vashti and Earle would start. "They never did get along perfectly, so I grew up hearing lots of arguments," Martha said. Sometimes they embroiled her in ways she did not understand.

"My father never really related to me at all," she said. But there was a woman in his office at the factory, a sophisticated woman—who smoked and laughed and was charming—who did. She took an interest. Martha went to the plant one day with her father. He was going to take her with him on an overnight business trip to Boston, leaving by steamer that afternoon. While her father worked in his office, the woman took Martha to lunch. "She was so nice and smiling and gracious," Martha said. Then she went with her father to Boston. He took her to Bunker Hill. "We saw all the sights. Had a lovely time." But when Martha and her father got home, her mother was furious. Martha never knew why. But Vashti—isolated as she was by having to care for Anne—and trapped in that role by herself for two days while her husband and helpful younger daughter were gone to Boston, somehow knew or sensed the attentions of the woman in Earle's office. It put her in a rage, and she took it out on Martha.

Her mother had one of the early sets of plastic brushes and combs made by DuPont, Martha remembered. "She took me upstairs and spanked me with that hairbrush. And then she made me go to the head of the stairs and yell down to my father, *'I hate you!'*"

Martha Cameron sat in her living room at Canterbury, a handsome, full-bodied, now gravely beautiful woman, recalling that day more than seventy years before. "That was the only real bad one," she said quietly. "I just didn't let it bother me. If anything, I became very shy."

The shy girl absorbed other lessons, too, lessons about female beauty and appearance, and about men, which she learned from Vashti and which stayed with her for decades, generations, after her mother died. We were sitting outside at lunch one day in Tampa, on an old brick street that had grown fashionable as a restaurant row, when a skinny young thing in a high tiny blouse and low-hugging jeans sauntered by—abdomen, navel, rib, and hip bones all swiveling, exposed to the air. Teenaged girls and twentysomethings all seemed to dress like this. Tightly half dressed. Available to the eye.

"So many *small* women, today," Martha said, her nurse's eyes appraising the saucy stick figure passing by. "There weren't any small women when I was young. People hid their skinniness. People worried about their babies if they were too skinny."

She had gone through a period of being skinny, but Vashti made her eat. Skinny wasn't considered healthy. It may have been because of the Depression, the bread lines, so many people without enough to eat.

"Growing up, young girls were afraid," Martha said, watching the stick figure disappear down the sidewalk. "One of the things they were afraid of was that on their wedding night, when her husband took off all her clothes, he would find out she was skinny."

CHAPTER SEVENTEEN

When They Were in Love

FEBRUARY 2001

Mary was not skinny. She was full breasted, sunny, and flirta-tious, and she was standing one morning in 1933 on the corner of Bayshore Boulevard just six blocks south of where Canterbury is now, when Wilber, driving past in his red Chevrolet Cabriolet, saw her, wheeled around, and stopped. Mary was waiting in a light cotton dress for the trolley to take her to town, to the merchants' association, where she had found a job in the collection department, at a desk under a ceiling fan. Filing notes of what people said when they were called and asked to pay their bills. Gas bills. Food bills. Store bills. She was just eighteen years old, but it was the middle of the Depression, and girls like her needed to work.

Her uncle Willie had lost his clothing store downtown, and with it had gone her father's job. Even the almost-new Henry B. Plant High School, named for the railroad baron who had built the silver-minareted Tampa Bay Hotel half a century before, had to close its doors, just five months into Mary's senior year. There was no more money to pay the teachers. Mary couldn't go up to Tallahassee in the fall either, to the Florida Seminary for Women (now Florida State University). The seminary had agreed to take the girls from her class who could afford the tuition—girls from families like the Garcias and the Cuestas, who owned cigar factories—even though their high school credits were incomplete. But Mary's family didn't have the money to send her.

She didn't mind so much being left behind. There were plenty of others who were. But it bothered her when she didn't have the seventy-five cents for admission to the tea dances on Saturday afternoons on the roof terrace of the Bayshore Royal Hotel—the one tall building that had been built on the boulevard before the boom collapsed in 1926. Mary hadn't cared about college. She had never been serious about school. But she was dark haired and buxom, with a sprinkling of freckles, dancing brown eyes, and an easy laugh. The dances were where the boys were, and she loved a good time.

It was then that Wilber had spotted her on his way to work. The cotton dress didn't hide her figure, and Wilber pulled up and stopped right beside her as she waited in the soft morning breeze for the streetcar by the bay.

It was a light fall day. Martha Cameron's mother, Vashti, had just died of cancer in New Jersey. Martha was fourteen. The Emyfish—depending on how old you believe she might have been at the time—was either in middle or high school in New Rochelle, New York, or had graduated and was enrolled in acting school in New York City, or was already auditioning for parts, trying to make her name on Broadway. My mother was a senior at Plant High in Tampa, in the school year just begun. My father was a young reporter for the *Clearwater Sun*, across the bay. They hadn't met. Karl Richter was one of the brightest students at the University and Jewish Theological Seminary of Breslau, Germany, less than three years from ordination as a rabbi. But the seminary was a cultural island in an angry and treacherous sea. The National Socialist Party had just won the largest number of seats in parliament—the Reichstag—in the national elections. The sky was darkening.

"How does a guy go about getting a date with you?" Wilber said, leaning out his car window to grin at Mary. He was twenty-three, and that was the way he talked, breezy, cocksure, and a little uncertain at the same time. Wilber was almost movie-handsome in those days, square jawed and blue eyed, with thick, wavy brown blond hair. His father was a railroad conductor—secure employment in the Depression—and Wilber had a car and a job. He was headed downtown, where he worked as assistant to the owner of the Chevrolet dealership, Mr. Ferman. No one in Tampa worried much about the Nazis.

"Why don't you take me to the tea dance this Saturday afternoon?" Mary said, her eyes smiling back at him. She had seen him around. Everyone in towns like Tampa felt they knew one another then, and in this case it was the right thing to say.

He became her morning ride, and steady date. Less than three years later, they eloped. A lot of couples were doing that. Church weddings, with receptions afterward, and gifts people felt socially obliged to give, were too expensive all around. Mary's parents weren't ready for her to be married. And she wouldn't sleep with Wilber until they were. That couldn't last forever.

So in November 1935, Dr. Duke, pastor of the First Baptist Church, agreed to marry them in his office, with just Mary's sister, Eleanor, and her boyfriend for witnesses. Then they drove north in the red Chevrolet. They spent a night in Savannah at the DeSoto Hotel, which had thin walls. A man down the hall snored so loudly that when they finally fell asleep—after the excitement of getting married, the long drive, and making breathless, awkward, pent-up love with Wilber for the first time—Mary had a dream. Her father had come and found them.

And was banging on the door.

O n the first Wednesday morning in February, the Piano Man came, unfolded his keyboard, and in a slightly reedy voice— the Piano Man was no spring chicken either—began to sing and play a song that had worried Wilber when Nathalie was sixteen and had a boyfriend:

> *It's NOW or never,*
> *Come HOLD me tight*

Kiss ME my darling,
Be mine tonight. . . .

Hearing it now, Wilber wanted to dance. Mary wasn't there in the recreation room, where most of the group activities took place, across from the physical therapy space. She didn't come over to the Health Center to see him every morning, and she didn't dance any-more, anyway. She hadn't in years. She treated her back like a fragile thing, and worried about falling. But Ernestine danced. She was full of music—always had been—and she sashayed over to where Wilber was sitting in one of the chairs that made a squarish circle around the edges of the room and, with a big grin, pulled him up. Wilber, as usual, was neat in gray pants and a striped shirt, a crisp image oddly blurred by his dazed expression. But Ernestine held him close. Still grinning, with one hand on his hip, the rest of her enfolding him like a warm cloud, she started to dance him around the clear space in the middle of the room. Tentatively, shuffling, he followed her lead. *Very* carefully, they began to boogie.

The Elvis number ended. But the Piano Man had apparently decided on a romantic morning. He adjusted his glasses, and shifted into

Let me call you SWEETHEART . . .
I'm in LOVE, with . . . YOUUUU!

Over by the windows along one wall, where a row of residents were parked and doddering in their wheelchairs, Louise, in white pants and blouse and a blue-striped overshirt, stood up, took my mother's hand, and, smiling down, began to dance beside her. Sister Barbara, the big, soft, pink-cheeked Jacobite nun who sometimes worked in the Health Center, started dancing and swaying on the other side. Mother turned her head back and forth, her expression as blank and curious as an owl's, looking first at Louise and then at the sister. She settled on Louise.

Wilber's eyes were a little glazed, but his feet were working, trying to get the rhythm. He had always loved to dance. In earlier life, he might have been the biggest dancer of all the men who were in the recreation room that morning. But now he had the added advantage of being the only one who could still stand up. The others were making little dancing moves in their wheelchairs.

Seamlessly, his white head rocking to the music, the Piano Man glided into another song.

> _I want a girl JUST like the girl_
> _That MARRIED dear old Dad._

Ernestine had moved away to dance beside one of the other men. Louise had shifted over to waltz with Wilber, leaving Sister Barbara swaying and floating beside Mother. Now Ernestine returned, clapping and laughing, cut in on Louise, and took Wilber back. The Piano Man was in good form. Wednesdays, when he came with his electric keyboard and synthesizer, were usually the liveliest mornings of the week. Some were livelier than others. One morning, the Piano Man fainted and fell off his piano bench. Some of the residents noticed sooner than others. But this morning he seemed fine. He came to the end of "A Good Old-Fashioned Girl," finished with a synthesized flourish, and returned to the Elvis songbook. With us boomers and our parents, you can always go back to Elvis.

> _Love me TENDER,_
> _Love me TRUE,_
> _NE-VER let me go. . . ._

Slowly—tenderly—smiling all the time into his eyes, Ernestine twirled Wilber around. He was smiling back at her. His eyes seemed less vague. He was beginning to look happy.

I t is a generation that loved music. People often sang along at social and patriotic and religious events, if there was a piano or some other instrument to follow, even if they weren't musical. Ruth

Richter had been bringing sheet music to her father, a trustee and professor at the Jewish Seminary in Breslau, when Karl first saw her coming up the stairs, fair and lovely and just sixteen. Often, as they began to spend time together, she sang as he played the violin, and her brother played the piano. They were bright, cultured young people of great promise. It was 1933, the year that Adolph Hitler became chancellor.

When Karl graduated and was ordained a rabbi, at the beginning of 1935, Hitler had already changed the German culture the young rabbi had just finished studying. Karl had been classically educated at a Latin school and then at university and seminary. He was steeped in history, philosophy, and religion. He spoke five languages. At the age of twenty-five, he had been in school almost nineteen years. He had earned a doctorate. But he didn't receive it. He never would.

"My doctoral thesis was never accepted because Hitler had already forbidden the graduation of Jewish students, and the Nazis had fired my professor," he wrote later, explaining the changes that had begun to occur.

The Nuremberg laws, which stripped Jews of the rights of citizenship, and marked the beginning of their expulsion from German culture and from life itself, were promulgated that year. The effects were immediate. When Karl and Ruth were married in March, the young rabbi and his bride could not be wed in the ancient rites and rituals of their own religion, in a service in a temple. Instead, they had a brief, spiritless civil ceremony in a government office, their marriage documented by the state with a cold, stark certificate stamped with a swastika. And then they left for Eastern Pomerania, then in Prussia and now a part of Poland.

Karl's first assignment was to service fourteen little congregations in different towns, none of them big enough to imagine having a rabbi of its own. The young rabbi would be a circuit rider, like the Methodist preachers in the small-town South when Helen Hill was a child—except that this was a generation later, and they had provided Karl with a used car. "A motorized Moses," the members of his scattered flock joked about him. The newlyweds' first home, a simple, one-story stone house, was behind the synagogue in the town of Schievelbein, and there they began to discover what their new life would be like.

"The house was next to the town laundry, which was next to the place where they kept the dead bodies," Karl said, "because there were no funeral homes in that part of Germany then. There was a half-wit man across the street on the second floor, a middle-aged man who lived by himself, who told us that he was assigned to write down when we left and when we came back." But the half-wit was not the only person who watched the young couple, and not all the attention paid to them was so clownish. Someone more serious shot bullets through their windows at night, a practice made easier by the fact that the house was just one floor. Karl and Ruth soon moved to a two-story house. It was a strange and anxious way to begin a marriage. After a nervous year, with Karl gone much of the time—he sometimes alone on the roads, she in the house—he was invited to take the pulpit of the main synagogue in Stettin, the provincial capital. They were glad, because it was one large congregation in a more sophisticated place—but there the Gestapo summoned him.

They had reports that he had made anti-Nazi remarks at Jewish funeral services. Karl denied it. "We are watching you," they said.

He and Ruth felt always under observation and threat. And yet the pattern of life also felt more stable. They decided to try for a family. Their first child was born in Stettin, and then, early in 1938, with their new baby daughter, Esther, they left for the last assignment Karl would have as a rabbi in Germany—the last time there was a substantial Jewish population *in* Germany. He had been asked to pastor the main temple in Mannheim. It was a move, they realized later, that saved their lives, because the Jewish community in Stettin was one of the first to be deported to Poland by the Nazis in 1940. But none of this—the lurking half-wit, the gunshots, the threats and surveillance of the Gestapo—was as surprising or frightening as it might have been to the Richters after the shock of the welcome they had received when they first arrived, in the damp cold of early April 1935, in the dreary town of Schievelbein.

Hung across the street from the little house that had been prepared for them—with its conveniently low windows, so accessible to someone outside with a gun—was a banner composed and painted just for them.

TO THE NEW RABBI, it said. WE WILL HANG YOU IN THE PUBLIC SQUARE THIS SUNDAY.

It was in 1938, as the Richters moved to Mannheim, and Mary and Wilber settled into married life in an apartment, having friends in for drinks, eating dinner out at Spanish restaurants for two or three dollars a couple, that my father's teasing, earnest, awkward notes and letters, cards and telegrams to my mother began. At least, that is when she began saving them. She was twenty-three then, an ambitious, sweetly intense, beautiful young woman of thick, wavy chocolate-black hair; large, dark, hazel green eyes; and a frequent, dazzling smile. She must also have begun to feel time passing, because she and a handful of the other young women who had been born and raised in Tampa and who were not yet married had formed a new group, the Spinsters Club. That's what they called it. They had a sense of humor, and the club began to sponsor dances and parties intended to enliven the Depression—and to provide social occasions where twentysomethings could meet and pair off.

I don't actually know how or where or when in Tampa my parents met. But I know that as young people in their twenties, they had two things in common. They had no money, and no fathers to turn to for help, advice, or introductions to the working world. It was the Depression, and they had to make their own way, reliant on their own talents and energy, and whatever connections or relations they had. My father's father had drifted off years before, unable to cope with the loss of his cotton land in Alabama to the boll weevil, in the years before World War I. My mother's father, the claims agent for Tampa Electric Company, had died of heart disease in

1934, which was why she, like Mary Davis, wasn't able to go to college, although her older brother and sister did. I don't know much more than that. Neither of my parents ever spoke much at all about their childhoods, or their romance and marriage, and I never thought to prompt them. It is one thing that all of us whose parents have died—or stopped being able to speak—most regret. Mother would probably have been glad to gush. She was a complete romantic, and adored my father, who became editor of the *Tribune,* in charge of its editorial pages, and was a powerful influence on the social and political culture of the state for more than thirty years. She loved him, loved what he did and what he stood for, loved being his wife. My father didn't talk easily about anything personal at all. But one of the chores that falls to us children, when a parent dies or has a stroke, is sorting through the personal things.

And so, when we had to break up Mother's apartment, I found, amid folders of old insurance and medical records, financial papers, and clutches of photographs, a large plain manila envelope on which my mother had written NOTES AND CARDS FROM JIMMY DURING OUR LONG COURTSHIP. Jimmy is what she called him then. She must have gathered the papers together in only the last year or two before her strokes, because the handwriting on the envelope was not the warm, graceful, instantly recognizable script that I had grown to both dread and cherish (my mother wrote a *lot* of letters) in the decades after I left home. It was small, cramped, and weak.

I held the envelope and looked at it—squeezing it to feel the weight of it, trying to guess at the volume and intensity of the feeling inside. What would my father have said in the privacy of his notes and letters to my mother when they were young? What would I find out about him that I didn't know? He had always been so reserved. He was a shy, formal, reticent man, and I couldn't recall his ever saying anything intimate to me (or to my mother or to anyone else, in front of me), about anything. *Ever.* He didn't talk well about personal things that mattered.

Were there notes and letters from my mother, back to him? What would she have said?

I couldn't imagine the contents of the envelope I was holding. I also couldn't imagine opening it to read the notes. That would be an invasion of their privacy. I didn't know what I would find. I didn't want to know. The idea scared me, and I put it aside. *Maybe,* I thought, *after she dies.*

But, of course, she didn't die. And I didn't open the envelope. Mostly, I didn't think about it. More than a year passed. I found the envelope again. This time I tucked it into the top drawer of a file cabinet, between two of a growing number of files on Mother: MOTHER HOUSE; MOTHER APARTMENT; MOTHER NOTES; MOTHER HISTORY; MOTHER FINANCE; MOTHER LETTERS; MOTHER LIVING WILL; MOTHER MEDICAL CHART; MOTHER FUNERAL PAPERS.

Several more years passed. I made scores of trips to Tampa, spent hundreds of days and nights at Canterbury. Digging in the file cabinet, I kept encountering the envelope. It got harder not to open. If I was having so many intimate conversations and candid interviews with so many other people at Canterbury—people who were friends of my parents, or parents of friends of mine, or strangers until recently—I couldn't choose to be incurious about my own parents. It didn't matter whether I wanted to know or not.

And so, finally, I opened the envelope. From 1938—which was when Hitler invaded Austria, and my parents began to date—to 1943, when the Allies invaded Sicily and first bombed Berlin, and my parents finally married, there were no notes or letters from my mother. She had saved my father's letters. My father hadn't saved hers. But then he was not the romantic.

He was not, in fact, that different in his notes and letters to the woman he was courting and would marry from how he was at home, or in social company a decade or so after their marriage, when I began to be old enough to pay attention. There was always a kind of humorous reserve, and distance. One night when I was a boy, sitting in the family sedan, a Studebaker Land Cruiser, watching a western with my parents at the Dale Mabry Drive-in, I said, "Daddy, how do you tell the good men from the bad men?" The cowboys were all shooting each other. I was too young to follow the plot.

"The good guys all wear white hats," my father said, chuckling in the darkness. In the westerns of the time, that was often—almost always—true. But my father thought some more about it and, at the office the next day, sat at his desk and wrote an editorial to his son, which he put in the paper, about how to tell good men from bad ones. That's the way he was. You knew what he felt and thought by what he wrote for the public.

The man who wrote to my mother was wry, guarded, self-conscious, rather formal, and gently—or awkwardly—teasing. He made jokes, poked fun, wrote self-effacing poetry, and sometimes made earnest amends, but he never seemed to take the risk of nakedly declaring his feelings, or committing himself in any way. The notes and letters aren't ardent. The feeling seems there—in the background—but it's masked. Given his family—a failed and absent father, two sisters who doted on Jesus but had no idea how to relate to real men (and were both hospitalized for emotional instability in early adulthood)—there is no reason to think that my father would have known how to be romantic, or open, or intimate, or smart, or even very relaxed and comfortable with women. Or that he would want to take the risk. He was cautious and shy. But he was also interested, and so he tried to be amusing.

He sent her flowers. On the undated card, he wrote, "I'll be along later to take you and the flowers to the dance."

From Washington, D.C., in October 1941, he sent her a series of postcards. On one, with an engraving of the Library of Congress on the front, he wrote, "Spent one day here reading *Congressional Record,* 1837–1941, inclusive. Very entertaining."

On another, with a picture of the National Archives Building, where the Declaration of Independence and the U.S. Constitution are housed, he wrote, "Spent a day and a night here, poring over valuable papers. Very cultural."

From aboard a little steamer, HMS *Monarch,* bound for Nassau, the Bahamas, in 1939, he wrote to her in pencil on the ship's stationery:

> Dear Barbara,
> I wanted to write this with a British accent, but upon discovering that my fountain pen had gone dry and not a drop of ink in the house, I concluded that I had best be my homespun self. That goes better with pencil.

She may have felt herself a spinster, but he seemed to view her as charmed and popular, and perhaps even unattainable. In February of that year, he sent her a poem typed with a red typewriter ribbon.

> *The giddy whirl in which you spin,*
> *Surrounded by a mass of men,*
> *Shrinks my ego to an atom;*
> *So I sit and mutter, "Drat 'em,"*
> *The while I study books on how*
> *To be a Killer and a Wow.*
> *Now, it says in Chapter Eight—*
> *Timid Suitor Gets the Gate—*
> *So I, on this romantic day*
> *Arise a bolder man, and say—*
> *(What the devil was that line?)*
> *Oh yes—Be my Valentine!*

Sometimes, like other young men in courtship, he suffered the agonies of foot-in-mouth disease. And sometimes, he drank too much.

"Dear Bobbie," he wrote on a Tuesday morning in February 1939:

> Sorry about my poor conduct of last night.
> I am a foolish fellow in many ways, one of which is letting small things sometimes get under my skin.
> In the cold clear light of day I can see how stupid this is.

But daylight, unfortunately, comes the morning after.
In sackcloth,
Jimmy

He was, in fact, a charming, gentlemanly—if reticent—man, in-
hibited about expressing himself, who came with shadowed feelings
about his family past. She might have been touched by that.

"Dear Bobbie," he wrote on a Thursday in February 1940:

Won't be here for Spanish class tomorrow. My father died suddenly, and we are leaving for Alabama.
Probably you are surprised to learn that my father was still
living.

He had never mentioned him.

Sometime after the United States entered World War II, following the attack on Pearl Harbor in December 1941, my father enlisted and became a staff sergeant, running a public information unit
composed of newspapermen at the Army Air Force Base at Drew
Field, in Tampa. He remained there, working at the airfield, living in
Tampa, for the duration. The war didn't really interrupt his and my
mother's dating, and in 1943, after five years of flowers and notes
and letters, parties and dinners and dances and who knows what, my
parents married.

For all his reserve and even diffidence, my father was handsome,
smart, serious, and principled, and I think my mother had believed
in him—and maybe even loved him—from almost the first. Certainly from early on in the notes and letters. She was an idealistic,
romantic, willful woman, determined about the things she believed
in and wanted—and in my experience, always adept at managing
and manipulating men, and social situations. Still, her friends, watching her long, unwed relationship with my father, had wondered
whether she was going to ever bring him home.

"Your father was *so* difficult. I didn't think she was *ever* going to
get him to walk down the aisle," the Emyfish said.

But in 1943 she did, and in 1945, my father, the uncertain suitor, perhaps even the un-ideal husband, whose experience of marriage and of women in his own family at home had been so unrecommending, sat down and wrote his still-new wife a poem. I was nine months old. They had been married two years. But he had been neglectful.

> *I just ignored St. Valentine's,*
> *Then Easter found me fast asleep.*
> *Mother's Day I clean forgot,*
> *And caused my little wife to weep.*
> *I am an unromantic gent,*
> *And stupid, too, you well may say,*
> *But this one date I bear in mind—*
> *The wonderful 22nd of May.*

It was their anniversary.

CHAPTER EIGHTEEN

Body Parts

SPRING 2001

As the azalea bushes began to blossom in March and April, coloring the green gardens along the Bayshore lavender and salmon and linen white, Mary Davis became perversely, even luxuriantly, grumpy. My mother got stiffer. And the Calendar Girls thought wistfully of their excitement, the year before, about posing nude for the sake of some good cause.

"Emy has given me uh new scale, an' it weighs me five pounds moah than the ole one," Mary said, over drinks in her apartment on the last Monday in March. She looked as if she could chew the rim right off her bloody Mary glass. "Ah am furious," she said, her eyes narrowed to little slits. "Ah thought ah had *lost* thuhteen pounds."

She was tired of her medications, too. "Ah *hate* takin' sevuhn pills a dayuh," she said. "And now theyah givin' me calcium, ah take *nighyun*—for cholesterol, high blood presshah, an aspirin uh day that evahbody takes foah theahr hahrt, and thuh calcium pill." I thought about that for a moment, adding up my own list of pills and puffers, and decided that she had me beat by only three a day. That didn't seem excessive for a woman of eighty-seven, who had smoked for sixty years, took no exercise, and still drank. But I didn't say that, and Mary changed the subject. She started complaining about Wilber, and church.

She had been with him the day before, for the 10:30 church

service in the Health Center, which is conducted in the recreation
room each Sunday by a group of unfailingly cheerful volunteer
laypeople from St. John's Episcopal Church, who arrive with
prayer books, hymnals, and robes, ready to lead the demented and
deteriorated in song and prayer. This Sunday had been a little different. A man named Ralph, with the dark mahogany color and
sunken look of a terminal cancer patient, expired in his private
room down the hall just before the service began, while a beaming,
all-white, middle-aged chorus on a videotape that Joyce had slipped
into the television sang

> *In the good old summerTIME*
> *In the good old summertime . . .*

That hadn't bothered Mary. Ralph's death didn't affect the service at all. The nursing staff just closed his door and told the funeral
home not to pick him up for another hour and forty-five minutes,
until after noon. By the time the unmarked blue van arrived at the
back door, with its wheeled dolly and driver-collector, church was
over. The Health Center residents were all in their dining room, eating lunch or being fed. Someone closed the dining room door, and
no one paid any attention as Ralph glided by, a long dark zippered
bag on an aluminum dolly. Mother and I had left during the middle
of the service to go sit outside, under the tree on the terrace by the
pool, and look at the roses. She had been grinding her teeth so hard,
she was louder than the psalm reading or the hymns. So I unwedged
her from the line of wheelchairs and rolled her out. But it wasn't the
racket of Mother's grinding that had bothered Mary.

What bothered Mary was that she was awake for the whole service, and Wilber was not. "He's sleepin' awll day long," she said,
fuming. "Ah'm not goin' tuh chuhch with him anymoah and watch
him *sleep* awll thuh time, and listen tuh him SNORAH! And when
Ah squeeze his han' and wake him up, he asks me out loud, 'Whut is
it? Whut do'yuh want? Whut do'yuh want me tuh do?'" What she
wanted was for him to be normal—awake and quiet and polite in

church, just as she had wanted him to be sociable and functional at the cocktail hour in the way he always had been. Wilber, of course, couldn't be that way. He was demented.

Which—actually—*was* normal for a ninety-one-year-old man. But Mary hadn't accepted what that meant. She seemed to expect him to be quietly, *politely* demented—to participate in things, do what he was told, remember her when she came to see him, and be grateful she was there—and then forget her so she could slip away in peace. But it wasn't working that way, and it especially vexed her that Wilber slept and snored and talked during church, because *he* was the one who had always prayed. Mary didn't think about God at all. That morning, however, she had discovered the joy of righteous feeling.

She was full of righteous indignation.

"That chuhch suhvice is the wors' thang Ah've evah seen," she grumped. "Who is that woman who goes roun' huggin' evahbody? She drives me crazy. 'Les' havah *hug*. Les' havah Sunday HUG!' *Hhhhmmmmmphhh!*"

Life's routine seemed to be losing its appeal. But the vodka and complaining—and someone to listen—seemed to do Mary good. When she was finished, we went down to the dining room.

As April slid into May, much of the thought and conversation at Canterbury turned physical. Martha Cameron and the Sweetso began to talk about vaginas. Sarah Jane Rubio discovered that her previous love life had caught up with her. And the precise, methodical Dr. Joel Shrager took some pleasure in seeing his naked reflection in the mirror again. It had been a while. He was short, and very near-sighted, and eighty-six years old. He and his wife, Miriam, had had no children. They were very bound to each other, and after she died—bravely, and also impatiently—of cancer at Canterbury ("If you want to know the truth, I'm ashamed," Miriam said, when another resident came to sit beside her, and asked how she felt. "I'm just lying here. *Let's get this show on the road!*"), Joel felt unmoored.

He wasn't social. He had no close friends, or any particular interest in film, or theater, symphony, museums, cocktail or dinner parties—or even in taking walks. His life had been his work, as an Army doctor and later, after he had retired from the service, as a medical school professor—and Miriam. He didn't know what to do with himself. But each morning, in the curtained silence of 801, the apartment they had shared on the right front of the building, six floors beneath the Sweetso, Joel rose early, as always. He showered, shaved, oiled and combed his straight brown hair, and dressed carefully but automatically, in gray slacks, a soft gray or white shirt, striped tie, tie chain, and maroon blazer. It was his daily uniform. Then, picking up the sword cane he had bought in the South Pacific decades before, and the retired U.S. Army officer's baseball cap, Dr. Schrager said good-bye to Miriam (her picture was hanging on the wall, and he always said good-bye going out, and hello coming in) and walked out the door.

He had no particular place to go. So he went to the dining room. Chanh was waiting. Joel was a person of structure, of order and ritual. It was his nature, and what made him feel secure. It was the same with almost all the residents of the Tower. It was what Canterbury was about. And so breakfast became a ritual. With a large white linen napkin tucked in his collar, so that it spread over the mounds of his short, broad chest and stomach like a bib, Joel methodically and completely consumed ever-larger breakfasts—eventually, three eggs, grits, pancakes, orange juice, toast, and coffee. Then he went to sit in the lobby, where, if anyone sat down beside him, or even stopped very long to say hello, he could tell them about the night his ship was hit by three torpedoes and sank in the North Atlantic, on June 12, 1942—and that other night, which was even more important in his memory. It was just eleven days later, and Miriam, on citizen patrol back in New Jersey, saw a German submarine surface at the very entrance to the Delaware Bay, and called the sighting in to a number she had been given for the Army Air Corps fighter group patrolling the coast.

"She got on her phone and got the group, and said, 'Get here in less than five minutes.' And, by George, they were there!" Joel said, smiling broadly. "They were there in less than five minutes, and confirmed the fact that it was a German sub, and sank it—in less than five minutes!" It gave him such delight.

He missed her terribly. He talked about her to anyone who would listen. In the years after she died, in 1995, other residents learned to avoid getting too close, and so Dr. Shrager mostly sat alone—a small, Buddha-like figure in a coat and tie, Army cap, and thick tortoise-shell glasses, perched on the couch, his right hand holding the black cane with its gold snake-head handle before him. No one seemed to realize that the cane contained a sword.

"I don't know how he can sit there day after day, with his hand on his cane," Marjorie Chunn Cochran said to Sarah Jane one evening over cocktails. Margy's first husband, Dr. Frank Chunn, had been a surgeon—curious, bold, decisive, and strong. She was used to more assertive men.

"Well, you *knowah*," Sarah Jane said, widening her big blue eyes and smiling her Cheshire Cat smile, "he wuzza pah-*thol*-ah-gist. He nevah haddah *live* patient."

Still, Joel was lonely. He felt the need to be around people. When Elizabeth Himes died in 1999, he had gotten on the Canterbury bus with a number of others and gone to St. John's Episcopal Church for the funeral service. As Elizabeth had instructed, it was a full service, with a choir, and Holy Communion. Joel was a Jew, but when people started heading for the altar, he stood up and got in line for the body and blood of Jesus, too.

Seeing the short, chubby figure on his way up the aisle toward the cross, Martha Cameron made a mental note to tell Rabbi Richter about it. She wanted to see what funny thing he would say. The rabbi listened without expression.

"He's just cramming for his finals," he said.

But as time passed, Joel Shrager did not depart. He expanded. Settled comfortably into a daily routine of rise and shine, breakfast-lobby-lunch-lobby-dinner-lobby-bed, he became a fixture on the couch between the front doors and the elevators. Each time I returned to Canterbury, there he was, a solitary tableau. Gradually, I realized that he was growing. Had been, for a long time. Joel was only about five feet tall, but he was getting broader. Rounder. He was, in fact, practically spherical. His belt was the equator.

Months slipped by, a year, and as I passed back and forth through the lobby, it dawned on me that something else was happening. The process had reversed. Joel Shrager was getting smaller. Sitting in his same place on the same couch, he took up less room. His shirt collar now seemed too big. The maroon blazer, which had billowed outward in soft, glorious ballooning curves for years, actually sagged here and there. He was shrinking.

One day, seeing him again on my way to the elevator, I stopped and introduced myself. Could we have breakfast or lunch, perhaps, or dinner?

"You choose," he said, without ado. "It doesn't matter."

We had breakfast. He tucked the white linen napkin in his collar, ordered a substantial plate from Chanh, and began to eat with methodical relish. Close up, though, his neck looked thinner, his cheeks not so plump.

"I noticed that you seem to be losing weight," I said, hoping the explanation wasn't heart disease or cancer.

Joel cut part of a fat, runny, poached egg yolk, pushed it into a pile of potatoes, and lifted it with his fork. "I have lost a hundred forty-seven pounds in the last year," he said matter-of-factly, blinking at me from behind his thick glasses. "Half my body weight." He put the fork in his small, wet mouth.

I was astonished. "How?" I said.

"I eat just one meal a day," he replied, lifting a piece of buttered toast.

I blinked back at him, considering. "Which one?"

"It doesn't matter which one," he said, in that same dry, clinical way, "so long as I eat only one." That was his new system. He was almost back to the weight he had maintained throughout his whole career in the army, he said—132 pounds.

He seemed so calm, so unaffected. What made him decide to do that?

Joel speared a wedge of pancakes with his fork, twirled it in some syrup, and paused. He had looked at himself in the mirror one day. "Did you ever see a tub of butter—three hundred pounds?" he asked, raising his eyebrows slightly. "I said *ixnay*."

I tried to think of something to say.

"You must feel *better*," I suggested.

"No," he said, in that same precise, expressionless tone, lifting the fork of dripping pancakes. "I feel just the same."

"The *same*?"

"The same," Joel said, patting his small mouth with the napkin. "I feel just the way I've *always* felt."

Sameness was important. Sarah Jane and the Sweetso felt the same way they always had about a few things, too.

When the phone rang in apartment 1504 after 10:30 one weeknight, it was late for Sarah Jane. Mauricio was down in Sebring. Even when he was away, she got up early. But it was hard for her to resist the telephone, and when she answered, she discovered that it was Carlos, on the security desk.

"At *this* ow-ah?" Sarah Jane said, peering at her bedside clock.

"Ah'ma sorreh, Missus Rubio, butta you haffa tah come down anna mooffah your cahr," Carlos said. Then she understood. She had forgotten and left her blue and white Eldorado in one of the visitor's spots under the protective overhang of the building near the front door, instead of in her own less-convenient assigned space. No cars can be parked in the outside visitor's slots after 10:00 p.m. It's a rule. But Sarah Jane had her own rule. Ladies don't go out in public unless they have their face and clothes on.

"Ah'm in bayed," Sarah Jane said. "Ah'm not comin' down tah do *anuh*-thang."

"Then bringuh me thah keys," Carlos told her.

"Carlos, Ah'm *not* gettin' dressed to bring down thuh keys," Sarah Jane said. Why didn't that man understand? He was supposed to be part of the support system, to make her feel attended to and secure. That was why she came here. Why was he bothering her?

The phone was silent for a moment. "Alla right," Carlos said. "Jus' puddah them onah thah ele-*va*-der. Senna them down. Ah'lla move id."

Sarah Jane thought about it. She would still have to get out of bed, still have to walk out of her apartment and down the hall to the elevator, still risk being seen by whoever else was up, and be watched the whole time, probably, by Carlos through the security camera. But the fifteenth-floor hall would probably be empty. On the other hand, if she insisted that Carlos leave the security desk to come up to her apartment and get the keys, she would have to face him at the door. Sarah Jane didn't face any men she wasn't married to without makeup on.

"Ohh, awhl *raaht,*" she said.

Carlos hung up, and dialed again.

The phone rang in 1501. The Sweetso was up. She and Martha Cameron, who was beginning to be called El Cee (phonetic for L.C., which was short for lieutenant colonel, the rank at which she retired from the Nursing Corps), had been conspiring about a trip to New York City. They were going to stay with the Sweetso's daughter and son-in-law, Meredith and Larry, on the Upper East Side. Meredith was getting them tickets for *The Vagina Monologues.* Trying to imagine all the funny and provocative things one might possibly say about vaginas made the Sweetso happy. She thought she might make a list. She was sitting in her living room, watching the news on CNN, when she picked up the phone by the couch and put it to her ear.

"This-issa Carlos ah-speakin'," the phone said.

"*Ah-ha*—the thought police!" the Sweetso exclaimed. She was feeling saucy.

Two could play that game.

"Wheruh isa yohr *cahr*?" Carlos asked.

Then she remembered. She had left it in one of the convenient visitor's spots under the overhang that afternoon, thinking she would park it in her own space later. She hadn't.

"You haffa to puddit insidah thah gates," Carlos said.

"*Who* says?" the Sweetso shot back. She was comfortable in her corner of the couch. She didn't feel like moving, and it cost her nothing to banter with Carlos.

"Ah'm *notta* puh-midded to haffa cahrs inna thah visitor's space ovah-nide," Carlos declared, in his best first sergeant's voice.

"Well, *I'm* not dressed," the Sweetso grumped, in her gravelly voice. It was a woman's best defense. Carlos also knew she wasn't easily pushed around.

There was a pause while he thought about it.

"Juss'a puddah yorh keys onna thah ele-*va*-der," he said.

And so, somewhere around 10:45 p.m., Sarah Jane and the Sweetso opened their apartment doors, stepped halfway out in their nightgowns to look up and down the hall, and saw each other standing there, each with car keys in hand. They began to laugh.

Giggling and tee-heeing, they tiptoed down to the elevator. They could hear the whir of cables as a car came up from the lobby. Carlos was watching on the monitor at the desk. The elevator car arrived. The doors opened.

Sarah Jane and the Sweetso pitched their keys into the car. And then—almost in unison—they put their hands on their hips, turned toward the security camera looking at them from up on the wall, screwed up their unmade faces, and stuck out their tongues. Then, wiggling their septuagenarian butts triumphantly, they sashayed back to their apartments, flounced inside, and slammed the doors. *So there.*

L ike Joel Shrager, Sarah Jane was particular about many things—especially those that had to do with beauty, form, and the care and preservation of body parts. Sitting down to lunch in the dining room one day late in May, she began retrieving from a bag on her walker the essential accessories and accoutrements to her dining experience. There were the usual little crystal containers of vinegar and oil, and shakers of sea salt and freshly ground pepper. But then she fished out a small thin tube that looked to me like lipstick, except much slimmer. She screwed out a colored point of something, and began expertly to rim the upper and lower edges of her own soft, glossy lips.

"Lip linah," she said, with a glance at me. She unsnapped a small glittering compact and admired her handiwork in its mirror. The slight tube in her manicured fingers looked cool, even crisp. Actually, it was.

"Ah put them in thuh freezah fuhst," Sarah Jane said, eyeing its shape, "so they sharpen bettuh."

It was one of the countless tricks she had developed, over the decades, to sharpen and enliven the endless small details by which life is either dulled or brightened. Like many old ladies—and, for that matter, men—who have weak hearts and slow arterial flow, Sarah Jane wore support panty hose. She hated them; they were hot and tight, and hard to pull on. They improved the circulation in her legs. But she much preferred to put onions and potatoes in them, and hang them in the kitchen. They made wonderful storage stockings, Sarah Jane thought, and the onions seemed a lot happier in them than she was, and stayed fresher longer.

She was a careful shopper, dedicated to the nuances, choosing shoes to match not only her clothes (color, texture) and the event (beachwear, casual, dressy, dressier, really dressy, formal) but also the season. Light in summer, dark in winter. But to be worth all that trouble, the match had to be right. One evening, some years before, when she and Mauricio were still living on the seventeenth floor of the Atrium, up the Bayshore toward town, the weather had reversed, turning suddenly cool. Sarah Jane had just finished packing up her winter shoes—each pair in its own plastic bag, all the bags tied up in one big bag—and putting them away. But that night, she realized that she simply had to dress for winter again, and so she asked Mauricio to get the bag of shoes back out of the storage space downstairs, where she had told him to take it.

"Oh," he said, looking suddenly attentive, "*that* bag." Mauricio, a doctor patient with his patients, was impatient with life. He was always in motion. He walked fast. He talked fast. And while he appreciated Sarah Jane's exhaustive and intricate attentions to the texture of life—he was, after all, the chief beneficiary of her charms—he paid little heed to what she did, or how. Or sometimes to what she said. Sarah Jane talked so much, one didn't feel obliged to catch every word.

Listening to her instructions with half an ear, Mauricio had taken the bag of lovingly chosen footwear and thrown it down the building's trash chute. Down it went, with all her carefully wrapped and tucked and bagged winter shoes, including some of the most expensive she had ever bought, from the Mall of America in Minnesota, in every color. Seventeen floors. Whoosh. Bump, bump. Bump. Bumpety-bump. Kah-bumpety-*fluump!* When Mauricio had turned to explain, in his cryptic way, that the shoes were not in—uhm—storage, his wife turned a considerably paler shade than her makeup, and made for the elevator. Within minutes, she was pawing through the trash bin.

Sarah Jane and Mauricio ran a little late that night. But she looked wonderful, as bloomingly colorful and coordinated as ever. And if there were the dimmest suggestions of scuffs and dents on her beautiful shoes, no one seemed to notice.

At this age, you had to keep the system working. It was the only way to know you still had a grip on life, instead of the other way around. But a woman like Sarah Jane also had to be careful not to let all her methods and defenses keep her from being open to new ideas. Living to an older age than she had anticipated, and sensitive to every small creak and shift in her own decline, she needed to be alert for any helpful, compensating clues of additional ways to cope. Most women her age—women like my mother—dreaded change.

"Ah *hate* change," my mother said one day, a year or two before her strokes. The nakedness of the declaration—and the fierce way she said it—took me by surprise. She had always seemed so curious, so graceful and good humored in the way she dealt with life, so flexible and warm—and still in control. It was the first time I had ever heard her sound resentful and angry, fearful of something with which she felt unable to contend.

It was the first time I realized that to women like my mother—accustomed to being able to manipulate life, but now old and fatigued, arthritic and frail—change was a threat to whatever perch they still had. Unable to defend themselves, they wanted to be protected. That's why they had come to Canterbury. But Sarah Jane believed in staying open to new possibilities. And so, on a Sunday morning in May, when she stooped to pick up the fat, ad-filled *Tampa Tribune* lying outside her door on the fifteenth floor, an announcement slipped out of the messy inner mass of throwaway supplements and circulars, fluttered to the hallway carpet, and caught her eye. It was for a portable medical-testing van.

"It wuzza company that goes awl aroun' givin' a stroke risk test, and a haht attack risk test," she explained one night, about two weeks later. Sarah Jane had arrived late for cocktails at El Cee's apartment, and was already talking as she glided through the front door with her walker—a voluble, animated vision in pastels, rouge, sleek blond hair, and jewelry.

"Ah know y'all thought Ah forgot," she was saying, "but *that's* why Ah'm lookin' foahwahd to mah carotid suh-gery." She stopped and swept her eyes around the room, smiling as she took the drink that someone held out to her. She had gotten their attention. She balanced the drink on her walker and kept on talking as she edged toward a seat.

"Theah wuh three differen' tests foah both thangs. Six tests in awll, foah ninety-five dollahs," she said. Her father, Sarah Jane reminded them, had died of a stroke. Her mother had had little strokes. She was determined to avoid becoming one more victim of the family pattern, and she was a practical shopper. "When Ah saw it wuz goan' tuh be at Bayshore Baptist, Ah went," she said. "If id had been ovah at WestShore Plaza, Ah would nevah have goan. But this wuz so *easy*.

"It came back that Ah haddah serious blockage in mah lef' carotid ahr-dery," she continued, pausing only long enough to give them all another look. When Sarah Jane took the results to her own cardiologist, who had never suggested that she have such tests, he was a little sniffy at being confronted with the work of a Sunday supplement medical van in a church parking lot. But he ordered a sonogram. And then an MRI. And then an angiogram. All of which cost a lot more than ninety-five dollars.

"An' when they did *tha-yet*," Sarah Jane said, with satisfaction, pausing as her audience—El Cee, the Emyfish, the Duchess, Mary Davis, and others, all held their drinks and stared at her, waiting for the rest of the story—"it showed a sa-veah blockage, *juss* as the road-show tests had sah-yed." Sarah Jane shifted the glass of bourbon and water to her right hand, placed the jeweled fingers of her left hand on the left side of her neck, where she could feel the impeded artery pulsing faintly, and gave them all a significant look through her large, lavender-tinted glasses. "This, of course, has *evah-thang* to do with the right side of yoah brain—yoah *speech*."

There was a silent moment while that sank in, followed by a small eruption of titters and giggles at the idea of a speechless Sarah Jane. Then she resumed. Her cardiologist had sent her to a surgeon, who told her, she said, "'At your age, which is seventy-four, and in your health, which is good, your chances of coming through the surgery are ninety-eight percent.' Mah chances of havin' a stroke if Ah doan' have id done arh fifteen puhcent," she continued. "*Nex* yeah, the chance of success goes dowahn, and the chance ovah stroke goes up. Eventually, they cross. So why havvid hangin' ovah mah heh-yed?"

She decided to have the surgery. "Too many fried egg sandwiches," she said, without explanation. There was a sly, mischievous light in her eyes. As soon as the test results came back, Sarah Jane had known what the problem was—the fatty residue from her second marriage. Her second husband—from the time they had spotted each other near the family lake house where she had retreated one summer to lick her wounds, after divorcing her crazy, drunken first husband, until the time she had divorced him, too—was an insatiable lover, whose horns grew late at night. "He was reallah ah sex *addig*," Sarah Jane explained, with a look intended to let me know that she

meant what she said. "So thuh sex was grea-yut. Aftahward, he didden' wanna cigarette. He didden' smoke. He wannid me to fix him
ah fried egg sandwich. Fry thuh bagan. Fry thuh egg in thuh bagan
grease. Buttah thuh breahyud. Jus' white breahyud. Withha big
glassa *whole* milk." It all smelled so good, she made the same thing
for both of them. Night after night, year after year, it was their routine: love and animal fat.

So now, she had decided, she was going to have all that carotid
plaque, from decades of high-cholesterol southern love and munching, scooped out.

"So many of mah friends have had face-lifts," Sarah Jane noted,
as weeks passed and the date drew closer. "Well, *Ah'm* goin' tuh
havah brain lift. And *then* maybe Ah'll be able to remembah somethin'."

No one questioned her decision. For the group in El Cee's
apartment, it was routine maintenance. They all had issues.
The Duchess, who had almost died of heart failure in the
pedicure chair the year before, took medications for her heart and
high blood pressure. She had osteoporosis and used a walker, too.
The Emyfish suffered from atrial fibrillation and spinal stenosis. If
she walked too far or too fast, she got out of breath. Besides, her
back and legs hurt. Her feet didn't always want to go where she was
headed. Sometimes, when she tripped and fell, she landed on her
prosthetic breast, which padded her fall. El Cee was arthritic. Her
neck and back ached. And sometimes she woke in the night with
burning sensations in her chest and throat, which worried her. She
was a nurse, after all, and her former husband had died of esophageal
cancer.

Mary Davis had almost expired before her heart valve was replaced. She had had surgery, years before, on her back. She walked
very carefully, and no longer risked leaning over to pick something up if she dropped it on the floor. The housekeeping staff
cleaned only once a week, and so a trail of coffee cups, glasses,

napkins, tissues, and crumbs and bits of this and that littered the carpet in her new apartment. She felt tired most of the time. She didn't know why, but she already knew as much about herself as she wanted to know. More, actually. She had never had much curiosity about her body, and she was getting tired of fixing it up so she could live a little longer. It just didn't matter that much to her anymore.

She was in the minority, of course. For most residents of the Tower, maintenance, detection, and repair were the order of the day. Whatever the problem, the idea was to stop the leak before it became a flood. They would all be carried away soon enough. They knew that. Their vulnerability was the reason they had come to live at Canterbury, where they could be monitored and supported, guarded, fussed over, and cared for by Mrs. Vinas and her staff. They lived every day with the feeling of sweet imminence. It was a part of the spirit of the place—always present. Usually unspoken, it affected everything.

"You buy everything in such *big* sizes," the Sweetso observed, looking up from her book one afternoon as I came through the door, carrying jugs of milk and orange juice, and a large carton of eggs for the refrigerator. "When you get older, you learn not to buy anything that will last more than two weeks—because *you* might not."

Sweet imminence. In the Health Center, on the last Sunday morning in May, as Mother lay in her chaise longue, grinding her teeth and watching as if from a distance, Ernestine heaved herself up in the front of the doddering crowd in the recreation room as the worship service came to an end. She flashed a big loving grin at Mother and the twelve or fifteen other decrepit old people parked there, closed her eyes, spread her hands out, palms up, and began, in a low, crooning voice, to sing:

> *Soon I will be done*
> *With the troubles of the world,*
> *The troubles of the world,*

The TROUBLES of the world.
Soon I will be done
With the troubles of the world.
I'm going home
To live . . . with my Lord.

Ernestine caressed the lines of the old spiritual, weaving her way through the lyrics, sometimes changing them as she went. Her gospel was sort of like jazz in that respect. It came out the way she felt. She was almost always at the worship service in the Health Center on Sunday mornings. She didn't have to be. She chose to be. And she almost always sang. It seemed to comfort her, and also the people around her. For Ernestine, music was a way to express love today, and faith in tomorrow.

At Canterbury, however, you never knew who might be going home. And not long after that, Ernestine, the sturdy pillar and spiritual well of the nursing wing—the one who was always there for others, always able to sense when one resident or another needed a little affection, a little attention, a little understanding or bucking up—stopped showing up. She wasn't there anymore. She just didn't come. She had for years been very overweight. She had never given herself the kind of care and attention that she lavished on the residents. Her diet was a horror of junk food impulse and absentminded neglect. Ernestine was only forty-eight years old, and she had had a stroke.

There was no immediate announcement or explanation. The staff at Canterbury is under strict orders not to talk about the health of residents or of members of the staff, and so it was a while before some understanding filtered out of what had happened. It was my mother's companion, Louise, who told me, because she and Ernestine had become friends. They kept up with each other by phone. Then I went to see Ernestine. She was lucky. It had been mild. She would be back in six weeks.

But before her absence had a chance to register among the residents of the Health Center, or in the larger community of the

Tower, a notice went up in the elevators and appeared on the Canterbury schedule, which scrolled endlessly across the screen of the in-house television cable channel: Mrs. Vinas had called a general residents' meeting, for Friday morning, the first of June.

Mrs. Vinas had also been away from Canterbury—just for a day or two the previous week. No one had noticed. It was hard to track her movements. Much of the time, she was in the building but out of sight. Sometimes she was away at elder care conferences, in Tallahassee or Washington. But she was usually in town and in her office by 5:00 a.m., when most residents were still asleep. She was sometimes visible at evening events, too, and was often popping up at odd times of the day and night, weekdays or weekends, so that people always assumed she might be somewhere in the building, even if she was not.

Mrs. Vinas had gone to the doctor on the previous Friday—an unusual appointment for her—for an examination she had finally scheduled, and with reluctance. "All right," she told herself, with annoyance, "stop fooling around." She was accustomed to being inexhaustible, but lately had been feeling fatigued. She had been given an antibiotic after some dental surgery. It had interfered with her digestion and made her nauseated.

"I couldn't eat," she said. The lack of appetite, the nausea, the fatigue led to all kinds of tests. Her Friday appointment was for a colonoscopy. It irked Mrs. Vinas to have to stop and attend to her body. She was used to its going where she wanted to go and doing what she wanted it to do, when she wanted to do it. She and Ernestine were practically the same age, very alike in their obsessive attention to their jobs, and to the needs of others. And in neglecting themselves.

But Mrs. Vinas was lucky as well. The heart attack hit her as she lay on the operating table in the doctor's surgical suite, just as she was coming out of the anesthesia for the colonoscopy—a sudden, paralyzing pain and pressure, exactly as she had always heard it described, like an elephant sitting on her chest. It wasn't a blockage, her cardiologist told her later. It was a heart spasm, like a clenched fist, and if it had happened at home, or in the car, she would have died. But it came when she was in the middle of a medical suite, surrounded by staff. "So they coded me," she said. "They pumped me with medications, and sent me straight into ICU. When they said 'helicopter,' I thought, *This sounds serious.*"

At the hospital, they didn't find a lot of damage. "It's minor damage," she said pointedly. But that night, about 1:30, in the intensive care unit, she started getting chest pain. It felt like someone's fist, pushing hard in the center of her chest.

"I called for the nurse. Nobody came." She looked angry, recalling the moment.

She willed herself through the night, waiting until morning, when a certified nursing assistant came to check on her.

"*Ring* the nurse," she said, dark eyes flashing. "*Bring* my chart!"

When the nurse came, Mrs. Vinas said, she told her, "You call my doctor, and I'm out of here, *now*! Because if I didn't die getting here, I'm going to die here!" With that, she got up, got dressed, checked out, and went home, furious at the sloppy care. That was Saturday. On Monday morning, she was back at her desk. No one at Canterbury even knew she'd had the heart attack.

"I wasn't going to say anything to them at all," she confided later, in the quiet of her office. "They have enough of their own problems. But I started picking up stories." In the intensely self-contained atmosphere of Canterbury, where gossip is circular, someone thought she saw papers being shredded outside Mrs. Vinas's office. The rumor spread that she was quitting—that she was shredding documents before she left.

Gossip, she knew, created a vacuum, which might soon pull up the fact that she had been to see the doctor or, even worse, been in the hospital. So she decided to call a general meeting of the residents. On Friday morning, as residents came into the assembly room on the first floor, they found Mrs. Vinas, in her conservative dark skirt, blouse, jacket, and low-heeled shoes, lifting additional chairs into place. When the room was full of gray and white and bald heads and old faces, all of them looking at her curiously, wondering what was up, she got right to the point.

"For those of you who heard the rumor that I was leaving—and for those of you who would rejoice in that," she said (and Lucie Cross was sure that Mrs. Vinas was looking directly at *her* when she said this, so she gave her a hard-eyed stare in return), "I hate to tell you that I'm not going *anywhere*." She had had a heart attack, she told them matter-of-factly, without going into detail. But she was lucky. It hadn't done much damage, and she was staying at her job.

People were stunned. *They* were the ones who were supposed to be worried about heart attacks and strokes. Mrs. Vinas had always seemed indestructible. Admired and even loved by some residents, she was also, from time to time, resented by many of them. But liked or not, everything—and everyone—relied on her.

In the days after the meeting, her office filled with flowers and notes and cards. Residents gave her tender smiles or appraising side-wise looks when they saw her. They watched her movements, her expressions, looking for signs, reporting their sightings to one another, gossiping about what they'd seen or heard. Everyone knew she worked too hard, that she needed to slow down.

"I don't know how she can relax," the rabbi said, solemnly, as he and Ruth sat at lunch in the dining room one day. "She's a micro-manager."

Ruth nodded, rolling her eyes slightly. "She's a driven person," she said.

"In the middle of the night," Karl remembered, "there was a water leak. It was dripping down the walls. It got on my books."

"And down Mrs. Vinas came," Ruth said, picking up his story, "in the middle of the night. And sat on Karl's bed." She paused, shaking her head at the idea of trying to get such a personality to relax. "I think her husband will have to put his *foot* down—if he cares."

"She should get an assistant. Or delegate more authority," Karl offered, looking at Ruth.

Ruth looked back at him. "It's not in her makeup," she said flatly.

No one really expected Mrs. Vinas to change.

But one thing that was true, after eight decades or so of life, was that nothing really surprised or distressed most residents at Canterbury that much, not anymore—and if it did, it didn't last that long. Illness, death, calamity—those things happened all the time. They couldn't let their own security or well-being depend on the content of other lives, or events. It was a self-protective wisdom, the shield of experience. Whatever occurred, tomorrow would follow today. Life was as it was, and would be.

"Do you know the story of the optimist and the pessimist?" the rabbi asked, a knowing twinkle in his old eyes.

No.

"This is the best of all possible worlds," the optimist said.

"I'm afraid you're right," the pessimist said.

And so, in a few days, everyone found something else to do or to think or talk about. A sense of normalcy resumed.

Dr. Shrager sat in his accustomed place in the lobby, looking calm and patient, and deflatingly plump.

The Sweetso and El Cee went to New York and returned, bubbling and fussing about *The Vagina Monologues*. "I thought the one on the left was Haley Mills," the Sweetso laughed. "She thinks the one in the middle was Haley Mills. We have been arguing about this for three days."

One night, at the Men's Table, Ben Franklin insisted that Martha explain *The Vagina Monologues* to the rest of them. "So finally, I did," the Sweetso said. "So Harold Tobin said *he* was going to write *The Penis Monologues*."

Sarah Jane went into the hospital to have her operation, which was uneventful. "She probably won't feel like talking for three or four days," her surgeon cautioned Mauricio, before Sarah Jane woke up.

"You don't know my wife," Mauricio said.

Within hours, she was on the phone. Within days, she was back at cocktails and dinner, giving the report on her operation, and the news on her second husband.

"He's juss had *botha* his carotid ahrteries done!" she crowed.

Even the Emyfish, who liked and admired Mrs. Vinas—and wanted her to stay well and be in charge for at least as long as she, the Emyfish, was there—found other signs of mortality and decay to fume about.

"Did you see the news about Imogene Coca and Arlene Francis?" she demanded one day. Her dark eyes were furious. "IMOGENE Coca and ARLENE Francis!" she repeated, as if she hardly could believe it. She sighed and shook her head. Arlene had just died at ninety-two. Imogene was dotty. It was incredible. Unimaginable. "Here are these two *brainy* women—Arlene Francis was *so* sharp. How can *they* get Alzheimer's?"

If *they* could, then . . . The Emyfish fell into a deep, gloomy silence, scowling out the window. She looked mad at the world. Or perhaps at the encroaching future.

"Old age is *disgusting*!" she growled. "I don't know why you can't be born old—and get younger!"

CHAPTER NINETEEN

War and Survival

JUNE 2001

I came in one night after dinner, expecting jokes and ice cream, and found the Sweetso, a ball of tears in a flowered size-16 nightgown, tucked as far back as she could get in the pillows of the big white leather couch, sniffing and blinking and dabbing her nose. The lights were dim. The television was on, turned to the History Channel, and it had taken her back to when she was young, a size 7, and the world was at war. On the screen, the U.S. Marines were fighting, foot by foot, even inch by inch, with flame throwers and mortars and howitzers, M-1 rifles and machine guns, fighter planes and the big guns of Navy ships offshore, for possession of the hard, hot, hostile gray rock of Okinawa. The old filmed scenes of battle reminded her, of course, of Charles. He had landed on Okinawa, and other islands before, as American forces moved westward across the Pacific toward Japan. It didn't matter to the Sweetso that those things had occurred long before she knew him. Charles had been her husband, her hero. Her own Marine.

She sat up with a pink, goofy, wet-faced smile. She wanted to repeat a Charles story. The advantage of being an officer during an invasion, he had told her, was that he could stand anywhere he wanted in the tightly packed landing craft, which had a shallow draft, and pitched and rolled in the waves as it moved toward shore.

"He said he always stood in the back, because it was the one place where no one could throw up on him from behind," the Sweetso said. She laughed in delight, coughing and chortling, blinking away the last of her tears.

"Wasn't he something?" She beamed.

It was June, and the great struggle that had altered all their lives so long ago had revived once more. It had ended more than half a century before. Yet each year, the memories and feelings came flooding back, testing them again. The flow seemed strongest from Memorial Day through the first week of June—the month in 1944 that the Allies had invaded Nazi-occupied Europe, landing on the beaches of Normandy. The date was June 6, the turning point in the Atlantic war—the greatest amphibious invasion ever assembled and executed in any war. But June had also been the decisive month of the American assault in 1945 on the Japanese island of Okinawa, a pivotal battle of the Pacific war. And one of the most ferocious.

It hadn't begun as the War to End All Wars. That was the name given, after the fact, to World War I. Some of the residents at Canterbury were old enough to remember it, too. But the name had proved to be shortsighted, its hope naïve. World War II was far worse: crueler, more violent, more global, murderous, and catastrophic—more evil, as everyone realized toward the end, when the death camps were discovered—than any war before. It had swept up many of the residents at Canterbury just as the Great Depression was finally ending, just as they were beginning to make their own lives. They went from the worst depression to the worst war. They were tested hard and early. They had lived long. Now, in the unexpected years of the new century, a millennium most of them had never expected to know, what they mainly wanted was to feel secure in their last years, and at peace. Surely, history was done with them by now.

Whether in the Atlantic, the Pacific, the Mediterranean, or the Caribbean, in war production work, or simply in keeping the faith at home, every American family had played some role in World War II. They prayed for those who were far away or who lost someone—or marveled, when husbands, sons, brothers, and daughters came back, at the dangers they had escaped. It changed almost all of them. Many of those who served in uniform were gone for two and a half or three years, or even more—a tremendously long time to be separated from parents and wives, lovers, brothers, sisters, and children. Separated by thousands of miles, lacking any knowledge of the events of each day, they had no way to keep each other close except through memory, photographs, and the thin, flyweight stationery on which they wrote back and forth, in letters that were censored, and frequently weeks—even months—late in delivery.

The ones who survived the war came back with a new sense of the great expanse and diversity of the United States, and of the world beyond, and a heightened—sometimes haunted—appreciation of life and luck. Some of the wives and girlfriends left behind did not wait. But most returning servicemen and servicewomen came back more precious than they departed, to families and lovers and spouses who swore never again to take them for granted, or let them go. And yet the odd thing, for my generation, was that our parents and their friends never talked about it. They didn't want to—at least not to us. It was as if it hadn't happened, except in books, in films, and on television. It was not until I came to Canterbury, and got drawn into the lives of people there, that I began to hear firsthand about the war.

By the time the Japanese bombed Pearl Harbor on December 7, 1941, Karl and Ruth Richter, and their daughter, Esther, had been safely, if strangely, tucked into the life of Springfield, Missouri, for two and a half years. The Jewish community, and the city, had been welcoming. It had seemed at first an odd place to be, but it was beginning to feel like home. Then came the sneak attack.

"The day after Pearl Harbor, we had to report to the police. We had to go down to the police station with our little girl, and take our camera, and our radio. But at least they didn't put us into camps—the way they did the Japanese," Karl said.

It was a strange time. The brilliant, sensitive, good-humored young rabbi with the beautiful wife and little girl—and awful, firsthand experience of the Nazis—had become a sought-after speaker in cities and towns across the Midwest. But the Richters were still German citizens, and when the United States entered the war against Japan and its allies, Germany and Italy, they instantly became enemy aliens. "I had to report to the U.S. district attorney whenever I left the city," Karl said, marveling. "And I had so *many* speaking engagements."

At the same time, he was made an air-raid warden. "Vat's de madder vith you Americans?" he joked, in his still heavily accented English, when he saw the mayor of Springfield one day. "In the mornig, ve are enemy aliens. In the eeff-ening, ve are en-thrusted vith civil defense."

"Don't worry," the mayor replied. "In Missouri, we know our enemies—and we know our friends."

In New Jersey, that Sunday of the attack on Pearl Harbor, Martha Cameron (then still the unmarried Martha Murrah) had worked the night shift on a men's surgical ward at the Jersey City Medical Center. She was asleep in the Nurses' Home, a tall, hotel-like building adjacent to the hospital, when news came of the attack. She was twenty-three. She had graduated from nursing school just six months before, and the quiet of the dormitory—a place where nurses who worked different shifts slept in different shifts around the clock—felt comfortable. When Martha woke that afternoon, however, the halls were full of noise. And when she made the rounds of the ward that night—"We saw every patient on the floor in those days," she explained, "took their temperature and pulse, and talked to all of them"—they all asked, "What service are you going to join?"

Just as she had been attracted to nursing by the experience of caring for her invalid sister and dying mother, family experience had also made military life seem familiar. Columbus, Georgia, the site of the army's big Fort Benning, was her mother's hometown. And

Martha had been to the U.S. Military Academy at West Point, with one of her cousins.

"The next morning, when I got off duty, I went to the nurse who took care of Red Cross applications," she said, "and signed up for the Army Nursing Corps." In March, she received orders to report to Fort DuPont in Delaware. When an overseas list went up, she put her name on it. She was sent to Fort Hancock, at Sandy Hook, New Jersey, to become part of a hospital unit being formed there. The young women lived in barracks, but basic training for doctors and nurses hadn't really been developed yet. All they seemed to do was train with gas masks, march in formation in their high-topped shoes, and march some more. Still, in July 1942, the hospital group crossed New York Harbor on a ferry to board a converted British ocean liner lying next to the huge, ghostly, burned-out hulk of the *Normandie,* the former pride of the French Line, which had been sabotaged as it lay at dock. Early the next morning, with an all-Indian Hindu crew, they slipped unescorted into the Atlantic, headed for war.

Martha Cameron was a newly commissioned second lieutenant in the Army Nursing Corps. "We had no idea what we were going to do," she said. "All we knew was that we would be in a hospital—some kind of hospital. That was all we knew." She would be gone almost three years, to England, North Africa, Sicily, France, Belgium, and Germany. She would land at Utah Beach, in the first company of nurses ashore after D-day, and follow the Allied front as it advanced, administering the drops of ether that rendered wounded and frozen young soldiers deeply unconscious during the bitterly cold weeks of the Battle of the Bulge, so that doctors could amputate their frostbitten feet and legs. More than fifty years later, after finally retiring from the career in civilian nursing that had followed the military one, Martha would try to organize her recollection of the war years, to see for herself if they might make the beginning chapters of a book. Her experiences would become part of two other histories of American nurses in the war, but in her own account, she got as far as a slim sheaf of typed pages, an outline entitled *The Life and Times of*

One Nurse of the Twentieth Century, which she kept in her apartment at Canterbury—in a drawer.

Tucked away, all over the building, were other experiences of the war. They were carried in memory by people who rarely, if ever, mentioned them. But there were also diaries, military records, yellowed letters, telegrams, and fading photographs—framed or stuffed into albums, or worn manila envelopes—of solemn or smiling young men in uniform. Some were in the formal, solitary poses made after they finished boot camp in the United States. Some were with their airplanes, or with their buddies, lounging shirtless on a ship deck, or wearily in a field in France, in the ruins of some shattered German town or blasted island in the Pacific, or under the sun in Algeria or Morocco, tanks and trucks and jeeps behind them.

Ben Franklin had been an Army officer in combat in North Africa and then in Italy. Ashby Moody had been an Army Air Corps glider pilot. Released by the C-47 transport that had towed his glider and one other from France, he had steered the flimsy canvas-and-wood craft, with a dozen nervous, sweating young soldiers aboard, and twelve hundred other gliders, floating silently through the air all around them, through the remaining ground fire, across the Rhine river. They landed safely, with bullet holes through the canvas, inside Germany. It was Ashby's last mission.

Joel Shrager had been a young Army doctor on his way to the war, just like Martha Cameron, when his auxiliary cruiser was torpedoed and sank—burning at both ends—on a Friday night. For two nights and two days, he commanded an overcrowded and underprovisioned lifeboat. They had just come through the Panama Canal that morning and were less than a hundred miles off the coast of Nicaragua when the ship was struck. The lifeboat was designed to hold nineteen, but there were thirty-nine men in it, almost half of them wounded, and it fell to Joel to keep them calm and still so the lifeboat would not capsize, to give them hope and enough water to survive. At first they thought they were going to die, because the submarine surfaced as the ship went down and ordered them to come alongside. But they rowed in the opposite direction, and for some reason the Germans didn't fire, leaving them alone in the pitch-black night. Joel doled out half a glass of water per healthy man per day, saving the rest for the wounded. They floated past other lifeboats, upside down with bullet holes in them. On Sunday, they saw smoke on the horizon and that afternoon were taken aboard a U.S. destroyer.

They all were lucky to come home alive. But as years and then decades passed, the drama, the suddenness, and brutality of combat slipped behind them. For the next half century or more, the papers and photographs they brought back became part of what they carried with them, from place to place, into retirement, and finally, to Canterbury. Mostly, the papers and pictures stayed in drawers. That is where, years later, they would be found by children or grandchildren, a nephew or niece, or perhaps by an old friend. The finders would leaf through them, trying to understand what they saw, wondering what to do with them. Often, not knowing, not wanting to dishonor them, they would put them in another drawer.

But in the solitude of their apartments, some residents at Canterbury went back again and again to those drawers—as to a deep, private well of memories and emotions from a time when they were young and deeply tested. The Sweetso wasn't the only widow who took her husband's letters out and reread them, time and again. Margy Chunn Cochran's first husband, Dr. Charles Francis Chunn— Frank, the great romance of her life—had kept a modest and vivid and detailed record of his experience as a combat surgeon in World War II. He had operated on hundreds of young soldiers, American and British (and even Italian and German), much of the time while being bombed and shelled in North Africa, Italy, France, and Germany. Frank was as faithful a letter writer as he was a diarist, and after she turned eighty and moved into Canterbury, a widow again from her second marriage to an old friend whose wife had also died, Margy began thinking that she should find some way to publish the three worn notebooks in which Frank had written, and some of his letters to her as well. Her daughter, Celeste Chunn Col-cord, edited them down, they hired a press, and the result was a book, *My Darling Margy: The World War II Diaries and Letters of Surgeon Charles Francis Chunn, MD.*

It pleased Margy. "It was a real love story," she said, with a smile. Frank had just graduated from Duke University Medical School, and she was a student nurse at the Duke University Medical Center, slim and dark haired, when he stole her away from her boyfriend, a cadet at the U.S. Naval Academy at Annapolis, Maryland. Frank Chunn was small, smart, ardent, and absolutely confident. And so *cute,* Margy thought. He told friends that he had seen a student nurse, the girl that he would marry. He asked Margy to help him change his patients' dressings, and then, with a sly smile, painted her initials in gentian violet on the skin around their incisions. She found him irresistible. His salary as an intern was all of ten dollars a month, and so, to make the trip home with her to Tampa to meet her parents, Frank sold his blood, and also his microscope. It was a successful visit. Her parents liked him and understood that he and Margy would marry later.

But when Margy and Frank got off the train that took them back to North Carolina, they decided they couldn't wait. They hailed a cab in Raleigh and went downtown to buy a marriage license, a ring, and flowers. Then they had the taxi take them to a Methodist church, where they were married by the pastor, with the grinning cab driver as their witness.

Five years later, after training in surgery in Detroit and in Ann Arbor, Michigan, and a year of residency in Vicksburg, Mississippi, they settled in Tampa. Frank Chunn had just opened his new office when the Japanese attacked Pearl Harbor that Sunday morning. And on Monday, just like Martha Cameron, he chucked his brand-new, hard-won career and volunteered for the Army Medical Corps.

It took him a while to get into a combat surgical unit. But four-teen months later, Captain Frank Chunn boarded HMT *Andes,* a fast British liner converted to a troop ship, and steamed out of New York. Like Martha, he didn't know what the future held, where it would take him, or whether he would survive. And so the night before embarking, he wrote his wife a letter.

My darling Margy,

This is absolutely the last un-censored note I will be able to write you for some time to come.

We are on the spot, and long before you get this letter, we will be on a big, fast boat going places.

I'm sure I'll come back to you just as I left you, but . . . if by any chance I don't see you again I have the thoughts and memories of a most wonderful love and happiness with you. This is much harder on you than I, because you may have to go on living. I couldn't live without you.

Please love me and think of me as I do you.

When the going gets rough, do as I do and will do. I will dream of you and have you with me in my soul.

We leave soon and will face a lot; I will do every bit of my part because I'll feel I'm doing it for us and what we love. I'm counting on you.

Love me as I love you,

Frank

What he could not write to her, he confided to his journal. The *Andes* left New York on February 28, 1943, and set out across the Atlantic with five thousand men and sixty-six nurses aboard. It was unescorted. "However, we are well-gunned and very fast."

March 6. "This ship has been dodging all over the ocean. We were in a hot spot yesterday. The Subs were quite close and several in number." What he didn't say then, even to his diary, was that the *Andes* had been attacked twice with torpedoes but had evaded them.

March 9. "Landed today at Casablanca. . . . Moon, stars, music, and wine." He was fascinated and enchanted. "Margy, if you could only be here. It's like living in a dream."

Frank had always been eager for new things. But for a boy who operated on rats, rabbits, and squirrels in his own small laboratory in an apple orchard behind the family house in Asheville, North Carolina—as for all his generation who went across the oceans to fight on foreign soil and came back—North Africa brought revelations. The French maid in Casablanca who drew his bath and washed his back. The good, cheap red wine. The casbah. But very soon, also, the brutal ephemerality of life.

He was young and brave, and inclined to see life as an adventure, and at first, as he watched from shipboard, from outside his operating tent, or from the bottom of the ditch or foxhole he had just jumped into, the duels of the German and Allied fighters and bombers, along with the exploding artillery and antiaircraft shells, were great sport to see.

But as the months unfolded and the war carried him through North Africa and onto the deadly beachhead at Anzio, Italy, it ceased being a show. British and American ships right next to him, and also ships he had just been on—converted passenger liners, hospital ships, cruisers, destroyers, minesweepers—were sunk before his eyes or just days after he left them. Repeatedly, he found himself in a hail of falling shells and bombs, mostly German but sometimes Allied. Patients, nurses, enlisted men, and other officers were killed and maimed all around him, and still he was not.

May 11. "Sweetheart, I'm back and am intact. . . . Since my last note, I've traveled 450 miles in my truck, was sniped at in Bizerte and shelled on Tunis road; then when I got back to our hospital we were shot up there. Had three patients killed and seven others wounded."

May 19, 8:00 p.m. "I've just finished 35 hours of operating and am a bit tired. Today I operated on 33 cases, not counting yesterday and last night. I have two little ole American nurses who stuck with me all the long hours and worked like hell. I've never heard one complaint and when we finished tonight they could still smile. They are grand girls and real soldiers. I'll never be able to say enough for the American Nurse. They shouldn't be here. It's no place for them but they are here and are doing their part. Some bastards in the States that I know should see them. Well, enough of that."

He operated when it was 116 degrees in the shade, and by flash-light, under fire, when exhausted, with a throbbing, infected thumb, and even with a deep shrapnel wound in his right hand, on American, British, French, Italian, and German soldiers—and also on civilians caught in the war, even on children.

In between the shelling and the surgeries, Frank missed his young wife terribly. "Margy, I wish you were with me tonight," he wrote in August 1943. "I need you so, now, darling. I'm blue and want you so. If I could only come across the miles to you tonight. Do you understand what my heart feels and is saying?"

Frank Chunn and Martha Cameron never quite overlapped. They were both in North Africa, but not in the same places at the same time. Then she landed in Sicily. Frank went ashore on the continent first, on January 22, 1944, at the Red Beach at Anzio, which became an infamous killing ground of Allied troops.

"We climbed into the landing boat and as we did a large mine-sweeper next to us was blown up and sank in about 5 minutes," he wrote. When they clambered out of the landing boat onto a pontoon, used as a bridge to the beach, the pontoon "was slippery with blood and large chunks of human flesh and meat were scattered about presenting a sight that I'll never forget and I'm a surgeon used to such butchery."

Frank didn't get off the beach at Anzio for four months, until May 26, performing often very complicated surgery, under fire almost the entire time. He reached Rome on June 5, the day before the invasion of Normandy began. The next morning, he watched as wave after wave of Liberator bombers, more than seven hundred by his count, passed over the ancient imperial city. He listened to the Allied radio and decided that they must be headed toward the German lines behind the beaches.

Martha and her hospital unit of twenty doctors, thirty nurses, and two hundred enlisted men—the 128th Evacuation Hospital—embarked from England on June 7 and reached the coast of Normandy in a Liberty ship three days later, D-day plus four. It had been a dangerous passage. The night before, crossing the English Channel, the nurses had been asleep—bundled in their shoes and fatigues, with a second set of men's fatigues specially impregnated with antigas chemicals over their own—when the chief nurse's whistle roused them. They grabbed their helmets and fell out to stand by the three- and four-tiered bunks, just in time to get knocked down by a tremendous explosion. A glider bomb had fallen between their ship and the next one. The explosion shook the ship so hard that Martha felt her teeth rattle as if they were loose. She thought they might fall out. Dazed, she looked around, expecting to see water pouring in, but the ship stayed on course, and in the morning, when they woke again, they were anchored off Utah Beach.

"Jeez. *Women!*" the approaching beach master exclaimed from his boat when he had threaded through the mass of ships waiting offshore and saw the nurses peering over the railing at him.

They climbed awkwardly down the rope nets thrown over the side and into the heaving landing craft, jumped from it into waist-deep water, and waded ashore to be scooped up by amphibious ducks and then by trucks sent to bring them inland. They had landed to the boom of artillery, but the beachhead by then was twelve miles deep. The doctors were already operating when they reached the field hospital. They were the first nurses, and so found the wards in disarray. There were ten or twelve beds per tent, a soldier who had died after surgery lying in one of them, and a line of wounded men waiting on litters on the ground.

"Boy, were they happy when they saw us," Martha said, "because they figured that they were safe then."

She and Frank Chunn were stretched beyond anything they could have imagined, in the operating tents in those years of war. But they were also both astounded at the wounds the soldiers could endure and survive, and at their increasing ability to save them.

"It's amazing what they can take," Frank wrote on February 19, 1944, on the beach at Anzio. "For example, on one lad, I closed a large sucking wound of the chest, explored his abdomen, and re-sected some small intestine, amputated his left thigh, amputated two right toes, and debrided 4 wounds of back and flank. Today, three days later, he is doing very well, and I believe will make the grade."

In the field hospital at Boutteville in Normandy, where she assisted on her first surgeries on shell fragment wounds (which became the most common wounds she saw), most of the wounds were in the belly, lungs, or brain. Martha was stunned that the surgeons "could reach down four inches from the top of the skull and drag out this huge piece of shell fragment," and that the young soldier survived to recover consciousness, and speak.

"All our cases had to wake up. We weren't through with our cases until they could talk with us," she said. It was Martha who administered the anesthesia. Once in the Nursing Corps, she had been trained to do that as one of the few nurse anesthetists. For more superficial surgeries, she gave the patients sodium pentothal, but for deep body and brain surgeries, she used ether, which was highly flammable and explosive (and later banned in the United States). She stood dripping it, in a method that seems very primitive today, drop by drop, on a mask over the patient's face, gauging the level of unconsciousness "by the breathing itself. As they got deeper and deeper, the breathing changed—first, normal chest breathing, then abdominal breathing. The main thing was that they didn't move. If they started moving a little finger or something, I gave them a little bit more. But you couldn't give them so much that they would stop breathing."

She and Frank both did things that amazed them. The day she walked into the field operating tent during the grim, cold days of the Battle of the Bulge and saw eight men with their frozen legs on blocks, waiting to be amputated, "was the only time I felt like turning around and going home. The surgeons' hands were so cold they couldn't feel to operate." They pleaded with her to let them light the Sibley stove, to warm the tent. That one time, Martha agreed, moving the operating table and patient away from the stove, praying that the ether would not explode and burn and kill them all.

Frank survived the war to celebrate the German surrender in

Paris. He returned to Margy with six Bronze Stars, a Silver Star, and a Purple Heart. They had three children. He became an accomplished and beloved surgeon in Tampa, and died of a heart attack that struck him on his boat at the yacht club, in 1970, in what was supposed to be the prime of his life.

The luck of the draw preserved Martha and brought her back to the United States, too, but too soon. She and five other nurses received orders for home just as the 128th Evacuation Hospital unit crossed the Rhine in April 1945. President Roosevelt died as Martha was on a ship in the mid-Atlantic, coming home. She had been gone almost three years. She was on leave in New York, in midtown Manhattan one day, when she heard the rising noise of crowds forming in the streets. "They were all rushing toward Times Square," she said. She moved with everyone else, not knowing what the excitement was, and when she reached Times Square, saw the news going round and round on the electric billboard: ALLIED VICTORY IN EUROPE. It was VE day. It caught her unprepared. The crowd was delirious. Martha was not.

"Oh, I was angry," she said, her face stern even now, more than fifty-five years later. She was not where she had wanted to be. She had wanted to see it through. She had wanted to be in Berlin.

CHAPTER TWENTY

I Can't Find My Wife

Wilber had been shipped overseas, too, although he was already in his mid-thirties when he put on his Army uniform, and the father of Nathalie, a baby girl. He served in the noncommissioned ranks, like my father, stationed with a support group in England for the last two years of the war. "I just hated for him to miss Nathalie's young years," Mary said, on a Friday evening in late June. "He left on her first birthday, and came back on her third."

We were talking over drinks in her apartment. I could see, from her windows, the long, browning stretch of grass and tired trees along the Bayshore toward town. It had been another very dry spring. But Mary had other things on her mind—not all of which she could remember.

There had been two messages waiting on my home phone line back in Baltimore when I called to check my voice mail the day before, after flying down to Tampa. The first was from the Emyfish. "Mary called," she said. "She's lost your phone number again. I gave it to her." *Click.*

The second was from Mary. "Dudley, this is Mary Davis in Tampa. I've forgotten what night we're going to have dinner. Call me." *Click.*

"Well, I was in the bedroom when we talked about it," she

explained when I called, "and I thought I'd write it down in my calendar in the living room. But by the time I got in there, I forgot what day."

The distance was about twenty feet, which seemed funny. That's what starts happening when you get old, if you don't have a social secretary following you from room to room. I pulled a pen from my pocket and fished for my notebook. I always carry notebooks at Canterbury. I fill them, and they stack up on a long table in my writing study at home, numbered and dated by month and year. But where was the notebook? I must have left it somewhere. I retraced my steps—and there it was. In the men's room. Propped on top of the urinal. Hhhmm. I'd done this before. In fact, I do it every time I come down to Canterbury and use the men's room. It's easy. Walk into men's room. Stand at urinal. Put pad down. Unzip. Whiz. Rezip. Walk off relieved. Of notepad.

At what age, I wondered, did normal people begin to have these moments? I've been absentminded all my life. That's why I write my name, address, and phone numbers on the front of every note-book, along with IF FOUND, PLEASE CALL . . . I had left car keys, dark glasses, my wedding ring, and cell phones in men's rooms before. But not with such regularity. Writing about things could get to be a problem if I lost my notes every time I had to pee. Peeing was getting to be sort of frequent.

"I had a friend, a man friend in Tampa," Judy Drake said, peering at me as she and Mary and I had lunch, "who wore a small note-book on his lapel. He wrote down things to remember. And if they were important, he tore out the pages and rolled them up and stuck them in his wedding ring." Judy was sitting across from me, a tiny figure, head and shoulders barely clearing the rim of the table, with a silver ponytail and serious blue eyes looming behind the lenses of her oversize glasses. She was looking at me as if she thought that was something I might try. I tried picturing myself with a yellow legal pad attached to my lapel, and rolled-up pages stuck like parchment scrolls through my wedding ring. The image didn't work. For one thing, I was divorced.

But Judy had given a lot of thought to the problem. She was a nurse trained at Johns Hopkins, and had twelve other nurses and doctors in her family line. She took these things seriously. She thought things should be properly labeled.

"I do *not* like 'senior moment.'" She sniffed, dabbing her nose. "I think it's tacky. I prefer *mild cognitive malfunction*. It has more dignity."

In my head, I tried it out. *Created moment:* "Thanks, Judy, I'd like to write that down"—pulling out pen—"but where's my . . . Damn. I must have had another mild but dignified moment of cognitive malfunction. Excuse me while I see if my notepad is on top of the urinal. I'll try to remember to come back. If I don't, and you re-member that I was supposed to, call me."

Remembering to come back, of course, is part of the issue. El Cee had recently had a call from a friend in Jacksonville who wanted to tell her about the man she'd gone out with. It was their first date, and she was tickled, especially because he could still drive. She thought he might be a new beau. He picked her up. They drove out of town, to a restaurant at the beach. Things were going well enough until he excused himself to go to the men's room. That was the last she saw of him. In the time it took him to whiz, he forgot about her, and lunch. He got into his car and drove home.

The main thing on Mary's mind—aside from her memory and her handwriting—was what was wrong with her. She had gone to have a physical exam, part of changing her Medicare coverage to an HMO. When the blood work came back, it showed that her white blood cell count was high. Her internist wanted to send her for more specialized tests, to a medical practice called Bay Area Oncol-ogy. He said the white blood cell count could mean leukemia. Mary thought about it, and decided that was one appointment she didn't want to go to alone.

"I'm not going to do it until Nathalie gets here," she said. She and Nathalie had discussed it on the phone. "She told me what to ask him: What else it could be if it's not leukemia; what I face if I don't take the chemotherapy; and a third thing—but I can't remember what it is."

All through drinks and dinner one night, in a slow, deliberate way, she talked about Nathalie, about Wilber, her memory, her handwriting, her eyesight. ("Nathalie's coming after the fourth," she said. "I wrote the date down in my calendar—but I can't read it. Nathalie's going to *die*.") She also talked about this strange new issue with her blood. For as long as I had known her, Mary had seemed to view life with either merriment or acceptance, a serenity that seemed sometimes to border on indifference. She had taken a mild tranquilizer for decades—for so long that neither she nor Nathalie remembered why she began it. She wasn't about to abandon it now. Whether it influenced her mood after so many years, no one knew.

But as life became more and more constricted, she seemed to grow calmer, more appraising. There was a dignity in her eyes. Without knowing what the additional tests would tell her, she seemed to have accepted that she might now have the condition that would kill her. But she didn't act frightened—not of leukemia, and not of death. And she didn't seem worried. Not about herself. From lifelong habit, Mary was worried about her husband. She was thinking of Wilber—the man who no longer knew her.

"I think he's happy over there," she said, pausing, her fork in midair. "I think he's satisfied, anyway." The thought seemed to comfort her. "He doesn't try to come home with me anymore. I go to see him about three times a week. I used to come home and cry and cry—all afternoon, every time I'd go to see him. But I don't do that anymore." She paused again. "I do worry about my *dying*," she said, "and his being over there all alone. With nobody to go see him, and care how he is." She looked very solemn as she said it. Sad.

But even her worry about Wilber wasn't the deepest feeling. Her deepest, primary feeling—which underlay everything else—was that none of this made any sense. It didn't seem right to her. The time for drama in their lives was past.

"Nathalie will be fifty-nine in January," she said, "which *astonishes* me. I'll be eighty-seven in September. I *never* imagined I would live to be this old. I used to think that eighty was the absolute dropping-off place. Eighty was old. *Really* old. And here's Wilber—who will be ninety-two on October first. Wilber and I will be married sixty-six years the seventeenth of this November. *Sixty-six years!*"

Mary stopped a moment, holding her glass, looking at me.

"Isn't that *terrible?*"

I n mid-July, when I came back to Canterbury, the issue that had dominated front pages and the television news for weeks was the disappearance in Washington, D.C., of an exotic-looking, dark-haired young graduate student and government intern, Chandra Levy, and the nature of her relationship with Congressman Gary Condit. The District of Columbia police had been searching for her for weeks with no result. But the Sweetso had an idea.

"If they really want to find Chandra Levy," she said, walking into the living room and glancing around, after I had had a couple of days to decorate her space with shoes and shirts, legal pads, magazines, newspapers, and cups, "there are a couple of places in this apartment where she might be." She cocked an eyebrow at me, and nodded toward my bedroom. "She's probably in there with Judge Crater."

In the Health Center that Wednesday morning (where the judge could have been, without any of his neighbors wondering why), the Piano Man was sitting on his bench, swaying and bouncing a little as he played

It's a long way to Tip-per-AR-Y.

The song predated Joseph F. Crater—the dapper associate justice of the New York Supreme Court who became the most famous missing man of his age when he walked out of a midtown Manhattan restaurant and disappeared the evening of August 6, 1930—by almost a generation. It was a British anthem, the romantic, hugely popular sing-along ballad by which young soldiers were waved gallantly off to battle on the Western Front in the summer of 1914, before everyone realized what a black, soulless, devouring maw the Great War would become. The song itself—too rollicking and innocent to associate with men getting gassed, machine gunned, and blown up, or contracting gangrene after living for months in the soupy mud and slush at the bottom of trenches—survived the conflict, enduring as a kind of rosy melody. Once or twice a month, the Piano Man banged it out. Not that he got much response from the nodding Wednesday-morning semicircle. He didn't. Much. But that didn't matter.

The Piano Man finished "Tipperary," and smiling his slight, fixed smile, shifted—with no apparent transition (which also didn't matter)—into

La coo-cah-RAH-cha! La coo-cah-RAH-cha! Da-da, da-da, da-da, DAH!

That got a response—in part because Ernestine, bless her musical soul, was back. A little tempered by her stroke, still feeling a little weak, she was still her loving, irrepressible self, and so, with a wink and a mischievous (if slightly wan) grin, she pulled Wilber out of his chair into the middle of the floor. Soon she, and Honduran Maria, and Sister Barbara, three pillowy, rhythmic women—one black, one brown, and one white—were all dancing with Wilber.

It was, hands down, Wilber's best hour of any week. Up and moving in brown pants and a gray cardigan sweater, his eyes vague but excited, his feet kicking this way and that, he was fixed on Sister Barbara, a symphony of motion, trying to follow her every move. It wasn't working. But it didn't matter.

Maria, her big brown eyes lit and teasing, moved in close and threw him a hip.

Bump! Her large right buttock collided softly with Wilber, who was getting pretty hippy himself, moving him slightly to the right.

"Oh *my!*" he said, as dazzled as if she'd just kissed him.

He stared a little wildly at Maria—who was arching her eyebrows dramatically at him—and with a gleam in his eye and a twitch of his rear, bumped her back.

Bump!

The place was hopping. Soon, the Piano Man was pounding out

Deep in the heart—of TEX-AS!

and Wilber and Ernestine were back on the floor together, dancing and throwing each other kisses. If the Piano Man could have stayed, they might have danced right through lunch.

The dramatic summer-afternoon rainstorms, which everyone who grew up in Florida, like me, remembers, had finally begun, ending the winter and spring drought. But just as the dry periods now sometimes seemed dryer and longer than the dry spells of our childhood, these rains also seemed different—coming in the mornings as well as afternoons, or in the evenings, slopping over from day to day. The days and nights dripped and poured. It gave a dark, wet, dramatic edge to life at Canterbury. One evening, about 7:00 p.m., when the dining room was full and the summer sky normally still rosy clear and soft and tranquil over the bay, the atmosphere outside the deep windows turned threateningly dark and luminous. Every growing thing—trees and bushes and grass, which had been soaked for days—glowed a deep lime green. Whitecaps tossed on the bay, and under the lowering sky, a line of rain advanced across the water, shrouding the southern end of Davis Islands in a silver veil. It sent a little shiver through the tables.

By July 23, a Monday, so much rain had fallen that the National Weather Service issued a flash-flood watch along the rivers that flowed into Tampa Bay. It had been a gray, ominous week. Jean Wilson, a University of Chicago graduate—a shy, quiet, but very bright woman in her early eighties, who ran the Canterbury reading and lending library that she and Harry had endowed before he died—fell down five steps in the dimness of a movie theater where she and Martha Cameron had gone to the afternoon matinee with Sarah Jane, landing full on her face.

When the paramedics arrived, they asked Jean if she knew where she was. She said Decatur—Decatur, Ohio. She had gone far away, and back in time. After weeks in the hospital, she would come back to the Health Center to be cared for, and return for a time to her apartment. But she was never going to be right again.

And in Boise, Idaho, Katharine Graham, eighty-four, the former chairman of the Washington Post Company, perhaps the most famous and powerful woman of her generation, and one of the richest, tripped over a curb while out walking and hit her head—proving that a person of her age can be intellectually able and disciplined enough after retiring as the chair of a major company to work for years writing her autobiography, win a Pulitzer Prize for it, and then fall and kill herself on a perfectly clean and ordinary public street, because she could no longer trust her feet.

The rain was blowing and cascading outside, the trees bowing in the wind, as Mrs. Graham's funeral service was telecast that Monday morning from the National Cathedral in Washington, D.C., Arthur Schlesinger Jr. and Ben Bradlee spoke. Yo-Yo Ma played the cello. Four thousand people stood to sing "Oh God, Our Help in Ages Past."

Across the bay, as the cathedral bells tolled, the city of Tampa disappeared in a pall of rain. In the dining room, Lucie Cross sat at a table, watching it pour and blow outside. She was ninety-eight years old. She might have tipped the scales at ninety pounds. But she was fierce. "Mrs. Vinas called my son two weeks ago, and told him I was creating a disturbance and she was going to *evict* me!" Lucie said, the jaw muscles in her thin face working under the skin. There was fire in her ice blue eyes. She looked so mad she could spit.

After the conversation with Mrs. Vinas, Chick Cross had called Lucie.

"Mom, what are you *doing*?" he said.

"You see," Lucie hissed, confiding again her darkest suspicion, "there is a waiting list for one-bedroom apartments. They want to get rid of me so they can sell my apartment to someone else. Well, I wish they would get rid of *her*!" she said, in a ferocious whisper. "I *hate* that woman!

"She told my son that I was falling *all* the time," Lucie said, her voice rising. She looked as if she'd been slandered. She straightened her bony shoulders and gave me a steely look.

"I have *always* been able to pick myself up!" she blazed.

At almost eleven o'clock one night not long after, Dr. Joel Shrager came down to the lobby. He was still dressed in his maroon blazer and tie, gold tie chain, and cap with U.S. ARMY, RETIRED stitched in gold thread above the bill. It was his uniform. But he looked distracted. Behind the thick glasses, his normally calm, dark eyes were worried.

"I can't find my wife," he said quietly to Rudine, one of the night security guards. "She's not in the apartment. I don't know what to do. I think we're going to have to call the police."

Rudine had two other jobs—which was why he always worked nights. He also lifted weights. He was black and enormous, very steady and kind, with a shaved head and a voice like oak. It was the fourth time since dinner that Dr. Shrager had come down that evening, and Rudine put his elbows on the desk and leaned forward, to be closer to the troubled little man, standing there with one hand on the gold head of his sword cane.

"Do you remember that she passed away a couple of years ago?" Rudine asked him. His voice was very gentle.

"I know she passed away," Joel answered, blinking up at Rudine. He stopped and pursed his lips. "*But she keeps passing.* I don't . . . I don't . . ." He paused. Blinked. Tried to collect his thoughts.

"The last time I saw her, she was passing by right over there," he said, pointing to his right, at a spot in his apartment, perhaps, that he was seeing in his mind.

"She was passing right by that bureau," Joel remembered, gazing at the sideboard on the wall of the lobby. He paused again. "And then she just disappeared," he said softly. "She passed away. And I lost track of her."

He stood very close to the desk, looking up at Rudine for help. "And now I can't find her. I think we ought to call the police."

Rudine gave him a comforting smile and pulled himself up. "It's getting late, Dr. Shrager," he said, coming around the desk. "Let me take you back up to your apartment."

He put a huge right arm around the little doctor's shoulders, and began guiding him toward the elevator. The doors opened and then closed on the two of them as the car began to lift. When Rudine came back down, about five minutes later, he was alone. It was after eleven o'clock, very quiet in the lobby.

Rudine knew the drill. There was no one to overhear. He picked up the phone and called Mrs. Vinas.

CHAPTER TWENTY-ONE

The Best-Laid Plans

AUGUST–SEPTEMBER 2001

By the morning of the staff meeting in mid-August, the rains had been so heavy for a month that the water stood in pools in the low places where the foundation had been dug for the failed building next door. Condominium towers had been planned—even begun—and then had failed on that big corner lot for as long as anyone could remember. Each successive failure had been a cause of great satisfaction at Canterbury. None of the residents liked the idea of some tall ugly new building next door, especially the residents on that side. And most especially the grumpy old ladies.

Lucie Cross had sailed out to give a piece of her mind to the owner of the house that stood on that property twenty years ago, as soon as she saw the FOR SALE sign go up.

"Are you *selling* that lovely house?" she asked, in a voice that suggested that there must be some mistake. Only a grinch would do such a thing.

"Yes," he said, giving her a level look. "A condominium is going to go up here."

"Oh, I don't like *that*!" Lucie gasped, recoiling.

"Do you live next door?" he asked mildly.

"Yes!" she snapped. Her blue eyes were hard.

"Well," he said with a tight little smile, nodding toward Canterbury, "how the hell do you think I felt when *that* went up?"

That first project had failed when the boom cycle in which it was begun ran out of steam—just as the construction of Canterbury had originally. The Tower was intended to be condominium apartments, too. But the developer ran out of money at the end, and it was bought by a largely Episcopalian group from St. John's, and then converted into a nonprofit life-care facility. Next door, the last two towers proposed for the site had gotten far enough to leave flowering clusters of steel reinforcing rods spiking up from the earth, bare and ugly, rusting in the air. The grim remains of the dead condominium drew so many complaints from Canterbury to the city's building and zoning departments that the corporation that owned the property sent some men out to pretty up the rods. They painted them white, which made the lot look like a cemetery and gave residents at Canterbury the creeps. The foundation work had also left various low places on the property, and a long, shallow depression at the back of the lot, which turned into an oval pond in rainy season.

On this Monday morning, the puddles and pond shone silver as the sun rose across the bay. The atmosphere was so thick with vapor from the recurring rains that the view from Canterbury to the east was of a great cave of warm mist and dark rippled water—and inside, a struggling light. The sun gained strength as it rose, burning through the clouds as the midnight shift—the nurses and certified nurse's aides, and the lone security guard—trickled out the rear of the building to their cars at the far end of the fenced parking lot just after eight o'clock.

By 9:00 a.m., when Mrs. Vinas convened the regular meeting of department heads behind the closed doors of the boardroom next to her office, to plot the management of the residents and the various systems in the building for another week, the sun was up. The misty cave had burned away. The day had become enamel bright, and the sweat was on the morning.

There were urns of fresh coffee and croissants and sweet pastries on the sideboard. But the meeting was business, and Mrs. Vinas, dark haired and brisk in her gray suit and white blouse, the whites of her eyes very white, the browns very brown and serious, moved the agenda quickly around the long table—from the social director to the head of food services, to the comptroller, the head of marketing, the director of nursing, and then to maintenance and housekeeping, patient services, and personnel. She had two or three serious things on her mind, the last major projects and concerns of the year—but first, the social schedule.

There would be a cocktail party in the social room of the Tower from 5:00 to 6:00 p.m. on Tuesday for new residents, and a prospective new resident who was coming to look the place over, with genial Joe, the bus-and-Lincoln-driver and deskman, at the bar, pouring the drinks and glasses of wine. There would be a separate happy hour to entertain the residents of the Health Center at 4:30 on Wednesday—a remnant of the life they'd once had—with hors d'oeuvres from the kitchen, nonalcoholic champagne and nonalcoholic wine, and Joyce, the director of social services and activities, supervising.

In three weeks, on September 11, the Hillsborough County Medical Association was having its quarterly dinner in a local hotel. Canterbury had purchased a booth to support the doctors, as it did each year, because the local doctors often recommended Canterbury and its Health Center to their older patients and their families. On September 23 and 24, the television station on which Canterbury ran advertisements was hosting another health fair at the Tampa Convention Center, on the river downtown. More than forty thousand people had come the year before to look over the skin creams; the health foods; the portable home defibrillators, props, and prosthetics—all the latest offerings of maintenance and rejuvenation, the medical procedures and surgeries, and facilities for care and comfort that were available to those with money, or good insurance. Robin, the head of marketing, thought Canterbury ought to buy a booth at the health fair again, too. It would be at the rear of the hall, strategically placed near the food court—always a good idea. Whether being so close to the other vendors on that row (glycerin-filled shoe insoles, the Body Image Laser Institute, the Dattoli Cancer Center, the Palm Harbor Plastic Surgery Centre, and the Foundation for Intimacy) was also a good idea, Robin couldn't tell. Every aisle was a little strange. You just had to pay your money and take your chances.

For those who wondered what the Foundation for Intimacy was all about—and were brave enough to ask—a tall, red-haired, blissed-out woman standing behind the counter of pamphlets and brochures would be glad to explain. Pellets inserted beneath her skin by the white-coated man next to her ("I'm an endocrinologist," he said, smiling) had "given me my sexual life back," she said. All weekend, she would seem breathless and amazed, as if dazzled by her good fortune. Or on some kind of pill.

Mrs. Vinas nodded as she listened. These were things Canterbury had done before. She approved the medical dinner and the health fair as good for sales, and moved on to maintenance and house-keeping, the province of complaints and problems. In room 119 in the Health Center, a chair had been found pushed up against the nurse call button. On Sunday, the day before, three fire engines had shown up, flashing and wailing, because a low battery in the alarm system had sent a false signal. Mrs. Vinas frowned and turned to the comptroller.

"Did the fire department charge us for coming for that?" she said.

And in apartment 702 in the Tower, a woman had complained that she smelled smoke at odd times, often in the evening. Mrs. Vinas rolled her eyes, and looked indulgent. "Sometimes the residents are smoking," she said, with a little smile. "And they're hiding. They go to the stairwell and hide there and smoke. Tell her the minute she smells it to walk out of the apartment and look in that space."

She knew all the tricks and recurring issues, all the quirks of the building and the people in it—and she tried to imagine all the possible combinations, all the things that might go wrong. She had to, because life at Canterbury could be so treacherous in unexpected ways. There were possibilities that simply did not exist in the world outside—and that would never occur to anyone who didn't work with old, infirm, demented people.

"Is it OK to give a flower arrangement to the new patients?" the newly hired patient advocate in the Health Center, a cheerful young woman, asked one Monday morning. "Like the ones we give new residents," she said, smiling, "but smaller?"

It seemed such a nice touch, pleasant and harmless and bright. But like my mother, almost all the patients and residents in the Health Center are brain damaged from strokes or Alzheimer's disease, Parkinson's, or some other form of dementia. Mrs. Vinas sat bolt upright, as if someone had buzzed her seat, and shot an intense look down the table toward Susan Conley, the blond, immaculate director of nursing, sitting in her tailored white uniform at the end.

"They can *eat* rose petals, can't they?" Mrs. Vinas asked.

The white uniform coolly nodded. Yes, they could—chew and swallow.

"What about carnations?"

The director of nursing thought for a moment. "A philodendron is more dangerous than a flower," she said, with a level gaze.

At that, Mildred, the rumpled, grandmotherly director of food services spoke up. "A carnation should be OK," she said, reassuringly. It was Mildred who supervised all the meals that people at Canterbury consumed. Vegetables. Starches. Beef. Pork. Fish. Fowl. Fruit. She had spent years weighing the nutritional needs of people in their seventies and eighties and nineties against their natural desires. She knew the limits and peculiarities of older digestive systems. If residents in the Health Center ate the occasional carnation, she thought, they could digest it. No problem.

Mrs. Vinas gave her new patient advocate, who seemed a little stunned, an understanding look. "I know it's such a tiny little thing," she said gently, shaking her head to indicate that the answer was no. "But you can't even give them a box of chocolates. They could be diabetic."

"What about a *picture* of flowers?" The mustached head of maintenance, Mr. Warren, laughed. (Except for Mrs. Vinas and Ms. Conley, all the women at the table referred to one another by their first names. But they all called Mr. Warren, Mr. Warren.) He leaned back in his chair with a hearty grin. He was the only man in the room.

Mrs. Vinas glanced in his direction and then ignored him. She

turned back to the patient advocate. "And *nothing* with water in it,"
she ordered, her eyes intent. "They could drink it." She stopped, not
wanting to discourage the new advocate. Her look softened, became
teasing.

"You see what you started?" she said.

Then she swiveled around to face the head of maintenance and
the rest of the table, and spread her arms out wide. "And it was *such*
a good idea!" she sang out. "You know what we *could* do—give
them a picture frame with all *our* pictures in it."

At that, the whole table laughed.

The department heads understood the joke. The residents of
Canterbury all had framed photographs on their shelves and
bedside tables. Of parents (dead). Of dead former spouses
(though not of divorced ones). Of children and grandchildren, if they
had them, or of nieces and nephews, and great-nieces and great-
nephews. Many of us aging children—whose younger faces were in
those photographs—held power of attorney for our parents. Some of
us were their trustees as well. Legally, we were in charge. But Canterbury was like a cruise ship, and as everyone knew, Mrs. Vinas was the
captain, and her staff the crew. We may have booked our parents on
board and paid for passage, but it was she who ran things, one eye on
the passengers, the other on the crew—watchful of the weather,
watchful for danger, for problems with the ship, for troublesome behavior or violations of the rules. It absolutely suited her nature, which
was controlling, conscientious, and organized to a fault.

She had been born with a flashing, endless, restless energy, but by August 2001, just three months after her heart attack, there was also an air
of strain about her, a thinness, and a shadow around her eyes. The quality and structure of the residents' lives, the services and support they
paid for each month and had grown to expect, all depended on her—
on her relentless mastery of detail. And it was not all about health fairs
and flower arrangements, cocktail parties, and smoke alarms.

There were *big* issues, the kind that hung over life-care communities and nursing homes around the nation—but especially in

Florida, the testing laboratory of all things old. The annual premium for Canterbury's liability insurance, which it was required to carry, had jumped by eighty-one thousand dollars the year before. And then the policy had lapsed. The insurance company simply refused to renew it. Florida had become a greenhouse of litigation by lawyers suing for wrongful injury or death on behalf of old people in nursing homes, in large part because Florida law made it easier to sue for damages than in most other states. The horror stories—of old people getting strangled by the cords and straps of their restraints, lying in filth, devoured by bedsores, dying of malnutrition and inattention—were drawing such large awards from sympathetic juries that the insurance companies, afraid to defend them in open court, were often settling the cases.

The lawsuits were almost entirely against commercial nursing homes, where the profit motive often reduced staff levels and the quality of care, rather than against nonprofit facilities like Canterbury. No one, Mrs. Vinas said adamantly, had ever filed such a claim against Canterbury. She ran too tight a ship—constantly second-guessing and checking on her department heads and employees, going over and over their lists of tasks. One reason she had placed herself on permanent twenty-four-hour call was to make it clear to all employees that there was no excuse for not notifying her anytime anything of consequence happened. She wanted no one unattended, and nothing left to chance.

But the company that had insured Canterbury was abandoning the field, dumping its Florida policies, pulling out of the state. Mrs. Vinas and the board treasurer had found other liability coverage, but it had cost. It seemed clear that each year was going to bring another premium escalation crisis. She also knew for a certainty that tomorrow, or next week, or sometime in the next four months, a team of state nursing home inspectors would appear at the Tower's front door. They would come unannounced and spend days in the building, especially in the nursing wing, examining the preparation and serving kitchens; the garbage and trash disposal systems; the emergency equipment; the staff nursing-to-patient ratios; the individual employee records; the patient care, feeding, medication, and recreation records; the medical authorization forms for each patient; the condition of the showers and laundry rooms; the pest control records—everything. It happened every year. Sometime between August and the end of January, they arrived.

"Has that leaky drain been fixed under the ice machine in the dining room?" Mrs. Vinas asked Mildred. "Are you ready for the survey?" she said, looking intently at Joyce, the social director. Joyce nodded but didn't speak. Her job had a million details and almost no boundaries. She was in charge of entertainment and recreation for residents of the Tower *and* the Health Center, and functioned as the go-to for many of their personal needs. Mrs. Vinas was not convinced. "Do you have your demonstration done?" she prodded gently.

And, of course, there was the weather. It was August—prime hurricane season—and Canterbury was not a bank, an office tower, or a government building. It was an aging residential structure filled with old, frail, dotty, crippled people, and it stood just a few feet above sea level, in a flood zone, directly across the street from Old Hillsborough Bay. That morning, even as Mrs. Vinas worked her way down her preparedness list, a storm was heading up the Gulf of Mexico. No hurricane in the twentieth century had blown up the Gulf and veered right, to come straight up Tampa Bay. It had been eighty years since a hurricane had even struck close enough to Tampa at high tide to cause a destructive storm surge inside the bay. It had occurred in October 1921, when a hurricane that had been clocked at one hundred miles per hour came ashore at Tarpon Springs, north of Clearwater on the gulf. Its winds pushed water in Tampa Bay eleven feet above high tide, in a surge that smashed buildings and piers all along the shore, and killed as many as eight people.

The main difference in risk since then was that 2.4 million people now lived around the bay. The vulnerability was huge. But from orbiting space satellites, it was also possible to see tropical storms and hurricanes being born, to know where they were centered at almost any hour, and where they seemed to be going. The building's designated official tracker was Murphy, the maintenance man, who kept a latitudinal and longitudinal chart of the Caribbean and Gulf of Mexico taped to the concrete block wall of the hallway leading to the back service door. Murphy was no meteorologist. But being responsible made him mindful, which was a good idea—because it was he who tended the building's mechanical systems, and who would have to plug the leaks and nurse the machinery if the air-conditioning failed, the lights went out, or the plumbing backed up.

Mrs. Vinas, however, wanted them all to be alert.

"Keep your eyes and ears on the weather out there," she said, her gaze sweeping the room. "There's a storm called Chantel that could turn into a hurricane."

I n the crowded little gym near the door to the swimming pool, as the staff meeting broke up, the Emyfish was performing her tai chi exercises in front of a videotape playing on the television. She had left Ashby to his breakfast in the apartment upstairs, making sure there were no seeds in anything he ate—seeds that could lodge in those little annoying pockets in his colon and cause diverticulitis— and had come down to work on her balance and form.

She was, by nature and theatrical training, a trouper, and tai chi was good for the shuffles and the stumbles that eventually tripped indomitable old dames like her. For several years now, she had been falling occasionally, inside the apartment and out—even elsewhere in the building and out. But her bones were good. So far, the Emy-fish had bounced, and tai chi had become a religious exercise with her, the latest means by which she intended to postpone mortality.

"She's fahtin' ole age evrah stepah' thuh way," Mary Davis had observed one evening, over her before-dinner vodka. "You haftah kindah admire huh foah that."

The Emyfish was in the gym five mornings a week. She let nothing interfere, because she was convinced that it helped. "I'm still short of breath," she said, "and I hate that." She had first noticed it on the dance floor one night four years before. That, of course, was before Charles Sweet fell like a giant loaf of bread onto the thin woman in the chair, and Mrs. Vinas took the dance floor away. "But it's better," she said. "And I think my equilibrium is better. I was getting wobbly even when I wasn't drinking. And I *never* wobbled, even when I drank."

As she turned and stretched, like some slow, ancient, silver-haired geisha, her mother's and grandmother's bracelets softly clinking at her wrists, she thrummed inside with excitement at the continued progress of the great retail inspiration of her elder years—the Emyfish Glamour Bib, which had completely replaced the nude calendar that she and some of the other women at Canterbury had first gotten so enthusiastic about over lunch and drinks and dinner a year ago. Ashby and the other remaining husbands had been grumpy about the calendar from the start. And anyway, it would have just been a later-age copy of what the Rylstone women's club in England had already done. The dressy dinner bib was Emy's own design, much closer to her heart. She and Martha Cameron and Sarah Jane had put together a thousand dollars, opened a joint checking account, and gone into business.

She, the Emyfish—as founder, symbol, and chief fashion plate—adorned herself at every meal with one glowing, glittering bib or another from her own considerable collection. She and Sarah Jane and Martha Cameron ate many of those meals together, sometimes with Mauricio and Ashby, sometimes not. The three women kibitzed and schmoozed and talked together all the time. They were plotting and researching, looking for some way to contract out the production and distribution so that they could lower the price and advertise and market the Glamour Bibs nationally. It was all very exciting. They had decided to adorn the Canterbury booth at the upcoming health fair with their bibs, and themselves. Her grandfather, Abe Maas, the department store founder, would be proud, the Emyfish thought.

Late that night, in her apartment on the second floor—early Tuesday morning, actually, about 4:00 a.m.—Helen Hill pulled the emergency cord in her bedroom. It was the first time she had done that in her twenty-four years at Canterbury, but she had chest pain that she recognized as angina, and it wouldn't go away. Her first heart attack, in 1976, had come as a sharp pain under her left shoulder blade. The occasional angina pain she had suffered since then could usually be dissipated with a nitroglycerin tablet. But she had taken three, and when she was still short of breath, sitting up in bed, she pulled the cord. In minutes, the late-shift security guard and nurse appeared in her bedroom. The nurse took her pulse, checked her blood oxygen, listened with a stethoscope to her chest. Then the paramedics came and gave her oxygen. She felt better.

"Do you want to go to the hospital?" one of them asked.

"No," Helen said tartly, eyeing him with her one good eye. "Who wants to go to the hospital?"

In the Health Center, farther down the hall on the second floor, Wilber, who had grown rotund from the regular meals and attention he received each day, was shaved and clean, dressed by the aides in checked slacks, yellow cardigan sweater, and brown laced shoes. He was napping in a chair in the recreation room at midmorning, as Mildred Tate began the cooking class with which the residents of the Health Center were entertained on Tuesdays. Usually, cooking class meant that the big, round, warm Maria, from Honduras, or Joyce, or Ernestine, or one of the other members of the activities staff, did something simple, like baking chocolate chip cookies, or warming sweet buns and pouring cups of lemonade. Having Mildred there to make real food was something of a treat, the big time, and the residents were arranged to face her in their accustomed semicircle of chairs and wheelchairs and reclining chairs. They were used to being moved around— parked here, parked there, turned to face this way or that. Some of them looked at Mildred. Some didn't. One or two, in addition to Wilber, were asleep.

But my mother was awake, and a light came on in her eyes as she lay motionless in her wheeled chair, propped and tucked in her cushions, watching Mildred work with the mixing bowl and pans, the eggs and flour, milk and breakfast meats. Mildred was making western omelets, biscuits, and sausages, just ten feet away.

Mildred knew that food had been my mother's life. And when she saw Mother look at her, saw her raise her left hand a little (the one she still could lift), Mildred brought the mixing bowl and sat down next to her. She reached for Mother's left hand, and with both their hands together, cradled a cool hard egg, cracked it on the rim, and broke it into the bowl.

Mother looked straight down, watching the yolk plop in. Mildred began to beat the mixture with a whisk, smiling at Mother across the bowl. My mother lifted her head, with that slightly awkward jerk that stroke victims have, and fixed her eyes on Mildred's face. She was following everything Mildred did. She rarely paid this kind of attention to anything anymore. Most of the time, she simply looked at me, as if I were some puzzle she was trying to divine, a performance she was waiting to see begin. But as she stared at Mildred that morning, there was something like pride and a brightness in her eyes—and around her mouth, just the suggestion of a small, conspiratorial smile, which Mildred shared. We're *cooking.*

In their apartment on the eighth floor, on the front left corner of the building, Karl Richter and Ruth had their morning pills and coffee—high blood pressure and arthritis pills for her, prostate and glaucoma medications for him—bantering with each other as they had for most of seven decades. With her strong features, thick white hair, and amused, appraising blue eyes, Ruth Richter was as handsome an old woman as she had been the softly beautiful girl in the framed photograph in their dining room, a picture taken far away and long ago. She still showed flashes of a sharp and mischievous sense of humor, an impatience with blather, euphemisms, and platitudes. But in the last year or so, her edge had dulled. It was not just her bad knees and arthritis, the physical slowness. Her pensive silences and vacant moments were getting longer. It was something the rabbi covered so well, with his eternally disarming humor and calm, that not even their son, David, the psychologist, had remarked on it. He didn't seem to realize that his resilient, opinionated mother—who had been strong and brave and clever all her life—was now failing mentally, even wandering from the apartment.

Just above them on the ninth floor, El Cee—who had put so many men to sleep in tents and operating rooms across the decades—had been awakened, deliciously, by Rudolf Nureyev and Dame Margot Fonteyn performing *Romeo and Juliet* on the arts cable channel she fell asleep watching every night. The sight of the famous couple, dancing romantically in the morning dimness of her bedroom, was so dreamlike and lovely that it distracted her totally from the ache of the deteriorating vertebrae in her neck, and put her in a rosy mood for a day of projects, most of which had to do with the residents' association, the Canterbury Players, or the Glamour Bib. The organized and unflappable El Cee was in charge of manufacture (meaning that she cut and stitched most of them herself, by hand). The irrepressible Sarah Jane, who had led the original recruitment drive for the nude calendar, was in charge of marketing.

"We doan think weah goan to get *rich,*" Sarah Jane had said, with her satisfied smile, as the three of them met one evening after dinner. "Weah juss goan tah do it until we each geddah new *cahr.*"

"Right," the Emyfish intoned, behind her. "The new *Jaguar.*"

O n the fourteenth floor, in the cool, quiet, freshly painted and carpeted less-expensive one-bedroom apartment to which she had moved after Wilber was placed in the Health Center—and from which she had a spectacular dead-on view of the city, three miles away—Mary Davis was asleep. She had woken at about 4:30 a.m., after almost eight hours of sleep, had some cereal and coffee, looked at the *Tampa Tribune,* and gone back to bed, leaving her coffee cup and the vodka glass from the night before—and others from other days and nights before—on the carpet and standing by the sink. She might or might not rise for lunch. Life had pretty much narrowed down to the cocktail hour and dinner following.

"Mah week consists of invitin' people in foah drinks, and goin' out foah drinks. And Ah have to clean up thuh apahtment befoah they come—and goan thuh bus to get hors d'oeuvres," she said.

It felt like too much trouble, and not enough fun. She didn't seem to have much energy. When someone did call to invite her to do something, Mary had trouble remembering the appointment long enough to write it down. Even when she did, she couldn't read her writing. And then there was the matter of her health—her elevated white blood cell count. Nathalie had come and gone. They had talked. Mary had thought a good deal more about it. She had decided that she probably did have leukemia. But she had refused the bone marrow test, which might have been conclusive.

"Whut's thuh point?" she had said, arching her eyebrows, looking at me with dead calm. "Ah'm eighty-seven yeahs old. Ah'm not going tuh do anythin' about it." In fact, she wasn't so sure anymore that there was a larger point "Ah'm boahd to death," she said. So there.

At the top of the building, in her corner apartment on the fifteenth floor, the Sweetso sat smoking a cigarette in one of the wheeled, cushioned armchairs at her smooth, molded, wine-red dining table. As usual, the strong, comfortable furniture, and everything else in the apartment, reminded her of her beloved Charles, dead almost two years. With an open book before her, sitting under the portrait of the censorious Episcopal bishop of Japan, the Sweetso squinted through her smoke, watching the morning news. She was on alert, ready to vaporize the dreadfully domestic Martha Stewart the moment *Good Morning America* went off the air and the maven appeared. It was her routine.

"*Aaargghhh!* It's that awful Martha Stewart!!" she yelled, jumping from her chair as that cool blond countenance materialized on the screen. She lunged for the zapper, lying on the coffee table by the couch, and *click!*—Martha disappeared midsmile, replaced by CNN's *Headline News.* It always made the Sweetso feel better.

"That takes care of *that!*" she grumbled. "That woman represents almost *everything* that pisses me off."

But her satisfaction was short-lived. It was a nothing news day. There were wildfires in the West, and a tropical storm that the weather report went on about. But nothing big or provocative had happened in politics or world affairs for days or weeks, and the resulting slack and blather had turned the Sweetso cranky.

"There is *no* news," she grumbled in a wreath of smoke, glowering at the television set from beneath her mop of sandy hair. "It's *August*. I could have sat here in July, and figured out what the news would be in August: fires in the West and some damn storm that won't ever turn into a hurricane!"

She fell silent and, to amuse herself, began to consider a couple new to Canterbury. "One wonders if they *copulate*," she said, thoughtfully, her gaze afar.

This was one of the things I loved about having coffee with the Sweetso in the morning. She wondered about things. Did she wonder that just about this particular couple, I asked—or about everybody at Canterbury?

"*Every*body," Martha answered in her gravelly voice, giving me a look that said, *What are you—slow?* "Everybody wonders that. About *every*body."

She smiled through the drift of smoke and retrieved a memory. "One man who was kind of drunk at a party here told me once that he didn't see how Charles and I could have copulated. Because Charles was six feet four. And I'm just five feet tall.

"Well," she said smugly, "I told him the difference was almost all in the legs, so it didn't matter." She paused, looking vastly amused, and began to laugh. "I wanted to say to him that some *other under-hung* man had asked me that once. But I couldn't bring myself to do it!" The Sweetso slapped the table and roared with laughter, which gradually subsided into chuckles and, finally, into silence. For a moment, she sat smoking.

"When I first moved in here, a lot of people told me they

thought I was too young to be here, and that flattered me greatly," she said quietly.

She paused. "But I haven't had anyone say that in a while."

As it turned out, the storm that came their way was not Chantel. It was not quite a hurricane either. Nor, by the time it arrived more than three weeks after Mrs. Vinas warned her staff to start watching the weather, was it the main event of their lives. But as Mrs. Vinas knew so well, you could never be sure which of the things you worried about would actually come to pass—or whether it would even be one of the things you had prepared so carefully for. It could be something you hadn't thought to consider. When you came right down to it, everything was like the weather—or rather, like the dramatic atmosphere around Canterbury—a mix of unpredictable, interacting systems.

To begin with, each resident at Canterbury carried his or her own unstable physical environment and climate inside. Each had some internal peculiarity—in bone, organ, or vascular structure. And all of them, like miniature individual weather systems, were calmed or agitated by their own high- or low-pressure systems, their own ebbs and tides of fluids, chemical emissions, and accumulations, or eccentric electrical impulses. They all had their own emotional dark clouds and sunny moments. Not to mention the individual differences in what each of them ate and drank, and the effect of that on their leaky old sewer systems.

Canterbury itself was sort of a larger weather system—the complex equation of all the individual variables of its residents and staff members and physical parts. Yet, for all its complications, it was just one small sphere within the great marine and atmospheric bowl of Tampa Bay, and the vagaries of the hemisphere and cosmos beyond. What it meant, Mrs. Vinas had long ago concluded, was that you never knew what would trigger what, or from where the next catastrophe might come.

In the first week of September, when the heat and humidity outside were thickest, and life around the bay felt slow and labored, a sudden change in blood pressure and flow stirred the sediment within Ruth Richter's aged vascular system and created a blockage. The stopper was just a tiny thing—a red flyspeck of material. The Richters had been prepared to deal with a hospitalization, because the rabbi was scheduled for surgery to relieve his enlarged prostate. But his operation had been uneventful, and their daughter, Esther, an author and playwright, had come from Arizona to stay with Ruth. It was a great comfort, and a good excuse for a family visit. Karl's stay in the hospital wasn't long. He emerged sore and a little weak, but ambulatory. He came back to the apartment, and he and Ruth resumed their long domestic routine—now two-thirds of a century old. The morning after he returned, she made breakfast for them. But an hour later, she seemed a little disconnected and, in a moment, said she thought she'd lie down for another hour.

Karl sat in the living room, sorting with his magnifying glass through the papers and the mail, and then, at almost lunchtime, he shuffled carefully back into their bedroom to check on Ruth. When he came through the door and saw her, struggling to rise from the bed, the left side of her face distorted, "I knew in an instant," he said, "that my life had been changed forever."

He yelled—he would remember afterward that he yelled and screamed and cursed ("It was a terrible shock to me")—and reached to pull the emergency cord by the bed. Within minutes, a nurse and a security guard were in the bedroom, and then another nurse. They called Mrs. Vinas, and then the paramedics. Within a few more minutes, a crew had come, ministered to Ruth, and rushed her away to the hospital.

There were so many people at Canterbury whose deaths might have been triggered in that next week or two, by any small event. A change in heart rhythm. Stumbling over a shoe on the way to the bathroom at night. A fall over a curb in the parking lot. A fainting spell at the wheel. Failure to see a stop sign in the rain, or to hear a siren. A diabetic sugar spike, forgetting to take medication, taking too much. An argument with a spouse or child. Financial worry. The shock of personal bad news.

So many of them were vulnerable: Ruth and Karl Richter, Helen Hill, the Emyfish, Wilber and Mary Davis, Lucie Cross, Sarah Jane. And, of course, my mother, who had already had enough last communions for three or four people.

The atmosphere was tightening. It was the height of hurricane season, and the tropical storm that Murphy began to track on his chart on the wall in the days that followed was Gabrielle. It was moving up the Gulf toward Tampa, still three days away, and no clear threat, on the Tuesday morning when something entirely different—something none of them had foreseen—occurred. After years of careful planning—after countless meetings and drills that must have been at least as meticulous as the ones Mrs. Vinas conducted—a group of devout and disciplined Muslim terrorists, bound for suicide and heaven, hijacked four passenger jets on the East Coast. They flew two of them into the twin towers of the World Trade Center, one into the Pentagon, and one into the countryside in Pennsylvania during a fight with a group of brave passengers, all of it right in the middle of *Good Morning America*.

The residents of Canterbury Tower learned of the attacks in the same way that the rest of the world did, by watching television in their apartments. Most of them, of course, were deep into their own eighth or ninth or tenth decades of history. They had moved to Canterbury with the feeling that all the major crises of their lives—with the possible exception of the ones involving their health—were now behind them. They could relax and be comfortable, secure within a system that permitted no surprises. They learned that morning, still in their pajamas, in their slippers and robes and housecoats—or already dressed, gripping the arms of their chairs, staring at the flickering horror on the television screens before them—that they were wrong.

Karl Richter, alone in his apartment, watched with a long tragic face, his old eyes taking in the ghastly images before him. It was only the fourth time in his life, he thought, that he was eyewitness to an act of evil so great that it left him without adequate words of description or understanding. The first time had been the Night of Broken Glass in Germany, sixty-three years before. The second, three years later, after he and Ruth had escaped to America, was the bombing of Pearl Harbor. The third, thirty-eight years ago, was the assassination of President John F. Kennedy.

"And now this," he said, sorrowfully. It was a dreadful shock to frail people to know that they were vulnerable to such evil. Karl turned to dress so he could go to Ruth. She would need his comfort.

In the Health Center, some of the residents who had not comprehended the destruction playing across the television screens mounted high on the walls of their rooms began to wonder, a few minutes later, why their sets had suddenly died. The screens, one by one, had gone blank, depriving them of the constant company of sound and image they were accustomed to, the endless murmur and movement of game shows and soap operas, news and old movies. Mrs. Vinas, as soon as she saw what was happening, had ordered all the televisions in the nursing wing turned off, lest the recurrent pictures of death and destruction disturb a population of people who were already damaged and needed no more bad news. As perhaps in many other nursing homes across America—and hospitals, mental institutions, homes for the mentally challenged, and various other places where captive, vulnerable, powerless inmate populations were housed— nurses and aides went from room to room, taking radios and pulling television plugs from the wall. The news would stay off for days.

I n their apartments in the Tower, all that Tuesday and Wednesday, the residents watched the news as the attacks began to gain a narrative line and plot in the days of commentary that followed, and the tropical storm with the frilly French name of Gabrielle drew closer, threatening to become a hurricane. There was no county medical association dinner for Robin, the marketing director, and Mrs. Vinas and some of the Canterbury board to attend that Tuesday night. It had been canceled, along with hundreds of other events around Tampa Bay. Everywhere, the normal rhythm of life had been broken. By Thursday, the Emyfish's cardiologist told her to stop watching television because her heart was fibrillating badly and her blood pressure was up.

"It was around one eighty," the Emyfish said, when she had it checked at the nursing station. "Or was that the cholesterol? Anyway, I've never had high blood pressure in my life. *Now* I do.

"They're ruining *all* our lives," she grumbled, in her deep contralto, sitting in her apartment with the television off. She felt deeply angry and anxious, distracted and fearful. The comfortable, customary pattern of her days was a shambles.

"And it's *just* what they want," she growled. "Those *bastards!*"

The sky was darkening, filling with thick clouds, rain, and wind. On Friday morning, *Gabrielle* arrived. Lillian Shepherd, a childless widow in her tenth decade, who lived to play bridge in the card room downstairs, was in her apartment on the south side of the fourteenth floor that morning. On television, the smoke was rising for the fourth day in a row from the Pentagon. It was where Lillian had worked as a secretary for thirty years. She could see the smoldering, cratered point of impact and imagine what lay behind it—the shredded airliner, the collapsed walls and rooms and hallways, the dead passengers and military and civilian workers. The destruction was still flickering on the screen when the winds from the back side of the storm, just shy of a hurricane, blew into Tampa Bay and began to push water over Bayshore Boulevard, smash windows, rip roofs, and tear the limbs off trees.

One large branch, on its way through the air, took two of the three main lines that brought electrical power into Canterbury with it. For a moment, as the rain howled and lashed Lillian Shepherd's side of the Tower, and the electric power lines separated, everything went dark.

Murphy, the maintenance man, was sitting in the social room downstairs, watching a Whoopi Goldberg movie on the big television. He was indispensable at times like this, because he knew how all the mechanical systems worked—and he could fix most of them.

Murphy had been in the building all night, alert for leaks, for signs of systems in trouble. Several times, Canterbury lost power, but each time, after a few moments, it had come back on. At some point the sun had risen, but the new morning was dim and violent. Through the big glass windows, Murphy could see gusts of billowing rain, illuminated by the lights around the pool. Then, all at once, his movie, and the lights inside and outside the building, went off. Murphy could hear the diesel engine of the big Caterpillar generator, the Tower's emergency source of power, cough and start with a roar. Then the power returned again, and the generator shut down. They might make it, he thought to himself. But they sure were going to have some drying out to do.

The rain was practically horizontal. Water was beginning to seep through the walls around the big windows in the Tower dining room when Martha Sweet came down in the elevator, looking for Murphy. The walls of her bedroom, on the south side of the Tower, were dribbling water, puddling the carpet. The storm was coming in, and it scared her. This didn't happen in the mountains of Pennsylvania, and she wanted Murphy to come do something. They got in the elevator. It began to rise, and then—as Murphy heard the alarm bell ringing in the elevator room below—abruptly stopped, about halfway up. There they stood, in a motionless elevator car, illumined only by the soft glow of the emergency light.

Now, why couldn't he be Robert Redford? the Sweetso thought, looking up at the balding, slope-shouldered Murphy, with his glasses sliding down his nose.

"You all right?" Murphy asked, peering down at Martha.

"I'm *peachy*," she lied, smiling at him.

Murphy turned, wedged his big rough fingers into the rubber seam between the elevator doors, yanked left and right, and pulled them apart. The car had stopped between the ninth and tenth floors. Murphy looked up and down the tenth-floor hall, and then leaned over, hoisted the short, round Martha onto his shoulder, and pushed her up and out through the top half of the doors, onto the tenth floor. She got on her knees, and stood up.

"My hero!" She grinned, spreading her arms wide, when he climbed out. She gave him a big hug. "I can make it fine from here," she said.

Ignoring her, Murphy took her hand and led Martha up four flights of stairs to her front door. The hallway lights were on by then. The emergency generators, which were intended to light the hallways, run the elevators and kitchen equipment in the Tower, and power the lights and the heating and cooling systems in the Health Center, had kicked in smoothly. But the blackout had erased the elevators' computer memory. The elevator cars didn't know how to operate, and they wouldn't for hours, until a repairman could come to reset them.

But people—especially old people, most of whom had stopped cooking for themselves long ago, and had nothing much in their refrigerators—had to eat. And so Mrs. Vinas, who had stayed in the building all night, along with some of her department heads and staff, had Mildred Tate and her skeletal kitchen crew make up 125 trays of ham and cheese and tomato sandwiches, and bowls of soup. And then Mrs. Vinas, and every employee on the Tower's staff who could be spared, began carrying trays of lunch up the stairs to all thirteen residential floors. On the fifth floor, the Emyfish saw Mrs. Vinas on her way up and tried to stop her.

"You shouldn't be *doing* that!" she boomed, giving the administrator a bulldog look. She was thinking of Mrs. Vinas's heart attack, just four months before. Climbing stairs was the worst kind of strain for a bad heart.

"I have a problem on the fourteenth floor," Mrs. Vinas said shortly, disappearing up the stairs. Calling to check on all the residents, the desk had been unable to reach Lillian Shepherd. Carrying the tray she had brought, Mrs. Vinas climbed eight more flights and opened the heavy door onto the fourteenth floor. She knocked on 1405, Lillian's door. There was no answer. Mrs. Vinas used her master key. She opened the door, walked across the dim apartment, and found Lillian, sitting dead in her chair, across from the blank screen where the smoke of her career at the Pentagon had been. She was ninety-two.

On her cell phone, Mrs. Vinas called Carlos at the front desk, and then her administrative assistant, to get her to pull Lillian Shepherd's file for instructions and family contacts. She knew the funeral home would send an unmarked van for the body, but they would have to wait until the elevators were working again, in order to carry Lillian down. Meanwhile, the staff would lock the apartment to secure it, so that no one could get in, and nothing could be taken out. Carlos was on his way up with the special half key to insert in the lock like a plug.

Mrs. Vinas looked around the apartment. There was nothing more she could do in 1405. And there were other residents to feed. She picked up the tray, carried the soup and sandwich to the apartment next door, gave it to Lillian's neighbor, and started walking back down the thirteen floors.

A day or two later, as always, a single red rose in a glass vase appeared on a small mahogany table in the lobby, between the elevators, with a framed picture of Lillian and a few lines about her. They remained until after the memorial service in the assembly room at eleven o'clock on Tuesday morning, and then the table, the rose, and the photograph disappeared.

The weather, and much of the litter from the storm, had cleared by then. It was a hot and bright day, and through the big windows of the dining room, the world outside looked vividly fresh and green. There had been so much rain.

CHAPTER TWENTY-TWO

Miss Osama

In those first few weeks after Gabrielle, the mood among the inmates at Canterbury was different from any I had known. They were used to living with the threat of storms and hurricanes. And residents died in the Tower from time to time—more often in the Health Center. But the events of September 11 had shattered the sense of sanctuary in which Canterbury had enfolded them, and on which they had come to depend. They now faced a kind of threat that nothing in life had prepared them for, and they were on edge, anxious, and gloomy. And sad.

With, of course, the exception of the Sweetso. She was pissed off.

"I would like to find *someone* in this goddamn building who knew who *Sisyphus* was!" she rumbled, scowling at the television screen.

"Do *you* know what the seven wonders of the ancient world were?" she would ask, with a superior arch of her eyebrows. I would get three. She would then proceed to name them all.

"Do you remember the *names* of Adam and Eve's sons?" she prodded me, another time. "Do you remember their *wives'* names?" Pause. "Did you ever wonder where those women *came* from?"

But her life and pleasures—and her peace of mind—had been upended by September 11. And the bad feeling wouldn't go away. She was sitting at dinner at the Men's Table on Thursday, nine days after the four airliners had crashed into the World Trade Center and the Pentagon, and the field in Pennsylvania, when Ben Franklin, her crony and political opposite, needled her for not being aware of some piece of the evolving story.

"If you read the *newspaper*," he said, with a smug glint behind his trifocals, "you would know these things." He knew she didn't read newspapers. She read books.

"You could read the newspaper every *day*," she shot back, "and not find out who *Sisyphus* was!"

Ben looked blank. "Who?" he said.

"You *see* what I mean?" the Sweetso rasped, triumphant. But it gave her no real pleasure.

Everyone was out of sorts.

"I have to go to the doctor tomorrow and Friday," the Emyfish said, the day after the attacks. She sounded off her feed. "I think all this terrible stuff has kicked my fibrillations back into high gear."

It was a significant admission, because one of the bonuses of life at Canterbury was that its location offered a built-in metronome for dealing with stress.

"When I came here for two days as a trial," Martha Cameron remembered, "one of the residents said, 'If you can't sleep, at least you can get up and count the cars going by.' "

"I did that," the Emyfish replied. "I did that when I first had my fibrillations. I got up and counted the cars."

Others had their own favorite comforts and remedies. "Whenevah Ah have been undah eneh kindah stress—happy stress, orah unhappy stress—the onlah thang that can make me feel beddah is fried chicken whangs from Kentuck-ah Fried Chicken," Sarah Jane declared in the dining room one day, about two weeks before September 11. "Awyund it *reallah* does." The kitchen was serving fried chicken.

But the usual therapies weren't working. "That damn Osama bin Laden has got me," the Emyfish complained at lunch, more than a week after the attacks. She sounded down. "I'm depressed," she said glumly. "And I'm not sleeping well at night."

It was making her mean.

When she and Sarah Jane had met in the lobby that morning, before driving across town to interview the manager of a sewing factory, filled with Vietnamese women, about the possibility of paying him to produce the Glamour Bibs, the Emyfish had greeted Sarah Jane with a silent stare. Sarah Jane was dressed as if she might be going to visit a sweatshop, which, in effect, they were. The Emyfish looked as if she were sailing off for lunch at the club.

"Well, I didn't know we were supposed to look like something the *dog* drug in," the Emyfish said, frosty eyes on Sarah Jane's rather nice sweat suit.

"Weh-yell, *you* don't," Sarah Jane stammered, caught by surprise.

"No," the Emyfish agreed. Certainly not.

"Does that mean you thank *Ah do*?" Sarah Jane asked. Her eyes were wide, and her voice was beginning to rise.

It did not prove to be a very successful morning.

Some people simply could not shake the grief and shock they felt.

"Ah cried *all* week long," Mary Davis said at lunch with Nathalie and me. Nathalie and I had both come down to be with our mothers.

"Evah-body had mah same reaction," Mary said. "They cried evah time they showed a picthah of somethin' patriotic oan TV."

For the first time in her life—which had embraced the First World War, the Great Depression, the Second World War, desegregation in the South, the riots and assassinations of the sixties, Vietnam, the Cold War, the collapse of the Soviet Union, the explosion of wealth and change in the age of the Internet, and now the New Old Age—Mary felt unprotected and vulnerable.

"Ah doan trust thuh United States anymoah," she said, shaking her head. Her dark eyes were pained. It was an amazing statement for a traditional woman and wife of her generation and region to make.

"Why not?" I asked.

"Septembah eleventh," she said flatly, looking dead at me. "Ah use' to think that thuh militarah could keep us safe from hahm. No moah." She shook her head again. "That such a thang could happen in thuh United States is unbahlievable."

Some people, tough-minded scrappy ones like Lucie Cross, had begun making preparations in case the terrorists should strike again, and closer. "I found a box, and I put in some raisins and crackers and fruit juice. And the bathroom has no windows. So I figured I would go in the bathroom, and close the door," Lucie said.

Others couldn't bring themselves to even talk about it.

"The funny thing is, they don't discuss it," Lucie said. "For two days I sat and watched TV, and didn't even come down for dinner, and the next night, I came down and sat at a table for six, and no one even mentioned it."

Every night since September 11, Lucie had talked on the phone to her son, Chick, the former Air Force pilot, who called from his home in New Hampshire to check on her. But "he didn't mention it," either, Lucie noted. "I said one night that we were probably sitting on a powder keg—being so close to MacDill Air Force Base. And he immediately changed the subject."

For the first time in the decade that I had been visiting and staying in the building, the formula didn't seem to be working. I began to wonder if the residents' basic contract with old age and Canterbury—that there is a time, late in life, to rest, and that it was possible in a place like this to be tranquil and secure—had not been broken. If the generation of the Great Depression and World War II could not believe that the worst of life was finally behind them, if they could not let their guard down now, at the average age of eighty-six, then when could they?

When could any of us? Ever?

If Social Security and pension checks, a nest egg, a nursing wing, a watchful service staff and security desk could not make them feel comfortable and safe, sheltered and separate, protected from whatever threatened the culture around them, then what could?

September 11 had shaken the premise of their final years, which was that their own lives might be longer than they had expected, but the hard times, at least, were behind them: They had found a place that promised to take care of them, a place where they could relax and make the best—the funny, forbearant, creative best—of whatever time they had remaining. Being at Canterbury had given them hope.

Now it seemed gone. It was as if they had lost their sense of humor.

On the eleventh day, with the rising sun a faint, shimmering white blotch in a curtain of mist, and the islands across the water veiled in a silver blue haze, the news was still grim. The television was reporting "six thousand three hundred thirty-three missing and presumed dead."

But the Sweetso, that contrarian, wasn't listening. She sat preoccupied in a cloud of idly drifting smoke at her dining table, shuffling some papers. She had something else in mind. She and El Cee had decided that the Canterbury Players should put on an entertainment, something light, to lift the mood. They had found a collection of funny answers children had given in school, and the Sweetso was sorting among them, trying to stitch some of them into a spoof of world history. So far, her favorites were these:

"His ships were called the *Nina,* the *Pinta,* and the *Santa Fe.*"

"One of the causes of the Revolutionary War was that the English put tacks in their tea."

"Thomas Jefferson was a virgin." (This one, she thought, was particularly funny.)

"Benjamin Franklin invented electricity by rubbing two cats together backward."

And "Beethoven was deaf. He was so deaf, he wrote very loud music."

"Boy," the Sweetso rumbled, shaking her head, "the things we do to keep this place going." Still, she thought the kids' comments had potential. Their goofy quality might be just the thing.

The Health Center, of course, generated its own protective layer of goof. Its weekly bingo game began about an hour later that morning, and at the table where Mother was parked in her reclining chair—turned out in a soft blue, white, and gold blouse, gold and white earrings, lipstick, rouge, eyeliner, and carefully brushed hair—Louise was waving one hand in the air.

"*Bango!* We got bango right heah!" she called to Big Maria, who was calling the numbers. "Brang Miz Clendinen huh money!"

"Look, Mama, at ahwll owah money!" She grinned, counting the small clutch of gray and white Monopoly bills. "We got two hundred fifty dollahs! We won two hundred fifty dollahs! We goan *shoppin'* this affahnoon!"

She held the money up close so Mother could see it.

Mother looked at the money, looked at Louise, and with what might have been a tiny gleam of satisfaction, ground her teeth. *Grind, grind. Grind.*

At lunch in the Health Center dining room an hour later, there was a new arrival. There were eight tables of four in the room that day, with feeders like Claudia or Marcia, Star or Louise, sitting at five of them, and three tables reserved for the residents who could still feed themselves. The new arrival, a short, plump, meticulous man with brown, slicked-down hair, tortoiseshell glasses, a brown tweed jacket, gray shirt, tie, dark pants, and cordovan loafers, sat down at a table of self-feeders, and carefully tucked the green cloth napkin at his place into his collar.

"Look, Mama." Louise grinned, patting Mother's hand and pointing. "We got thuh Doc with us, nowah!"

Dr. Joel Shrager raised the stemmed glass of cranberry juice by his plate in a toast to the three others at his table. They looked back at him blankly.

"Well," he said, smiling, "good things!" He held the glass out toward them, then paused, staring at it. "Is this wine?" he asked.

Toward the end of the second week, the calendar began to take hold again. At first, of course, all events had been canceled. But after a few days, it began to seem better—a sign of strength, and normalcy—to go ahead with whatever had been planned.

And so the Health and Fitness Expo opened at the Convention

Center as scheduled. Canterbury had booth number 827, under the SENIOR WELLNESS sign at the rear of the hall. To get there, one passed down an aisle lined with booths hawking discount vitamins, cell phones, Cool-Shade sunglasses, and Altra Medical Heartstream Automated External Defibrillators.

"We've put them in a lot of places," the tall tanned woman at the Altra counter said with an easy smile. She looked too young and lean and fit to be a candidate for defibrillation herself—not anytime in the next four or five decades. But, she said, looking cheerful at the prospect, there were now devices waiting for people to go into arrhythmic collapse in "golf clubs, airplanes, health clubs, senior centers, and shopping malls. In fact," she added, brightening, "Countryside Mall just put *three* in."

Sarah Jane, the Emyfish, and El Cee took a bagful of Glamour Bibs and some light folding chairs to sit on, and parked themselves that morning at the Canterbury booth, under a large picture of Elizabeth Himes's living room, with its red walls, glued-on moldings, fake fireplace, and view of the bay.

CANTERBURY TOWER—INDEPENDENT RETIREMENT LIVING AT ITS BEST! the sign proclaimed. They stayed through lunch and into the afternoon, answering occasional questions from those who stopped. They sold three bibs. It was a long way for the Emyfish and Sarah to walk, back and forth across the depth of the convention hall. But it was good to get out.

There was no way to know how September 11, or the change in atmosphere it had created at Canterbury, might have affected Mother. She seemed a little distant and preoccupied—if it was intellectually possible for her to *be* preoccupied. Except for the one glint of interest she showed at bingo, when Louise held up the money, she hadn't been very expressive. Then, suddenly, two weeks after the attacks, as I came into her room on a Tuesday afternoon, she was different, alive again.

She still had a small bandage on her left forearm. It was dated August 23, the day that someone, moving her in or out of bed, or in or out of the shower chair, had bumped the arm on something, creating two small tears in her fragile skin. But that was business as usual. Mother always had a Band-Aid or bandage on one appendage or another, usually on her arms. Her skin—thin and brittle as old fabric—tore easily. But the little tears, which the nursing assistants carefully salved and tended, never seemed to bother her. It wasn't her frail, shrinking, stiffened body that I paid most attention to. It was her eyes.

As I came around the corner of the door that afternoon and bent down to kiss her, her eyes were alive. She gave me the glad, excited look I had seen so many times in years past—when I came home at Thanksgiving or Christmas from college, from the military, or from working and living away. She didn't say anything, of course. She just looked thrilled at the sight of her son. I could have been a good son or a bad son. It didn't matter. It was a motherly flare of emotion that quieted, as I sat with her, like a light being turned down, and was replaced, as I held her hand and made conversation, by a calm, still clear-eyed look. I took it as contentment. She looked pleased at being together, the two of us. No questions. No expectations. Just being.

It made me feel better.

And it wasn't just Mother whose spirit had come out of hiding. Ruth Richter was bouncing back from her stroke.

"She's very determined," the rabbi said with a smile. He was walking over to see her in the nursing wing three times a day. "Yesterday, she was the champion of the bingo." He rolled his eyes, to be pleased at such a thing.

"Suddenly, she came into her own again. The first few weeks, she could neither cry nor laugh. Now she has both back. And she knows everybody. She remembers names and places," he said happily. She had recovered her edge.

"The speech therapist, at the end of a long session one day, asked, 'Can you say something in German?' "

"Gehen Sie nach Hause!" Ruth snapped. She was tired.

"What does that mean?" he asked.

"Go home!" she said.

But it was the medley performance the Sweetso and El Cee put together, at the end of the month, that finally cracked the residents' sense of gloom. The assembly room was filled. Except for meals, it was the first gathering of the building since September 11, and the residents filled the room, glad to have an entertainment, hoping it might lift their spirits. The monthly performances were miniature variety shows, usually goofy sketches intended to be light and funny. But when Martha Sweet, who always emceed the evenings, appeared at the microphone, she seemed solemn, and she announced, in her gravest gravelly voice, that they were going to depart from the norm and start on a more serious note.

"And here is our own Martha Cameron," she said, without further explanation.

El Cee got up with a piece of paper in her hand. She stood looking out at them all for just a moment, and then began to read from it. It was a Dr. Seuss–like poem that one of the inmates had found on the Internet. It was a crude piece of work. A poet—or anyone who cared for poetry—would have found it witless and banal. But it had lots of patriotic flourishes and celebrations of the American way, and lots of *U*'s and *S*'s in it. The writer was evidently a big fan of Dr. Seuss, and when El Cee finished, the room was smiling. Then everyone stood. They sang "God Bless America," several times over. Then they played some simple category games the two Marthas had chosen: the names of rivers in Europe, the names of songs with hearts in the title.

As the Sweetso said later, "Everybody made a lot of noise, and seemed to feel better."

After that evening, people began to be able to talk and think aloud more easily about the strange, terrible, singular thing that had happened, and one night, at the Men's Table, the Canterbury sense of humor came back.

After the initial horror, as the story of the plotters emerged, day by day, the regulars at the table had begun to discuss it, tentatively at first. Sitting in their circle of chairs, dressed as always in jackets and ties, their white-haired or bald old heads gleaming, they had tried to imagine the minds of the bronze-skinned, fanatic young terrorists who hijacked the planes, determined to die in them. They tried to imagine the lure of the seventy-two virgins who were said to await Islamic martyrs in heaven.

It was too much. All things considered, Ben Franklin finally said, he'd rather have a couple of experienced widows. They all agreed.

When that conversation got around, it raised the mood in the building considerably.

But the final lift came when the United States invaded Afghanistan in early October, looking for bin Laden, and Karl Richter one evening suggested the perfect strategy for dealing with him. It was equal parts King Solomon and Milton Berle.

"We capture Osama bin Laden," the rabbi said, a wise look on his old face. "We bring him to the United States. Give him a *complete* sex-change operation. And send *her* back to Afghanistan. To the *Taliban*."

Everyone thought that was brilliant.

CHAPTER TWENTY-THREE

He Wants Our Ashes

DECEMBER 2001

C anterbury was again the place I had come to love. I went home
without worrying any more about it—or about Mother—at
least not any more than usual. Then five days later, on a Monday afternoon in mid-October, the security desk at the Tower called,
and transferred me to the nurses' station. It was Wendy.

"I was just feeding your mother lunch, and she showed signs of
having another TIA," Wendy said. "What she had was facial drooping on the left-hand side—which is a sign a person makes just prior
to a severe stroke. It's like a presymptom of a stroke," she said, to
make sure I understood.

Everyone knew that Mother was on a DO NOT RESUSCITATE—
even a DO NOT TREAT—set of orders. But drawing the line between
care and treatment isn't always easy. Wendy asked if they could start
her on 225 milligrams of aspirin a day, a mild preventative. In principle, I could have said no. But deny my mother aspirin? I said yes.

The next day, Canterbury called again. This time, it was Carlos
on the front desk. I could hear the sound of the parking lot gate
bing-bonging in the background as he let a car in or out.

"Ah, Heidi wouldah likah to talkah to youah, suh," he said. Heidi
was the patient care representative. "I havuh Mr. Clendinen onnah
thah line," Carlos said, speaking on another phone. Then Heidi
came on. She is very direct.

"Right now, we're seeing a severe change," she said crisply. "A big change, where she can't swallow. She's almost unable to swallow. Last week, around Thursday, she wasn't too bad. But on Friday, at breakfast, there was an incident"—nurse talk, in this case, for choke. "Today, I tried just giving her smaller bites with the honey-consistency liquid." Anything Mother was given to drink—water, cranberry juice, apple juice—was thickened so it would move slowly down her throat, giving her time to swallow. "But she choked and turned red," Heidi said.

She was in dying mode again.

Two days later, I was in Tampa, sitting beside Mother at lunch. She looked listless. Dull. She hadn't been excited to see me when I walked in, and she wasn't swallowing anything but spoons of the little cup of custard supplement, which is silky and light. The scene, the moment, the sense of a formula breaking down, felt glumly familiar. We had been this way before. I stayed awhile, but Mother had no energy and there wasn't much passing between us. After a little, I left.

I had dinner that night with the Emyfish and Ashby, Sarah Jane and the Duchess, and Phyllis Sutton Russell, in the blue and gold dining room at a table by the window. Thin and big busted like Ethel Merman, with a brassy, mischievous personality and come-hither eyes, Phyllis was seventy-seven. She had been married twice and, with another woman, Connie West, ran a little company that helped widows sort through and pare down their household possessions so they could move into Canterbury. For an hourly fee, Connie and Phyllis would manage the move as well. Arrange the furniture. Hang the pictures on the wall. They would also keep the books, pay the bills, take people to the hairdresser, communicate with the children, or do anything else for twenty dollars an hour that widows didn't know how to do. Or want to do. Or want to do alone.

They had made a business out of helping older women deal with life, especially after their husbands died.

Phyllis was full of stories, usually about other people's relationships—which are always the best gossip. She was talking that night about a married friend the Emyfish and Sarah Jane also knew, who was inconsolable because her husband had left her for *an older* woman.

"It's almos' the wors' thang Ah evah huhd!" Phyllis laughed merrily, as if it were one of the best things she had ever heard.

"Ohh, *nooah*." Sarah Jane smiled serenely. "The worst thang *Ah* huhd was a husbin' who leftah woman Ah know—for *nobodeh*! It wuz becuz she didden' undahstan' his *mew*-sic!"

The Emyfish, next to me, was looking faintly amused. But her mind was elsewhere. She was thinking about her old friend, my mother, who might once again be on the way out. Which had gotten her to thinking about her own mortality. And where she might end up.

She leaned in close. "You know," she said, her deep, smoky voice dropping to a confidential murmur as Phyllis and Sarah Jane volleyed stories back and forth across the table, "when your mother was still well, she and we were talking about our arrangements. We said we were going to be cremated. And Bobbie said, 'Well, you know, Dudley will take you. He has the ashes of *a lot of people* around.'"

I was sort of stunned. It was sometimes astounding to discover what my mother told people when I wasn't present. I had concluded long ago that we were probably all better off if we *didn't* know what our mothers said about us. But the Emyfish had remembered, and she wanted to talk about it.

And Mother was actually right. Or partly right. I didn't have a *lot* of people. But I did have two—Florence and Bessie. About half of them. The other halves were in the ground in Florida. My cousin Florence was in the square golden box in which she had come from the crematorium on a shelf in a bookcase in my living room, behind the rosy, unfired clay bust of her that her husband, Louis, had made. Aunt Bessie was in the gold, red, white, and green Medaglia D'Oro Espresso coffee can in which I had put her, behind the terra-cotta face of a handsome young Greek whose features had adorned the corner of a roof gutter on the island in the Mediterranean where I had found him, years ago, and brought him home.

I looked at them every day. It was Florence who had first drawn me into the issues of the New Old Age, when she turned ninety and her lungs gave out. She was sort of a distant cousin. Her mother's sister had married one of my mother's father's brothers. I never knew her aunt, or my great-uncle, or my grandfather. But Florence and I had always clicked. The long conversational martini lunches we enjoyed at a restaurant on the bay in Dunedin, all through her eighties and my forties, had finally turned into quiet talks beside her hospital bed, plotting how I might help her die. Florence's mind was wonderful. She hated being trapped by her breathless body in bed. Her dilemma, and the question of what, if anything, she could do about it, had developed at about the same time that I became responsible for my aunts Bessie and Carolyn, which wasn't very long before Mother gave me her power of attorney and made me her trustee, and moved into Canterbury.

Florence was on the west side of the bay, in Clearwater. Bessie and Carolyn and Mother were on the east side, in Tampa. My involvement with them in their last years was in 1992, 1993, and 1994, a period I have come to regard as the time when my own life began to be diverted a generation ahead, into the lives of the family members and old friends I had always known as adults, and who had now begun to fall apart—and to fall, in a way, on me.

By the summer of 1996, after much nursing care, time, and money, a lot of conflict and angst, a good deal of unhappiness, but a great deal of discovery and love, my old cousin and my two aunts were dead. I told the Emyfish that night at dinner how I had ended up—not by plan, but by a sort of piecemeal process—with Florence and Bessie in my bookshelves, and why it gave me a warm feeling to have them there. When Florence died in December 1995, I asked her sister-in-law, Dot, in California, if I could have a portion of her ashes, and Dot had kindly agreed. Otherwise, Florence would have disappeared from my life—into some anonymous ash ground in Pinellas County. When the bronze metal box came, I put her up on the shelf, behind her bust. When Bessie died, the next April, I had asked Mother if I could pour some of her ashes around Dad, in Myrtle Hill. Bessie was a pauper. She had nowhere else to go.

"Ah think that would be lovahlee, deah," Mother said, "juss not *oan* yoah fahthuh."

And so I flew down to Tampa, bought a red rubber bucket and a green watering can from the hardware store, drove out to the cemetery, and poured about half of Bessie around my father. I don't think, actually, he would have liked it. He didn't much like being with her when she was alive. But that's the advantage of dealing with dead people. They can't complain. It was a brilliant day in May, noontime at high drought season, sweating hot. I dripped on Bessie as I watered her in. And then three days later, I flew back to Baltimore with the rest of her, and put her in the coffee can. Coffee was the only thing I knew that she really loved. She drank it all the time. So I figured she'd be happy up there in her can on the shelf, with a handsome Greek for company. He had to be the best-looking man she ever had.

The Emyfish remembered them, of course. She had known Florence and Bessie slightly. But what amazed me was that my mother had decided, on her own, to invite Emy and Ashby to join them. To join *her*.

Usually, when Mother spoke for me that way, giving or accepting invitations, it irked me. It was part of a lifelong pattern of control and direction. She was an extraordinarily charming and thoughtful and also artfully manipulative woman, skilled at moving people around like puppets while smiling at them fondly. Especially her children. Mothers do that. Children rebel. Sometimes, the mothers just get sneakier. It wasn't until I got into therapy and realized the extent of it that I decided enough was enough. I told her to quit, or lose me. Mostly, she had. But this time, coming as it did when she seemed to be slipping away, I was touched to hear what she had said. It was so classically Mother.

I planned to put her in the bookshelves, too. Part of her. It had become my personal burying ground, and the thought of her being there made me happy. But I wasn't sure she understood that. I couldn't remember how much we had talked about it before her strokes—and so I didn't realize how taken she was with the notion of being the center of a company of dear, departed old souls in my living room. My mother was deeply sentimental. She *loved* being wanted. She loved being at the center of things. But I think what she probably liked most was the prospect of being a perpetual presence in her only son's life. Hovering was one of her favorite things. It drove me crazy. But that was when she talked.

I had thought about the Emyfish and Ashby, of course. I didn't like the idea that relationships with people you cherished had to come to an end. That you prayed over them, put them in a box in the ground, covered them over, and that was that. Thanks for the memories. Having Emy and Ashby around felt cheerful to me, and right. It always had, and I could conjure them up a lot better if they were actually there. Besides, if they had souls that needed to go somewhere after death, I don't know why they couldn't come to my house. But I hadn't known how to raise the subject with the Emyfish. Death and its aftermath weren't things she had ever wanted to talk about. Much less plan for.

Mother, of course, understood all that. So she had made the offer for me.

"I would *love* to have you," I told the Emyfish at dinner. "Just not soon." She chuckled and sort of winked at me, and turned back to the other side of the table. It was time for dessert.

"Ah'll have thuh black cherrah yogurt," Sarah Jane was saying, looking up at the waitress, "with some Grape-Nuts."

I ordered pecan pie. Warmed. I was glad that the Emyfish seemed to like the idea. It gave me a rosy feeling. But I wondered if she had discussed it with Ashby. We didn't have a chance to talk about it anymore that trip. Mother got better in a few days—she started eating and swallowing again—and I went home without knowing.

The answer came not long after, on one of my next times down. It was the cocktail hour, and the three of us were sitting in Emy and Ashby's living room before dinner. The Emyfish and I had our feet up on a pair of creaky old footstools with crocheted cushions, sipping drinks and munching salted nuts. We were looking across the water toward the city, which was changing colors with the setting sun. Being there in the amber glow of old lamp shades, surrounded by the familiar fabric, crystal, furniture, and art that had been her parents' and grandparents', with the city turning deeper shades of bronze and silver in the distance, and a litter of old maps and documents, papers and bulletins spilling across the couch and dining room table—the product of Ashby's continuing curiosity about the past (and his inability to throw anything away)—made me feel part of some long, fond, secure continuum.

It was what I wanted to feel. I didn't want the arrangement to end. I liked it. I was slurping cold, nonalcoholic chardonnay, the closest I get to real wine anymore. The Emyfish was in her favorite wing chair with her shoes off, idly twirling a vodka and diet Sprite with lots of ice around in one of her grandmother Bena's etched, tall-stemmed, gold-rimmed goblets.

I don't recall what we were talking about. There was no crisis that needed discussion or decision. Mother had seemed stable for the last couple of months. There were no events to deal with. We were just sitting together as we had, off and on, in one way or another, for more than half a century, ever since Mother dumped me into Emy's arms.

The Emyfish was staring off now with a thoughtful look, as if she was sorting something out. Her eyes were fixed on a big antique blue and white bowl on the dining table, an island of porcelain in a sea of drifting books and paper. She looked as if she had made up her mind. She turned toward Ashby, who was sitting across the room, his nose buried in some journal.

"Ashby, don't you think that Chinese bowl would be good? *Ashby,* are you listening to me?" She stared at him over her drink, raised her arm, and rattled her ice and her grandmother's bracelets.

"Ashby!!"

He lifted his head from what he was reading and peered at her over his glasses, his white eyebrows knit in a craggy scowl.

"Good for what?" he said. He had heard her. He almost always heard her. He just didn't always answer.

"For my *ashes*. For *our* ashes. For Jughead. He wants our ashes."

Ashby gave her a dour look, as if this would go away if he ignored it, and went back inside his paper.

It was a brief moment, and passing. But I knew them. He hadn't objected. And I thought I knew, from that point on, that we had reached an understanding. A piece had come into place. There was a plan. It wasn't written out, but it didn't need to be.

I would keep coming back to Canterbury for as long as Mother lived, for months or years. Perhaps even beyond. Someday, I knew, she had to die. She kept threatening to. One day she would. She might go before Wilber and Mary. Before the Emyfish and Ashby, the Sweetso, the rabbi and Ruth. Before Sarah Jane and Mauricio, El Cee and Helen Hill and Lucie Cross. She might not. She might outwait them. There was no way to know. I had given up predicting.

But one day—one way or another—the core of this village, the people I had always known, and the ones I had met and grown part of since I began coming to Canterbury, would begin to fail. They couldn't simply keep growing old. But they wouldn't all go at once. It would happen through the years. For a long time yet, I would keep returning to the plump, off-white little tower by the bay. It was the natural thing to do. Canterbury had become my other home. Baltimore-Tampa-Baltimore was the axis of my life. At some point, however, the path would change—just as my understanding had.

The long, day-by-day, week-by-week, year-by-year experience of this indeterminate, enduring New Old Age had altered my conception of relationships. I had begun to think of them as eternal. Not the people. But the relationships. The ones we cared about, the ones we were prepared to nurture and maintain, could live as long as we do, I thought—as long as we were prepared to keep them. They'd just change form. It could be arranged.

Whether Mother was the first or not, the people I had grown to love at Canterbury would begin to die. I would hope to be there when they did. I would try to be there for the services. Some, I knew, would be buried, whole body, in caskets, in the ground. But more and more, like Mother, they were choosing to be cremated. It made them very portable. At some point, whether I was there to sing and pray and speak over Mother, or the Emyfish, or Ashby, or someone else, or not, I wouldn't come back alone. I had the feeling that it would just be the first of more trips with company in my briefcase.

Who knew how many souls can live in a living room?

Hello, Mother, Good-bye

JANUARY 2007

There has been no more talk about ashes since that afternoon late in 2001. The Emyfish and Ashby are still at Canterbury. And the Sweetso. And Sarah Jane and Mauricio, and El Cee, and many others. I still see them when I'm there.

We have breakfast and lunch and dinner, and we make conversation. There have been some changes. The nursing wing has been refurbished—wall coverings, carpets, furniture, the dining room, the recreation room. There are now more single rooms, and a section called assisted living, whose residents have their own rooms in a nursing environment but are free to come and go. The Duchess lives there now. Solar panels have been installed on top of the covered parking, to capture the sun and warm the pool in spring and fall for the Sweetso and Doris Garcia, and others who like to splash around. The exterior of the Tower has been painted, a very soft khaki-cappuccino color, and an automatic fire sprinkler system installed in the halls and all apartments.

Mrs. Vinas finally banned smoking everywhere in the building—including the apartments. The Sweetso, to her own disgust, had quit, which may have been what Mrs. Vinas was waiting for. The Sweetso had gotten a cold she couldn't shake, which became bronchitis, which seemed to leave her breathless and disoriented. When the nurse checked, her blood oxygen count was down to 89. In the hospital, the doctors told her she had chronic obstructive pulmonary disease. Emphysema, for short. While she was in the hospital, her daughter, Meredith, came down from New York, and she and Mrs. Vinas threw out all the cigarettes and ashtrays, had the carpets replaced, the walls scrubbed down, and a lot of things laundered and cleaned. The smell of tobacco tars and nicotine, which had been overpowering—to everyone except the Sweetso—became faint, tolerable, and less suggestive.

"I am *so* pissed off," the Sweetso said. "I thought I was so smart. And now I feel so *stupid*." She came home with an oxygen machine, which she uses only at night. And though it was a battle—and you couldn't have gotten odds anywhere in the building that she would succeed—she hasn't smoked again. Everyone was very supportive. No one said I told you so. But I was tempted.

The Emyfish still likes to play bridge and have a drink before dinner. She still does her exercises in the morning. Her lunch and dinner calendar is still full. She still thinks Ashby doesn't know how old she is. They both have more doctor appointments than they used to. Her heart seems weaker, and her spinal stenosis and neuropathy have progressed. After falling on her tailbone coming out of the dining room in December 2003, trying to fake it by leaning on an umbrella—whose metal point slid on the floor—the Emyfish finally consented to use a cane. She named it Cary Grant, so she wouldn't mind being seen with it in public. After some cramping and spotting, she was diagnosed with uterine cancer in 2006. But as of this January, she was not going to do anything about it. The surgeon didn't want to operate, given her weak heart, and after a nurse told her that radiation treatment would burn her privates, she said the hell with *that*. Ashby, who had been successfully treated with radiation for early cancer of the larynx about five years before, was diagnosed with early bladder cancer, and had chemotherapy. After a period of looking thin and wan—though dapper—he bounced back. Sarah Jane developed breast cancer, and had the affected tissue and lymph nodes cut out. With some reluctance, she started the chemo treatments the doctors advised, but they made her feel so rotten, she decided she'd rather have cancer than chemotherapy, and stopped. That was it. No chemo. No radiation. God could take it from there. That was five years ago, and she seems fine.

Some of the others have died. The first was in December 2001, just after we thought Mother might do it. It was Ruth Richter. She had a second stroke, from which she would not have recovered. The rabbi and their son, David, the psychologist, stayed up late and wept together and drank bourbon, and decided to disconnect her. She was eighty-four. And there have been other departures since. Lucie Cross fell again and broke her hip in January 2002, and died under anesthesia on the operating table. It was the perfect way for a scrappy old nurse to go. She wanted to get fixed or die trying, and she did. She was ninety-eight. Wilber died in the nursing wing that December. He was ninety-three, and just finally slipped off. Mary died of congestive heart failure in July 2004. She was eighty-nine.

And the rabbi died in September 2005, of prostate cancer. He was ninety-four, witty to the last. When a young and comely nurse came to take his blood pressure and pulse, two days before the end, his heart rate jumped.

"I'm not dead yet," he said.

Herbert Carrington, the old maître d' and host at the yacht club, finally died of prostate cancer, too, which he had developed, along with bad knees and diabetes, after he turned 100. If he had attended earlier to the prostate cancer, he might still be here. But he was 107, and lively almost to the end. The last time we had lunch, the waitress asked him if he wanted a drink.

"No," he said, "I gave it up."

"I didn't know that, Herbert," I said. "So did I."

"No kidding?" he exclaimed, looking surprised. "When did you quit?"

"When I was forty-four," I said. "When did you quit?"

"When I was ninety-seven," he said.

We talked about this and that, and Herbert told me, before we left the restaurant to go see Mother—they had always liked each other— that he didn't think he would marry his current lady friend, who was in her sixties, or live together either. "The children wouldn't approve," he said. He was 104. I went to his grandson's wedding in Alexandria months later. Herbert was still driving. He worked until he was 105, and it occurred to me that he might be the oldest independently living, loving, working, driving man in America.

But Mother's time still didn't come. Not in 2001. Or 2002. Or 2003. Or 2004, or 2005. Or 2006. She had just been practicing, when we thought she might die, in late 2001. There were several things that had long made it difficult for her to swallow—and made her choky when she tried. The strokes had left her with a slow, weak swallowing reflex, and a fluttery valve cover over her windpipe. She had also suffered from acid reflux for years. Decades, probably. Over time, the stomach acid splashing up can irritate and damage that area of the throat. Every morning, she was given a dose of Prevacid, mixed in with a little applesauce, to reduce the acid. It was one of the few medications she still took. When the choking subsided and her appetite returned, she had begun to float along again. She was, after all, only eighty-six at the end of 2001. It was the average age at Canterbury Tower—and roughly the life expectancy of well-cared-for, affluent white women of that generation in America.

More than five years have passed since then. As of January 2007, it has been nearly nine years since my mother's two strokes. Nine years of being woken and brushed and cleaned, dressed and made up and transferred to the wheeled reclining chair so she could be taken to the dining room, the morning entertainments, the games and cooking classes and therapy groups, the visits of the Piano Man, the group birthday parties, the picnics on the second-floor terrace, or across the parking lot in the little St. Francis of Assisi Park. Whatever was planned, Mother almost always went along. Twice, when hurricanes in the Gulf threatened to come up Tampa Bay, Canterbury was evacuated. She and the other residents of the Health Center, along with all the nurses and certified nursing assistants, were driven away from the coast in ambulances and vans, east or north to safer places at higher elevations.

Then, with much shifting and shuffling, they all came back, and the routine resumed.

I have now spent almost four hundred days and nights at Canterbury. Every hour or two, as the months and years slipped by, Mother was rotated a quarter turn—and then propped and retucked in her pillows and blankets, in order to avoid exerting constant pressure on any one area of her fragile skin. So meticulously cared for, with her beloved Louise beside her three times a week, she lived, and seemed content. And around her, the brave, dotty, poignant, surprisingly spunky life of the village continued to unfold.

Other people, inmates and staff, came and went. Some staff members were fired by Mrs. Vinas: two of them—one the supervisor of the other—for having an affair. Some found higher pay elsewhere. One, an older security guard, a tall, bony Brit with wonderful big muttonchop whiskers who looked like something out of Gilbert and Sullivan, fell and died in the front hall in the middle of one day. He stopped breathing, and no one could revive him. But most of the staff members who make Canterbury what it is are still there: Mrs. Vinas, of course, and Mildred, Chanh, Murphy, Susan Conley, Ernestine, Claudia, Marcia, and Star. The loss that shocked everyone was Carlos—Carlos Vera—who had seemed so indestructible. He developed a very aggressive cancer, which had already metastasized when it was discovered. He was given only months to live. He told Mrs. Vinas he wanted to die at Canterbury. She made the arrangements. Carlos worked sitting down, at a newly created guard post, as long as he could do that. Then he moved into a room in the Health Center, to be cared for by the rest of the staff. He died with his family and his big dog, Spike, around him, in 2006. He was fifty-eight. Mrs. Vinas still cannot talk about it without tears welling in her eyes.

The working staff, I have come to realize, seems to die much younger than the residents. At least four—perhaps five—of the women residents lived to be one hundred in the time I have been there. One of them, Helen Hill, made no bones about it, and let her family have a party for her in 2005. The other ones just smiled. At least two long-term residents lived so much longer than they had anticipated, they decided they had outlived the usefulness of life at Canterbury, and moved out—leaving the money they had paid as endowment behind. One was Judy Drake. Most of her old friends, and also her generation of her family in Tampa, were gone. She could barely see over the dashboard, and had started running into other cars in the parking lot.

When her daughter, Julie, died, I think Judy made up her mind that she should be with Sally, her remaining child, and her grandchildren—the three generations of them together, the way families used to do it. So in May 2003, she moved to a town in rural Virginia, to live in a mid-nineteenth-century house with her gregarious, high-energy divorced daughter, a private school teacher there, and her children. They seem happy. The other one who decided to leave, who had been there since Canterbury first opened, was a man named Ira. He called bingo every week, and was involved in good works for the needy outside Canterbury, but ate alone when he was there, and hardly ever spoke. He was so reticent that Helen Hill, who is polite but no patsy, had quit saying hello to him fifteen years before, because she realized one day that in the previous twelve years, he had never returned the greeting. When he left, he didn't say why.

The ones who remained went on as usual. They had tiffs and squabbles. They were saddened, or relieved, or indifferent, when others died. They made new friends. Found new loves. Inspired, amused, annoyed, and sometimes infuriated each other. Got caught up in surprising mysteries. Were afflicted by strange ailments. And discovered, when they began to lose their memories and charms, that others drew away. They suffered uncomplainingly, for the most part. Only occasionally insufferably. They exhibited great dignity; said terrible and also hilarious things, some of them intentional; and died quiet, usually long-delayed but also sudden, quixotic, dramatic, determined, and even violent deaths. In one or two instances, having carefully considered the likely quality of the days and months and years to come, they decided, without fuss, to kill themselves. And did.

There are more tales to tell of life at Canterbury in these last five years. But that is not what this last chapter is about. This chapter is about what brought me to Canterbury in the first place—my mother. And about the thing that has come to mystify so many of us, because it has become so elusive and unpredictable.

The end.

When it finally came, after so many false starts, so many course corrections, so many years of gradual descent, I was surprised.

But I had let down my guard. Mother had lasted so long—deteriorated, threatened to die, recovered, endured—that she had lulled me again into thinking she was eternal. Dressed and made up and carefully laid in her padded chaise longue, nestled in pillows and afghans, she had become a cameo, a cocoon around which the air—and life itself—flowed. And slipped away.

She was still a part of life. She was awake to it. She turned and sometimes smiled at the sight and sound and touch of it, the presence of those of us who loved and attended her. She was hungry and thirsty enough for it to eat and drink at mealtimes. Because she did those things, she lived. But as time passed, she had ceased to react or contribute in any except the most subtle and nuanced ways.

Certainly by the last couple of years—and perhaps for considerably longer—my mother had achieved an effortless, free-floating state of existence. It is one that occurs, I think, only in systems of compassionate and total care, among people who have no life-threatening disease, but also no remaining capabilities or responsibilities, and therefore no stress, no anxiety, no worries about or anger at life, and in fact, little or no awareness of the world, near or far, at all. Nothing to think or wonder about. And nothing left to do. It is the ultimate, end state of life in a place like Canterbury, where the contract is care for as long as you live, whether you're aware of it or not.

If Mother had remained at home, like her own mother or my father's mother, living by herself, or cared for by her children, she would certainly have died years before, from the strokes, the pneumonia, some other infection, or—which always terrified me—by choking to death. The first two ends are how my grandmothers went.

If she had been in an inferior nursing facility—a more typically understaffed, for-profit nursing home like the one I put my aunts Bessie and Carolyn in, where most of the residents were wards of Medicaid—I don't think she would have lasted more than a year or two. An unnoticed or untended skin tear, a broken bone from a careless move, a urinary tract infection from soiled pants and sheets might have spread an infection to her bloodstream that without antibiotics, or perhaps even with, would have killed her. And we had pledged no antibiotics.

But at Canterbury, Mother was watched over for almost a decade by loyal, patient, mindful nurses like Sally and Stacey, and constantly tended by a group of certified nursing assistants: by Meva until she retired, and Claudia and Marcia, Star and Yvonne—and of course, by the devoted Ernestine, and Louise. They treated her as they might have their own mothers. That's how Louise thought of her.

"She's likah mama tuh me. She always been like that tuh me," she said. Some of those women, in fact, missed work at Canterbury only to tend to their own parents when they sickened and died. Then they returned to my mother's side, and to the care of the other old people in the Health Center.

That kind of care is a calling. Only people of great compassion do it. And after a while, their devotion raises a question: How long can a serenely brain-damaged but otherwise disease-free person like my mother be maintained, in an existence with no physical or emotional stress, by a system of nearly perfect care? Obviously, years longer than if she had not come to Canterbury.

But how much longer? And to what purpose?

The conversations Mother and I had had more than a decade before—in the last century, in the last millennium—when she was crippled by arthritis and osteoporosis, troubled by high blood pressure, beginning to experience transient little cerebral events, but still thoughtful and aware, and determined to avoid precisely this state of affairs, had long ago come to seem naïve, not to mention irrelevant.

Neither of us could imagine then what would happen to her. What she would become.

And then it happened. When it does, you become accustomed. Instead of thinking of my mother as gone—and devoutly wishing that she were, because that is what she originally would have wished—I simply came to think of her as *this*.

She no longer wished to go. I ceased to wish it for her.

She was as she was. And while being with her was some days awful, it was also sometimes very sweet. Mostly, I just sat and talked to her. There were almost always other people around. There is very little privacy in nursing homes. You just act as if there were, knowing full well that there isn't, and that others are listening in. Visitors, after all, are entertainment. In the group of chairs next to us on the porch one afternoon about four years ago sat a long-necked, sharp-eyed old lady who had lived in the nursing wing for years. Thin and bent, she reminded me of a hawk on a limb—always peering around. She had visitors that day—some lumpish relatives I had never seen before. They were ill at ease, uncertain how to conduct a social visit in such a place. They didn't come often enough to know. The tall old lady was clearly bored with them, and their lame attempts to inquire about the weather and the food. She was watching us, and suddenly decided to give her relatives an example of real conversation.

"Look at that," she said to them, gesturing our way. "He's *so* nice to her. And she's just *gone*."

Not to me. But "gone" was what I feared. I had come to dread Mother's infections, her periodic inability to swallow, the possibility of her choking, the likelihood of another stroke. I'm not sure whether I was afraid of feeling responsible for her death—because my instructions were no treatment—or afraid of the disruption, the trauma it would cause. Perhaps I would be fine with her death. So much of her had already departed. Maybe I had done all my grieving. Maybe not. I didn't know, and I feared the unknown.

As the years went by and these tales began to near an end—and as Mother grew duller and stiffer and more shrunken—I began to hope she would live to see them published. Having survived this long, why shouldn't she stick around for the finish? It's her story. It's what she would have wanted when she could think and feel. I didn't know that she could do that anymore. But I didn't want her to die.

"I don't know why she's still here," said Cathy, the physician's assistant and geriatric nurse who came twice each week from the University of South Florida Medical School to check on Mother and about twenty others in the Health Center.

I didn't either, but my mother was a woman who liked to see things through. She kept on living, and I kept coming back. In between visits, I ended an eight-year relationship with a man she liked. Sold my house. Bought another with some friends. Sold it. Bought a third. Began a new relationship. I didn't tell Mother all of that. I didn't want to trouble her. But each time I went to Tampa, six or ten or twelve times a year, she was there, waiting to look at me with those questioning eyes. What happened, I think, though it may seem odd, was that she became the rock of my changing, evolving life. She was, much of the time, not much more expressive *than* a rock. But she was *my* rock, my mother. And I was afraid to lose her.

W hat seemed the greatest threat to her survival was also the tiniest—the little skin tears that occurred so frequently, and about which the nursing desk always called me. It happened once or twice a month, or more. They would tell me how big the tear was, how they were treating it, with what kind of salve. The tears were usually less than an inch long, and typically on her forearms or lower legs, the backs of her hands, or along her bony spine. They always healed. Then, late in 2006, I realized that the calls had become more frequent. And the nurses had started speaking of a bunion, a sore bunion on her foot, on the big joint of her right toe.

That was different.

Her feet had been misshapen for decades by her lifelong love of fashionably high-heeled shoes with pointed toes, and probably by her later arthritis and osteoporosis. But Mother hadn't walked in almost nine years. Why should a bunion be an issue? I didn't understand. But I was out of touch. I had lost visual continuity. In the previous six months, I had been working to finish writing, had sold the third house, moved, ended the last relationship. I had not been down to Tampa. I hadn't ever been away so long. But I had been freed of guilt by a conversation with Cathy, the physician's assistant, more than a year before.

I had been sitting with Mother, feeling inadequate. She was giving me one of her "So where have YOU been?" looks. That's how I interpreted it. I had the guilts. When I left her room, Cathy was standing at the nurses' station.

"How are you?" she asked, looking at me.

Frustrated, I said. I wished I knew what was in my mother's mind. She had largely quit seeming glad to see me, and I translated that as criticism, of the son who didn't come to town frequently enough, didn't see her often enough when he did, and didn't stay long enough. Her gaze had become increasingly cold, and noncommittal. Increasingly, I ran out of things to say. She seemed withdrawn. Inert. It was harder and harder to relate. But I didn't know whether she really missed me when I wasn't there. I didn't know whether she remembered that I *had* been there, or how long ago. I didn't really know whether she remembered me at all.

I couldn't tell that she knew me. For more than a year, I had doubted that she did.

Cathy looked at me levelly for a quiet moment and then, very matter-of-factly, told me several things. That my mother had almost certainly had more strokes in the last years. That she had probably developed arteriosclerotic or Alzheimer's dementia as well. That in any case, she had no sense of time passing. No memory of the past. No intellectual ability to think about the present. To comprehend the things I said to her, or probably even to know who I was. I might look familiar to her, Cathy said, but when or how often I came, how long I stayed, or what I said, had no effect on how my mother felt.

No one had ever talked like this to me before.

"How long do you think that's been true?" I asked.

"For as long as I've been seeing her," she replied.

"How long is *that*?"

"Five years," she said simply.

I was dumbfounded.

"You don't think it matters whether I'm here or not?"

"Not to her," Cathy said. "After all this damage, her brain is probably mush."

She looked at me, to see if this was sinking in. "So do what you need to do for *yourself*," she said. "Don't worry about her." To hear a medical professional—someone with years of experience working with the demented in university and veterans' hospitals and at Canterbury—describe my mother as (what had the sharp-tongued old lady said?) *gone* was dismaying. I couldn't believe that I had been talking for the last five years to someone who had no idea who I was or what I was saying.

In fact, I *didn't* believe it. I don't. There had been too many times when she had seemed absolutely present—even warm, comprehending. I had gotten her to laugh at stories I knew my mother would have found funny. And she had shown stern disapproval at my behavior once, when I knew my mother would have disapproved. That had been only about a year before.

I had my own experience of her. I also knew that everyone who had regular experience of her—from Louise, to Ernestine, to the nursing assistants, the licensed practical nurses, and the registered nurses, to Cathy, the physician's assistant, and the doctors—had a different opinion of the level of Mother's awareness. Louise, Ernestine, Marcia, Claudia, Star, and the other nursing assistants all believed that Mother was still animated by her own spirit. Her spark was still visible to them. They were the people most intimate in her life, and they felt that she knew them, could understand them, knew me, and brightened—even ate better—when they talked to her about me, and told her I was coming.

Each of us experienced her individually, according to our relationship.

We weren't going to agree. But disturbing as the conversation with Cathy was to me, it was also very freeing. It allowed me to quit worrying about whether my mother missed me when I was nine hundred miles away.

And so, as one event in my own domestic life connected to another, I stayed in Baltimore, tending to business, talking by phone to Louise, to Melissa, to the nursing desk at Canterbury.

Then, on January 6, I got the answer as to why, after all these years, a bunion should be a problem. I didn't know the person who called. Some of the nurses and nursing assistants in the Health Center are part-time, especially on the weekends. This time, when the security desk rang, I was connected to a registered nurse named Donna, who worked one or two weekends a month at Canterbury, but whose main work and experience outside for thirteen years had been in intensive and hospice care.

She had taken it on herself to call and warn me.

"You know she's got that wound on her foot?" she said.

I was aware the bunion had turned into a sore. No one had used the word *wound* before.

"It starts as a reddening area, but underneath it is festering. And then it comes to the surface and opens up," Donna explained. "Now it's open. And it's kind of deep." This, she said, was what eventually happened among elderly patients with advanced dementia. Sores tended to develop on the legs, the heels, the coccyx at the end of the spine, and in bunions—the areas where blood circulation was poorest.

"These wounds sometimes go straight to the bone," she said.

I still didn't understand. The skin tears had always healed. Why now?

"I think probably the reason for that was that her appetite remained pretty good," Donna said. Mother had absorbed enough nutrition for her skin to heal.

"But this morning, she would not open her mouth for me." So there it was. Mother had an infected bedsore. Her skin could no longer heal itself because she had no reserve left, and she wasn't eating. If we did nothing, the infection would spread into her bloodstream and she would die of sepsis. We had finally come to the juncture that her doctor, Susan Zimmer, had warned us about in 1998.

"And it's not a bad way to go," Donna said. She sounded encouraging. We could treat it with antibiotics, either given by mouth, or more aggressively through an intravenous drip. I would have to authorize it.

"But I really don't think it's going to heal," she cautioned. "I think it will get worse, and she will probably acquire some more." There was a pinhead area on my mother's butt bone that was just a little pink at the moment, she said, "but I can tell right now, that is going to be the next area."

And there was another issue. My mother was in pain. The nursing staff was trying to remove the infected tissue on the surface, to keep the wound clean and pink. They were cleaning it regularly, and applying antibiotic ointment. But that morning had been different. "During her treatment, she actually grimaced and sat up," Donna said. "She's definitely feeling it."

So there were two questions. Should we give her something for the pain? And should we give her antibiotics to try to kill the infection, or let the wound fester and deepen, proceed to the bone, infect her bloodstream, overwhelm her white blood cells, and take her life?

So far as I knew, my mother hadn't been in real pain since that first stroke gave her a sudden blinding headache and sick stomach that Wednesday evening before Easter, in 1998. There was no reason for her to hurt now. I said yes to five milligrams of liquid morphine, placed under the tongue half an hour or so before they cleaned the wound. I would have said yes to more. But the bigger question was whether to try to heal the wound.

We weren't about to do an intravenous drip. That was too invasive, too aggressive. It was what Melissa and I had agreed, years before, that we would not do. No tubes.

But there was a middle ground. The doctor could prescribe twelve days of antibiotic by mouth. It probably wouldn't be powerful enough. It would also violate my agreement with my sister. But if my mother swallowed the capsules, it might work. It would be up to her—and Mother Nature.

I recoiled from the idea of doing nothing while my formerly immaculate old mother was devoured by an infected sore. She wouldn't want that. But that was my former mother. I was being a wimp. It was what I wanted to be. I wanted her to have one more chance, in case she wanted to stick around.

Out loud, so we both could hear me say it, I said, "But that's all we're going to do. Just this. No more."

"With or without the antibiotic, I don't think it will matter," Donna replied. Her best guess was that Mother could last "thirty to sixty days. And it could be less." The last time she had worked at the Health Center had been Thanksgiving weekend, she said, "and I can really see the decline."

I, of course, could not. I hadn't been there.

I called Melissa to tell her about Mother, and that I had weakened, and authorized twelve days of antibiotics.

"But that's got to be it," she said, sounding a little grim. "No more." I knew she might have made a different decision. No, I promised her. "No more."

On Monday, the nursing desk called again. This time, it was a licensed practical nurse named Peggy. Mother hadn't passed any urine in four days, she said, so they had catheterized her, to see if there was a blockage or an infection. They had found only thirty cubic centimeters of urine, about an ounce, in her bladder. There was no blockage or infection. Mother was just dry. She was eating and drinking so little, she was dehydrated.

"It's been for about the last week that she hasn't been eating," Peggy said.

She was down to 72.6 pounds. She had entered the Health Center at almost twice that. They were giving her 5 milligrams of Roxanol, the morphine sulfate solution, every few hours. The Levaquin, a 500-milligram dose of antibiotic, had begun the day before.

We would see.

On Tuesday, Cathy called. "She's got the dwindles," she said. "She's not eating. She's not drinking. She's got that wound on her foot. I don't think she's going to improve. And honestly, it's a tragedy that she's lasted as long as she has. Bless her heart. She really needs to let go."

"I wouldn't be surprised if you got a call any day," she said.

I'd better get down there, I thought. On the other hand, Cathy added, "This could vacillate back and forth for weeks."

I couldn't stay in Tampa for weeks. I asked if she could have Dr. Perron, the geriatrician with whom she came to the Health Center each Tuesday, call me. In an hour, he did.

"As dementia advances, you just eat less and less," he said, "and she's eating a little applesauce, but that's all."

How long? I asked. The New Old Age is his specialty. But like many others, Dr. Perron has come to have an almost mystical regard for people my mother's age. It may have been mainly the men whose courage and service in World War II moved Tom Brokaw to describe them as the Greatest Generation. But it is mainly the women who now survive.

"You never want to second-guess that generation," Dr. Perron said. "I think it is the toughest generation America has ever had. If she stops eating and drinking altogether, it would be a matter of three or four days. But if she's eating a little, drinking a little, I'd say a couple of weeks."

I wanted to see my mother while she was still alive and conscious. But I couldn't go down to Tampa and wait for two weeks.

On Thursday, another nurse, Stacey, called. Mother's pulse and blood pressure had dropped.

On Friday, Stacey called again. The blood pressure was down another twenty points. "I think it may not be long," she said.

On Sunday morning, when I walked in, Louise was sitting by the bed. At the foot of the bed, on top of the covers, was a big, fluffy white teddy bear covered in purple hearts. It was from Louise. At the head of the bed, curled under the covers, was an emaciated little bird. My mother.

"Yestuhday, Ah could feed huh," Louise said, looking down sadly at the tiny S-shaped form. "But Ah cain't feed huh no moah. She tightens huh mouth up tuh where you cain't get any food in theah. But you givuh some juice, an' she opens up," she said, wonderingly. "Ah doan know how she knows thuh difference."

It was hard to imagine. She was so small on the pillow. So drawn down. All bones and shadows. Her eyes were dull, a kind of muddy blue, half rolled up behind the lids. I didn't think she could see me. When I bent down, her cheeks were cool to my kiss, her forehead warmer.

I looked up to see Ernestine, her big dark eyes on Mother. For days, she had been sitting sentry anytime no one else was in the room. "I think she's a little weak now," Ernestine said softly. "I think she's decided to give up on her own, now."

As we looked, Mother stopped breathing. Louise frowned, and reached down to rub her shoulder. She touched her cheek, her forehead. She put her right hand palm down on Mother's upper chest and patted, gently, staring at her. Mother resumed breathing.

I had told the nursing desk two days earlier to stop taking her to the dining room. Now another aide, Alison, a surgical assistant at MacDill Air Force Base who worked two weekends each month at Canterbury, came in and spent a patient half hour trying to slip small spoons of supplement into Mother's mouth from a four-ounce cup. In all that time, Mother took less than an ounce of it, and about the same amount of the water. Her eyes were more open, but I couldn't tell what she really saw. Then another aide came in, and asked if they should bring a lunch tray from the dining room. No, I said. We weren't going to try to feed her anymore.

I walked down to the nursing station, and asked them to call hospice.

O n Monday, she began to look very peaceful. She was getting the morphine solution every four hours. It relaxed her, so that more and more, she simply looked as if she were asleep, instead of in some vegetative twilight zone. It was a comfort.

I sat down beside her. "I think you're going to float off, Mother," I said. "I think you're going to see all the people you love who are already gone, pretty soon. Nana, and your daddy, Baya and Louise and Nicki-Nat." I paused. I hadn't talked to her about heaven in years, not since Melissa and I had decided to withdraw her blood pressure medications at the end of 2000, in hopes that she would die. I can still remember her look when she realized I was trying to shuffle her off.

But she wasn't going to turn back this time. I started to name all the friends who would be up there, waiting. My mother's days had been filled with good deeds and social engagements. She had a talent for making all kinds of people feel connected to her. There ought to be a big crowd in heaven. "Patti and Frank," I said, "and your friend Heebie . . ."

But I couldn't remember where the list went from there. In the last six years, I'd forgotten the whole chain of names. There were scores of them, hundreds at one time. Thousands, maybe. But they were gone, and I couldn't call them up. I felt like a dodo.

Mother didn't look as if she cared.

Dr. Perron walked in. He touched two fingers to her chest, here and there, put a hand down to knead her soft stomach, and stood back up, looking at her. He was tall and fair haired, with a sensitive face.

"A priest described this time to me once," he said quietly. "He said the soul is gone. We're just waiting for the body to depart." He patted my shoulder and left.

The hospice case manager came that evening at 6:15 to get all the necessary information. Her name was Deborah. She was very thoughtful and nice. A nurse on the Silver Team—there were several teams in the bay area—would come on Tuesday to do the actual assessment of Mother, Deborah said, as she explained the process to Melissa and me. The Health Center staff would continue to care for her, but under the management of the hospice system. A nurse would come two or three times a week to monitor her care, and an aide two or three times to bathe her. We all looked at Mother. None of us thought she would last that long.

"I wish we had been called sooner," Deborah said, a little ruefully.

When I came back at 8:30 Tuesday morning, Ernestine was already there. Melissa and I and Brad, her husband, had spent a lot of time together Sunday and Monday and Tuesday, with Mother, and at meals outside with one another. Almost every time I came back to the room, Ernestine was there. When we left for lunch on Tuesday, she and Louise and Claudia and Marcia and Star and Yvonne closed the door to the hall, gathered in a semicircle around Mother's bed, and prayed.

"We asked the Lord to bless her going out, and to be with her the same as when she came in," Ernestine said. "We gave her back."

Mother's feet and hands started getting cool on Tuesday, and as the day passed, the cool began to work up her legs. By the time we left, around eleven that night, her knees and forearms were feeling cool. Her eyes had been closed for two days. She hadn't eaten or drunk anything since Sunday.

Ernestine's husband brought her back to work at 7:20 Wednesday morning, and she went straight to Mother's room, sat down by the bed, and started talking to her about heaven. Mother began to make some different sounds, so Ernestine moved around to the other side of the bed, where she could sit closer to her head. She put her warm plump hands on Mother's arm and forehead and began to hum some tunes—spirituals and hymns.

Mother made some more sounds. *I'd better sing "Peace in the Valley,"* Ernestine thought. She began to croon to Mother, singing the old words about the blessed peace at the end of life that Thomas A. Dorsey, the father of gospel music, had written for Mahalia Jackson, seventy years before.

And that's how my mother died, with Ernestine singing to her.

Ernestine held her, and then called out through the door to the nurse, who called Mrs. Vinas, who called me.

When I got down from the Sweetso's apartment, half an hour

later, Star had already been in to make her up. Mother was tilted up on the pillow, with the light of a lamp above the bed falling on her face. She had a prominent, slightly hooked nose, beautiful features, and that thick, wonderful hair. She was almost ninety-two. Her face had never wrinkled. The hair was brushed and luxuriant. Her makeup, rouge, eyeliner, and lipstick were on. Her eyes were half open. All the signs of dementia had fallen away. It looked as if she had come back, as if she had been transported from the pitiful shrunken state to which she had sunk and in which she had just died, and was now in some golden, regal, strangely radiant form. I was mesmerized. She was gorgeous in a way I had never seen before, glowing and restful, a portrait of complete repose.

I touched her cheeks and forehead, kissed her, and sat down. I couldn't take my eyes off her. Mrs. Vinas and the nurses and nurse's assistants began to come in, to say good-bye. Melissa and Louise came and stayed. I left to shower and change and cancel a plane, and came back.

The funeral home had been sold to another small chain in the years since Mother had made and paid for the arrangements. The phone number on file was wrong. It was almost six hours before the attendant came. Melissa and Louise had to leave. I stayed with Ernestine, looking at Mother, and got Ernestine to sing "Peace in the Valley" again.

The attendant's name was Wayne. He wore a dark new suit, a white shirt, and a tie. He had a nice smile and manners, a wheeled dolly, and a long vinyl zippered body bag.

"No," Ernestine told him. "She has her own sheets and blanket." And she did. Melissa had seen to that. The staff had remade Mother's bed with her own linens, and the soft white blanket stitched with loving words that Melissa had brought.

I touched Mother's cheeks, her arms, her hands, her legs, her feet. She was cool all the way down now. Wayne began to fold the sheets around her. He folded her up the way a Marine detachment folds the flag. Then he paused. Mother was in her own hooded white shroud, sheets, blanket, pillow and all. Just her face looked out.

"Shall I leave the face uncovered?" Wayne asked, looking toward us.

"No," Ernestine said softly. "We don't do it that way. We cover the face."

Wayne carefully folded the sheets over the face. Mother disappeared. He and Ernestine lifted her onto the dolly and strapped her down. He rolled her out the door. Ernestine and I followed, and as we passed down the hall, I became aware that all the noises of the nursing wing, all the conversations, had stopped. All the doors to the patient rooms were closed, and every so often, a nurse or a nurse's assistant stood silently along the wall. Mother had lived here almost nine years. They were paying their respects.

The security guard escorted us to the elevator, down and out the back door. There was the white unmarked van. Wayne opened the doors, slid Mother in, closed the doors, and waved good-bye.

He drove off, and Ernestine and I walked arm in arm inside.

I flew back to Baltimore that afternoon, to write. In two days, Mother would be ashes. In about six weeks, we would have the celebrations, the Episcopal services and parties, the hymns, eulogies, grits, and bourbon that she had waited for so long. Most of her friends were now dead, but there were still some alive, and there was our generation of children. We would lower her into the ground next to her beloved Jobie. Part of her. But Melissa had decided that she would like to put some of Mother in the columbarium in the shaded garden at St. John's. It's her church, too, just blocks from where she and Brad live, off the Bayshore. She can go there, to be with Mother, anytime.

And there was a serving dish I remembered, back in Baltimore, that I wanted to find.

It was fairly high in the shelves of the butler's pantry. An elegant footed dish of English china with handles and a lid. I think Mother had gotten it in London. It was perfect—soft, rosy pink and white, with touches of gold. It was about the right size. It looked just like her, and the tables she used to set, in rooms filled with flowers and family and friends. She loved arranging things, food, and people, and being at the center of them. She radiated good feeling, and that's the way I see her now in my mind, not as the woman in the bed, watching me always, but as my mother in earlier life, face uptilted, laughing gaily, lighting up a room.

She was like an angel that way, omnipresent. It used to bother me. But I discovered, as she began to dim and then to crumble, piece by piece over the last twenty-five years, that I cherished what remained, until there was nothing, finally, but her eyes. Looking at me. Until they closed. I don't know, even then, that she really wanted to leave. If she knew anything, she knew that she needed—that we needed—for her life to have an end. But that didn't mean that she wanted to be gone. Not entirely. And she won't be. Mothers never really leave us. Not so long as we have memories. But we will be able to feel her presence, too.

In Tampa, Melissa and Brad and I, and Christopher and Whitney and Louise, can stand among the stones in Myrtle Hill. Or can sit in the garden at St. John's, and watch the light play across the wall where she lies. In Baltimore, I will have only to look up at the bookshelves by the fireplace in my living room, at the elegant, soft pink and-white serving dish she always kept in the center of her dining room table, which was, for her, the center of the house, and of life.

So there, Mother. I hope you're happy. I am. We'll all be together. Everywhere at home.

ACKNOWLEDGMENTS

Nothing good happens without the love, understanding, and support of family, friends, and colleagues. I sometimes wonder why mine don't wear out, or get bored with the subjects that absorb me for years on end. In fact, they may get bored. And weary. But they have the grace and good heart not to say so. I cherish them for their tolerance, their faith, their good humor, and their encouragement. They make my life feel rich and bright, funny and right. I think they're angels.

No book like this, of course, gets published without the special kinds of emotional and financial commitment, deep patience, and intellectual, legal, and literary support that authors require. I think of it as a very professional kind of love, because these relationships are about much more than just the ardent hope that the damn book sells.

For that reason, I am very fondly and gratefully indebted to Kathy Robbins, my unfailingly smart, tough, loving shepherd and literary agent, with whom anything feels possible and without whom this book would not be; to Rick Kot, my quiet, strong, deeply civilized, *patient* editor at Viking, for believing in and betting on the idea of this book and on its author, and for staying faithful to both through years and various frustrating phases, which he helped resolve; to Rachelle Bergstein, my artful and indispensable in-agency editor, who channeled me through the last restructuring, cuts, and rewrites necessary to get the manuscript in shape to go to the publisher, and to the ever-efficient and good-humored Kate Rizzo and Cory Hunter; to Alessandra Lusardi, who guided the manuscript at Viking with great calm and dispatch—and handled the author with considerable sensitivity; to Deborah Weiss Geline, for truly superb and detailed copyediting and thoughtful suggestions for tuning and tightening the manuscript; to Jasmine Lee and Roseanne Serra, for their wonderfully perceptive and charming cover design—and redesign; and to production editor Bruce Giffords. And I am grateful to Andrew G. Celli Jr., for his deft and careful—and entertaining— legal advice. And for demonstrating that northern lawyers can be funny.

There are others who gave these Canterbury tales very meaningful exposure and support. I am grateful to Jackson Boggs, chairman of the Canterbury board of trustees, and to the rest of the board, for understanding this project and not opposing it; to Penny Duckham, executive director of the Kaiser Media Fellowship Program; to Alex Ward of the *New York Times,* for soliciting a large and early excerpt from the working manuscript to run in the *Times;* to Marilynn Yee of the *Times,* for the lovely photographs she took to illustrate that piece; to David Andelman, editor of Forbes.com, for soliciting and publishing a piece of the manuscript there; to the judges of the J. Anthony Lukas Work-in-Progress Award, given annually by the Nieman Foundation for Journalism at Harvard University and the Columbia University Graduate School of Journalism to assist in the completion of a significant work of narrative nonfiction on an American topic of political or social concern, for citing *Canterbury* as a finalist in the awards competition in 2006; and to Patrick O'Connell, the chef and owner of the Inn at Little Washington and pope of American cuisine, for collaboration on the book's title and on life.

But this book, which is so personal, and which took so much longer than I expected, has had many angels. Some of them lent or gave grants or contracts, or gave money outright, to keep the author afloat and the project alive. Some gave employment, garage space, office space, guest space, counseling, or cars to drive while in Tampa. All of them listened, laughed, panged, and marveled at the stories of life at Canterbury and made me think the whole thing was worthwhile.

The special angels of these last years, beginning more than a decade ago, include Florence Hosch, my fiercely inquiring and indomitable old cousin, who taught me much about love and principle and giving to those you believe in; the Kaiser Family Foundation, which gave a grant in support of this book project; Jim Ferman, chairman, of the Bank of Tampa, the only bank I know that bets on writers; David Kennedy of Tampa, the only real estate investor and banker I know who bets on books and friends; Howell Raines, then editor of the editorial page of the *New York Times,* who employed me part-time there in the first year of this research and who published the Mother's Day column ten years ago that was the germ of this book; Joy McCann Culverhouse, who is both a joyful friend and one of the great philanthropists and personalities of Tampa Bay; my sister, Melissa Spring, who has been lovingly patient and supportive of a brother she knows all too well, and of a book whose contents she did not know; the inimitable Laurence Miller of Austin, Texas, a patron of creation, who loves his friends more than we deserve; Dr. John and Jane Payne of Baltimore, New York City, Key West, and Maine, who are so generous and humane—and such good company—in so many places and in so many ways; the bountiful Rebecca Hoffberger, founder of the American Visionary Art Museum in Baltimore, and the only truly magical personality I know; and my dear and endlessly intuitive old friend David Hall, as well as Jane Cralle Hall Witt, Cralle Hall, Gail DeLoach, and Ron Goldstein; Ronald Steel, the distinguished author, historian, and foreign affairs expert, who has been a cherished and generous friend and guide in life, literature, and contemporary culture for many years. In one way or another, at one time or another, they have all helped keep the wolf from the door.

There are many others who have repeatedly extended themselves, in all kinds of concrete and meaningful ways, to feed my spirit; to give me advice, space, and organizational aid; to shape the book; to help the work along; and in general to keep body and soul together. I owe much to the inexhaustibly empathetic and encouraging Gary Cohen and also to Bill Kovach, Dr. Tom Bryant and Brandt Petrasek of Washington, D.C.; to the incomparable Nathalie Dupree of Charleston, South Carolina; to my old friends Alex Jones and Susan Tifft in Boston; to Cathy Clayton and Greg Thomas, Marian and Hal Flowers, Ken Hardin and Armando Maiquez, Tom and Anne Henderson, Carla Kelly, Jean Kelly, Jeanne and Jeff Kronsnoble, Anne Lippe Phipps, Harriett and Philip Plyler, and Lee and Tommy Touchton, all for good deeds and life support in Tampa; to the wonderfully insightful and generous Eileen Rhea Brown of Atlanta; and to Tom Hall and Linell Smith, Jon McGill and Linnet Jones, Tom Mayer and Sally Jacobs, for love and logistical support in Baltimore. Hackey Clark, Robert Wagner, Frank Poppen, Nicholas Conti, Don Peyton, Paul Ritterman, the brothers Majid and Sajid Rana, and David Smith all kept me informed, advised, and operational in Baltimore. They are wise counselors, craftsmen, and friends, and they could have charged a lot more.

Joshua Batten has for years filled my house with art and pleasure, love and support. Taylor Branch and Christy Macy; Steve Wigler and Norrie Epstein; Sandy Goolsby; Dr. Jimmy Duke; Steve Bolton and Jim Magruder; Dr. William and Tizzie Benedict; Adam Nagourney and Ben Kushner; Lem and Barbara Coley of Stony Brock, New York; Anne Raver and Rock; Alexandra and Dr. Ron Dworkin; Gregory King and Peter Sultan; Lois Blum Feinblatt and Ellen Halle; Joe Lazarro; Marchant and Ron Martin and Stephen Salny, the Babycakes, have all been wonderfully supportive and inspiriting friends. My cousin Baya Harrison of Tallahassee, whom Mother loved, has acted repeatedly and selflessly as the family lawyer. We owe him much. And I have long appreciated the counsel and company of John Germany, my mother's lawyer and dear friend—and mine.

This book began with Mother, and it was she who gave it its

ending. I am grateful to her not only for inspiring it in so many ways but for letting me know that she understood I was doing it, and was glad.

My daughter, Whitney, my deepest joy, is also a good reader and a smart and candid editor. She gets some of that from her mother, Nancy Barritt, who is also good-humored and understanding. I'm grateful.

But my most grateful thanks go to Caridad Vinas, the administrator of Canterbury, and the residents and staff of Canterbury Tower and Health Center, for their trust and welcome and for taking me into their schedules and their lives, knowing that the notes I was always taking were intended for a book that would depict them, as the Emyfish said with a sigh, "warts and all." Given that, and some of the very tender and intimate moments related in these tales, I am profoundly and particularly grateful to my lifelong friend Nathalie Davis Wood. She and I shared the last years of our parents' lives. It was a comfort. And a treasure.